The World of
Túpac Amaru

D1472217

Ward Stavig

THE WORLD OF
TÚPAC AMARU

*Conflict, Community, and Identity
in Colonial Peru*

WITHDRAWN

University of
Nebraska Press
Lincoln &
London

BOWLING GREEN STATE
UNIVERSITY LIBRARY

© 1999 by the University of Nebraska Press
All rights reserved
Manufactured in the United States of America

∞ The paper in this book meets the minimum requirements
of American National Standard for Information Sciences—
Permanence of Paper for Printed Library Materials,
ANSI Z39.48-1984.

Library of Congress Cataloging-in-Publication Data
Stavig, Ward.
The world of Túpac Amaru : conflict, community, and
identity in Colonial Peru / Ward Stavig.
p.   cm.
Includes bibliographical references and index.
ISBN 0-8032-4271-9 (cl : alk. paper). —
ISBN 0-8032-9255-4 (pa : alk. paper)
1. Indians of South America—Peru—Quispicanchis—
History—Sources. 2. Indians of South America—Peru—
Canchis—History—Sources. 3. Indians of South America—
Peru—Quispicanchis—Ethnic identity. 4. Indians of South
America—Peru—Canchis—Ethnic identity. 5. Ethnohistory—
Peru— Quispicanchis. 6. Ethnohistory—Peru—Canchis.
7. Quispicanchis (Peru)—Social life and customs.
8. Canchis (Peru)—Social life and customs. 9. Peru—
History—Insurrection of Túpac Amaru, 1780–1781.
I. Title.
F3429.1.Q86S73   1999
985'.37—DC21   98-35769
                                                   CIP

In memory of
my father,
George Stavig,
and my grandparents
Dora Buck Doolittle
and Roy Doolittle,
and for my mother,
Lois Stavig—
decent, hard-working,
honest folk.

CONTENTS

ILLUSTRATIONS

TABLES

PLATES   *Following page 128*

Acknowledgments

I am forever grateful to the people who helped shape this work and made my life so much richer in the process. While I cannot possibly thank them all, I would like to express my profound gratitude and mention a few specifically.

My experience in the archives and national libraries of Peru, Bolivia, and Argentina was very fruitful thanks to the directors and staffs of the Archivo General de la Nación in Buenos Aires, the Archivo Histórico de Potosi, the Archivo Diocesano of Potosi, and the Archivo Nacional de Bolivia—especially to Doña Anita and the late Gunnar Mendoza. In the Archivo Nacional del Peru and the Archivo Arzobispal de Lima the staffs were most helpful as were people in the Biblioteca Nacional. In Cuzco I wish to thank the Archivo Departamental de Cuzco (Archivo Histórico de Cusco), the Archivo Arzobispal de Cuzco and the Archivo Arzobispal de Sicuani.

Institutional support made this work possible. The Fulbright Foundation supported my research in Peru, Bolivia, and Argentina, and a special thanks is due to Carmen Pardo in Bolivia, to Marcia Koth de Paredes in Lima, and to the very friendly Fulbright staff. The Organization of American States supported travel, the University of Pittsburgh awarded a grant to study Quechua, and the University of California, Davis, supported my work with Humanities Travel Fellowships, a Regents Fellowship and a Humanities Dissertation Year Fellowship. The USF Publications Council at the University of South Florida provided a valuable subvention to publish this study.

Acknowledgments

From Peru I would like to thank Manuel Burga, Mariella Corvetto, Franklin and Mariana Pease, and especially Luis Miguel Glave. Alberto "Tito" Flores Galindo befriended and helped me and is greatly missed.

I also wish to express my appreciation to Nicolas and Janice Cushner, Christine Hunefeldt, Eric Langer, Brooke Larson, Benjamin Orlove, Louis A. Pérez Jr., Karen Powers, John Rowe, the late Michael Sallnow, David Sweet, and two very special friends—Phil Dabel and Priscilla High.

One cannot ask for more consideration and support than I received as a graduate student from the History Department at U. C. Davis. Wilson Smith, James Shideler, Luis Arroyo, Bill Hagen, and Karen Hairfield deserve special thanks. Three people gave more of themselves than anyone has the right to expect—Daniel Calhoun, Rollie Poppino, and Arnold Bauer. Dan kept me on my intellectual toes. Rollie was my first teacher. With his open door, kindness, and dry sense of humor he encouraged and supported me in every way possible. Arnold shared everything from debates over world-systems theory and the properties of good tortillas to the harvesting of turgid clusters of zinfandel. A constant source of intellectual curiosity and humane consideration, he taught me through deed and example.

At the University of South Florida I wish to thank Marianne Bell, John Belohlavek, Giovanna Benadusi, Robert Ingalls, Gary Mormino, Fraser Ottanelli, Kathleen Paul, Carole Rennick, Gail Smith, and Sylvia Wood.

Finally, I wish to thank Ella Schmidt for waving to me from the back of a restaurant in Sicuani as I walked by late one rainy morning and for what we have shared since then, including a great deal of work on this book, but especially Lucía and Mariana.

Introduction

*Observations from the House
of Garcilaso "El Inca"*

Queremos un cacique de nuestro ayllo nuestro sangre que sepa criarnos con aquel amor cariño e estimacion que necesitamos. *Naturales* of *ayllu* Chumo

It ain't the things you don't know what gets you into trouble; it's the things you know for sure what ain't so.   Rural American expression

---

A SHORT block up a narrow cobblestone street from the Plaza de Armas in Cuzco lies an attractive, smaller square, the Plaza de Regocijo. Despite its charms relatively few tourists linger on its benches, although many visitors—foreign and Peruvian—pass by on their way to the market or train station, or they duck into the Cafe Varayoc for some espresso during the day or a hot pisco punch on those bone-chilling Andean nights. In the morning local folk, taking a respite from the day's activities, tarry in the plaza enjoying the warm rays of the sun. During the day young boys scurry to shine shoes, people from outlying communities patiently observe the bustle of urban life while engaged in the seemingly endless waiting that is a part of their lives, and near midday friendly women sell steaming tamales. In the late afternoon and early evening, lovers often stop to share a few precious moments together. On the darker side, gangs of youthful pickpockets sometimes rob trusting souls who have not experienced the harsh reality of Dickensian thieves, drunks sleep off their overindulgence sprawled on a bench, and the homeless—without a safer and warmer doorstep on which to sleep—take what refuge they can in the Plaza de Regocijo.

Introduction

On one corner of the plaza still stands the house in which Garcilaso de la Vega (El Inca), the son of an Inca princess and a Spanish conquistador, spent his formative years absorbing knowledge of both the indigenous and European worlds that informed his *Royal Commentaries of the Incas*. While I was researching this book, the Archivo Departamental del Cuzco, the repository of many of the ancient and yellowed documents that give life to this work, was housed on the second floor of this colonial structure. In the dim light of the unheated reading room, with a portrait of Garcilaso staring over my shoulder, I pored over bundle after bundle of documents filled with rich details of the lives of the men, women, and children who are the focus of this work.

One of the more striking aspects of working in Cuzco is that vestiges of the past live on in the present, making the past even more vital. Perhaps this is most clear in the architecture of the city, which includes Inca, colonial, republican, and modern construction. While conducting my research I not only worked in Garcilaso's house but lived in a nearby colonial building that had an Inca wall as the base on which later centuries of construction rested. Now a hotel, the widowed owner informed me that this had been the colonial home of the Marques de Casa Xara whose lands were in Quispicanchis, one of the provinces of Cuzco I was studying. Indeed, the widow was a descendant of the Marques and despite considerably declined fortunes still owned a small portion of the original Casa Xara family lands in the community of Guaro(c). Leonidas, a young man of indigenous heritage from Guaro, worked in the hotel (just as his ancestors had most likely worked for the Marques) and knew the widow because of the property she held in his community. One evening I asked Leonidas about his community's history. He proudly related an account of a *curaca* from Guaro who had forcefully and successfully defended his people's lands against the incursions of the neighboring community of Urcos and maintained control of the fields so necessary to their existence. As we continued to talk and gaze into the night sky above Cuzco, Leonidas also explained to me that part of the constellation we refer to as Orion represented a hand plow, such as those introduced to America with the Spanish conquest. Even the understanding of the heavens had been transformed by contact with the Old World. For Leonidas, as for the widow, the past really lives on in the present.

This book is a "ground up" ethnohistory and colonial history. Its primary focus is on the indigenous ancestors of people such as Leonidas, who lived in the two provinces of colonial Cuzco—Quispicanchis and Canas y Canchis—that are at the center of this work. The book also examines the complex relations and interactions these indigenous peoples developed with their neighbors of European and mixed heritages such as the ancestors of the widow of the Casa Xara line. Analyzing the colonial world through the lens of rural Cuzco allows me to penetrate deeply into the lives of the ordinary people who formed the vast majority of this society and to more thoroughly understand Spanish colonialism not just as it existed in decrees, centers of power, or among the elites but as it functioned in the day-to-day existence of these ordinary men and women. This is not, however, a regional study. It takes up issues of broad concern in the colonial world and of concern to those who study this world. It places the families and communities of Quispicanchis and Canas y Canchis in their colonial and global, as well as regional, context. Thus, it brings together two sorts of history that are usually kept separate. It is a close, even intimate, view of the daily lives of indigenous villagers and a broader account of the economic and political institutions of colonial society and the ways these institutions functioned on the ground. In this way it welds together a micro- and macroanalysis of the Andean world.

One of the main objectives of this work is to understand and bring forth the historical agency of the men, women, and children whose lives were filled with the (extra)ordinary human experiences that are the substance of this work. In getting at their lives this book deconstructs certain widely accepted notions in Latin American historiography, but this deconstruction was not, I must confess, my original intention. It emerged on its own in the analysis of new archival materials. Likewise, while authors like Nathan Wachtel have pointed to the "destructuring" nature of colonial policies after the encounter, my investigations indicate that some of these policies also had within them the unintentional seeds of solidification, even enforcement, of the new ethnic realignments and identities that were created from the early colonial turmoil and which persisted and became sources of strength—of inadvertent restructuring—to indigenous peoples.[1] Thus, Spanish policy in Quispicanchis and Canas y Canchis did not lead down a direct path of homogenization of ethnic groups into generic *campesinos*, or at least this path did not go far before detouring onto different trails of identity.

In addition, the values of *naturales* in rural Cuzco were not necessarily at odds with those of the Spanish, but instead they were often surprisingly similar. This complementarity or intersection of values created a complex reality in which interaction with Europeans both protected indigenous values and strengthened the ties between colonizer and colonized. Some have seen this meshing or complementarity of values that allowed the colonial system to survive as leading to the decline and eventual collapse of indigenous ways.[2] Perhaps in the early colonial period this argument has more merit; however by the late colonial era the Andean world was different. Spanish and indigenous worlds were not—if they had ever been—seamless or separate spheres. In the eighteenth century such differences were seldom so sharply defined, and, prior to the Thupa Amaro rebellion at least, there was much cultural fluidity. The bounds that provided meaningful identity still had parameters, but they were often flexible and depended on each peoples' (ethnicities) own concepts of what made them who they were. The binary-like contrasts that seem to explain much in earlier periods shed less light on the late colonial period, and the indigenous-European intersections that have been viewed as destructuring frequently provided mechanisms for survival in later periods in Quispicanchis and Canas y Canchis. This, in turn, may help us understand at least one reason why, despite all the grief caused by colonialism, Spanish rule in the Andes endured as long as it did.

Introduction

The provinces of Canas y Canchis (also known as Tinta, the capital of the province) and Quispicanchis are today best known for being the explosive heart of the Túpac Amaru (Thupa Amaro) rebellion.[3] This upheaval, the most serious challenge to Spanish authority since the sixteenth century, shook colonial society to its roots and made manifest indigenous discontent with the rapidly changing and increasingly harsh conditions of the mid– to late eighteenth century. This "close to the earth" view of the core of the rebellious zone in Peru provides a strong sense of the period and illuminates the complex and concrete reasons that informed people's actions while creating a fresh perspective for understanding the movement, but the rebellion is just one aspect of this work. The book is about much more than the rebellion. It is about the world that gave shape to Túpac Amaru, the everyday world of the peoples of Quispicanchis and Canas y Canchis, and the colonial-indigenous society they formed. It examines the lives of these Andean women and men to better understand them and the ways they shaped their lives and reshaped colonial society. The chapters that emerge are like a series of time-lapse photos. There is movement in them, but rather than building chronologically toward the events of 1780 they analyze issues and themes that were vital to this world and which, in turn, help us better understand not only the colonial world but the rebellion as well.

Above all I focus on the efforts of indigenous peoples to continue living in a manner that made sense to them, examining the alterations, accommodations, and struggles in which they engaged to maintain or redefine themselves in a world that was changing, but in which custom and tradition weighed heavily. The historical debate is taken beyond the realms of state and economy by analyzing the ways factors such as mentalities, concepts of identity, and population also impacted daily life. I place special emphasis on the role of culture in the material, political, and social life of indigenous peoples, especially on the ways cultural considerations affected native peoples' interactions with a world in which they did not overtly set policy or make laws. And I engage a variety of questions that are at the center of debates related to non-Western peoples and colonial societies such as the role of ethnicity, gender and familial ideologies, the retention and construction of values, the dialogues between cultures, and strategies of survival and "adjustment."

Many aspects of the pre-Columbian and early postencounter Andean world no longer existed by the late seventeenth and eighteenth centuries, indigenous societies having been partially overlaid by and intermingled with European society. To a degree the Spanish had encouraged this mixture by tailoring certain colonial demands to indigenous customs. By the late colonial period many aspects of indigenous life and culture persisted, but the context and form had altered. Likewise, after more than two centuries of Spanish domination, rural Cuzco was a mature colonial society in which native peoples not only understood their rights and obligations and those of the state but also understood that aspects of the relationship were not immutable.

The provinces or *partidos* of Quispicanchis and Canas y Canchis were selected for several reasons. While contiguous, there were significant differences in geography, climate, production, settlement patterns, and the ratio of Indians to Spaniards that made these provinces especially interesting. Together they reflect a diversity of conditions that could be found in many regions of the viceroyalty of Peru and provide a more representative base for understanding the colonial world than either would have alone or than many other regions might provide. Both *partidos* were linked to local, regional, and international economies, albeit in somewhat different ways. The royal road, the major artery of the empire, passed through Quispicanchis and Canas y Canchis connecting them with Cuzco, Lima, and, ultimately, Spain in one direction and with the Lake Titicaca basin, La Paz, the silver mining centers of Oruro and Potosi, Tucumán, and regions beyond in the other. In addition, Canas y Canchis and Quispicanchis were the only Cuzco provinces subject to the massive forced labor system or *mita* that impacted much of highland Peru and powered the engine of the empire—the silver mines of Potosi. And even though near the center of the former Inca empire, Quispicanchis and especially Canas y Canchis had not been just extensions of the

Cuzco-based regime as might, at first glance, be expected. These provinces had been brought into the empire by force or the threat of force. People in much of the zone originally did not even share a common tongue with Cuzco. Thus, while strongly influenced by Cuzco, it would not be correct to see these peoples as being one and the same with the Inca.

To better convey a sense of the peoples and the time, I have endeavored to let the historical actors speak for themselves. I want the reader to smell the fresh turned earth and the smoke rising through thatch roofs, to feel the anger and apprehension of having lands threatened and taxes increased, and to share the anguish of illness and death and the joy of fiestas and births. Hopefully, this invites the reader more fully into their lives. As James Scott put it, "example is not only the most successful way of embodying a generalization, but also has the advantage of always being richer and more complex than the principles that are drawn from it."[4] Thus, when beneficial I use their own words to "construct" an analysis that reads like a narrative rather than directly inserting myself into the history by drawing attention to my analysis (as I just did).

The rich ethnographic data that inform this work come from research in local, departmental, and church archives in the Department of Cuzco, as well as from investigations in Lima, Potosi, Sucre, and Buenos Aires. In reading their words and "listening" to their voices, I came to fully appreciate the daunting nature of the task in which I was involved; probing the lives, the inner worlds, of peoples and cultures so different from our own.[5] Much of the surviving documentation revolves around conflicts or violence. I have carefully gleaned these materials for their social content, not just the tensions around which they are centered. Nonetheless, the sources are especially fruitful on antagonisms, and I have made use of this rich material to explore the issue of conflict. At times I have also had to rely on older, and to some degree questionable, chronicles and accounts such as that of Felipe Guamán Poma de Ayala to provide historical and cultural context to the events and understandings of the late seventeenth and eighteenth centuries. The documentation is problematic in yet ano-

ther way, testimony often having passed through the filters of inter-
preters and scribes in addition to the normal pressures that influence
public words. In writing I have tried to be aware of these influences,
as well as my own "filters."[6] Recognizing the problems involved, I
nonetheless have sought to understand the peoples of colonial Peru as
they represented themselves and their world while also being aware of
the ways they were represented. A truly "emic" view of the distant past
is, of course, impossible. However, the effort to understand these
people on their own terms brings us closer to them and lends even
greater vibrancy to their humanity. It also brings home the importance of local and cultural, even individual, concerns in the shaping of
history from the microcosmic to the macrocosmic level.

The significance of this "close to the earth" analytical vantage
point cannot be overestimated. The role of the state vis-à-vis indigenous peoples in colonial society is quite different if viewed from an
hacienda veranda or the viceregal palace rather than the village plaza.
In the daily give-and-take between ordinary folk—indigenous, European, African, and mixed—simple dichotomies of oppressor and
oppressed often lose much of their starkness, and more of their humanity has a chance to come forth. I would hope that *naturales* (a colonial term for indigenous peoples) from Cusipata, Tinta, or any of
the other communities in this book, if brought back to life, could recognize contours of their lives instead of lifting their eyes in disbelief
and saying, as people in Peru are wont to do for outlandish notions
that make their way into print, "*el papel aguanta todo*" (anything can
be said on paper).

Naturales, like human beings everywhere, brought their understandings of the world to the problems and situations that confronted them. World views and ways of life developed in "time immemorial" affected actions in later periods. However, their world was
not static, and neither was their understanding of it. Their way of life
changed, and certain aspects of their cultures disappeared while
others gained in strength and new "culture" was added. Complicating
questions of identity or consciousness was the issue of ethnicity. The
peoples of rural Cuzco, deeply aware of the differences among them-

selves (even more so than Europeans), acted on these variances. By the late colonial period crown policies had further exacerbated the tendency toward fragmentation, and the primary ethnic identity of many Andean peoples, such as those of Quispicanchis and Canas y Canchis, was centered in their *ayllus* and communities instead of in a larger regional, ethnic, or racial awareness.

The state played a major role in shaping the lives of native peoples, and most of the primary sources for this book were generated by contact with the state. This unavoidably makes the state loom large. However, one should be careful to not overstate its importance, for it was not central to all aspects of indigenous life. Indigenous peoples had their own agendas, their own concerns, and their own priorities that they pursued independent of, or despite, the state. Likewise, as important as material conditions were they alone did not determine behavior. In traditional societies culture and economy are not easily separated, for in these worlds, as Karl Polanyi noted, "man's economy, as a rule, is submerged in his social relationships."[7] Culture gave form to material conditions at the same time that material factors altered culture.

Old and New World systems of governing were not the same either. Although the actions of particular colonial officials and the state may have outwardly coincided with Andean notions of state-subject relations, Spanish precepts of government reflected European heritages, not those of Andean America. Thus, while *naturales* tended to function out of values related to a hierarchical system of reciprocity, colonial rule stemmed from the supremacy of the crown. This authority, when at its best (which it seldom was), could be akin to state paternalism, but it did not have the same depth of reciprocal responsibility that informed indigenous relations. On a daily basis, however, colonial officials and native peoples often conducted themselves in a manner that obscured these more subtle differences. This, in turn, allowed colonial society to function despite these structural disjunctures.[8]

The depth and complexity of the lives of people in Quispicanchis and Canas y Canchis resist any analysis that compartmentalizes or restricts their humanity and the contradictions with which they lived. Their relationships within their own world and with the larger colonial world were multidimensional. The analysis that results from addressing these complexities is full of the "stuff" of life and is richer, more troubling, and more contradictory than a more restricted, less complex, treatment might have been. My attitude toward the analysis of this complexity concurs with that of Clifford Geertz, who argues that "the force of our interpretations cannot rest, as they are now so often made to do, on the tightness with which they hold together, or the assurance with which they are argued. Nothing has done more . . . to discredit cultural analysis than the construction of formal order in whose existence nobody can quite believe."[9]

In examining the colonial Andean world, I have benefited greatly from the research, ideas, and theories of colleagues. However, this work does not test or employ any single one of these analytical concepts or tools, but instead draws on understandings attained from a wide range of sources dealing with topics within Latin America and beyond. Indeed, the closer one gets to the blood and sweat of real people the more it is almost impossible to "be blinded by the glare of a perfect and immaculate consciousness."[10]

Among the helpful notions encountered for analyzing this world were those related to "the social dialectic of unequal mutuality," which in recent years in the area of peasant studies has become known as "moral economy."[11] At the crossroads of culture and economy, certain aspects of moral economy seem particularly well suited to aid in the understanding of Andean peoples.

E. P. Thompson first gave birth to the term "moral economy" in explaining why rural folk in eighteenth-century England protested and committed acts of violence against property or symbols of traditional authority when the social and economic fabric of their lives began to unravel under the impact of the flying shuttle, spinning jenny, and the world they represented. Since its first use the concept has been expanded and transformed. Thompson generously acknowledged that "I have no patent to the term" and observed that, "much of the very interesting discussion which is now extending under the rubric of 'moral economy' from African and Asian to Latin American or to Irish Studies has little to do with my [1971] usage but is concerned with the social dialectic of unequal mutuality [need and obligation] which lies at the centre of most societies."[12] Thus, though first used in the European context to help understand the transition from traditional to modern societies, "moral economy" has itself been transformed into an analytical tool—more a style of questioning than an actual theory—helpful in understanding societies as distant in time and place as early twentieth-century Southeast Asia, eighteenth-century Chiapas, and nineteenth-century Bolivia and the United States. It also has important analytical value for the study of Andean indigenous peoples during the colonial period.

The emphasis placed by *naturales* on face-to-face relations; the long and varied tradition of reciprocity; the importance of custom and tradition, on the validating force of history[13]; the dominance of subsistence and barter, with market relations only partially developed (and then often under direct or indirect economic coercion); and a communal approach to dealing with the outside: all these factors make the types of inquiries posed by the new moral economy (and related or similar analyses) particularly well suited to understanding the actions of native peoples in the colonial Andes. This vein of inquiry is also quite apt in the examination of a changing society such as late colonial Peru, for it not only applies to the defense of tradition but helps us comprehend the actions of ordinary peoples in new situations and new sets of relations. Just as tradition and culture are not static, neither are the rationales of defense and restructuring for survival.[14] As the saying goes, "If things are going to stay the same, things have to change."

Native peoples emphasized the importance of custom and tradition but at the same time recognized that the rights and obligations that defined Indian-state relations were subject to change and revision. These relations, often rooted in unwritten but understood norms of conduct and reciprocity, gave meaning to the more formal agreements that required indigenous people to render service and tribute to the colonial state in exchange for access to rights and resources that they needed to maintain their way of life. However, rights that the native people claimed to have held from "time immemorial" were not necessarily as ancient as the term might suggest, for, as Brooke Larson has noted, "what came to be called customary law, land rights, and reciprocities in the Andes were modified, even invented, by colonial authorities. *Ayllu* claims to lands, held from 'time immemorial,' often had their origins in the Toledan period, or later. Even when colonial law and practice did respect certain precolonial social patterns and norms, they had the effect of making Andean customs more rigid and precise through colonial codification."[15]

At the same time, however, indigenous peoples often used Spanish customs and laws in ways that were not intended by the conquistadors. Michel de Certeau argues that this usage diverted Spanish colonization "from its intended aims":

> Even when they were subjected, indeed even when they accepted their subjection, the Indians often used the laws, practices, and representations that were imposed on them by force or by fascination to ends other than those of the conquerors; they made something else out of them; they subverted them from within—not by rejecting them or by transforming them (though that occurred as well), but by many different ways of using them in the service of rules, customs or convictions foreign to the colonization which they could not escape. They metaphorized the dominant order: they made it function in another register. They remained other within the system which they assimilated and which assimilated them externally. They diverted it without leaving it.[16]

In the absence of fully developed market relations, with few realistic economic alternatives (especially ones that were better), and with access to land tied to fulfilling communal responsibilities and state demands, what can be seen as moral economic actions were often also the most economically rational actions.[17] Even if alternatives had existed, the considerable efforts by *naturales* like those in Quispicanchis and Canas y Canchis to preserve their communal well-being suggests that few of them found the "bright lights" and market of Cuzco or

Potosí more appealing than life in their own villages except when conditions were perceived as oppressive beyond the colonial norm.

Communities had to be ever vigilant and as tough as nails to preserve themselves and their interests against the intrusions and demands of others—indigenous peoples as well as Spaniards. In this process resistance, in its violent as well as everyday forms, was an important weapon in the indigenous arsenal of defense. It allowed them to adjust and redefine their relationships with their own *curacas* and other communities, as well as with colonial society and the state. Like other peasants and oppressed peoples around the globe have often done, the peoples of Quispicanchis and Canas y Canchis sought to restore what they considered to be a proper order and to alleviate or minimize their burdens while avoiding, as much as possible, direct confrontation with their colonial rulers. Confrontation was risky, desperate business, but if offenses or threats to their way of life were serious enough violence could erupt. However, nonviolent forms of resistance, the "weapons of the weak," were the tactics most frequently employed to alter conditions that were objectionable or that exceeded the parameters of acceptable burdens or behavior.[18] These subtle forms of resistance were often more effective than dramatic, violent protests.[19]

Imperial power was not *"todo poderoso."* The real power of those who control is constrained by the power of the weak. As Barrington Moore, among others, has noted, "In any stratified society . . . there is a set of limits on what both rulers and subjects, dominant and subordinate groups can do. There is also a set of mutual obligations that bind the two together [and an] unverbalized set of mutual understandings. . . . [In this situation] what takes place is a continual probing on the part of rulers and subjects to find out what they can get away with, to test and discover the limits of obedience and disobedience."[20]

In this context indigenous resistance was often compatible with, indeed vital to, the long-term maintenance of Indian-state relations. Without the testing and probing, without the ability to be altered or informally readjusted, the colonial system quickly would have proven too rigid. Unless or until resistance challenged the system, rather than righting wrongs within the system, such actions typically functioned (although this does not imply conscious intent) to preserve rather than destroy the relationships and agreements that collectively guided indigenous interactions with the state. The occasional loss of the life of a corregidor or tax collector was the price paid by the state for the preservation of its legitimacy.

Seeking to maintain control over their lives and a semblance of harmony, communities resolved as many problems as they could internally. When necessary or to their advantage, however, they did not hesitate to use the colonial legal structure and very frequently obtained favorable adjudications. The Spanish legal system became one of the most effective "weapons of the weak" as Andean peoples quickly came to understand and use Spanish courts to fight their battles and redress their grievances. In the process indigenous reliance on the colonial legal structure, when it functioned in their favor or at least with credibility, certainly did not erode Indian-state relations and may have enhanced colonial legitimacy. The effective use of this tool of the state made it less likely that indigenous people would mount "a frontal assault on the existing balance of power."[21] Thus, use of the colonial legal apparatus, what Eric Hobsbawm calls "working the system . . . to their minimum disadvantage," was very important to the preservation of both indigenous and colonial society and is an underlying theme that informs this work.[22]

Why did Andean peoples accept some burdens, work through legal channels to change others, and rise in violent protest against yet others? And why did attitudes toward specific demands change? In other words, why were some demands seen as legitimate while others were not, and why did this evaluation sometimes change? By placing issues such as economic demands in a cultural context that includes the sense of justice and injustice that guided indigenous relationships with the Spanish crown and colonial officials, our understanding of the importance of nonmaterial concerns on material life is enhanced. Relations that seem clearly exploitative to the modern reader must be reevaluated to determine if the "exploited" agreed, in whole or in part, with this categorization. The difference is important for it is the perception of an action, not just the action, that determines behavior and response.

While people certainly worked to minimize or avoid state-imposed burdens, many of the obligations tended to be viewed by the native peoples as part of the uneven reciprocal exchange that defined and guaranteed, sometimes loosely and sometimes rigidly, certain rights to them.[23] The *naturales* of Quispicanchis and Canas y Canchis endured tribute payment, the *reparto,* service in the Potosi *mita,* and a variety of lesser obligations not only because they had little choice, but also because they understood this service as guaranteeing access to land and water, a traditional reciprocal relationship with their *curaca,* and a legal system that maintained these and other rights. However, long-term changes in the economy or population, a temporary crisis such as a drought, or the demands of individual corregidores or *curacas* could alter or severely strain relations and even cause temporary ruptures such as riots, revolts, and, once in a great while, open rebellion if events were perceived as serious transgressions of the norms that guided relations.

Obligations or exchanges between communities and the state, or exchanges between individual Indians (or *ayllus*) and their *curacas* were uneven. Equality was not a key factor, however, in determining the strength of the reciprocally binding set of obligations and rights that helped guide native peoples' lives. Uneven exchange was not a novel reality imposed by Spanish colonialism, inequality of exchange being the norm under the Incas as well. Ultimately, though the levels of exaction were important the most relevant question was not "How much was taken?" but "How much was left?"[24] People struggled to maintain a culturally, as well as physically, determined level of existence. If that level was met the social system would most likely remain stable. What James Scott wrote of Southeast Asian peasants in the twentieth century rings true for the Andes in an earlier period: "While a minimum income has solid physiological dimensions, we must not overlook its social and cultural implications. In order to be a fully functioning member of village society, a household needs a certain level of resources to discharge its necessary ceremonial and social obligations as well as to feed itself adequately and continue to cultivate. To fall below this level is not only to risk starvation, it is to suffer a profound loss of standing within the community and perhaps to fall into a permanent situation of dependence."[25]

The Spanish colonial system, while imposing its laws and obligations, left the indigenous communities largely self-governing. Communities were allowed, and expected, to resolve most of their internal difficulties, and reliance on internal structures normally helped preserve the integrity and solidarity of community relations. However, the perpetuation of internal control under circumstances altered by colonial rule could also exert pressures on these relations and serve as forces of disintegration and disunity. If resolutions to problems were found using the community's internal structure, the strength of bonds and traditions tended to be enhanced, but if not, outside forces might be drawn into communal affairs, which might undermine village authority.

Although Spanish-Indian relations were very important, they alone did not determine the nature and strength of native peoples' relations with colonial society and government. The relationship between *curacas* and the communities and *ayllus* under their rule was also critical in assuring that the glue that bound colonial society together held firmly. Throughout the colonial period as the economy and society changed so did the role and actions of *curacas*. Some were hereditary, others were elected or appointed. Some were rich and powerful, others were not. In rural Cuzco, as elsewhere in the Andes, there were always *curacas* who were tempted to abuse their relationships with their communities.[26] However, there existed "definite cultural limits to a *kuraka*'s ability to turn the labor and goods of his Indian subjects into his own personal wealth. The *kuraka*'s access to labor was defined in terms of Andean society as a reciprocal exchange. In order to be able to call upon the labor of his Indian subjects, the *kuraka* had to continue to observe, to some degree, the norms of Andean society by reciprocating in some way for those services."[27]

Introduction

In Quispicanchis and especially in Canas y Canchis the relations between *curacas* and *ayllus* and the communities functioned along traditional lines of reciprocity and respect to a greater degree than in some other regions of the Andes that have been studied and, indeed, to a much greater degree than my present research on the area surrounding Potosi demonstrates.[28] Thupa Amaro is just the most obvious example of a Canas y Canchis *curaca* who was both a businessman and a protector of the people he served. Economic activities, however, were just one source of potential friction that could cause sparks in this vital relationship. Problems connected to land, tribute collection, abuse of authority, and favoritism also bedeviled *curaca*-community relations.

The *curaca* was expected to provide guidance, organization and protection to the community. In turn, the community was expected to defer to his power and judgment, and to provide him with labor and with a greater share of communal lands. The *curaca* also represented the community to the outside world. Erosion or abuse of this relationship weakened traditional bonds and caused intracommunity tensions. Thus, in the Andes dual reciprocal relationships—one between *naturales* and the colonial state and one between *naturales* and their *curacas*—were vital in maintaining the polity.

Other sources of internal discord also existed. Community members (*originarios*) were sometimes at odds with those who had taken up residence (*forasteros*) in their *ayllus,* and though there were fewer *forasteros* in Quispicanchis and Canas y Canchis than in many other regions they were still an important group.[29] Moreover, intracommunity conflicts involving different *ayllus* and the opposing halves or moieties (*[h]anansaya* and *[h]urinsaya*) were very much a part of daily life.[30] The documentation attesting to internal community divisions is considerable, and often the differences do not involve just a few individuals but large factions, as one would expect when *ayllus* and moieties were at odds with one another. Tensions such as those relating to *curacas, forasteros, ayllus,* and moieties did not exist everywhere, yet they were common enough. Reinforced through daily experience, they could lead to serious rifts within communities. Many of these problems were exacerbated, if not created, by the state, but when they occurred along lines of internal division these tensions were focused inward rather than against the state. These internal conflicts, addressed within chapters of this book, were very important for they divided *naturales* against one another and thereby functioned to blunt, or divert, tensions away from the state and even caused people to turn to the state for resolutions.

For *naturales* the conditions of life sometimes improved, but more often if conditions changed they deteriorated. To meet increased demands communities and individual families responded with ever increasing levels of work (self-exploitation), although flight and relocation were options as well.[31] Until demands became so great that the social reproduction of an entire region was threatened, rebellion was an unlikely response to changing conditions. However, smaller scale violent protest or revolts increasingly punctuated the lives of *naturales* in the mid- to late eighteenth century, but they were directed against particular individuals whose actions or behavior were seen as abusive and excessive—outside Andean norms. When the degree of *abusos y excesos* was severe enough to transgress the Indians' sense of justice, the authority a person such as a corregidor may have enjoyed was delegitimized, leaving the offending individual open to attack. These face-to-face relations between *naturales* and local officials were very important in determining the course of events.

Although Andean scholars have observed conjunctures between state demands, changes in the colonial economy, and revolts and rebellions, we must also ask ourselves if there were additional reasons why protests and challenges to authority occurred when they did and why they took the forms they did. As conditions made it more difficult for the native peoples to meet colonial exactions, were officials who enforced the demands increasingly perceived as excessive and abusive? Did colonial officials actually resort to increased threats and force as villagers, unable or unwilling to meet the demands, became more resistant? Why, under the same combination of demands and problems, were some officials attacked while others were not?

Introduction

Rural Cuzco was never a peaceable kingdom. In addition to antagonism between indigenous and nonindigenous peoples, and between communities and *curacas*, must be added conflicts between communities. In a world in which survival meant having access to resources, it should come as no surprise that neighboring communities were often at odds with one another. However, most *naturales* lived their lives absorbed in the joys, sorrows, burdens, and routines of existence. Crops, fiestas, food, health, animals, tribute, birth, marriage, death, weather, water, and religion were just a few of the factors that dominated daily life. These factors are at the heart of being and are vital to this work, but because they are so enmeshed in peoples' lives they are dealt with indirectly as they affected life rather than as the subjects of separate chapters.

The chapters of this book expand outward from the village plaza in ever growing circles of involvement between indigenous and nonindigenous peoples and the state. Chapter 1 acquaints the reader with the peoples, cultures, and environments of Quispicanchis and Canas y Canchis while drawing attention to the rhythms of the *natural* world and of everyday life. It also introduces the reader to important features of the pre-Inca, Inca, and colonial history in the region that provide context and understanding for events in later chapters.

Though struggles over colonial exactions and forced labor have drawn a great deal of attention from scholars, equally important but more subtle struggles were waged between indigenous peoples and Europeans over cultural values and religious beliefs. Chapter 2 focuses on the issues and conflicts that developed between Andean peoples and the Spanish church and state over values related to sex, gender relations, and religion. Sometimes similar and sometimes conflictive, indigenous and European values made gender, sexual, and familial ideologies significant points of cultural contention, resistance, and articulation between *naturales* and Europeans. These colonial "dialogues" over personal relationships make this chapter vital in our understanding of questions of culture, identity, and colonialism in their eighteenth century indigenous and European forms.

Personal violence and robbery between indigenous peoples, as well as between Indians and non-Indians, irregularly punctuated daily life. Cultural values were very important in determining the attitudes and responses of the *naturales* to crime, and these relations are explored in chapter 3. Likewise, racial connotations in crime and violence are scrutinized and questions raised concerning common assumptions and perceptions of violence in indigenous lives. In the control of crime a certain symbiosis sometimes developed between indigenous peoples and the state that enhanced community solidarity and, at the same time, facilitated the functioning of the colonial regime. This relationship, fraught with ambiguities, had far-reaching implications for *naturales* and the state, which includes the question of social banditry (or lack thereof).

Land was basic to a community's survival, and individual access to communal lands was the right that most clearly defined community membership. As population fluctuation, state action, and usurpations made land an even more precious resource, and as ethnicity became more closely identified with the community or *ayllu*, control of land became even more important in the community's understanding of themselves as a people. The significance of land to the *naturales'* way of life, and their struggles to maintain their lands, are the subject of two chapters, one on Indian-Spanish land problems (chapter 4) and the other on the conflicts between indigenous communities and individuals over land (chapter 5). These chapters also make evident the very real importance of indigenous ties to the state through the legal system on which the communities relied, as well as examining the complex day-to-day and face-to-face interactions between *naturales* and Europeans that were vitally important in determining attitudes and actions of people—indigenous and otherwise—in rural Cuzco.

The toil and sweat of native peoples drove the colonial economy. The Spanish were dependent on indigenous labor, and their work in and for the European sector is the subject of chapter 6. Spurred by direct and indirect economic coercion, and sometimes by their own interests, *naturales* produced for the local, regional, and colonial markets through labor on their own lands, on Spanish haciendas, in *obrajes,* in the transport of goods, and in a myriad of other ways. From early in the colonial period the *naturales* of Quispicanchis and Canas y Canchis played vital roles in the colonial economy not only as centers of production but also of distribution.

The forced labor system known as the *mita* inextricably linked the *naturales* of Quispicanchis and Canas y Canchis and much of Alto Peru to the European political and economic systems. Compelled to labor in the bowels of Potosi, indigenous workers extracted enormous quantities of silver that helped maintain the Spanish empire and the growing world economy. However, this system of forced labor threatened the communities' well-being by transferring human and physical resources to the Spanish economic sector, causing internal discontent, and by provoking villagers to flee to avoid the rigors of Potosi. *Naturales* developed strategies to resist or ameliorate the impact of the *mita* while at the same time developing yet other strategies that ensured compliance with this demand to safeguard the community vis-à-vis the state. Disliked by virtually all Indians, the *mita* produced disjointed but continual protest and was a constant source of tension between *naturales* and the state. The complex and troublesome relationship between Potosi and the peoples of rural Cuzco, which parallels the problems of indigenous peoples in much of the southern Andes, is discussed in chapter 7.

In 1780 the contradictions and burdens of colonial society, combined with "Inca" leadership, led to a violent explosion in the Andes, and the peoples of Quispicanchis and Canas y Canchis were at the heart of this eruption. The rebel leader was a *curaca* in Canas y Canchis with an extensive network of family and associates in both provinces, and the rebellion is known by his name: Túpac Amaru. The deterioration of conditions, the development of conjunctures that led to this upheaval, and the rebellion itself are the focus of chapter 8. The movement, rooted in its local and cultural context to give it depth and to better understand human agency, is related to the complex events and changes—governmental, economic, and cultural—that heightened colonial, regional, and local tensions to the boiling point.

Finally, chapter 9 provides a brief overview of the heritage of rural

Cuzco in the wake of independence and of the continuing importance for modern Peru of what the villagers of Quispicanchis and Canas y Canchis did in the eighteenth century.

In this book I try to tell the story of the women, children, and men who fill its pages in a way that does justice to their lives, their perceptions, their problems, and their struggles with all the contradictions, the joys and sufferings, and the good and bad, in short, with all the humanity that this implies. In attempting to understand how they shaped their world at the same time they were shaped by it, I hope the reader's appreciation of the complexities of the colonial world, and the vitality of the people who lived in it, will be given new light.

The World of
Túpac Amaru

1

Nature, Society, and Imperial Heritages

WHEN THE Andean creator-God Viracocha arrived in Canas y Canchis he called out to the people, but they did not recognize him: "They all came at him with their arms to kill him. When he saw them coming, he understood what they were coming for and instantly caused fire to fall from heaven, burning a range of mountains near the Indians. When the Indians saw the fire, they feared they would be burned. Throwing their arms to the ground, they went straight to Viracocha and all threw themselves to the ground before him. When he saw them thus, he took his staff in his hands and went where the fire was. He gave it two or three blows with his staff, which put it completely out."[1]

In this way, according to one legend, the Canas people, who along with the Canchis inhabited the upper Vilcanota and surrounding region, came to know their creator.

Today, on the site where Viracocha made fire fall from the heavens, dark lava and boulders from the volcano Quimsachata rest at the edge of towering stone and adobe walls of an Inca temple dedicated to this god. Off to the side a small colonial church, nestled at the edge of the lava, marks the European intrusion into this world and Christian efforts to supplant Viracocha and other indigenous gods with their own vision of the creator. In late June, at the commemoration of the Inca festival of *Inti Raymi*, local people annually gather under the shadow of the volcano to celebrate and renew traditions. Through dance, children of the largely indigenous community, dressed in "indigenous" clothing and carrying war clubs, reenact the conquest. In this dance, however, there are no Europeans, for the conquest depicted is not that of Pizarro but of the Incas who brought the region under their control as they pushed south from Cuzco into the Aymara-speaking regions of Lake Titicaca and beyond.

This reenactment reflects two important realities. First, the indigenous world was embroiled in turmoil long before the arrival of Spaniards, conflict that would not be forgotten even in the wake of the tumultuous encounter with Europeans. Second, the early history of the Canas and Canchis peoples remains opaque as myth and history overlap. This chapter explores these realities and other heritages of human society that contoured the region's history prior to the eighteenth century. It also examines the impact of the natural world and of Inca and early Spanish imperialism on Quispicanchis and Canas y Canchis and in so doing lays the groundwork for understanding the chapters that follow.

Although it is certain that the Incas brought the Canas and Canchis under their imperial umbrella, when this took place and the nature of the interaction is less clear. Garcilaso de la Vega, the great mestizo historian and Inca advocate whose mother was of royal Inca blood and who grew up surrounded by Inca nobility, believed that Sinchi Roca, the second Inca ruler, brought the Canchis into the empire.[2] Pedro (de) Cieza de Leon, an early and generally trustworthy Spanish chronicler, understood that it was much later—under the reign of Viracocha Inca—that the peoples of the upper Vilcanota succumbed to Cuzco. According to Cieza de Leon, the Canchis at first not only rejected the Inca's emissaries but fought a pitched battle with Cuzco forces before being defeated. The Canas manifested a similar independence, but after learning of the Canchis' defeat they became more disposed to accept the terms of the Inca's envoy who offered jewels, fine clothing, and good treatment in exchange for service and subservience.[3] Father Bernabé Cobo, one of those amazingly curious friars who came to the New World, concurred with the peripatetic Cieza de Leon, but added that "these provinces of the Canas and Canches were always held in high esteem by the Inca Viracocha and his successors . . . because from the time that they yielded obedience to this Inca, they helped and served the Incas with notable effort and fidelity in all the wars and conquests that he undertook."[4]

Long before the armies from Cuzco carved the empire of Tawantinsuyu from Andean ethnicities, Canas y Canchis was a center of ethnic conflict, and these early battles left an important stamp on the region. The Vilcanota river drainage system makes the region especially desirable. The wider bottom lands were not only a relatively easy route for moving goods and people between the Lake Titicaca basin and Cuzco, but were more fertile, lower and better suited to agriculture than much of the surrounding territory, which was higher and used more for pasturing and the cultivation of a restricted number of high altitude crops.

Originally populated by Aymara speakers, the quality of the land and its strategic importance led to ongoing tensions and intrusions, making the region a buffer zone between the Aymara and Quechua worlds with a diverse ethnic population. This human mosaic did not prevent people from uniting under duress to confront intrusions by powerful neighbors. Neither the Canas nor the Canchis, however, seem to have had a strong central authority in the period just prior to Inca domination. By the time of the Inca conquest of the Colla (Aymara) center in Hatunquolla—the region beyond Canas y Canchis en route to Lake Titicaca from Cuzco—"no lord politically the equal of the king of Hatunquolla was to be found in either Canas or Canchis."[5]

This may have been due, in part, to the settlement patterns of the region, where, outside the valley, the rugged terrain and the focus on pasturing not only led to disperse habitation but to the interspersing of peoples from various communities and ethnicities.[6] The majority of the Canas lived on the west bank of the Vilcanota, while the Canchis were concentrated on the east side. There were, however, significant exceptions to this pattern and in outlying *ayllus* divisions tended to be more ambiguous.[7] In this situation the martial skills that were honed confronting outside threats were further sharpened against neighbors in land conflicts and other disputes. While the Incas sought to limit conflict in territories under their rule, Tawantinsuyu's imposition of settlers (*mitimaes*) to assure Cuzco's dominance only added to the ethnic complexity and division.[8] Some of the tensions between communities, *ayllus,* and moieties were released in ritual conflict known as *tinku,* which was also culturally vital in ensuring fertility. Among the most famous *tinku* are those in what, prior to modern boundary realignments, was Canas y Canchis, especially between the *ayllus* of Langui and Checca. These battles were frequently fought in the last days before lent—between the Sunday mass before Mardi Gras and Ash Wednesday, the time known as *carnestolendas.* The tinku tradition still persists, and modern participants dress in their finest to do battle, but the ritual nature of these encounters does not mean that they are less serious or bloody. Not only are lives and goods placed at risk, but women are sometimes captured and treated as concubines. Men are often seriously injured or killed, but the death is believed to ensure prosperous harvests and fruitful livestock.[9] When asked why they fight, one modern respondent stated so that "we will continue to exist and we will have potatoes all year long." During the colonial period officials expressed displeasure with these encounters, one such Spaniard referring to them as "bestial games." After tinku deaths colonial authorities sometimes jailed those responsible, but the weight of communal opinion normally led to the release of those implicated. When the young men of Marcaconga and Sangarará met to "*jugar las carnestolendas,*" as had been their custom, a villager from Marcaconga was struck in the forehead by a rock, and others continued to throw at him while he was on the ground. He later died. His cacique complained that the encounter had been more of an attack on his people than a traditional battle, but those who had been detained were later released due to the customary nature of the fight.[10] Likewise, in 1772 a young girl, Sebastiana Lazo, was killed when the two moieties of Langui, *hanansaya* and *hurinsaya,* fought after drinking chicha during *carnestolendas.* Spanish authorities complained of the "abuse and *mala costumbre* they have in entertaining themselves in such a dangerous way in . . . the pueblo of Langui and the rest of the province as is well known" and detained the young man believed to be responsible. Sebastiana's father, as upset as he was, complied with custom and asked the corregidor to release the prisoner. The corregidor acceded to the father's wishes, but warned the young man not to participate in *carnestolendas* again. The ritual, however, persisted.[11]

Unity was further hampered by the diversity of tongues, which made Canas y Canchis, if not quite a "Tower of Babel," a linguistically distinct zone. Originally Aymara speakers populated the area, but contestation and Inca influence brought Quechua, the imperial tongue. The process of linguistic change, however, was not an even one. According to the lexicographer Ludovico Bertonio some Canas continued to speak Aymara until the seventeenth century. The languages that emerged were hybrid dialects of Quechua strongly influenced by Aymara, but they were distinct enough for Guamán Poma to refer to them separately and include Canche and Cana among the "*muchas lenguaxes*" of the realm.[12]

This regional fragmentation persisted, and the Canchis and Canas entered the colonial period precocious in their internal divisions. Spanish policies further accelerated the fracturing of ethnic identity and provoked new tensions, especially over land. Before the arrival of Europeans, most people had lived in small, relatively dispersed settlements. The desire to organize native peoples for purposes of extracting labor, meeting economic demands, converting them to Christianity, and bringing them more fully under governmental control led Spain to resettle people into larger communities known as reductions (*reducciones*). Established by Viceroy Toledo in the early 1570s, these reductions eroded older forms of regional and ethnic identity.[13] However, over the sixteenth and seventeenth centuries *ayllus* often rekindled old bonds and reestablished more extended patterns of settlement to meet the pragmatic needs of everyday life. An *ayllu* of Layo cultivated lands some distance from the village and built homes and kept livestock there.[14] Though the cacique of this *ayllu* eventually asked for recognition as an independent settlement to "be spared exploitation by other groups in the village," in most instances the reduction communities, also organized into parishes, persisted as centers of political and administrative life throughout the colonial period and even beyond.[15]

Disease also stimulated fragmentation. Ravaged by epidemics, indigenously controlled lands that the state determined to be in excess of needs were sold or distributed. Likewise, the horrors of *mita* service in Potosi also led people to flee their natal communities while *naturales* from other regions rented vacated lands to live as *forasteros* and, thus, escape the *mita*. Often these people were eventually incorporated into communities, but they too had diverse origins. The 238 *forasteros* in the mining center of Condoroma (Canas y Canchis) reflect the eclecticism of this process as they came from some 94 different *pueblos*, 197 different *ayllus*, and were subject to 201 different *curacas*.[16] By the eighteenth century colonial pressures and changes in the indigenous world had led to "ethnic" identities in Quispicanchis and Canas y Canchis that were at least as complex as they had been prior to the European encounter, this despite a plummeting population. And this identity was expressed most clearly not at a regional or broad ethnic level, but at the level of the community, moiety, and *ayllu* that became, in effect, "ethnicities."[17]

The peoples of rural Cuzco were not alone in this process. Ethnic fragmentation was widespread in the Andes. For instance, Roger Rasnake, in his study of the Yura in Bolivia, argues that one consistent Spanish policy through the centuries was that of "turning Inkas and [ethnic groups such as the] Wisixsas into 'Indians,' the goal of conquest through homogenization and destructuration." Rasnake sees Toledo's reductions as an important part of this process for "a consciousness of wider ethnic identity was lost; 'new' loyalties based on the *reducciones* were evolved, demonstrating a more localized sense of ethnicity . . . [and] by the middle of the eighteenth century the wider sense of loyalty had disappeared."[18]

Although the Spanish may have sought to "homogenize" native peoples by undermining more inclusive and larger senses of ethnicity, the end result was often nearly the opposite. The communities in regions such as Quispicanchis and Canas y Canchis became both sta-

TABLE 1. Prominent Parishes, *Ayllus,* and Settlements
in Quispicanchis and Canas y Canchis

Quispicanchis	Canas y Canchis
Acha	Ancocaba
Acomayo*	Cacha (San Pablo de)*
Acopia	Cacha (San Pedro de)
Acos*	Cangalla
Andahuaylillas*	Checa*
Ccatcca	Charrachape(i)
(San Juan) Caymana	Checacupe*
Guaiqui	Checasupe(i)
Guaraypata	Com(n)bapata
Guascarquiguar	Condoroma
Guaro(c)	Coporaque*
Lucre	Hancoba
Marcaconga	Hilave
Marcapata*	Langui*
Mohina	Layo
Munyapata	Lurucache
Ocongate	Marangani
Oropesa*	Pampamarca*
Pomacanche*	Pichigua*
Pomachape	Pitumarca
Papres* (San Juan de la Cruz)	Senca (Singa)
Pirque	Sicuani*
Quehuar	Surimana
Quiqujana*	Tinta*
Quispillacata	Tungasuca
Sallac	Yanaoca*
Sangarará*	Yauri*
Urcos*	

*Parish centers

[7]

ble and flexible, allowing people to survive as a unit but with a multiplicity of localized identities. Thus, the Spanish achieved part of
their goal in that communal identity was not as threatening as larger
regional and ethnic identities, but the reductions also inadvertently
provided a mechanism for indigenous peoples to redefine or restruc-
ture themselves, to preserve a cultural identity, and most importantly
to survive.

In the short run the very process of creating reductions exacerbated indigenous disputes over land. Toledo's upheavals set in motion
forces that led to decades of tensions between certain communities.
This was just one aspect of European land tenure policies that affected native life. Taking lands dedicated to the Inca state and religion, the granting to (or purchasing of) property by non-Indians,
combined with the appropriation of the labor and resources needed
to work lands through the distribution of encomiendas also transformed life. However, one of the most lucrative of the first two dozen
encomiendas granted in Canas y Canchis went not to a Spaniard, but
to Inca royalty. Paullu Inca cooperated with the Spanish, while his
half-brother, Manco, led the resistance against the Europeans. For
his cooperation Paullu Inca was bestowed many privileges, including
an encomienda over the former Canas center of Hatun Cana (Santa
Lucía de Pichigua). His grandson, Melchor Carlos Inca, was still
listed as holding this encomienda in the 1580s.[19]

Due to climate, distance from Cuzco, and smaller concentrations
of fertile soils, Canas y Canchis was not as attractive to Europeans as
Quispicanchis, where many of the Cuzco elite had lands and homes.
The late colonial traveler and geographer Cosme Bueno, scrutinizing
rural Cuzco with his keen eye for the economic underpinnings of
life, wrote of Canas y Canchis (see plate 1):

Because there are many snow covered mountains, its climate is extremely cold most everywhere. Nevertheless, wheat, barley, corn,
potatoes, *ocas* and quinua grow there and in warmer regions—ra-
vines near the rivers—some fruit although not in abundance. In
the higher regions where pasture is abundant cattle are raised as

well as great numbers of *vicuñas, h(g)uanacos, vizcachas*—that are similar to hares or rabbits—deer (*ciervos*) and partridges. In the rivers large *bagres* are caught. There are many lakes on which aquatic birds such as ducks . . . breed. . . . Many silver mines are found in this province, but they are not worked at present due to flooding in some and cave-ins in others. Those of Condoroma, that have suffered the first accident, are an exception. . . . In the jurisdiction of . . . Yauri there are two copper mines that are worked. There are also some gold mines; but not of consequence.

Of Quispicanchis Cosme Bueno observed (see plate 2),

Its climate is diverse. The climate of the valley of Oropesa which is the closest to Cuzco is temperate and desirable. It is for this reason that many distinguished *vecinos* from Cuzco and members of religious orders have haciendas where they grow corn, wheat, and other grains, fruits and vegetables. . . . Almost all the rest of the province is cold although wheat, corn, and other crops (*semillas*) are also grown; in the higher regions there are several estancias that supply Cuzco with cattle and other livestock (*ganados mayores y menores*) especially towards the east of the province where the Cordillera (mountain range) de Vilcanota runs. . . . Passing the *cordillera* one finds the *montaña* of Andes de Cuchóa where a broad river, named Araza, flows. . . . On a mountain named Camanti near this river there is a gold mine, and in the surrounding region various coca haciendas where bananas, pineapples, papayas, limes, granadillas and other fruits of the *montaña* are harvested. Also various poisonous insects live. For protection against barbarous Indians, those with interests in the mine continually maintain some armed guards.

This province is watered by two notable rivers, with some fish and many arroyos—among these the Huatanay that passes Cuzco . . . [and] flows into the Vilcamayo river that exits in the north of the province . . . and it enters from Canas Y Canches. The other notable river [is the] Apurimac. . . . A half league from Oropesa . . . there is a lake that today is named Mohina . . . where many reeds . . . some fish and water birds grow. . . . There are some other small lakes and also a large one named Pomacanchi.[20]

Although colonial descriptions of the peoples of Quispicanchis and Canas y Canchis are not abundant a few, reflecting the lenses of the authors perhaps as much as mirroring the observed, do exist. Cieza de Leon noted that the Canchis were

> intelligent and homely (*domestic [domésticos]*) Indians, without malice, and always skilful [*sic*] in working, especially gold and silver. They also had large flocks of sheep (*ovejas y carneros*). Their villages are like those of their neighbors; they wear the same clothes, with a black . . . [braids] round the head, the ends of which hang down as low as the chin. While the Canas all wear clothes, both men and women, and they have large, round, high woolen caps on their heads. Before they were subjugated by the Incas, they had their villages in the mountain fastness, whence they came forth to make war; afterward they descended into the valley.[21]

Guamán Poma, perhaps influenced by Spanish views, used skin color as a factor in his descriptions. The peoples of Quispillacta (Quispicanchis) were "somewhat white and gentlemen (*gentilhombres*)," while the Canas were "somewhat dark (*moreno*) and of tall stature."[22] Almost two centuries later the *Mercurio Peruano* provided another portrait that appears to reflect the distancing of the indigenous and nonindigenous worlds, as viewed by Euro-Peruvians, in the aftermath of the Thupa Amaro rebellion:

> [The Canas] were distinct in their character as well as customs and dress. They were very arrogant, serious and melancholic, their music was mournful and very slow and even their attire was doleful: their shirts, and their blankets and capes were black. . . . The Canches were happy, festive and lazy, but very poor; therefore they dressed in rags and skins.

TABLE 2. Tributary and *Forastero* Population of Canas y Canchis in the Mid–Seventeenth Century

Community	Tributaries	Forasteros	Total
Sicuani	198	150	348
Lurucache	124	59	183
Marangani	119	17	136
Cacha	134	25	159
San Pablo	202	36	238
Tinta	154	46	200
Pampamarca	96	13	109
Tungasuca	65	13	78
Surimana	39	31	70
San Juan de la Cruz	122	10	132
Combapata	151	22	173
Checacupe	192	12	204
Cangalla	10	14	24
Pitumarca	115	11	126
Coporaque	215	54	269
Yauri	302	44	346
Condoroma	0	238	238
Pichigua	354	43	397
Checasupa	144	64	208
Languisupa	162	15	177
Layosupa	99	30	129
Yanaoca	152	86	238
Totals	3149	1033	4182

Source: Luis Miguel Glave, *Vida símbolos y batallas. Creación y recreación de la comunidad indígena. Cusco, siglos XVI–XX* (Lima, 1992), Cuadro 7, 75.

The Canches are medium of height, and very bold, fickle, restless, disloyal and deceitfully obedient; for when they can get away with not observing . . . orders . . . with impunity, they do so. They are hardworking and not at all lazy. . . . The Canas, even though of darker skin are corpulent and better shaped: they almost have the same proportions as the others; they . . . ride horses and have their houses adorned with tiles, tables, and other furniture. But for the most part, all of them are dull and faint-hearted, taciturn and lovers of solitude: they build their huts in the most rugged and remote of mountains: at the sight of travelers they flee like wild beasts: in their conduct they are harsh, and are even curt with their own wives; and they have a great tendency towards the most ridiculous superstitions.[23]

Nothing was more vital to these *naturales* than their lands. Land allowed them to survive and socially reproduce and, ultimately, defined them as distinct peoples. The *naturales* knew their lands, the microclimates, and the signs of changing weather and seasons as well as they knew the backs of their hands. Their lives depended on the land and this knowledge. Where possible they remade nature to fit their needs. They altered the landscape with terraces that turned steep hillsides into more gently sloped, productive land. They brought life-giving water to their fields with irrigation canals and aqueducts similar to those that Cieza de Leon observed in Urcos where "water was conducted with great labour from a river."[24]

Over the centuries a productive relationship had evolved in the southern Andes between cameloid herding, agriculture, and land preparation. This *"papa, llama, y chaquitaclla"* (potato, llama, and foot plow) complex was a mainspring in the region's livestock and agricultural regime.[25] Soils in the higher reaches were often weak and needed to lie fallow for years. Llamas and alpacas grazed on these and other lands and fertilized them. Manure was also collected to enrich the soil at the time of sowing. The *chaquitaclla* allowed steep hillsides to be worked, as well as valley lands, and its long spade turned the earth deeply. By not breaking the soil the same way as a plow, the *chaquitaclla* helped avert problems of compaction and erosion.

After the conquest the herding tradition of many Andean peoples such as those in the highland zones around Cuzco left them better prepared to deal with European livestock than those without such a tradition. Accustomed to llamas and alpacas, these *naturales* readily incorporated European cattle and, especially, sheep into their way of life. The extensive pasture needs of the herds and flocks with high summer pastures and lower winter pastures was an important factor in maintaining extensive land use after the arrival of Europeans. The herder-agriculturist tradition based on transhumance was preserved, and as an added bonus sheep fertilizer proved to be even richer than that of cameloids.

This was quite a different scenario than occurred in areas with a weaker herding tradition, such as Cajamarca, and especially in New Spain where nature had not blessed the region with large domesticable animals and therefore people had no livestock tradition. This was important to the evolution in Mexico of a system of large livestock ranches dominated by Europeans, for native people had no strong use-based claim to the extensive pasture lands. In New Spain native peoples eventually came to own sheep in some numbers, but cattle, other than as draft animals, were not typically adopted to any great extent by most core-area Meso-American people. Contrast this with the situation in the southern Andean highlands where even in the late eighteenth century indigenous people still owned a majority of the livestock in the region, and the holdings of Europeans were nowhere near as significant as in New Spain. "In the Andes . . . the extension of the *mancha india* was practically identical with what may be called the *mancha cameloida*. . . . In other words, the survival of an Indian community peasantry was most marked precisely where the continuity of Indian livestock raising had been strongest."[26]

Although the natural world could be beneficent to its human inhabitants, as in endowing their world with cameloids, it could also be cruel. Frost, hail, drought, torrential rains, and plant diseases all threatened crops. Earthquakes also shook the region. Late 1746 and early 1747 was a period of unusually frequent and severe seismic activity. The Marques de Valle Umbroso, living in Cuzco but with his hacienda near Oropesa in Quispicanchis, recorded some of the violent shaking and other calamities of that period. On one October day alone there were fifty *temblores* at the *obraje* of Lucre (Quispicanchis), and the people moved outside for fear that their houses might collapse. Later in the month earthquakes again disturbed the zone. On Christmas night the streets of Cuzco came alive with commotion and panic after an earthquake or loud noise startled people. A couple of days later the residents of Oropesa and other nearby Quispicanchis communities heard a thunder-like noise that came from within the earth as sometimes occurs before earthquakes hit.

The populace wondered as to the cause of so much violent shaking. Some speculated that the mountain behind Cuzco was full of water and about to overflow, others affirmed that they had seen a comet which was interpreted as a sign, while still others had had a revelation of a Chilean nun who would bring ruin to the kingdom. On the next to last day of the year a devout religious procession dedicated to the *Señor de los Temblores* and the Virgins of Belén and La Soledad made its way through Cuzco. Some five thousand people filled the streets, and penitents flogged themselves until wounds opened and blood ran while others carried large crosses or scourged their flesh with thorns. But the earth continued to quake. Quiquijana, Urcos, Andaguaylillas, and Lucre were all hit. In Oropesa forty *temblores* rattled nerves one day. With rumors of an earthquake that was supposed to strike on 5 January 1747, crowds took to Cuzco's streets on the night of the fourth with "such noise and clamor that a woman aborted." Only two days later the residents of Oropesa rapidly organized a religious procession to implore God's relief after being violently shaken from their sleep in the early morning hours. Mixed with all the earthquakes were heavy rains that also put a strain on adobe buildings. On the second Sunday of 1747 parishioners had just left mass in Lucre when the chapel collapsed. The following Sunday another earthquake hit. Over the next month, rains, earthquakes, and fierce lightning storms pounded the region. On 24 February the moon even disappeared as a total lunar eclipse further darkened the night sky.[27] To the residents of Quispicanchis and Canas y

Canchis it must have seemed that something had gone wrong in their relationship with nature and the gods, or God.

Too much rain caused buildings to collapse and fields to flood, but drought struck communities even harder. Seeds didn't germinate, crops died in the field, and animals grew skinny and weak, as did the people. In addition, communities found it difficult to meet their tribute obligations, which threatened their right to lands. After a season of sparse precipitation the *curaca* of Mohina (Oropesa, Quispicanchis) requested to be allowed to pay tribute in silver instead of in wheat and corn.[28] Frost, hail, unseasonable snows, and other such calamities also threatened life. In Marangani (Canas y Canchis) a particularly cold and harsh year left pastures in bad shape and villagers feared that their animals were going to be in total ruin.[29] But in other communities people feared not just for the animals, but for their own lives. When a heavy frost blanketed Quispicanchis one April maturing crops were killed. In the especially frigid villages of Acopia and Mosocllacta where the freeze had been even harder "all the miserable people . . . [were] perishing from hunger and without having the means . . . to sow [new crops] and pay their tribute."[30]

While Andean peoples sought to contour or harness nature with the construction of irrigation systems, terraces, and so forth, in actuality the rhythms of nature contoured their lives. Rains, frosts, breaking the soil, planting, weeding, harvesting, storing, times of abundance, periods of dearth and hunger, and the birthing and moving of livestock; all these natural events and forces played a part in determining the cycles of indigenous life. The first months of the year—January through March—were the times of heaviest rains, which, in combination with the relative warmth of the Andean summer, brought new life to the fields. People busied themselves caring for young plants and protecting them against the predation of birds and other animals. Crops such as potatoes and ocas had to be hilled. Fields that had been fallowed were also broken for the next planting. Despite the sprouting crops January was often a time of scarcity and hunger as the old crops had been used up and the new ones had not matured, but it was also a time of anticipation as the last corn, potatoes, and wheat were sown. By February and March the worst had passed. Vegetables began to ripen and livestock gave birth, which ensured the future. From April through June and July crops ripened, fields were harvested, and new grasses put flesh back on the protruding ribs of livestock and people. Families needed to guard their fields more intensely as maturing crops provided temptation to both man and animal, but for the most part these were good months as stomachs were full. In May corn began to be harvested, and by June potatoes, *ocas*, *ollucos*, quinua, and other crops were mature. Frosts also made it possible to process the *chuño*—freeze-dried potatoes—that converted bitter high-altitude potatoes into an edible food that could be stored and used when needed.

After the major growing and harvesting seasons, time was set aside to make repairs or improvements on homes, religious sites, roads, and irrigation ditches. Corresponding with this work, before the arrival of the Spaniards, had been the festival of *Inti Raymi*, which paid homage to the sun for the generosity that brought life to the earth. In the colonial era this period, near the summer solstice, continued to be observed. The day of San Juan, 24 June, remained a time when many *ayllus* gathered to make decisions related to communal business and duties, to feast, and, in places such as rural Cuzco, to pay half their annual tribute, which the colonial regime made due at this time. By July the harvests were largely finished, but work continued as fields demanded further attention before the upcoming plantings, including fertilizing the fields with dried, and sometimes burnt, cameloid and sheep dung that had been gathered for this purpose.

From August through December the fields continued to be worked and planted, particularly those in areas that could be irrigated. As spring came and the climate warmed seeds began sprouting in irrigated fields. August was a time for plowing and for sowing early corn (*michica sara*) and some varieties of potatoes, particularly small potatoes (*mauay papa, chaucha papa*). Guamán Poma thought that this was a good time of the year, for not only were vegetables available, but "in this month there is no sickness or pestilence and food is cheap, the wine (u[v]ino [chicha]) sufficient and the meat good." September was known as the month of planting corn and, because the winds blew, it was also a good time to thresh grains, but for those who did not have irrigated lands for early crops a scarcity began to haunt them that would last until near the end of the year. October was a time of shearing, as sheep, llamas, and alpacas had their wool cut and mange tended to, and with new seeds in the fields people once again had to be on guard against birds and animals. November was normally a time of drought when, at least in Inca times, people implored Viracocha to bring them the rain that would sprout seeds and bring forth new crops. It was also the time in which people traditionally worshiped the dead who were seen as the link between the surface of the earth and the "inner world" where the seeds and roots were. December was a busy month. The rains began and those who didn't have their dry-land (not irrigated) fields ready would no longer be able to work the earth. Dry-land or seasonal corn (cochaca sara) was planted as were potatoes, ocas, and quinua. Guamán Poma warned of all the disease that appears at this time of year. But he closed his comments in December in a positive manner noting that melons, lucumas, avocados, and peaches were all ripening, this despite the Christian colonials making the other half of tribute due at the time of the birth of their savior.[31]

As a result of the Columbian exchange the Andean diet incorporated new foods, both plant and animal, as well as beasts that altered the way in which work was done. However, much of the new agricultural and livestock production, especially wheat and cattle, was destined primarily for the nonindigenous market. But cabbage, Swiss chard, onions, garlic, barley, habas, chicken, pork, and mutton added further complexity to Andean stews, while eggs, cheese, and a variety of fruits and nuts such as apples, pears, figs, peaches, citrus, olives, and almonds were among the many other foods that enriched diets. These foods complemented a cuisine that varied from region to region but which centered on potatoes, quinua, ocas, ají (chili), squashes, avocados, *tarawi* (lupin), *huacatay* (a pungent herb used in sauces and cooking), *cuyes* (guinea pigs), llama, alpaca, and occasional fowl such as doves and ducks.

Spuds, however, were the staple around which meals focused. Potatoes were selected for their appropriateness to different soils and altitudes as well as gustatorial properties and length of survival after being dug. Bitter potatoes, with alkaloids that protected them from extreme cold, could be grown high in the Andes. The long lasting, freeze-dried product made from these potatoes, *chuño,* was a great boon to the food supply. Farther down the mountainsides, in valley floors, and in special ecologic niches such as canyons or near water, other crops and a staggering array of regular (nonbitter) potatoes were cultivated. Diverse varieties sown in a range of soils and climatic zones provided insurance against diseases and natural misfortunes. The long lasting and flavorful *ccompis* might be a most valued potato, but generations of experience and knowledge taught people not to rely solely on it. These "safety-first" agricultural practices were "designed over centuries of trial and error to produce the most stable and reliable yield possible under the circumstances."[32] Even the furrows for the potatoes varied to meet the needs of the plants and the supply of water. Near lakes or lowlands where standing water was a problem higher furrows were built in special patterns that allowed the fields to more readily drain, but in dry areas furrows were constructed to maintain water (see plate 3).[33]

Community lands were worked on a communal basis, and individual plots were worked by the family and others who might be involved in labor exchanges. On family plots men and women performed separate but complementary tasks. Men turned the soil with the *chaquitaclla* or Andean foot plow, and women, the bearers of fertility, placed the seed in the earth.

Although the steadfast rhythms of nature were not susceptible to Spanish influence, Europeans quickly made their presence felt in Andean villages, particularly as they sought to control labor and extract wealth from the *ayllus.* Initially, the extension of colonial rule was haphazard, based primarily on need, convenience, and desire. In the upper Vilcanota one of the first prolonged contacts between *naturales* and the Europeans was a foraging (pillaging) expedition sent out by the besieged and desperate Spaniards in Cuzco who were being hard pressed by the forces of Manco Inca. Some seventy Spaniards scoured the region for almost a month bringing back to their compatriots some two thousand head of livestock.[34]

The granting of *encomiendas* further tightened the Spanish grip over the region for with *encomiendas* came greater supervision, control, and demands. When the crown tried to limit the power of *encomenderos* in the 1540s with the passage of the reformist "New Laws" these lords of the land rose in rebellion. The rebellion was crushed, but the crown had learned there were limits to its power, and part of the process of stabilization was stripping the rebels of their encomiendas while rewarding others with new grants.[35] Thus, for the peoples of the upper Vilcanota the situation changed little, except that the crown had learned that colonial realities could place limits on pro-indigenous reform.

In the 1560s *corregimientos* were established, and the corregidor, the most powerful local representative of the colonial state, became a fixture in indigenous life. The corregidor enforced labor assignments, collected tribute, served as judge in legal disputes, saw that the *mita* was complied with, and sold goods in the *reparto*. In addition, the corregidor might have lands, relatives, businesses, and labor needs that impacted his functioning in office. To a large degree the reputation of the corregidor depended not just on the colonial policies he enforced but on the character, habits, needs, beliefs, and conscience of the individual in the office. These personal variations had a profound influence on indigenous perceptions of the state and thus on the reciprocal relations that guided their dealings with the colonial regime.

Although local officials such as the corregidor were dealt with on a face-to-face basis, the Spanish monarch was typically viewed with a deference and respect similar to that which the Inca had commanded. The king, for the most part, was considered to be above the evil and exploitation done in his name. This special tie to the king was perhaps most clear in indigenous compliance with the Potosi *mita*. The Inca had extracted *mita* labor as part of the reciprocal relationship of obligations and rights that linked the Inca and his subjects. In the colonial period *mita* work was also viewed by the indigenous people of the upper Vilcanota and other places as a vital, though increasingly onerous, part of the pact of reciprocity they believed existed between themselves and the crown and which guaranteed their rights to land and other fundamental aspects of life that preserved their existence. *Mitayos* from a province neighboring Canas y Canchis even argued that their service to the king through the *mita* endowed them with special rights. They made demands of other Indians en route to Potosi, rioted, remained defiant, and even meted out punishment in the name of the king: "The *mita* Indians did not fail to note that the *mita* was a 'painful task,' and that in Potosí they would 'undergo hardships,' but it is also evident that compliance with this obligation was perceived as part of a peculiar relationship with the colonial state, or more precisely, with the king himself, which permitted the *mita* workers to establish an equivalency, or identification, between themselves and the monarch."[36]

Like the *mita*, Toledo's other impositions penetrated deeply into local life. His orders restructured ethnicity and even put a new face on the *ayllus*. Although geography and other natural factors could cause modifications, the Spanish symmetry of a grid pattern village with a central plaza, church, and official buildings at its core was decreed. The viceroy also stipulated the type of house—one story, rectangular, with a door that opened on to the street—in which families were to live. Toledo even tried to control the size of communities with a target population of not more than 500 tributaries or a total population of 2,500 to 3,000 people. "This population size was determined by the number of Indians that one resident priest could effectively catechize rather than the quantity or quality of subsistence resources."[37] During his years of work reshaping Andean life, Toledo took a prolonged break from his travels in Checacupe (Canas y Canchis) to write to the king and issue new mandates that would transform the world around him. One wonders if the viceroy spent any restless nights in Checacupe contemplating the value and values of the world he was altering.

In the century or so after the Toledan "reforms," the period before this study begins, Quispicanchis and Canas y Canchis went through the pains of population decline, out-migration, and continuing exploitation, but at the same time *naturales* learned how to better cope with, accommodate, challenge, deceive, and live alongside Europeans. They became active and knowledgeable participants—vital historical actors—in a maturing colonial society.

The process of dealing with the Europeans was somewhat eased by Spanish reliance on indigenous self-rule. While imposing their demands and establishing a regional governance structure, *curacas* were left in charge of *ayllus* and moieties. The Europeans also made provisions for village governments that mirrored their own but with communities selecting their own officials. Men, but in reality couples for both man and wife had responsibilities in many of the offices, were nominated and selected by the adult males of the village to fill offices in the church and civil structure. These offices or *"cargos"* marked a man's (couple's) standing and stature in the community. Though a burden, to be selected was an honor. And it was after fulfilling several of these offices well that a man (couple) rose in esteem within the community and could be considered for the higher and most honored positions in village life.

Naturales in the more prosperous zones of Quispicanchis were under the close scrutiny of Spanish eyes due to the extensive non-indigenous population and land holdings. More remote zones remained relatively free to control their internal functioning within the parameters established, or enforced, by the colonial system. To aid in the articulation of Andean and Spanish judicial systems, which brought indigenous subjects more fully into the European orbit, the crown appointed a "protector of Indians." This official assisted native peoples with legal cases that could not be resolved by internal means alone, and indigenous people became incredibly adept at understanding and using Spanish law.

If the state made demands and meddled in village affairs, the church went to the core of life. In addition to serving crown and God, friars and priests often had their own economic interests including haciendas, mines, trade, and so forth. Thus, the person who said your mass, baptized your children, married you, heard your confession, and buried you also made demands on your labor and production. You plowed his fields, cooked his meals, cleaned his house and stable, pastured his sheep, and often provided gifts such as fresh eggs, fish from the river, or an old hen for Sunday dinner. These demands came in addition to those that were due the church—work on its lands, building projects and repair, religious celebrations and pageants, sextons, choir members—all were part of this world.

Many of these burdens, personal as well as institutional, were not resented, and some were even remunerated. Few people resented service to a good priest, but in the course of their lives most *naturales* experienced two, three, or even more priests. Like corregidors, the priests' characters, habits, demands, concerns for the people in the *ayllus,* and their ties to nonindigenous peoples varied. Catholic personnel were powerful economic and political forces in community life. Priests sometimes rivaled *curacas* in strength and community following. These two poles of power could also work together to the benefit—or detriment—of villagers; other times they became the magnets around which communal factions adhered. But while temporal concerns were central, the harvest of souls was vital.

Priests worked in overt and subtle ways to bring people into the Christian fold. The apparent fierceness of the Spanish and their God and saints was not necessarily a hindrance to acceptance of the European belief system for people who already had been subjugated to Inca religion by force and who had come to know another creator through the fire he rained down on them from the heavens. Giving up their own gods, however, was quite a different matter. For the peoples of Quispicanchis and Canas y Canchis, as throughout the Andean world, the natural world was ripe with divinity. Mountains, lakes, springs, rocks, and passes, the sun and moon, lightning, and untold numbers of *huacas* and household or field gods known as *conopas,* not to mention ancestors, were part of the supernatural world.

To migrate not only meant leaving behind home and kin but the divine world that provided spiritual meaning to your life. Father Cobo thought the "Indians of Peru were so idolatrous that they worshiped as gods almost every kind of thing created."[38] Cobo and others sought to change this by bringing the world and ways of the Christian God to people. Many of the Europeans saw this as a special challenge, for it was not the *naturales,* but "the common enemy of mankind [who], using malice and astuteness, succeeded in usurping from these blind people the adoration that they really owed to their true Creator, and he [the devil] kept them prisoners in harsh bondage. . . . [H]e reigned over them for many centuries until the power of the Cross started stripping him of his authority and ousting him from this land here as well as from other regions of the New World."[39]

As appealing as Jesus, Mary, and a host of saints were, pantheistic peoples did not easily abandon old beliefs just because they might have accepted new ones. The profundity of Andean religion made the Europeans' project of extirpation or erosion of faith in *huacas, conopas,* and the natural world Sisyphean. As one indigenous man inquired, "Father, are you tired of taking our idols from us? Take away that mountain if you can, since that is the god I worship."[40]

This interchange and conflict over religious values, this moral-cultural dialogue, began early in the colonial period, and though the intensity waxed and waned, it persisted because at stake were fundamental values. *Cofradías* (sodalities or brotherhoods), saints days, and syncretic Christianity became central to most villagers' way of life. Through the introduction of these beliefs and institutions European Catholics provided Andean peoples with powerful spiritual and temporal resources that proved to be extremely important in shaping their identity and assuring their survival. However, the conflict and redefinition—this praxis—of community and selves over the issue of values was ongoing, and one of the arenas in which this interaction or cultural dialogue took place was in the realm of intimate life and relationships.

2

Sexual Values and Marital Life
in the Colonial Crucible

... hay costumbre entre los indios casi generalmente no casarse sin primero haberse conocido y hecho vida maridable entre si. ... Ordeno y mando que se procure, así por los sacerdotes, corregidores, caciques y alcaldes, persuadir y quitar a los dichos indios esta costumbre tan nociva y perniciosa a su conversión, policía y cristiandad, haciendo castigos ejemplares. ... VICEROY FRANCISCO DE TOLEDO

BY 1759 Doña Maria Hincho and her husband, Don Mariano Puma, had been married for some forty years. More fortunate in a material sense than many others in their community, this indigenous couple owned land—a small hacienda—and animals. Perhaps this derived from Don Mariano's heritage as a noble Inca and being the son of a cacique. Doña Maria and Don Mariano, however, had no children. When Don Mariano was seventy-four years old the couple, being Christians and not having offspring, decided to donate much of their wealth to the church. In so doing they also showed concern for the members of their community, Santa Lucía de Pichigua, as well as love for each other. They specified that some of the rent from the hacienda and the animals donated to the church be used to help defray community religious expenditures, especially expenses for the fiesta of San Francisco Javier. And they specified that "for the salvation of our souls," a *capellanía* (chaplaincy) also be established with the rents of the hacienda. The respect and love this aging Indian couple had for one another was very clear. Even though Don Mariano was the one who formally donated the lands, he made certain that it was "their" act and that the *capellanía* was for "their" souls, the donation of the hacienda reflecting their commitment to one another, their

Christian devotion, and their concern for their community. Indeed, the donated hacienda was named Pumahincho, a combination of their two surnames.[1]

The values this couple expressed reflect the complex nature of Indian society in the late colonial period. By aiding the community in meeting its religious expenses they demonstrated the persistence of the value of communal solidarity. In expressing their devotion to one another they represented the ideal for married couples in both indigenous and Spanish society. And through their donations to the Catholic church the couple showed their commitment, and that of the community, to the religion brought by the Europeans. As native people in late colonial society, Don Mariano and Doña Maria saw no conflict or contradiction in subscribing to an array of values that reflected the complicated world in which they lived. Some of these values were primarily of indigenous origin, some were Spanish, and some were a mixture or were indigenous values (recognizing that indigenous peoples did not necessarily share the same values and that values change) that paralleled and coexisted with those of Europeans. This created an ambiguous relationship between Andean peoples and European culture and the colonial state, as compliance with Spanish ways sometimes involved little if any change, native peoples even using the state to enforce accepted indigenous-European values at times. In other instances, however, the values were in conflict, and tensions rose in the subsequent struggles. Thus, at least by the eighteenth century the value systems of native peoples in rural Cuzco and other regions of the Andes, while sometimes reflecting their distinctive roots, were not clearly separated from European convictions but were intricate and heterogeneous systems of belief and understanding. Yet the dialogue between cultures was ongoing, and the peoples of rural Cuzco not only were "working the system" to get their way, as Eric Hobsbawm suggests, but they also understood this system through their own eyes, operating in a different "register" as manifested in the arguments of de Certeau.

The analysis of colonial Latin American realities through values related to personal and intimate behavior is a relatively new but rapidly growing field. Most work has centered on criollos and mestizos, but this chapter focuses on native Andean peoples. It examines the personal lives, as well as the beliefs and values, of indigenous people such as Doña Maria and Don Mariano, and it focuses on those points of interaction with European society, especially with the church and priests, in which indigenous and European convictions came face to face with one another. In this colonial crucible indigenous and Spanish values rubbed against one another in the course of day-to-day existence, though this did not necessarily lead to fusion or amalgamation despite a great deal of occasional "heat" sometimes having been generated. I will first focus on topics in which cultural and legal norms were violated—rape and incest—and then I will turn our attention to attitudes and values dealing with the formation of heterosexual relationships, marriage, and marital conflicts.

Religion, a source of comfort and strength for many, was also a focal point of much contention. In the postconquest world most *naturales* became Christians; and in late colonial Cuzco indigenous peoples overwhelmingly considered themselves to be believers—Catholic Christians. Their conversion and the depth of their devotion to Christian values, however, were tempered by their continued adherence to Andean beliefs, as they brought Mary, Jesus, and a host of Catholic saints into their spiritual and cultural world of household, field, and mountain deities. The result was a mixture, a syncretic intertwining and blending, of Andean and European religions and beliefs. Syncretism provided indigenous peoples with a means to help them cope with and adjust to values from two worlds, values that in turn allowed them better to contend with colonialism.[2]

Not all indigenous and Spanish values coexisted or meshed so easily. Some priests and church officials informally winked at syncretic beliefs that they did not view as important or as threatening to "Christian" ways. But even in matters as personal as love and sex, conflicts between Indian and Spanish values developed and persisted. Often this dissension stemmed from differing views of gender relations and the "proper" roles of men and women as envisioned through indigenous and Spanish lenses. When Europeans sought to

[26]

impose beliefs and morality that collided with deeply held Andean convictions, native peoples, even those like Doña Maria and Don Mariano who considered themselves good Christians, often struggled tenaciously to maintain their cultural ways despite threats and actual punishment. When values and beliefs coincided, however, and *naturales* lived within accepted Indian-European norms, the practical effect was to preserve, if not bolster, the existing legitimacy of the colonial church and state.

Documentation

Late seventeenth- and eighteenth-century rural Cuzco had no Dr. Kinsey or Masters and Johnson conducting systematic surveys of indigenous sexual habits.[3] Therefore, data on this aspect of indigenous lives remain impressionistic. Yet even if the documentation yields only glimpses of what went on "behind closed doors," it does provide an idea of public morality and the values that guided daily life.

Although Don Mariano and Doña Maria may have represented the ideal Andean marriage, most couples whose lives are revealed in colonial archival records appear there because of marital conflict or violence. Mutual interdependence and loving, emotional attachments between men and women may have been the norm, but in daily life such sentiments were usually limited to personal conversations and private correspondence. However, the spoken words have disappeared, and in a world in which most Indians—especially nonelite indigenous women—did not read or write, few personal documents pertaining to private life were generated and even fewer remain. Though colonial observers do provide a few insights, the leading sources of information on the more personal aspects of indigenous life are the documents generated by civil, criminal, and religious legal proceedings. The rich, detailed testimony in these cases brings us face to face with the people of Guaro, Sicuani, Coporaque, and other communities of Quispicanchis and Canas y Canchis. The criminal records focus, quite naturally, on what was considered abnormal or illegal. Although "it may seem paradoxical, at first, to be trying to learn something of marriage by looking at troubled ones. In fact, however, 'trouble' is the catalyst that moves us to order our thoughts about most matters. As long as norms and experience roughly coincide, one is unlikely to change course or analyze experience; the awareness of a disparity between them is what spurs thought and action."[4]

Thus, these documents dealing with abnormal and criminal behavior shed light on what both Spanish law and local indigenous peoples deemed customary and acceptable, even as they show how the emotions and passions that normally bound people together often had been violated or ruptured and instead of solidifying relationships took conflictive, even violent directions. Family violence and sexual disputes were the leading causes of homicide in Quispicanchis and Canas y Canchis. These types of murders were more common than those resulting from robberies, tax disputes, or conflicts over land. Out of forty-three violent deaths tabulated in the late seventeenth and eighteenth centuries, twenty-eight of them (65 percent) derived from problems concerning love, jealousy, or other aspects of male-female relationships.[5]

The legal records, in combination with sources such as the manuals used by priests to confess *naturales*, also illuminate Spanish efforts to instill European values in the native people—to make the "other" more like themselves.[6] As Asunción Lavrin notes, "confession and penitence, two essential elements in Roman Catholic spirituality, were the tools to correct errors and mold consciences into proper doctrinal observance."[7] And in the Andes, even though the use and availability of confession was very uneven from priest to priest and village to village, it "became a means of instructing the Indians in norms of sexual behavior."[8]

It was in questions dealing with the biblical commandment against adultery and other sexual practices that the church focused its efforts to inculcate Christian sexual mores and root out indigenous practices that contradicted those mores. The questions confessors addressed to their indigenous flocks ran the gamut from bestiality, homosexuality, incest, and masturbation to the proper positions for intercourse, sexual dreams, and even sex with priests. So meticulous were the written inquiries—a manual from 1631 contained 236 questions on the commandment regulating sexual behavior and noted that many others could be asked—they lead the modern reader to "wonder if in fact the Church was not serving to disseminate knowledge of sexual pleasure that perhaps never had crossed the minds of their newly converted Quechua-speaking parishioners."[9]

Although many confessional manuals of the era did not focus on gender-specific questions, those used in the Andes asked many distinct questions of men and women.[10] For instance, men were asked "Have you 'forced' a woman?" or "Touching the private parts or the breasts or some other part of the body or kissing or embracing your wife, or your mistress, or a woman relative of yours, or of your wife, have you polluted yourself or did you have an ejaculation?" Women were asked such questions as "Have you agreed to men sleeping with you utilizing other than your natural vessel [vagina]?" and "Have you kissed the private parts of a man or have you agreed that he may kiss yours, enjoying this very much?"[11]

The impact of the church's efforts, as varied as they were, are very difficult to determine; thus, "the degree of acceptance by the common folk of the behavioral models set by the church" remains questionable, for there "was always a gap between religious canons and the actual behavior of people. Adaptation, confrontation, enforcement, and elusion in matters of personal behavior, especially in its sexual aspects, became important elements in the daily lives of many people."[12]

In colonial Mexico, however, Serge Gruzinski argues that confession did have an impact on the transformation of indigenous ways, although it is not an impact that is easy to measure. "It would be difficult to deny that confession contributed in an indirectly [sic] and intellectual manner to the erosion of mental, social, and familial structures and to the crumbling of ancestral codes and ancient forms of solidarity that regulated the functioning of pre-Hispanic societies."[13]

By the late colonial period these efforts were hardly new, and, unfortunately, in the communities and ayllus of Quispicanchis and Canas y Canchis the historical record does not reveal information about the confessional in sexual matters during this era.[14]

Although Don Mariano and Doña Maria were not the only couple to express loving sentiments, many other such expressions involved violence or tragedy. Offended husbands became embroiled in violent, sometimes fatal, disputes defending their wives'—and their own—sense of honor. Likewise, women often tried to protect their husbands, lovers, family members, or friends by biting or throwing rocks at those who assaulted the men they held dear. Expressions of loyalty within the family were quite common. Adult children often turned to their parents or brothers and sisters for help, while these same children normally, but not always, helped care for their parents. Care and succor were extended to other relatives as well. When the son of a sick woman from *ayllu* Quehuar in Sicuani (Canas y Canchis) approached his *curaca* about being allotted more land to plant, the *curaca* informed him that there were no more communal lands to distribute. However, the *curaca*, also a relative of the sick woman, volunteered use of a portion of his own lands if the son would give some of the harvest to his sick mother. The son accepted the offer, but it seems that the *curaca* may have been more concerned for his sick relative than the son, because the ailing woman never received the promised share of the harvest.[15]

Concern and anguish racked parents when confronted with the illness or death of a child, and sometimes the intensity of these emotions were so strong that the distraught parents created further problems. When Maria Puma fell from a bridge and drowned, her father, overcome with grief, was not willing to admit an accident had taken his daughter's life even though community members had witnessed the tragedy. After consulting "*brujas*" or sorceresses, he accused his son-in-law of murder. In defending the son-in-law community members testified to the importance of the strong emotional bonds between couples in community life when they stated that the husband "was living with his wife so lovingly, giving an example to everyone."[16]

Rape

If a mature, loving relationship between married adults was one of the important binding components of community life, among the acts that most offended community values were sexual assault and rape. The archival records for Quispicanchis and Canas y Canchis reveal few cases of rape, but the crime may have been more frequent than the recorded legal proceedings indicate. For instance, the goods of an indigenous rapist from Quispicanchis were embargoed and sold and the proceeds used to compensate the victim and to establish a fund for "Indian women who were deflowered by Indian men."[17] In this case the word deflowered was almost certainly a polite term for rape, although there were differences between local indigenous and Spanish society over when rape was a matter of legal concern. That such a sentence would be handed down suggests the crime might not have been as infrequent as the few archival cases might infer.

The indigenous chronicler Guamán Poma suggested the same for an earlier period when he observed that wives, daughters, and sisters were taken from poor Indians by Spaniards and "forced" (raped) under threats to their husbands, fathers, or brothers.[18] This rape, this sexual intimidation, of indigenous women was just one form of oppression native peoples suffered. While legal recourse was possible, the usually private nature of the act pitted the word of an Indian woman against that of a Spanish man, a situation not likely to lead to a conviction. Thus, even though they considered the crime to be very serious, *naturales'* experiences may have led them to conclude that it was unwise, or not worth the effort, to follow through with accusations of rape against Spaniards due to the fact that such charges frequently were not pursued by the government or the accused was "exonerated." In this situation few accusations of rape were brought against Spanish men for the violation of indigenous women.

Accusations of rape were frequently included, however, when a litany of charges were brought against powerful individuals. Captain Don Pedro de Roda had served the royal government in rural Cuzco, but later, during his *Juicio de Residencia*, he was accused by *naturales* of murder, abduction, owing debts of various kinds (money, llamas, and mules), having beaten people, having drowned a young woman after raping her, and having "forced" another woman. The captain was acquitted. He may well have been innocent, but the power and influence of the accused, combined with his ability to create doubt, also could have kept him, and others like him, from paying a legal price for their actions.[19] Indigenous peoples did become adept at using the legal system and were quite capable of making false charges to strengthen their case, a practice for which they undoubtedly had ample European precedents. It is also possible that newly appointed Spanish officials, in cases similar to the one against Captain Roda, encouraged *naturales* to present testimony that otherwise would not have been forthcoming, or even coerced false testimony from them to strengthen their own position by discrediting the former office-holder. Spaniards, just like Indians, were often divided by their particular interests.

In rural Cuzco, attitudes toward, or perhaps definitions of, rape may have varied from our own, and this variation could have lowered the number of documented rape cases. With one possible exception, charges of rape among indigenous people in rural Cuzco involved either young girls or married women. The scarcity of rape cases involving single adult women is notable. It could be nothing more than a lapse in the documentation, but it may well signify a difference in attitude toward, or in ways of dealing with, the violation of a single woman as opposed to that of a child or married woman.

The rape of a child was regarded as an abhorrent crime that was not only an affront to the victim, but to the parents and the community as well. In much the same way, the sexual violation of a married woman was perceived not only as an offense against her but also against the husband and the community. Community values supported the monogamy of married couples, and the rape of a married woman not only did violence to her but transgressed those values. These attitudes did not apply equally to single women, even though they usually lived at home and were subject to parental authority. This may have been due to the fact that premarital sex was the norm, and in some courtship and ritual practices the lines between rape and culturally acceptable force were blurred.[20] Likewise, drinking was often involved, and actions while "under the influence" were frequently considered in a different light by indigenous people.[21] With unmarried women any censure of behavior that in other circumstances would have been considered rape was apparently left to the families of the individuals involved or at least was kept an internal community matter. Not one document was encountered in which the community or family complained to the state about the rape of an unmarried woman by an indigenous man. Only the church pried into the matter of rape using the confessional to make general inquiries such as "Have you 'forced' a woman?"[22]

The rape of a child was not only a grave violation of cultural norms, it also threatened the life of the victim. Seven-year-old Agueda Aguilar bled to death after being raped by a drunk. Petronia Turuco barely escaped the same fate. Petronia had been gathering potatoes when Gregorio Leon, a *cantor* (choir member) in the church and a person well known to the victim, attacked her. She fled but he caught her, and even though she tried to fight him off, biting and shouting, he forcibly violated her. Petronia escaped and ran until she encountered a woman who was out gathering greens. This woman testified that "blood was flowing down the girl's legs." Outraged, the woman shouted at the *cantor,* "How could you have done such knavery, forcing a girl," at which he begged her not to tell the girl's parents. The mother could not stop the bleeding and sought the aid of Mariana Arias, a neighbor of Spanish descent. Instead of telling Arias what had happened, however, the mother said that a dog had bitten her daughter. Arriving at the house, the woman found the girl with blood running down her legs and a puddle of blood on the floor. When told that the girl had been raped she "opened the girl's legs and saw that she was injured and her virginity defiled." Speaking in Quechua (even though of Spanish descent and married to a person of Spanish descent she spoke the language of her surroundings and needed a Quechua translator to give her testimony "not being very fluent in the Spanish language"—*[por] no ser muy inteligente en la len-*

gua castellana), Arias inquired why she had not been told what had actually transpired. The mother, giving an indication of her values, replied, "because of the shame she had for her honor and that of her daughter."

Asked how he could rape a nine-year-old virgin, the *cantor* claimed not to have forced her. He maintained that she had voluntarily had sex with him, that they had had intercourse often, and that she had been teasing him. Besides, he stated, she was really fourteen years old, not a girl of nine. And she was sick because she had fallen ill after getting wet crossing a river and being out in a shower and that women ordinarily fall ill with their *achaque* or period. Thus, the rapist claimed that the girl was really a young woman and then used a defense culturally appropriate if she had been older.

The *cantor*'s claims of innocence were not believed. Having been convicted of rape, Leon was taken from the jail in Sangarará (Quispicanchis) and with the town crier shouting out his crime for all to hear, he was paraded through the streets on a beast of burden and then given fifty lashes. In addition, his goods were embargoed and sold, and the proceeds from the sale were used to compensate Petronia, who received twenty-four pesos, the remainder being used to establish the aforementioned fund for indigenous victims of rape.[23] The punishment publicly shamed the criminal in full view of the community he had offended and provided compensation for the victim.

Severe punishment of rapists had deep cultural roots in Andean society. According to Guamán Poma, who tended to idealize Inca sexual morality while contrasting it with Spanish (and sometimes contemporary indigenous) behavior, rapists paid with their lives when the Inca held sway. However, Bernabé Cobo qualified this claim stating that the Incas imposed the death penalty only if the victim was a noble; if she was not of the nobility the rapist was tortured.[24] In these penalties no distinctions were made for the age or marital status of the victim, but in practice such differentiations may have existed.

The rape of a married woman, sometimes referred to as "forced adultery," was extremely serious. The legal implications of forced adultery, if any, are unclear. Perhaps the term was used just to denote the marital status of the victim, but more likely it further emphasized the gravity of the crime, the husband as well as the victim being perceived as having been injured. With cultural sanctions reinforcing personal emotions, it is not surprising that the rape of a spouse provoked strong reactions. When Blas Conde discovered that his cousin, Rafael, had attempted to either rape or seduce his wife he bludgeoned his relative so severely that his cousin died from the resulting injury. The husband's action was apparently viewed with some understanding or leniency, for instead of being sentenced to work in an *obraje* he was ordered to serve six years in the convent of La Almudena in Lima to "purify himself of the crime."[25]

At times the rape of an Indian woman by a *natural* in a position of authority, as in some cases involving Spaniards, was an exertion of dominance by the powerful on the less powerful. In 1752, when the *curaca* of Pomacanchi demanded tribute a second time from Miguel Lloclla, a quarrel ensued and Lloclla cursed his *curaca* stating that he had already delivered his contribution. This, however, was not an isolated incident. Tensions already existed between the ethnic lord and many members of the community. According to Lloclla other *naturales* had fled to get away from this oppressive *curaca*, "in particular those of [Lloclla's] *ayllu.*" One evening, after drinking with other *curacas*, and knowing that Lloclla, a *cantor*, was away assisting at a burial, the *curaca* raped the wife. Upon his return the *cantor* found the *curaca* with his wife whom he "had forced to commit adultery." Lloclla complained about the *curaca* who then, with the aid of his family, beat the *cantor* and threw the couple in jail. When testimony in the case ended, the wife, the victim of the rape, remained in jail. Lloclla and his wife, suffering at the hands of the most powerful figure in the community, were forced to seek redress outside the communal structure. Lloclla turned to the church not only to free his wife, but to seek the removal of their tormentor from his position. Religious authorities responded with threats of excommunication, but the *curaca* had used rape as a demonstration of dominance and as an act of revenge. The husband's use of the term "forced adultery" involved no malice or suspicion toward his wife, rather it represented a violation of their marriage by another.[26]

Thus, rape was considered a most serious offense by *naturales*, a morality shared by Spanish Catholics. Powerful figures in both societies used their influence to avoid punishment, especially when the victim was a nonelite Indian. The major difference between the values of *naturales* and Spaniards concerned rape in situations involving unmarried women, the indigenous peoples of rural Cuzco apparently dealing with such matters privately or within the communal structure due to different cultural practices and expectations.

Incest

Legendary tales of the origin of the Incas involved the first Inca, Manco Capac, taking his mother for his wife. Another version has the royal roots evolving from the marriage of four brothers and four sisters. For the Inca elite such relationships underscored their status and were not considered incestuous. For the commoner of the Inca empire, however, Guamán Poma claimed the following rule prevailed, "We order that no one may marry his sister, nor his mother, nor his first cousin, nor aunt, nor niece nor other relatives, nor with his godmother. Under penalty both eyes shall be gouged out, he shall be quartered and shall be placed on the hillside, for punishment and for others to remember, for by law only the Inca can marry his sister (*ermana carnal*)."[27]

Although the Spanish considered incest a serious crime, they most often invoked a pecuniary penalty rather than the sentence of death as called for in the Old Testament. Thus, while punishments, or enforcement of the punishments, may have differed, European prohibitions against incest reinforced Andean tradition.[28] Nonetheless, the Spanish expressed concern about incestual practices among Andean peoples, and these anxieties were reflected in warnings from priests such as "Do not sleep all tumbled together like piglets; instead each one alone by himself." A 1631 confessional manual listed the following questions for priests to ask of their flocks. "Have you slept with your mother? Have you slept with your daughter? Have you slept with your sister? Have you slept with your cousin? Have you slept with your granddaughter? Have you slept with your grandmother? Have you slept with your step-mother? Have you slept with your sister-in-law or your mother-in-law? Have you slept with your sister-in-law's mother or her daughter? Have you slept with a mother and her daughter? Have you slept with two sisters and how many times with each of them?"[29]

Despite the attention given to incest by the church only two accusations of such behavior, both between parent and child, made their way into the European legal system from communities along the upper Vilcanota in the late colonial period.[30] In neither case did the parent and child force themselves on the other. Due to the bond or attraction between parent and child, however, emotional coercion may be implicit in such relationships even if neither of the involved consciously sought to take direct advantage of the sanguine ties. These cases also suggest a hesitancy by villagers to expose such private matters despite their moral values.

Diego Montesinos and his illegitimate daughter, both residing in San Pablo de Cacha, were accused of being lovers. Montesinos had given the daughter, Monica, a ring and spoke to her with "extraordinarily affectionate words." Monica, seven or eight months pregnant at the time of the accusations, denied that she and her father were sexually involved, although she admitted to having slept in the same bed. The father also denied their sexual relationship, but others in the community testified that they had seen them "*en fragante delito.*" Having been accused and ordered to remain in the community, the father and daughter fled. It was Montesino's wife who had first pressed the matter. She had tolerated his adultery with Monica's mother, a woman from the same community, but when years later he began seeing the daughter born of his adultery she could no longer remain quiet. Once the veil of silence had been lifted, other community members came forth with their observations and deductions.[31]

Another case of incest, worthy of headlines in the most sensational of modern tabloids, involved a mother and son from Sicuani.

The son, Faustino Espinoza, told friends that his wife was suffering from a stomach ache and that he feared for her life. Later, his wife and two children were found dead. Faustino first said they had died of the cold. Then he maintained that they had been crushed by potatoes, often stored on the rafters above the living area, when the hut they were in collapsed. The wife and children had broken necks and their bodies showed evidence of abuse. The wife's body was badly bruised and swollen, perhaps indicating a struggle prior to death. An *ayllu* official testified that the wife had confessed to him that she feared Faustino "would kill her like a dog," because he was afraid that she would reveal he was having sexual relations with his mother. She was right. The mother, Maria Malqui, was a widowed spinner. From her jail cell she maintained that her son lived with her because she had a loom and that her son wove to help pay his tribute. After the bodies had been found, Faustino spoke publicly of his oedipal involvement.[32] Community members had suspected the relationship but had not acted on the hearsay. In this instance their reluctance to interject themselves into such a personal matter did not protect community members but meant that the wife's worst fears came true.

Sirvinacuy (Trial Marriage)

The sexual habits of unmarried indigenous couples were a source of serious tensions between native peoples and the Catholic Church. Indigenous men and women lived together before marriage. This cohabitation was part of a process of relationship formation that has become known as "*sirvinacuy*" or trial marriage. The period, or process, of "trial marriage" was a fundamental cultural practice designed to ensure the strength of a couple's relationship and thereby assure the success of the marriage. These "marriageways" were very important, for the married couple was the basic unit on which the social and biological reproduction of the community rested.[33]

Although trial marriage was a source of continuing friction, more casual premarital sexual relations, though not condoned, provoked less hand-wringing among church officials. This attitude parallels those in more Spanish and mestizo regions, such as Argentina, where "poor girls, regardless of their race, were presumed to be sexually experienced past the age of puberty."[34] The church also tolerated ongoing liaisons between people of different social status, such as Spanish men and Indian women, for marriage was not expected due to social distance. But when people lived together whose status or race made them suitable partners, then the church might well object.[35]

Evidence conflicts concerning indigenous attitudes toward premarital sex in the pre-Columbian and early colonial periods. Some differences undoubtedly stemmed from regional and ethnic variations. Other contradictions were rooted in class-based behavioral distinctions.[36] Although the Inca elite made an issue of female virginity in some situations, such as for the "wives of the sun" or *acllas*, they did not always do so.[37] For commoners in Tawantinsuyu premarital intercourse was not only "common" but "socially sanctioned."[38] In contrast to Christian Spanish society, female virginity typically was not considered precious by indigenous people. Virginity bestowed no particular honor or moral superiority on a woman or her family. Loss of virginity did not stain a family's honor or threaten the legitimacy of offspring, as it might in the Spanish world.[39] The coming of Spanish rule and the introduction of Christianity, in which virginity was "emblematic of a chaste life and respect for the moral canons of the church," did not alter this aspect of indigenous sexual behavior for the common folk.[40]

Spaniards who commented on the lack of indigenous concern for virginity, such as Pedro Pizarro ("their fathers did not pay any attention if they were good or bad: nor was it considered to be shameful among them") and Father Acosta ("virginity, which is viewed with esteem and honor by all men is deprecated by those barbarians as something vile"), condemned not only Indian women but also indigenous men for not giving virginity what they considered "proper" importance.[41] Neither indigenous men nor women were living by, or—in the value system of the Europeans "up to"—the moral codes of Spanish society and the church. Early in the seventeenth century Father Arriaga reported that "mere fornication is not regarded as sinful." He related the following incidents, which must have been jarring to even this world-wise Jesuit. "In a town I was passing through an Indian boy asked me to marry him to his betrothed. One of her brothers, however, objected strongly, giving no other reason except that they had never slept together. I also know another Indian who refused to see his wife after their marriage and treated her harshly. He alleged that she was a woman of low condition since no one had ever loved her or had carnal knowledge of her before marriage."[42]

Even though condoned culturally, the harmonious acceptance of premarital sexual relations had significant exceptions, especially when it came to the relations of women.[43] Sometimes fathers and husbands, their senses of morality and honor apparently transgressed, reacted with anger or violence to innuendoes of premarital sex or the knowledge of such relations involving their daughters or the women who were now their spouses. Did these feelings reflect the influence of Christian teachings and the impact of the confessional? Although the messages of the European religious did not necessarily transform everyone, and certainly not all to the same degree, aspects of the new teachings undoubtedly influenced some people toward beliefs that did not resonate with most of their neighbors. Or did these feelings stem from contradictions between accepted cultural norms and individual beliefs that are part of life, to some degree, in most every society? Not everyone dances to the same tune.

In 1766 Visente León was killed as a result of the abuse he heaped on his wife because of her premarital relations. His wife had lived with another man before she and Visente were married and had borne a child from that relationship. Visente, consumed with his emotions, would get drunk and then proceed to beat his wife and accuse her of "having been a bad woman." After one such incident the wife's brother, angered at her treatment, clubbed Visente and killed him.[44] Unfortunately the record leaves no clues as to the rationale behind Visente's actions, nor does it tell if the brother reacted to the abuse alone or if he was further spurred by the cultural "irrationality" of Visente's actions.

Visente was not alone in holding feelings that seemed to contradict cultural norms. In Pomacanche a *natural* named Pascual Colque, incarcerated after being accused of committing a crime by a fellow villager, maintained that the real reason he was jailed was his public comments about the sexual activity of his accuser's daughter. Colque claimed to have seen the daughter in *"fragante delito"* on three different occasions, and that it had been his comments about her behavior, not any wrongdoing, that had led to the charges against him.[45] Why would Colque testify about his observations, true or not, if he did not believe that they would undermine the accusations against him? In a society in which premarital sex was supposed to be open, why were his comments objectionable? Did her relations jeopardize the honor of her family, an indigenous family of considerable standing in the community? Could her family, because of its status, have been more influenced by or sensitive to Spanish teachings or opinions than others in the community? Did the father's reaction stem from the influence of Christian sexual values?[46] Unfortunately the archival record does not even hint at an answer to these questions.

Church officials may have decried indigenous attitudes toward fornication, but they did little to alter this behavior until relationships took on a more permanent character. It was the period of cohabitation before marriage, lasting from a few months up to two or three years, that most concerned them. While Manco Inca was still threatening European control of Peru, Spaniards were already making reference to the "diabolical" practice of trial marriage, and complaints about the institution continued throughout the sixteenth, seventeenth, and eighteenth centuries.[47] In the 1550s the Augustinians reported that the Indians "have a custom, and until today there is not anyone who can stop it, which is that before they marry with their woman they have to live together [*probar y tener consigo*]."[48] In the 1570s, no less a figure than Viceroy Francisco de Toledo observed that if a couple did not live together before marriage, they claimed that they would not have "peace, contentment, and friendship." Toledo, not sharing the Indians' sentiments, thought this practice to be "noxious and pernicious to their conversion and . . . Christianity" and recommended punishment for offenders.[49] Despite admonitions and threats, the church had little impact on this deeply rooted practice, which *naturales* maintained was necessary to ensure stable, compatible marriage relationships. In 1649 church officials in Lima, aware that their efforts to instill Christian values opposed to premarital sex had been unsuccessful, noted that indigenous marriages not preceded by *tincunakuspa* (*sirvinacuy*) were quite rare.[50]

The strength and tenacity of the Spanish reaction to *sirvinacuy* are in some ways puzzling because the practice was in some ways akin to the "promise of marriage" (*palabra de casamiento*) or betrothal in Spanish society. Although the European ideal was to not have intercourse before marriage, once the *palabra de casamiento* was exchanged, the marriage process was considered to have begun, and church and society looked on the behavior of couples, particularly the woman, with more understanding.[51] Children of such unions could be legitimated, even if the couple never married, and though codes of honor could lead to the societal rejection of mother and child, in practical day-to-day living such was not the case. Instead, neighbors apparently moved with ease and familiarity in and out of such houses. The illegitimate children of these unions played and were educated with legitimate offspring of equal rank.[52]

In the eyes of one's neighbors, in both the indigenous and Spanish worlds, much depended on the character or morality of the persons involved. For the Catholic church, however, morality was also related to discretion. It was perhaps this sense that separated *sirvinacuy* from betrothal in the minds of priests. *Sirvinacuy* was public, and although trial marriage usually led to formal marriage, this was not always the case. Not everyone turned out to be compatible, and indigenous men and women terminated relationships without stigma. The children that resulted from these unions were accepted in indigenous society and constituted a public affirmation for the Europeans of a relationship that existed outside the bonds of Catholic matrimony.[53] Thus, while there were some parallels between *sirvinacuy* and Spanish relations after the *palabra de casamiento*, there were also marked differences.

Though colonial courtship practices are rarely glimpsed, mutual attraction and parental influence appear to have been the forces behind most indigenous relationships.[54] Parents influenced the process of "mutual attraction" through their observations and comments about community members and in even more direct ways. If colonial Indian parents were like their modern counterparts, they sometimes took the initiative in seeking a spouse, not necessarily with the child's knowledge or permission. They might approach the parents of the prospective mate and speak for their offspring, as well as encourage good feelings between the families, for marriage linked families, and such kinship ties were very important in the Andean world.[55]

Because most people married within their community or region, potential marriage partners were not often strangers. Before entering into the semiformal arrangements of trial marriage, a period of courtship and sexual experimentation passed. Young people started noticing or flirting with one another; then chance or arranged meetings while working in the fields or tending to chores, such as herding llamas or sheep, provided opportunities for sexual encounters. Community festivals, with their high spirits and gaiety, often aided by the consumption of *chicha,* also created a mood and setting conducive to growing affection and sexual experimentation. A modern observer of courtship practices in the not very distant Lake Titicaca region writes that

> Courting is informal. The suitor finds occasions to be with the girl. A popular site for casual encounters is provided by the hills. . . . Young men seek out the girls who are pasturing their animals on the hills. And there they converse, fight or make love. During the early stages of courtship the girls tend to offer resistance. The potential mates may engage in mutual insulting. They try to steal items of clothing from each other. But they may also give one another gifts of food, e.g., bread, candy and so forth. Eventually, if all goes well, they fall in love. Then they may arrange meetings. They may get together on market day . . . or they may see each other at fiestas, possibly dancing together in one of the dance groups formed for such events. . . .

[43]

Serious courtship leads to sexual experimentation. The potential mates may sleep with each other regularly. These encounters are supposedly clandestine, of course, but the parents of the girl and the boy may know that this behavior is occurring. If they approve of the match they will not interfere. On the other hand, if they do not approve, they might try to put a stop to the courtship. If the girl becomes pregnant, the end of the courtship phase is hastened.[56]

If the couple got along well and the relationship progressed, the woman, although in some instances the man, eventually moved in with the lover's parents until the couple married and were ready to establish a home of their own. The purpose of this period of cohabitation was to assure compatibility, a stable marriage being important not only to the couple but to the family and the community. During this period the man and woman deepened their relationship and learned more about one another. A sixteenth-century Augustinian noted that the process functioned not only to assure sexual compatibility but to determine if the woman was a good worker and cook. This observer commented that if this trial period went well, the young man asked the woman's parents for permission to marry their daughter. If they said yes, the father would inform the young man of his daughter's faults so that "the son-in-law does not complain or quarrel if his daughter is a '*mala mujer*' or lazy."[57] Father Cobo also claimed that men lived with women before being married to determine if they could "*bien servir y regalar.*"[58]

Indigenous efforts to ensure stable, compatible relationships through trial marriage were seen very differently by the European Christians, whose references to the practice are numerous and condemnatory. Typical of these attacks are those made in the *Sinodales del Arzobispado* in 1613. "Cap. VI. That you endeavor to end the abuse that the Indians have of first living with those that they are going to marry: Because the Devil has introduced among the Indians, that, when they agree to marry with an Indian they live with her first, living in offense of Our Lord. It is just that it be remedied: We order that the priests in their Sermons very regularly exhort and threaten them that what they do is an abusive and grave sin; that they investigate those that are guilty of it and that the evidence be sent to the Curate so that they may be Punished."[59]

Sermons, admonishments in confession, and personal advice were used by priests to encourage adherence to Catholic morality. For the most part, however, priests did not use religious courts or the power of the state to force cohabiting indigenous couples to formalize their relationships. Far from the centers of religious authority, and knowing their parishioners on a more personal basis, most priests in rural Cuzco were tolerant or understanding of behavior that their urban-based superiors ordered expunged. This understanding may have been enhanced by the complex nature of Catholic theology. The church "had the power to impose stern spiritual condemnation but was also bound to pardon the sinners. In practical terms, it was often forced to forgive and forget."[60]

Nevertheless, from time to time a priest did attempt to force young people to marry, and this evoked strong responses from the *naturales*. In some of these instances, the relationship between the priest and the parishioners had soured, and the priest's efforts to compel marriage were motivated by deeper tensions. Forcing marriage could also involve pecuniary gain for the priests, although in none of their complaints in Quispicanchis or Canas y Canchis did indigenous parishioners mention excessive demands (see plate 4).

The tactic used to force the sacrament of marriage was simple and direct. The priest detained *naturales* in the church under lock and key until they acceded to his demands, even though this contradicted church teachings that marriage should be by consent and was invalidated by coercion.[61] On occasion this heavy-handed action was also hasty. One religious official, at odds with both the *naturales* and the non-Indians in his community, locked up a *chola* and tried to force her to wed, only to discover that the prospective groom was already married.[62] In another case the people of Checacupe and Pitumarca complained that their priest, Don Jose Loaisa, locked young men and women in the church with "the end that they marry by force: this fact is public and notorious." The community sought an end not only to matrimony under duress but the tragic consequences such measures provoked. So strong was resistance to coerced matrimony, village spokesmen claimed, "some single women have killed their children at birth and thrown them in the river and only in this way do they free themselves of punishment and being locked up . . . [and] forced to marry."[63] In Yanaoca and San Pablo de Cacha, community elders argued that efforts to force their young people to wed were misguided and created hardships for the parents. They pleaded that not only was their children's labor lost while they were incarcerated, but the parents had the additional burden of bringing food to the "inmates."[64]

In circumstances such as these, when European Christians sought to impose beliefs that clashed with deeply held cultural values, the *naturales* of Quispicanchis and Canas y Canchis aggressively defended their way of life. Pointing to the disruptive and harmful effects of Spanish mores, the villagers of rural Cuzco struggled to maintain their time-honored customs of courtship and marriage. The persistence today of premarital cohabitation as a cultural practice demonstrates how determined indigenous people were and how effective, despite occasional setbacks, such as those represented in these cases, day-to-day resistance could be in thwarting colonial demands that clashed with fundamental indigenous values.

At the same time that *naturales* were resisting efforts to eliminate trial marriage, they also filed complaints against priests for having sexual relations with unmarried women.[65] Indigenous protests against such relations were common but seemingly less frequent than the activity. Just as most priests tolerated trial marriage, most villagers tolerated priests' indiscretions. And just as priests sometimes brought up the issue of cohabitation when they were in conflict with a community, Indians sometimes brought up the sexual conduct of a priest when they were at odds with him. The *naturales* of Checacupe and Pitumarca brought a long list of charges against their priest for abuses and dereliction of duty. The charges included having an "illicit friendship" with a woman with whom the priest lived "like a married couple" and another "illicit friendship" with a widow in Pitumarca.[66]

These accusations were made against the same priest, Don Jose Loaisa, who later tried to force Indians to marry.

When conflict was not an obvious factor, the basis for indigenous protest against the sexual activities of a priest with an unmarried woman is unclear. It is always possible that the *naturales* had reasons they did not wish to express openly, and of which the priest was unaware or also did not wish to make public. In most such cases, however, knowledge that such conduct was not in keeping with priestly morality was given as the root cause of the charges. It could also be that because priests were not allowed to marry, the Indians believed that relations between unmarried women and priests served no acceptable social purpose.

Typical of such charges was the case brought by the people of Quiquijana (Quispicanchis) against their priest in 1758 for causing "great harm to his own conscience and the souls of his parishioners." The priest had lived with and had children by a woman who had moved to the parish with him and then died. Another lover was rumored to have had a child by him, and it was "public and certain that the said priest was presently living, with scandal to this community and the parishioners, in public concubinage with the daughter of the sexton."[67] The syncretic mixture of Andean culture and Christianity formed a belief system that made it completely acceptable for *naturales* to justify cohabitation for themselves as Catholic believers but also allowed them selectively to deny—operating in a different "register"—the right to priests who were supposed to be celibate. In the colonial crucible right and wrong were not absolute values for the *naturales* but depended on individual and cultural perspectives.

Marriage

Marriage was the normal condition for adults. In the Andes, to a greater degree than in many other regions, there existed a recognized complementarity and equality between men and women. Writing of the Inca period Irene Silverblatt states:

Andean men and women experienced their lives in gender-specific worlds, yet these worlds were also interdependent. Perhaps no Andean ritual more clearly expressed the interdependence and complementarity of male and female spheres than marriage. . . . Rituals surrounding marriage shouted an ideology of gender equality. Whether that ideology was true to the substance of gender relations is another question. . . .

Marriage rites, whether binding together peasants or the Inca elite, celebrated the formation of a new unity made up of equals. Accordingly, wives and husbands saw themselves as contributing in complementary but commensurate ways to the formation of the household.[68]

In addition to uniting a couple, marriage brought together a network of kin who could be relied on for labor and mutual support. The married couple worked together to provide for the family and meet the demands of the state and community. In agriculture men broke the ground and, with their wives' help, prepared it for planting, while women, the symbolic bearers of fertility, sowed the seed. In the preconquest period, "the Incas implicitly recognized male and female labor as forming a unity necessary for the reproduction of social existence."[69]

In the colonial period the state recognized this unity in some aspects of life and not others, but it remained a fundamental part of life in the *ayllus* of Quispicanchis and Canas y Canchis. For instance, although only men were subject to the *mita* for the mines of Potosí, wives invariably accompanied the husbands. In the eyes of the couple and the community, the man's required service was a requisition of the wife as well. The husband could not be expected to serve without the support of his spouse.

In community political matters the husband represented the family to the outside world. This does not mean, however, that the wife's voice was not represented. If the past was like the present, men in rural Cuzco did not normally make decisions before consulting their wives. Thus, while wives may not have had a public voice in community affairs, it does not necessarily follow that their concerns were not represented. And in confrontations with European authorities, indigenous women often figured very prominently.[70]

The unity, especially the economic unity, of the married couple was attested to by authorities, both indigenous and Spanish, who held the wife responsible, even incarcerating her, for debts of the husband. A cacique in Sicuani who had previously jailed a wife for her husband's debts took the concept of shared obligation a step further when he jailed a woman whose betrothed (*en palabra de casamiento*) fled without paying his tribute. The cacique hoped to force the woman to reveal her lover's whereabouts. Unfortunately for the woman and the cacique, the betrothed had beaten and robbed his fiancée before disappearing and most likely had no intention of returning.[71] Such actions went against Spanish legal tradition, but the power of the cacique within his own community allowed him this latitude. In this way caciques could use the colonial system when they chose, or interpret their powers (*à la* de Certeau) in a different manner, or perhaps they were at times just ignorant of the law, and local officials saw no reason to set them right, especially when it served their or the state's interests, until a situation became public. When a cacique's ire was aroused, or even when he was just being abusive, both husband and wife might suffer his wrath. Such was the case in 1790 when the Spanish cacique of Checacupe not only took the land of an indigenous couple but jailed the husband and beat the wife.[72]

The vast majority of men and women, having passed through courtship and trial marriage, assumed their rightful position in the community as an adult couple and became a source of stability in village life. They dealt with the pains and agonies that life presented. They raised and buried children, and they met their communal and state obligations. Though such couples represented the norm, many relationships did not live up to those standards. Honor, jealousy, adultery, and spousal abuse disrupted private lives and made male-female conflict, as noted earlier, the leading cause of murder in Quispicanchis and Canas y Canchis.[73]

It was the defense of honor that led to the tragic death of Philipe Apacyupa. Apacyupa had purchased a quantity of coca from a Spaniard, and to celebrate closing the deal they drank *aguardiente*. Somewhat inebriated, Apacyupa and his companion went out into the street, where the Spaniard, according to witnesses, accidentally bumped into the wife of Melchor Cansaya. Cansaya had been drinking too and took offense. He "offered to cut out the entrails" of the Spaniard. In the scuffle that followed Apacyupa was mortally wounded. Cansaya maintained that his stabbing of Apacyupa had been an accident; he was coming to the defense of his wife, who, as he perceived it, had suffered an indignity. Despite the testimony of eyewitnesses who said the encounter had been accidental, Cansaya maintained that his wife had been kicked. Described as a tranquil man of good conduct, Cansaya became a different and dangerous person when his sense of honor—enhanced by *aguardiente*—and perhaps an underlying antagonism toward Spaniards, was aroused.[74]

Premarital sex and the changing of partners after failed relationships was normal behavior, but after marriage *naturales* expected spouses to be faithful. Here indigenous and Spanish values once again coincided. Adultery and suspicions of adultery could give rise to jealousy and sometimes led to quarrels and violence.[75] Javier Rafael "took the means of homicide . . . [to] free himself of jealousy." Believing his wife had been "trampling the marriage" with Ventura Cusimayta, Raphael killed Cusimayta, who was hardly more than a child, being described as twelve or fourteen years old.[76]

Adulterous spouses were also subject to attack. Wives, however, seldom physically assaulted their husbands to the point of inflicting serious harm, but the opposite was less true. Irate husbands or their relatives vented their wrath on both the lover and the marriage partner. Juan Humpiri, no longer able to tolerate the long-standing illicit relationship between his sister-in-law and the *curaca*, went to the house where they lived late one Sunday night. Finding them together in bed, he chased the *curaca* away with blows and then reviled his brother's wife, stating that "she was an easy woman and that it was her fault that the *curaca* treated them with ignominy." Humpiri hit her on the temple, and when she tried to strike him back with a weaving staff he wrested it from her and used it to hit her on the head again. The Humpiri family was especially upset at the public dishonor the relationship caused. The wife and the *curaca* had even given the husband a baby to care for that had been born of their illicit relationship, but the baby had died. The situation endured for so long because the *curaca* was powerful and, according to the brother-in-law, took lands away from the poor Indians and "thr[ew] them a bone" while renting the best lands to Spaniards. The family finally received backing when a priest, whose lands the *curaca* had also tried to take, came to their support. However, for several years the power of the *curaca* had forced humbler Indians to compromise their personal values and put up with humiliation out of fear of losing their lands; that power had also allowed the wife to live outside accepted community norms. The mounting sense of dishonor, plus the support of a priest who could use the power of the church to confront both the adulterers and the economic situation, finally permitted the family to respond. Why the husband's brother and not the husband himself took the initiative remains uncertain. The eldest brother normally looked after married sisters, but it is unclear if the same was true of all brothers or if the action stemmed from the brother-in-law's own shame and anger.[77]

Adulterers who became especially attached to their paramours sometimes abused or even killed the slighted spouse. Lovers also tried to break up marriages by suggesting violence and resorting to more than just their charms. In 1706 a *natural* from near Ocongate (Quispicanchis) confessed that he had killed his wife "because the devil tempted him," and because his lover had told him that if he killed her "she would marry him and treat him very well."[78] Likewise, in 1773 Agustín Masa told authorities that he had killed his wife, and accidentally his own child who was on the mother's back when he struck the lethal blow, because his widowed lover, Maria Cama, had urged him to do it. He claimed to have been living in "*ilicita amistad*" with Cama and that she had told him his wife was "useless" and that they could go away and get married.[79] Cama said that she had not fa-

vored the murder, but she also maintained that she had not influenced or had "illicit commerce" with the accused.[80] Some of those
involved with a married person took direct action to clear the way for
their own marriage. Maria Mamani was the lover of, and the mother
of a child by, Domingo Utcca (Udcó). When Utcca's wife awoke in
the middle of the night with "a pain in her stomach and all of her
body," he went out in search of something to relieve her suffering and
brought back a "cure" that Mamani had provided. On taking the
"medicine" the wife's tongue immediately swelled up, and she vom-
ited blood for the next three weeks.[81]

Wives trying to rid themselves of unwanted husbands typically
sought the aid of others rather than confronting their husbands
alone. Esperanza Malqui, in an illicit relationship with Blas Condori,
urged Condori to kill her mate whom she described as "useless." She
wanted to marry Condori and was, according to Condori and his
accomplice, not only willing to pay to have her husband killed, but
very happy at the news that they had lured him to a remote area
under the pretext of stealing cattle, killed him, and thrown the body
into a river.[82]

Domestic violence was a normally tolerated aspect of married life,
although it had personal and cultural limits. The Inca, according to
Guamán Poma, had sought to control the physical abuse of women
through legal sanctions. It is likely that spousal violence increased
during the colonial period, because drinking became more common
and much of the violence—most often but not always against
women—occurred after the partner had imbibed.[83] Spanish society
also tolerated some physical abuse or "punishment" of wives by husbands as a patriarchal corrective for behavior that the husband
deemed unacceptable. Excessive abuse, however, became a concern,
and "arbitrary punishments severely administered . . . [were] a mortal
sin."[84] As long as the violence remained within personal and cultural
bounds, most spouses accepted the bruises as a part of married life.
All too frequently domestic violence in both indigenous and Spanish
society went far beyond tolerable limits, leaving spouses severely bat-
tered and in fear for their lives, if not dead. In 1749 a young Spanish

boy in the community of Pichigua witnessed an Indian beating and kicking his wife to death. After the assault the husband tied his wife to a horse and had the horse drag her body to make her death appear accidental.[85] Such violence certainly was not limited to Indian culture. Martina Calle, an indigenous woman, lived on an *estancia* near Pichigua with her mestizo husband. When her body was found the husband had disappeared. No one knew what had happened.[86]

Community members did intervene in marital conflicts, but such intervention was not always effective. On the night of Corpus Christi, 1691, screams shattered the silence in the community of Quiquijana. A Spaniard went to investigate and found Sebastián Poma whipping his wife. Trying to appeal to the Indian's religious values, the Spaniard asked how "he could do such cruelty being a Christian," but Poma responded by threatening him. The next day the witness returned to the house where he found the parents crying over their daughter's lifeless body. The cadaver was horribly cut, "the flesh in pieces," the result of being whipped.[87]

Many spouses tolerated some abuse, but few would endure continual or severe abuse, and some countered violence with violence. Women often relied on family members, particularly brothers, to protect them.[88] For example, Faviana Paucara appealed to her brother for help after repeated beatings. She had wed Pablo Guana at the age of about thirteen, and in their year and a half of marriage Pablo hit her often, and because of this they had even lived apart for six months. Finally, after yet another beating Faviana and her mother urged her brother, Pasqual, to kill Pablo. Faviana gave her brother a sharp rock, and, while the husband slept, Pasqual struck him on the head and killed him because "he gave Faviana a bad life."[89]

When a relationship deteriorated or abuse became intolerable, the wife traditionally fled back to her family. This was the culturally accepted way of getting out of a bad relationship in the Andes.[90] In colonial society, however, the church and the state sometimes exercised their considerable muscle to enforce the marriage contract by ordering couples to live together. On occasion, moreover, husbands and wives appealed to the church or the state to restore their marriage when a third person came between them. In 1771 several villagers from Coporaque sought such help from the church. Mathias Yanquera wanted his wife's lover removed from their lives. Three months earlier, Mathias had left home in search of work to support his wife and children, but he began to hear bad things about his wife. On returning, he found a *natural* named Bernardo with her, and he turned to the church to get something done about this "Indian and wife stealer." Yanquera testified that he tolerated his wife's behavior because of his love for the children and for her.[91]

In another case a woman asked the same church official to get her released from jail. She had been incarcerated for not living with her husband, but she maintained that he had been living with another woman and had treated her badly, even whipping her. Because of his violence and "diabolic cruelty" she, in keeping with indigenous norms, no longer recognized him as her husband.[92] The documents do not reveal what action the church took in these cases, but as a matter of policy the church typically went to considerable lengths to maintain marriages. For example, a Sicuani priest brought legal action against four men who had Indian "concubines" (though the men were most likely indigenous, their race was not specified) to force them to live with their wives.[93]

Legal terminations of marriage in the colonial world were not unknown, but they were fairly rare. Even then, the term *"divorcio"* referred to a legal separation that did not include the right to remarry.[94] Such permanent separations tended to be a tool of the more well-to-do, although in Lima a wider spectrum of people including those of the lower class sought *divorcio.* Violence and adultery were the most common, but not the only, reasons given by spouses—most often women—wanting to end a relationship.[95] Joana Ynquillay of Oropesa was one of the rare indigenous women from the sierra who sought *divorcio.* Joana had long been aware of her husband's adulterous relationship with a woman from Pisac, but she had tolerated it and endured being beaten until she was "bloody and full of welts." However, she finally turned to the church for help and sought *divorcio* after her husband sold their team of plowing mules and later tied her hand and foot in a corral and whipped her. Having sold the mules that sustained them, she feared that her husband really planned to kill her and flee with his lover. She was eight months pregnant at the time.[96]

Besides making it difficult to end a marriage, the church also imposed severe penalties on those who ignored the law and formed new relationships without legally terminating the first marriage. Men and women who wanted to be married, for cultural, economic, or religious reasons, were in a very difficult position if one of them previously had been in a failed relationship. The suffering caused in the clash between Spanish Catholic values and indigenous syncretic values over cultural definitions of bigamy is revealed in the case of Teresa Sisa, an Indian woman who married twice.[97] Sisa had wed Diego Quispi, but after a year of marriage she fled due to "bad treatment." A few years later, with her parents' blessing, she remarried. When Sisa and her new husband, because of his work, returned to the region where her first husband lived, she was recognized by former in-laws. The church brought charges against her for being married twice. The second marriage was declared null, and Sisa was sentenced to be "punished exemplarily." She was mounted on a "beast of burden" and led through the streets, stripped nude to the waist except for a *corosa* (dunce's cap), while a public crier called out her crime. After this public shaming she was lashed one hundred times. Sisa was also ordered to serve six months in a convent, after which she was to resume married life with her first husband, whom the church admonished not to hurt or maltreat her under threat of severe punishment.[98]

Such punishments may have served the example the church intended, but people caught between a violent spouse, their desire for a married life, and a rigid church had good reason for despair. Most priests in rural Cuzco understood that human weaknesses existed and that profound changes could not be wrought overnight. When priests were not so understanding life could be made harrowing and painful for indigenous men and women, most of whom, nevertheless, considered themselves to be Catholic Christians.

In conclusion, the aftermath of conquest and the introduction of Christianity affected the lives of *naturales* at even the most personal levels. The rejection, acceptance, or accommodation of European cultural norms and attitudes was an uneven process that depended a great deal on how extensively indigenous and European values meshed or conflicted, as well as on face-to-face relations. By the late seventeenth and eighteenth centuries, many indigenous and European values had been overlapped and intermingled, but significant areas of conflict also existed. In defense of their culture and their way of life, the peoples of rural Cuzco tenaciously resisted certain European mores, and this day-to-day resistance could be very effective.

At the same time, however, even though Europeans imposed their values through conquest and colonial rule, Andean peoples actually shared many of these values, at least in their outward manifestations. Such overlapping tended to maintain, if not strengthen, colonial legitimacy. However, while *naturales* in Quispicanchis and Canas y Canchis accepted, at least to a certain degree, some European beliefs, they put their own stamp on them. Almost all villagers became Catholic believers, as Jesus, Mary, and a host of saints were incorporated into their spiritual world, but it was a syncretic, indigenous Catholicism, not Spanish Catholicism. The syncretism functioned to allow the *ayllus* to adapt, adjust, or accommodate European beliefs to their own value system in the manner that best suited their own cultural meaning. In addition, the *naturales* of rural Cuzco learned to use the colonial legal system, along with European values, to defend and enforce their own values against those, both nonindigenous and indigenous, who threatened their way of life. Most often, Spaniards and Indians were not overly rigid and tried to find ways to exist together. On certain issues, however, the church and state were unwilling to compromise, and they used their considerable coercive powers to impose their beliefs, making the *naturales'* lives difficult.

The interaction of indigenous and Spanish values has often been dealt with in terms of resistance and accommodation; however, indigenous peoples lived and functioned with a wide array of convictions that reflected the complexity of their lives. Seeking to understand the intricate and entangled nature of the values held by peoples in Quispicanchis and Canas y Canchis is helpful in comprehending and analyzing a wide range of Indian-European relations, not just sexual values, in the colonial world.

3

Robbers, Rustlers, and Highwaymen

Mandamos que no ayga ladrones en este rreyno ni que ayga salteadores. GUAMÁN POMA DE AYALA, *Hordenansas del Inga*

Stealing

IN 1773 Andres Quispe, an *originario* from Checacupe, was accused
of stealing a calf by members of his own community. This was not
the first time he had had such troubles. A village official testified that
Quispe was a known cattle and llama thief who had been in jail many
times. In addition Quispe neither paid his tribute nor fulfilled his
community obligations and was described as rebellious by nature.
The official summed up his pejorative attitude toward Quispe stating
that he was "indolent, lazy, and a vagabond." Others in the community shared this opinion. Francisco Guamantilla, the *curaca*, referred to Quispe as a "dog." And one woman called Quispe "the most
animal thieving Indian in the world." In addition to stealing the calf,
Quispe had stolen an ox from his own brother to pay for "*droga
suia*"—"his drug" (it is not clear what the "drug" was). Other stolen
property had been found in his house, and meat was found hidden in
a nearby canyon. Quispe had also broken out of jail twice.[1]

steal

Two years earlier, in the not very distant community of Checasupe, another Indian, Andres Quecaño, had been accused and convicted of stealing several horses and mules. Apparently these were
not Quecaño's first crimes either. Witnesses stated that from a
"tender age" he had supported himself by robberies in the pueblos of
Canas y Canchis and Belille (Velille, Chumbivilcas), and he lived a
"disorderly" life. He had been caught and jailed several times, but had
always managed to escape. The Quehue resident who filed the com-

plaint, apparently not an Indian, asked that Quecaño be sentenced to an *obraje* for the rest of his life and that he make restitution for his crimes. Nicolas Guaicho, a Checasupe *curaca*, also maintained that Quecaño was a "well known rustler." In addition to the crimes for which he had been detained, others testified that Quecaño had stolen a gelding from the *curaca*, six good horses from Melchor Guaicho, a mule from Bartolomé Ordoñes (he later paid for it), two horses from Joseph Calavetta, and a mare from Clemente Guanco. Quecaño was sentenced to two years in the *obraje* in Lucre (Quispicanchis) "in order that with his own work he pay the Royal tribute and the value of the 6 horses and 2 mules of Pedro Narverto Davila." In passing sentence the corregidor of Canas y Canchis, Pedro Muñoz de Arjona, stated that Quecaño's punishment "may serve as a warning to other delinquents."[2]

Quecaño and Quispe were not the only *naturales* involved in crime, and this chapter explores the attitudes and values of the people of Quispicanchis and Canas y Canchis in relationship to the issues of criminality and good governance. It analyzes how the villagers along the upper Vilcanota sought to use the colonial legal system for their own ends and how the Spanish, having empowered communities with the primary responsibility for maintaining their own internal day-to-day social order, made the apprehension of criminals such as Quispe and Quecaño a force in the preservation of community solidarity. Crime was typically seen as a threat by villagers, and thus for *curacas* and community officials the control of crime became an important function of office, their honor and prestige being linked to their ability to maintain safety and security. In this situation theft and violent crime had little possibility of being viewed as protests against the state but instead were perceived as breeches in the communal order. Though the supervision and control of crime enforced communal solidarity and communal values, it also strengthened the colonial system by maintaining order and giving cultural importance to the control of crime.[3] In turn, the state found itself in the position of defending traditional indigenous values, but in so doing it also strengthened the legal knot that bound colonizer and colonized.[4]

Thus, by the eighteenth century indigenous understandings and use of the colonial legal system meant that this system was enforcing new structures and providing the underpinnings of the communally supported "restructuring" that had taken place, but the state was an integral part of this new indigenous order.

The cases of Quecaño and Quispe illustrate important aspects of indigenous criminality in late colonial Cuzco and make clear the attitude of the overwhelming majority of *naturales* toward all criminals, indigenous and otherwise.[5] First, in late colonial Quispicanchis and Canas y Canchis there were *naturales* who led criminal lives. Second, these thieves stole from Spaniard and Indian alike, but most victims were other indigenous peoples. Third, there is little evidence to support what has become known as "social banditry."[6] Villagers did not lend support to, or harbor, criminals. If criminals viewed themselves in a way that might suggest they were social bandits they never gave a hint of such sentiments in their testimony. This is significant, because documents dealing with other topics often do reveal subtle and indirect tensions, as well as major rifts, between local indigenous peoples and the state and non-Indians. Indigenous people were often frank and outspoken in their protests against state or individual actions, and much of the historical record for these cases comes not from colonial officials, but from the testimony of victims or witnesses and the accused. There is no reason to suspect that *naturales* would mask their true intent more in cases of theft or violent crime than they would in more politically loaded testimony against the state or people of European, African, or mixed descent. Fourth, the punishment Muñoz de Arjona imposed on Quecaño—"[the sentence] may serve as a warning to other delinquents"—indicates that these cases were not all that uncommon. Fifth, animals were among the most commonly stolen items. Because not all the rustled livestock could be readily eaten or easily hidden, it suggests that there was a market for such animals and people who purchased livestock with few or no questions asked. Sixth, criminals were often notorious, but relied on their knowledge of the terrain, the remoteness of some regions, their mobility, and the fear they invoked for protection. Seventh, few criminals escaped the grasp of the law for long. Those who did lived outside society or if living in or on the margin of society they worked at concealing their activities, especially if they preyed on their own or nearby communities. Sometimes thieves were protected by family members, friends, or associates. However, this was individual, not communal, support or tolerance and stemmed from personal ties or association. And finally, the *naturales* of rural Cuzco viewed thieves with disdain and apprehension. If personal risk was not too great, criminals were captured by community members who then often used the state to prosecute and punish the offenders.

State, Community, and the Illusory Social Bandit

Spanish colonialism imposed demands on its indigenous subjects that, if not complied with, made people criminals in the eyes of the state, but these are not the types of acts under consideration here. The robberies and violent crimes being examined were committed primarily for personal gain and do not include such things as punishments for not paying tribute, overt political actions such as riots, or conflicts over land. The infractions at issue were not limited to the indigenous population.[7] Mestizos and Spaniards figure prominently in a number of robbery complaints, but in a region where 80 to 90 percent of the population, if not more, was indigenous it should come as no surprise that the majority of perpetrators and victims were also indigenous.[8] More than forty-five thieves and over fifty victims out of over fifty thieves and sixty victims identified in the roughly eighty years prior to the Thupa Amaro uprising were *naturales*.[9]

James Scott argues that rural theft "is a nearly permanent feature of agrarian life whenever and wherever the state and its agents are insufficient to control it" and that such theft by itself is unremarkable: "When such theft takes on the dimensions of a struggle in which property rights are contested, however, it becomes essential to any careful analysis of class relations."[10] The ordinary rural theft that seemed "unremarkable" to Scott in Southeast Asia was, however, most remarkable in rural Cuzco.

When people in the communities of rural Cuzco felt abused by powerful individuals, government officials, or colonial policies their reactions normally did not include what has become known as social banditry. Objection and resistance took various forms. They sought legal redress, fled to avoid demands, hid community members to keep them off tribute lists and out of forced labor, rose in tumults to restore an acceptable equilibrium (their moral economy), and, once in a great while, even exploded in rebellion. They were not inclined to use or see theft, however, as a form of social protest.[11] Thus, the *naturales* of rural Cuzco were similar to many other rural peoples in that "much, if not most, of the prosaic but constant struggle of the peasantry to thwart those who seek to extract labor, grain, taxes, rents, and interest from them takes forms which cannot satisfy [the] definition of a social movement."[12]

Villages resolved minor criminal cases through their internal governing structure, elected officials or *curacas* determining justice. But indigenous officeholders did not have the legal authority in Spanish colonial society to impose severe physical punishments, although they sometimes did this, or to sentence criminals to jail or to an *obraje*.[13] Crimes that carried harsh penalties such as whipping or forced labor or those that could not be resolved within the existing community structure fell under the jurisdiction of the colonial state, usually in the person of the corregidor.

In those cases not dealt with internally, once a suspected criminal was apprehended he or she was held for the legal apparatus of the state to determine guilt or innocence and to pass sentence. Resolution of the case was typically based on the testimony of those involved. Thus, the victims and witnesses, most often *naturales*, were vital in such proceedings. In this way the state became a tool for the defense of traditional values, which could also serve to enhance faith in the justice system as an arbiter. When the villagers' sense of justice was not upheld, the opposite could be true. In this situation crimes such as rural theft were quite "remarkable" due to their impact on indigenous culture, and Indian-state relations as indigenous values were maintained and ties to the functioning legal system of the state increased. Although it is not appropriate to speak of colonial hegemony because indigenous ways were reinforced at the same time that colonial structures were also maintained and accepted, it is good to remember that hegemony "develops not because people collaborate in their own subjugation but because the dominating power has been able to institute practices and beliefs that rational people choose to adhere to, often because of coercive threats, but that over time come to appear normal, even natural."[14]

When the colonial legal system functioned in this way, it made it even less likely that native peoples would view criminality as, or that criminality could evolve into, social banditry. The contradictions of state exploitation and support of traditional values gave form to the complex and ambiguous mental world in which the *naturales* in the upper Vilcanota drainage lived. Attitudes toward the state varied depending not only on its policies, but on the particular individual enforcing those policies. The quality of the face-to-face relations between community members and Spanish officials was, in part, determined by actions involving criminality. It is ironic that while governmental policies may have driven more people to criminal activity, community values and state authority not only prevented criminality from emerging as legitimate resistance but may have reinforced bonds between Indians and the colonial state.

Thus, resistance and political protest manifested itself in many ways in eighteenth-century rural Cuzco, but it did not take the form of social banditry. *Naturales* considered most common criminals to be just that, not social bandits. However, I did encounter one case that from the macro level might be regarded by some as social banditry, although I view it as more akin to guerrilla warfare.

In 1789 indigenous "social bandits," "rebels," or "thieves"—the nomenclature depending on interpretation and point of view—killed guards (*soldados*) on each of two different haciendas in the warmer ecologic zone of Quispicanchis known as the Andes where coca was grown. Confronting one hacendado, a government official argued that not enough *soldados* had been employed to protect hacienda workers and complained of the "great lack of care and little esteem with which the hacienda owner and his administrators look on the lives of the workers and rest of the people." In trying to explain the situation and defend himself against accusations of neglect, one hacendado replied that his property had been ruined by "the rebels [Thupa Amaro]" and he was only slowly getting the hacienda back in order. But the group of about forty Indians who killed a guard with arrows and a spear and made off with goods were not remnants of the Thupa Amaro rebellion. These social bandits–guerrilla warriors were chunchos, the indigenous peoples who lived near the coca zone and in the jungle and who had defied both the Inca and Spanish conquests. These "*indios infieles chunchos*," as the official referred to them, maintained an ongoing struggle with those who intruded into their territory or established settlements in border areas between the sierra and their homelands. The resistance and struggle of the chunchos often took the form of theft and raids on these settlements, and when their territory was encroached on there was no reason for distinction to be made between native peoples from the sierra and Spaniards: both were traditional enemies and represented a threat. Thus, as in so many situations in the colonial world, this case had its ironic twists. At least one of the *soldados* killed was a sierra Indian named Juan Choquehuanca who had been guarding the hacienda and workers, presumably other *naturales* from the sierra like himself. And it was a colonial government official, not the *naturales,* who took the initiative in chastising hacendados for not having enough concern for "*las vidas y almas*" of the workers who had been killed by the chunchos.[15]

Culture and Crime

Even though state policy and internal conflicts broke down a larger sense of ethnic identity, individual communities and *ayllus* remained remarkably cohesive.[16] One aspect of this cohesiveness was a cultural heritage, reflected in the ancient Andean admonition "*ama qhella, ama suwa, ama llulla*"—"neither lazy, nor a thief, nor a liar be," which held criminals in very low esteem. Disdain for criminals was a shared value that enhanced unity in the face of potentially disruptive criminality. The opprobrium in which thieves and violent criminals were held was deeply rooted in Andean society. Felipe Guamán Poma de Ayala stated that in the time of the Inca the following laws concerning thieves and murderers prevailed:

Item: We order that there be no thieves in this kingdom nor highwaymen, *suua poma ranra,* and that if caught for the first time, be punished with 500 lashes and if caught a second time, be stoned and put to death and their bodies not buried, so that foxes and condors can eat them.

Item: We order that what was found be given back and paid for, so he won't be punished as a thief and so the records should show.

Item: We order that nobody in this kingdom can possess poisons, nor potions nor witchcraft to kill somebody or be killed by it. He who would kill somebody with them is sentenced to die quartered and thrown into a precipice. And if this action was against the Inca or the Lords; rebellious and deceitful, that drums be made from their skin, from their bones flutes, from their teeth and molars, necklaces, and from their heads, vessels to drink chicha. That is the fate of the traitor and it has to be publicly announced, and you say *yscay songo auca* [traitor].

Item: We order that anyone that kills, be killed in the same way, if he used a stone or a club, that this will be his sentence and execution.

These punishments are especially significant because, according to Guamán Poma, in normal circumstances the deceased were buried in tombs along with items that would accompany them in the afterlife. Thieves were to be denied the cultural vision of a proper life after death. Likewise, the use of terms such as "lazy" in association with criminals carried cultural weight, because being considered lazy was very negative. Guamán Poma maintained that in the Inca empire the following rule prevailed:

Item: We order that those lazy and dirty as pigs should be sentenced to drink in a vessel the dirt and filthiness of their
fields or houses or dishes with which they eat or that their
heads, hands and feet should be washed and they should be
forced to drink that water, as a sentence and punishment
throughout this kingdom.

Even though Guamán Poma's views of Inca morality were idealized, and orders, such as those cited above, might not be followed
to the letter, they do give an indication of attitudes. It was a reflection
of these attitudes and a severe warning, if not the actual punishment,
to criminals that on a second offense they could be stoned to death
and that their bodies would be left for condors and foxes to eat rather
than being buried with the goods they would need in the afterlife—
"fuesen apedrado y muerto y que no la enterrasen su cuerpo, que lo
comiesen las sorras y cóndores." However, even Guamán Poma implies that differences in types of thefts were recognized. For instance,
the theft of mature corn from fields was so common that vigilant sur-
veillance was required to protect the crop from pilfering, the emphasis in this case being placed on prevention rather than deterrence
through punishment (see plate 5).[17]

To view indigenous criminality as an outgrowth of colonial society is tempting, but the relationship between colonialism and crime
in Quispicanchis and Canas y Canchis remains vague and complex.
We do not know what caused people like Andres Quecaño to turn to
a life of crime from a "tender age" disregarding the laws, customs, and
culture of their own people. Had they been abused by colonial society, or was colonial society abuse enough, to lead them, directly or
indirectly, to embark on a life of crime? Under Spanish rule measures
to control crime were less draconian, and most likely less effective,
than under the Incas, and this may have permitted criminals to survive. However, the actions of these criminals could have stemmed
from personal or familial problems or character traits that had little,
if anything, to do with the circumstances of colonial life. The development of urban markets and increasing consumption in the Euro-

pean sectors, though not a prominent part of life in rural Cuzco, also created a supply of goods and animals that had value as well as a market for them. In the colonial world there were also more people who were not under the direct moral supervision of villagers or who were coming and going from work in regions outside their communities and who may have been tempted to rob the "other."

The relationship between colonialism and the criminality of *forasteros* is equally intriguing. Were *forasteros* such as Andres Quillilli, who was caught in Guaro in 1747 with goods that "could not be his," victims of colonial policies that led them to become *forasteros*?[18] The state certainly did impose demands that led many *naturales* to give up their lives as *originarios* to become *forasteros*. But people also gave up their status as community members and became *forasteros* for reasons not directly involving the state. And *originarios* sometimes dealt with the *forasteros* in their community in a less than cordial manner. If an Indian became a *forastero* due to colonial policies, was treated harshly by the *naturales* in the community to which he moved, and at some point turned to crime, who was responsible—the individual, the community, or the state? Then as now, causal relationships between the circumstances of life and criminal activity are very complex and almost impossible to substantiate.

Consider the case of Ysidrio Condori, a *natural* from Sicuani who had moved to Pitumarca. Condori had been living as a *forastero* in Pitumarca for some three years when he was accused of "*robos triviales.*" Detained by several villagers and one Spaniard, Condori was lashed ten or twelve times with a pizzle (*miembro seco de toro*) to make him confess. Then Javier Quispetuma, a *cofradía* steward in the church, took over the punishment. Quispetuma had been drinking and with Condori "hanging from a joist naked, he laid on such cruel blows and punishment with the bull's penis [pizzle] to the point of having left him unable to speak." Quispetuma bragged of the lashes "with much imperiousness and pride," but the *forastero* died. The body was not only black and blue, but it was flayed and swollen with visible blows and lashes from the buttock to the ankles. There was a deep cut on the head and abrasions all over the body. In his defense Quispetuma stated that neither the Spaniard nor any of the other community members present "impeded him in the act of carrying out the punishment that he executed." Although *naturales* held thieves in low esteem, one has to question whether such violence would have been tolerated for minor thefts if the accused had been an *originario* of their community, not a *forastero*.[19]

Culprits were expected to pay the price of their actions or at least make restitution for their crimes, but they often used finer points of the law to lessen or avoid punishment. For instance, in 1747 two *naturales* were accused of stealing a large silver candlestick (*blandón*) from the church in Coporaque. The theft took place the day after San Juan (24 June), the day tribute was due. It would be tempting to see this robbery, coming on the heels of tribute payment, as a form of social banditry. However, one of the accused, Juan Julio, was a known thief and the other, Estevan Cazeres, admitted to participating in several other robberies. Pasqual Sullai, an Indian from Coporaque, claimed that Julio and Cazeres had robbed him twice taking "55 *varas* [*vara* equals 33 in.] of *jerga* [rough wollen cloth]," rags and old dresses, and 8 *varas* of another coarse cloth that he had woven with his own hands. Sullai recovered the stolen items by chance when a woman who had been visiting the estancia where Cazeres lived recognized certain goods and informed Sullai. Accompanied by the *alcalde* and *curaca*, Sullai went to the estancia where his goods were recovered and the missing candlestick was discovered.

Julio confessed to robbing Sualli and to being present at the theft of the candlestick after a witness identified him as the person accompanying an unidentified suspect who wore a poncho. The wind had lifted the unidentified man's poncho, and a long silver item had been seen. Julio maintained that it had been two mestizos who robbed the church, and though he had been in their company he had not participated in the theft. Cazeres denied involvement in the robbery of the church, even though he admitted helping in earlier thefts. No mestizos were found and while the two confessed thieves pleaded their innocence of the church robbery, villagers and the prosecutor sought to convict the accused pair. Only the *Defensor de Indios* supported their denial. The *Defensor* argued that Julio had not taken the candlestick and that because the other stolen goods had been "returned" there had been, in effect, no crime—an attitude that may also have reflected Inca law. The accused fled, along with their wives and children, before a verdict was rendered.[20] Even if this theft had reflected a prepolitical action against colonial rule, it certainly was not viewed in a positive or tolerant light by the people of Coporaque. And the criminals disassociated themselves from the Church robbery even though they confessed other crimes, most likely due to the social condemnation reserved for such a crime and to avoid more severe punishment.

As noted, the role of the state as a causal factor in indigenous criminality is difficult to assess. Another case that reflects this complexity involved a complaint made by Favian Quispe and other "*yndios principales y tributarios originarios*" from the community of Sicuani. They maintained "that in the necessary and indispensable trips that we make to the city of Cuzco [to sell our goods] we suffer unspeakable extortions and frequent robbery in three places and [having gone there] only with the hope of paying our tribute, we return more in debt." One of their complaints concerned "extortions . . . made by the *caminero* [sales tax collector who assessed the commerce traveling on the royal road] of . . . San Geronimo [who] with the greatest cruelty, whether we carry a pass or not, demands the sales tax and besides this he makes us haul rocks, cut alfalfa and do other jobs." After receiving the complaint the crown replaced the abusive *caminero*, but the people from Sicuani also complained of being robbed in two other places:

> The first is on the plains of Andaguaylillas and the second . . . in front of the *obraje* of Lucre in the parish of Oropesa, Quispicanchis, a place known by its reputation; . . . in both [places] they rob us. [The people of Sicuani asked that the government official] . . . give orders to the *alcaldes mayores*, caciques and their delegates in the villages of Andaguaylillas and Oropesa that it should not be allowed nor permitted under any circumstances in these plains

that these men—so mischievous and harmful—be more in numbers than the common hidden robbers [and that they] be punished with the most severe sentences to help us in our endeavors.[21]

The two locations complained about were at, or near, junctions in trade routes and were natural locations for thieves to congregate. Both Andahuaylillas and Oropesa were communities with large *forastero* populations due in part to the work available in nearby *obrajes*, and *forasteros* were more than proportionately represented in local criminal complaints. Labor in an *obraje* was also the most typical sentence for *naturales* convicted of theft and other crimes, and the *obrajes* of Quispicanchis were the beneficiaries of much convict labor. After their sentences were served, criminals may have plied their trade in their new surroundings. State actions were insufficient to prevent or control crime in places such as Andahuaylillas and Lucre where people traveling through, like those from Sicuani, were robbed. The law-abiding, tribute-paying villagers of Sicuani wanted community officials in Andahuaylillas and Lucre, as well as the state, to exert a firmer hand against the thieves. By not doing enough to control crime, the state, in a sense, fostered criminality with the victims primarily being native peoples. The same, however, could be said of the local indigenous communities, but if most of the thieves were *forasteros, yanacona,* or vagabonds—not community members—and they robbed from travelers not the community, perhaps it was just easier for local indigenous officials to not see what was happening.

In the prosecution of crime, sentences were meant to punish and provide restitution, although in some instances it is clear that deterrence was also a desired end. In Quispicanchis and Canas y Canchis indigenous criminals were frequently sentenced to forced labor in an *obraje.* The wages did not go to the criminal but were used to make the aforementioned compensation or pay fines or debts to the victims or the state. Such sentences also supplied much needed labor for the textile mills that were vital in the regional economy. *Naturales* were occasionally condemned to *obraje* service on flimsy or trumped up charges (see chapter 6) that could occur in the colonial world but which are not included in the type of criminality being discussed.

Obraje workers labored under harsh conditions. Although no list of jobs performed by convict laborers is available, they, as with other forced laborers, most likely were employed in menial or unhealthy work. The 1768 sentence of a *natural* from Checasupe makes it clear that atonement was intended in the sentence. The thief received one year in the *obraje* of Lucre "in order that he may be purified of his crime and that he may pay with his personal labor the costs and remaining obligations."[22] A similar sentence was imposed on a pair of indigenous horse thieves in 1780. They were to serve two years in the textile mill of Pomacanchi "so that they may purify themselves and that . . . Royal Justice be satisfied and publicly restored."[23] And when Andres Quecaño, the rustler discussed earlier, was sentenced to *obraje* labor, the colonial official noted that his punishment "may serve as a warning to other delinquents," which made manifest that deterrence, as well as punishment, was a concern of the crown.

No sentences in rural Cuzco, except that of death, included mutilation.[24] Corporal punishment, however, was common. Lashes were inflicted for many lesser crimes and were frequently ordered in conjunction with other punishments for graver offenses. Such was the case of a notorious thief from Canas y Canchis who was condemned to two years in an *obraje* and given one hundred lashes. The sentence also made it clear that the reasons the culprit was ordered to a Quispicanchis *obraje* instead of one in his home province was for "*destierro*" or exile.[25] Several indigenous criminals from Canas y Canchis received sentences to *obrajes* in Quispicanchis that included *destierro*. Being forced to labor in a distant *obraje* compounded the punishment by removing the convicted person from family, friends, or associates who might physically or psychologically support him or help him escape. There were numerous exceptions to this practice. Nicolas Quispe, a *natural* from Guaro, stole from Thomasa Sisa, who resided near the *obraje* of Pomacanchi. Quispe was ordered to work in an *obraje* in the community next to his village instead of a more distant *obraje* in the same or a neighboring province where exile would have been a factor. It appears that while Indians from Canas y Canchis suffered *destierro*, usually to *obrajes* in Quispicanchis, the reason for the exile was not just punishment. The labor demands and influence of powerful *obraje* owners in Quispicanchis, such as the Marquis, who owned the *obraje* to which Quispe was sent, made these textile mills the recipients of convict labor from both Canas y Canchis and Quispicanchis.[26]

Capital punishment was almost never imposed on common criminals. Execution was normally reserved for serious crimes against the state, such as rebellion, and even then it was used sparingly. *Naturales* who killed someone in an assault, or even intentionally murdered, very rarely were executed. For instance, Matias Usca, a resident of Yauri (Canas y Canchis), had been jailed for stealing a mule. He escaped along with prisoners from nearby Coporaque, but during the escape the jailer was killed. When captured, Usca maintained that it was another Indian who had planned the escape and killed the jailer. There was some suspicion, however, that Usca had also murdered a woman in the neighboring community of Pichigua. The prosecutor sought the death penalty for this crime, which he termed "impious, atrocious and un-Christian," but Ucas was condemned to labor in "one of the *obrajes* of Quispicanchis [in which] he be jailed for five years."[27]

Although common perceptions of colonial practices dictate that crimes against Europeans were punished more harshly than crimes against *naturales* this was not always true in Quispicanchis and Canas y Canchis where there was little, if any, difference in the sentences imposed. For example, Agustin Guanco and Joseph Guamani confronted a pair of Spaniards after the Spaniards' dog attacked some sheep. An argument ensued, and one of the Spaniards hit Guanco causing blood to flow. Guamani then smashed the Spaniard in the face with a rock and killed him. The Indians were jailed, but they broke the lock and fled. Sentences were passed in their absence, when one assumes that harsher penalties would be imposed, but the sentences were not extraordinarily severe. Guanco was sentenced to six months in an *obraje* or the mines of Potosi and one-half of his goods were to be taken. Guamani, the one who delivered the fatal blow, was to receive two hundred lashes, have "goods confiscated to pay costs of the case, and be exiled to an *obraje* or mines of Potosí" for three years.[28] The length and severity of the sentence was in keeping with those imposed when the victim was Indian.

Only one case of murder was uncovered that led to the execution of the indigenous culprit. This involved a particularly brutal crime that occurred shortly after the Thupa Amaro revolt. In 1784 Yldefonso Mamani confessed to having killed Angela Castro, a Spaniard, just to rob her. His accomplices were two indigenous women, the most culpable of which was Juliana Llamoca. The three planned the robbery together, although the third woman opposed the murder. Mamani claimed to have stabbed the Castro woman only six times, but those who examined her body said it was "made a sieve" with fifty-three wounds. Mamani gave his accomplices thirty pesos to keep quiet. Both women also took mules, while Llamoca carried off five hundred *varas* of cloth that the victim had been selling. The women escaped, although rumors circulated that they had died during their flight. For his part in the crime Mamani was sentenced to be hanged and his body "quartered and his pieces placed in all the pueblos of this Jurisdiction [Canas y Canchis]," and if Llamoca was found alive she was to receive the same penalty. A judge in Lima pleaded for Mamani's life. He pointed to the lack of witnesses, the use of only one interpreter, and the age of the accused—he was only twenty-two—as reasons to grant mercy, but the pleas of the judge were ignored. The *Subdelegado y Comandante de las Armas* submitted this report:

At 11:00 in the morning, after having been spiritually comforted, the criminal Yldephonso Mamani was brought out from one of the cells of this Royal Jail, guarded by a party of 12 men, and a sergeant . . . and 5 companies of dragoons, . . . and comforted by 5 priests. He was hanged by the executioner Diego Gonzalez an Indian, and died there, naturally; He was left there until 4 in the afternoon and was lowered by the executioner himself. His head was cut off and his body quartered, having his head sent to the place where he killed Angela Castro and his right hand sent to the village of Checa where he was born so they could be placed on poles, as his other members should be, and having done this, they buried the rest of the body in the cemetery of this holy Parish church.[29]

Why was this young man executed when so few received the death sentence?[30] Perhaps the victim was Spanish, but other Spaniards had been killed by Indians, and they had not been executed. The fact that the killing was premeditated and particularly brutal could also have influenced the punishment, because excluding murders between spouses, for which native people in Quispicanchis or Canas y Canchis were not executed, there were few premeditated killings. Most likely, though, the sentence of death reflected the fear that still flowed through Spanish hearts, for the murder occurred just after the Thupa Amaro rebellion and in the region that had been the center of the upheaval. The colonial government was making a powerful statement to help preserve the order and protect its Spanish subjects who lived in a largely indigenous world.

Trade, Fiestas, and Crime

Throughout the colonial period trade was very important to the peoples of Quispicanchis and Canas y Canchis. Being situated on the royal road only enhanced rural Cuzco's links with colonial markets, and locally produced cloth, food, coca, and livestock were sold in destinations as distant as Oruro, Potosi, and Cochabamba. Canas y Canchis, in addition to having emerged as a hub of transport early in the colonial period due to its llama herds, was also home to important fairs including one in Tungasuca—part of Thupa Amaro's *curacazgo*—and the great mule and livestock fair in Coporaque. These fairs articulated local peoples with regional and even international trade networks. While this articulation created some economic opportunities in the region, it also provided local thieves ample opportunity to convert stolen goods into silver or other desired items. The fairs attracted people to the region who took advantage of their mobility and knowledge of markets to rob and to buy and sell stolen goods.[31] Apart from the riches of the church and whatever silver individuals may have had, the most frequently purloined items were clothes, cloth, crops, and animals. Being a center of livestock production and trade, the peoples of Canas y Canchis were especially hard hit by rustling.

In 1751 Ygnacio de Aparicio, a Spaniard from near Urcos (Quispicanchis), complained of being robbed by a muleteer from the Lake Titicaca region. Accused of stealing ten pesos and several articles of clothing, the *arriero* only admitted to pilfering a few pieces of clothing, including a cape. He had sold some of the apparel, and after being captured he returned other clothing he had not been able to sell. He even presented Aparicio with two pesos, part of what he had made in the sale of the cape.[32]

Most theft related to regional trade involved livestock, the various fairs and markets providing opportunities to steal, as well as sell, animals. Many of the mules in Quispicanchis and Canas y Canchis, indeed in the entire Cuzco region, came from Tucumán in the northern part of Rio de la Plata and were sold at the Coporaque fair. People connected with this trade passed through rural Cuzco, and the less scrupulous among them stole or received stolen animals. Agustin Gonzales, a *natural* from Coporaque, was traveling with *arrieros* when he stole a mule from another Indian named Joaquin Anco. He also admitted to previously having stolen other horses and mules. The thief had converted the stolen mule into cash by selling it for three pesos "to some of the transients from Tucumán."[33]

Neither the market for stolen animals, nor the theft of animals, declined after the Thupa Amaro rebellion. Testimony by *naturales* in 1806 revealed that a butcher from Arequipa offered to buy livestock from them, even if the livestock were not their own.[34] Through people such as the Tucumán transients and the butcher from Arequipa, the more persistent and successful rustlers in Quispicanchis and Canas y Canchis transformed their depredations into lucre.

Thieves, especially gangs, presented serious threats to the property and lives of people where they operated. In 1794 people from Yauri, plagued by a gang of rustlers from the province of Lampa, complained that "we find ourselves gravely hurt by the continual theft of beasts that these individuals commit on the pampa of our *ayllu*." They knew their livestock was hidden on the desert of Llangacagua, but they "dare not enter . . . fearful of some murder by so many bad men." Although various members of the gang were of indigenous origin, the head was a Spaniard named Estanislao Marroquin. After his capture Marroquin gave an indication of underlying social tensions in the sierra when he complained of being held on the testimony of a *cholo*.[35]

Simon Gamarra and Thomas Condori, rustlers from Chumbivilcas, a province bordering Canas y Canchis, stole numerous horses and mules in both *partidos* but were captured after one of their fruitful sprees. The pair had taken nine horses from Francisco Succo and Martin Guarocaya, *naturales* of Coporaque who made the formal complaint, and two horses from Miguel Ramirez in Velille (Chumbivilcas). While on the move they rustled four more horses, which they entrusted to Francisco Choquetaypi of Pomacanchi, where they then stole nine more horses. Two more horses were taken from Pedro Montalvo near Checa before they robbed an Indian on his way to Cuzco of four horses and a mule.[36] Such plundering caused concern among all peoples in the region, indigenous and otherwise, and led to cooperation in the apprehension of the thieves.

Enterprising thieves typically embarked on their careers near their home territory and then either enlarged their scope of operation or found it convenient to operate elsewhere. Lucas Chancairi of Pichigua complained that another *natural* from the same community, Luis Acsana, stole ninety of his sheep. The theft had occurred three years earlier, but Acsana had moved his activities, operating with three others, to the province of Lampa. The gang had been rounded up and jailed in Lampa, but they escaped and fled to Canas y Canchis only to be recaptured. Chancaiari, hoping to recover his loss, sought to have Acsana sentenced to an *obraje*, where he would be forced to work until restitution was made for the sheep.[37]

Such prolific thieves as Gamarra, Condori, the gang of Marroquin, Acsana, and their associates were a serious nuisance and threat to the livelihood of the people in the communities and haciendas on which the thieves preyed. The dynamism of the regional economy made thefts, especially rustling, lucrative for the robbers by providing a ready market for stolen goods. Hence, the problem persisted.[38]

These rustlers and robbers not only disrupted life but offended the social order of the communities they disturbed. Outlaws "earned" their living not as part of the community, but apart from it. Don Rafael Poma Ynga, an upstanding *alcalde* of Acomayo (Quispicanchis) described as an *"yndio noble ladino comerciante,"* was attacked by two of the community's lesser lights, Miguel Balderrama and Fermin de la Torre. Charges were brought against the two "for resisting Royal Justice and for having tried to kill the said *alcalde* and for other excesses that they have committed against the public tranquility." According to Poma Ynga, Balderrama was "full of a thousand vices [and a] known horse thief," and both men associated with "vagabonds and women of public life." The community stood behind their *alcalde*. Several *naturales,* including Visente Vilca, who had been enjoying a game of checkers on the evening when he heard the commotion, supported Poma Ynga's testimony. Spaniards also testified in support of Poma Ynga and against Balderrama and de la Torre. The only defense for the miscreants came from the mother of de la Torre, who claimed Poma Ynga was out to get her son, who, she reminded the court, was still a minor.[39] There was little or no support in villages such as Acomayo, either among Europeans or *naturales,* for those who disturbed the public order or transgressed acceptable bounds of behavior.

Such cooperation between Indians and Spaniards in criminal matters was not uncommon in rural Cuzco, both races wishing to preserve public tranquility and control criminality. This does not mean that racial tensions did not exist, but numerous cases demonstrate that *naturales* and Europeans both testified against members of their own race or the opposite race to bring to justice those who threatened the public well-being. Relations were guided by daily experience, by face-to-face contact, and in this situation most *naturales* and Spaniards subjugated whatever racial loyalty that may have existed to the security of their person and property.

Rustling created a great stir and public outcry, as many people were usually victimized in a short period. Also common, however, was the occasional theft of livestock by individuals in the community who sold, used, or ate the animal and sought to keep their identity secret. In 1705 Francisco Pichacani, a *forastero*, was jailed for stealing a pair of plowing oxen. He had not tried to leave the region nor had he sold the animals. Apparently he needed the oxen to work his fields, although it would take a fairly desperate person to believe he could keep the acquisition of oxen secret.[40]

The efforts of two local rustlers to protect their anonymity had tragic consequences. Using the cover of darkness to hide, Diego Cajia and Mateo Colque, both young boys, were stealing sheep when Colque slipped while negotiating a canyon and fell to his death. Cajia, like many other criminals, took refuge in the church.[41] Except in very serious crimes, or in the heat of pursuit, the church remained a sanctuary. Authorities normally did not enter the church to remove a criminal but waited, sometimes for days, for the criminal to give himself up or to attempt escape.

Acting alone to settle accounts or bring a criminal to justice could be dangerous business. Pasqual Chulluncuya, a tributary from Pichigua, got more than he bargained for when he decided to settle a score over some stolen sheep with another tributary from the same community. A couple of months earlier his son-in-law "lost" ten sheep, and four were found in a herd belonging to Antonio Atajo. A few years before other sheep had disappeared, and he had long suspected the Atajo family. Teresa Cayllo, the wife of Chulluncuya, testified that her husband had left home with the intent of confronting Atajo. The next time Chulluncuya was seen he was dead, and his body had been quartered. The head and chest were not found. Atajo, however, had not killed the hapless victim. En route to deal with one suspected thief, Chulluncuya encountered two others—Francisco Chaguara, also of Pichigua, and Melchor Pacco, an associate from Ayaviri. Chulluncuya accused them of rustling, and they later confessed to attempted horse theft. A fight broke out and Chulluncuya was stoned and kicked to death, but, perhaps due to the cultural and religious implications of such actions, the killers denied dismembering him.[42]

Many thieves, especially those from within the same community, relied on their knowledge of the victims and their property to avoid being apprehended, but not all were successful. Gregorio Mamani, a wool spinner by trade, was caught trying to sneak off with four loads of *chuño* that were on his llamas but which did not belong to him. This was not Mamani's first crime. He had taken a sheep belonging to Santos Thenco, but even though he had been convicted and received lashes for the crime he maintained his innocence. Accused once more of theft, Mamani admitted that about a year earlier he had rustled a horse and sheep from Thenco but claimed "he had not stolen more from him."[43] Robbing from those in his own community, Mamani, like other such thieves, did not go on crime sprees that would attract attention, but he did persist, if not always successfully, in his occasional thefts. When caught, his neighbors hauled him before colonial officials to be punished.

The weak, the old, and those without family support, in short the vulnerable, then as now, were frequent victims of crime. Ana Ayma, widowed only fifteen days, was robbed of sheep, cows, and other items including "five pieces of cloth, four *varas* of dark brown Castillian cloth, a new shawl [*yacolla*], . . . *varas* of fine linen, a basket of coca, . . . two purple *llicllas* [cloaks] of wool, a new cloth of vicuña neck fleece, [and] *varas* of wide ribbon." It could have been coincidence that Ayma was robbed at this point, but more likely a cold-hearted thief was taking advantage of the situation. The same *natural* who victimized her, a tributary from her own community named Pedro Cansaya, also had rustled fifteen head of cattle from another *natural*. Cansaya had no compunction about stealing from his neighbors, nor did the victims feel remorse in detaining a fellow tributary and testifying against him before Spanish officials. Acting on their complaints, Spanish authorities sentenced the thief to be whipped and to be exiled to labor in an *obraje*.[44]

Cansaya's wife, though not convicted, was implicated in one of the crimes. This was not unusual in that although men dominated criminal activity, women also were among the ranks of common criminals, and husband-wife teams preyed on their victims together. Josef Lerma and his wife were both sentenced to two years in the *obraje* of Quispicanchis after having been caught stealing from the cacique. Perhaps their sentence was harsh, because the accusations against them for "various robberies" also included the charge of "breaking exile."[45] Apparently, this was not the first time they had fallen afoul of the law.

In the communities of rural Cuzco, as elsewhere in the Andes and beyond, the routine of everyday life was broken by the celebration of fiestas and religious holidays. Easter, Christmas, saints days, and days devoted to fairs, marketing, and community labor were often festive occasions. Ironically, these were also the moments of greatest crime.[46] In 1777 the house of the priest in Pampamarca, another community in which Thupa Amaro was *curaca*, was robbed during a fiesta and fair. Those testifying noted that many people attended the fair from "different places and provinces," implying that the criminals came from outside the community and took advantage of the festivities to steal. Celebrations typically involved alcohol consumption, and people were less vigilant at these moments, which provided criminals an additional opportunity.[47] For instance, on Christmas of 1705 the house of Doña Juana Aguirre was robbed during church services. An indigenous official detained a Spaniard named Juan de Buenaño for the crime. Buenaño maintained that he had been on his way to the church when someone threw a bundle out of Aguirre's house and hid it. He claimed to then have removed the bundle and given it to a friend to sell in Cuzco. The thief, whether the accused or not, took advantage of the fact that most of the community was in church celebrating the birth of Christ.[48]

Juan de Buenaño, despite being described as a Spaniard (almost certainly a *criollo*), not only needed a Quechua interpreter to make his statement, but he did not even know his age. Buenaño was not the only Spaniard in Quispicanchis and Canas y Canchis who could not speak Spanish. Many poorer people of European descent lived in a dominantly indigenous and Quechua-speaking world and spoke the tongue most often heard. In 1689 the priest of Coporaque wrote

that the community "does not have Spanish haciendas nor estancias.
. . . It has six poor Spanish [men] . . . and eight women. It has, more
or less, a thousand souls, large and small, among the *naturales.*"[49]
How often did people such as these actually speak Spanish? Too often it is assumed that Europeans in indigenous society were rich and
powerful persons, but the *naturales* of rural Cuzco also knew poor
Spaniards. Spaniards such as Buenaño were more likely to be perceived as deserving derision rather than as part of an oppressive colonial structure, especially when they turned to crime.

Francisco Guanca was another victim of holiday theft. On Corpus
Christi, while Guanca served as "steward of the Sacrament," Diego
Mamani and Mateo Caucata entered his home and stole several
items of clothing. Guanca testified that among the stolen goods were
"a black woolen cloth of Quito [*ongarina*] that was once part of a *reparto,* two cloaks that we call shawls [*yacolla*] with which we cover
ourselves when we go to church, two hand cloths, a red undershirt, a
pair of trousers made of thin black woolen cloth, one *vara* of fine
British linen, two *varas* of yellow ribbon . . . another good ribbon . . .
of *reparto,* . . . a light-blue skirt, two cloaks or carrying cloths [*llicllas*]
of red baize . . . a small money bag [*chuzpa*] worth 5 reales, [and] two
colorful bags from Caytas." This *natural* owned considerable goods,
including items distributed in the *reparto.* The thieves were caught
while trying to sell their loot in Yanaoca and in Pampamarca. The
year was 1780, the year of the Thupa Amaro rebellion, which was, in
part, against the *reparto.* A common complaint from people in the
communities was that they had no use for many *reparto* items or that
their need for such goods was saturated. Though this may have been
true in general, these two culprits were not only marketing *reparto*
goods, but they were doing it in Thupa Amaro's curacazgo. The market may have been saturated at the prices corregidores were forcing
people to pay, but in the informal economy at least these thieves believed there was a market for such goods.[50]

Just the year before, in 1779, on the eve of Corpus Christi, Feliz
Vayalla of Coporaque complained that his mother-in-law had been
robbed of items including a blue cloak that was a *reparto* item and a

blue woolen waistcoat and that he too had lost pots and pans. Other *naturales,* including Asencia Vaihua, Antonio Quecane, Sebastian Cana, and the widow Thomasa Guamani, had also been victimized. At least three thieves, all Indians, were involved. Two were apprehended in Yauri with stolen booty, including the blue *reparto* cloak belonging to Vayalla's mother-in-law. The thieves were turned over to the colonial state to be prosecuted by none other than Thupa Amaro.[51]

In conclusion, by the eighteenth century the peoples of Quispicanchis and Canas y Canchis lived in a complex and contradictory world that, not surprisingly, created complex and contradictory responses.[52] Overwhelmingly, the victims of indigenous crime were other *naturales.* If richer Indians and people of European descent were also robbed it did not necessarily indicate a political or preconsciously political motive. Those engaged in criminal activity saw no reason to exempt anyone from their talents, especially those who had more. Criminals were pursuing their own economic interests, and they were not supported in their criminality by indigenous villagers.

The people in the communities of the upper Vilcanota were struggling to maintain the most vital aspects of their culture, their way of life. One structure that helped preserve community solidarity was the system of office holding. Though the system had been created by Spanish colonialism, the *ayllus* successfully adapted and used it and were largely self-governing in their day-to-day existence. Demands of the colonial state and internal community differentiation caused tensions in this structure, but crimes such as theft and murder did not normally create internal community dissension. By controlling thieves and violent criminals, community officials served their people, enforced the community structure, and in the process also served the colonial state. Once the suspects were apprehended, *naturales* provided the state with the testimony to convict. When the state did this, as it normally did, the impact was to enforce community values as well as maintain the colonial order. When the legal system functioned in this manner it also reinforced the relationship between colonizer and colonized by lending greater legitimacy to this important aspect of colonial justice. Thus, even while there was extensive discontent with the Spanish colonial system, there was a fundamental reliance, perhaps enforced due to a lack of other realistic choices, on Spanish justice. The Indians used the legal apparatus of the state "working the system . . . to their minimum disadvantage."[53] The result was to further deepen the ambiguities that riddled their lives. But unlike the decades after the European arrival in the sixteenth century—when a more binary division separated indigenous and European societies and cultural cooperation perhaps aided the survival of the new colonial society and also led to a certain destructuring of Andean society—in the eighteenth century the more fluid nature of culture and the multiplicity of cross-cultural contacts created a much different environment as reflected in the treatment of criminality. Indigenous people accepted certain aspects of the colonial regime and used them to their own benefit. This created a growing interdependence and a certain legitimation of colonial authority, but it also strengthened or reenforced and "restructured" communal values, which helped make the *ayllus* of Quispicanchis and Canas y Canchis ongoing and vital.

4

Indigenous-Spanish
Struggles Over Land

El . . . valle de Oropesa, que es lo mas immediato al Cusco, es tem-
plado, y apetecible. Por esta razon tienen en ella muchos vecinos dis-
tinguidos del Cusco, y las Religiones diversas haciendas de Maiz,
Trigo y otras semillas, frutas, y hortalizas, con hermosas casas de
recreo. . . . COSME BUENO, description of region of Quispicanchis
closest to Cusco, 1767

IN 1571 Pedro Atahualpa, the *curaca* of Urcos, complained to colonial
authorities that Captain Diego Maldonado had violently taken possession of community lands, built huts, and installed his *yanaconas* on
their lands. This was one of the first of numerous confrontations between Spaniards and *naturales* that stretched the duration of the colonial period in which the villagers of Canas y Canchis and Quispicanchis were forced to defend their fields and pastures against
usurpation by people of European or mixed descent.[1]

This chapter explores the relationship that developed between the
peoples of the upper Vilcanota and the Spanish legal system in the defense of village lands. It examines the impact of this relationship on
the reciprocal ties between villagers and Spaniards. It also draws attention to the importance of power, face-to-face relationships, and cross
racial cooperation as loyalties were guided more by self-interest and
personal ties than by strict racial divisions. Indigenous communities
were, after all, often in disaccord with one another, and the same appears to have been true for Spaniards and their European neighbors.

The defense of community lands against European encroachment
was one of the hallmarks of indigenous resistance to colonial domination. Identification with and dependence on communal lands

maintained culture and sustained life. Access to land also provided *ayllus* with the means to meet many of the state's economic demands such as tribute. Thus, a threat to the *naturales'* control of the land was a threat to their very existence. However, while European and mestizo usurpers often resorted to threats, violence, or other real or implied force to occupy lands, peoples in rural Cuzco infrequently responded with an "eye for an eye." Instead of force, *naturales* in Quispicanchis and Canas y Canchis most often turned to the colonial legal system to restore their lands and thus assure maintainance of the proper social order.

Using this system of justice, the peoples of the upper Vilcanota region were amazingly successful in the defense of their lands. While they did not win every case involving claims of illegal appropriation, decisions went in their favor more often than not. Understanding that they could "work the system," community leaders became skilled legal strategists, and the Spanish legal apparatus functioned as an effective weapon of the weak.

The Spanish crown encouraged this "legalism" by establishing a system that included a legal representative for the Indians, the *protector (defensor) de naturales*; creating a special legal status for Indians, albeit a second-class status; making special laws that governed Indians; and rendering a high enough measure of justice that indigenous confidence in the judicial system was maintained. The reasonable functioning of a protective system of justice, so important to the *naturales'* understanding of the reciprocal rights and duties essential to the colonial equation, helped maintain the bonds that tied the villagers of rural Cuzco to the system that also oppressed them, for colonial law also legalized the alienation of indigenous lands through various means deemed justifiable by the state.

In reality, the communities had little recourse but to use the legal system. Court battles were not only the safest form of resistance or vindication but also offered greater opportunity for success than more militant actions. Likewise, the limited scope of land occupations and the nature of law, most often involving individual communities or individual actions, militated against widespread collective actions.

With the aid of the Spanish *protector* who helped craft legally powerful claims, *naturales* developed arguments that curried favor with colonial officials. High on this list were the inability to meet tribute payments, their weak position requiring governmental protection, and the disruption of religious life. For instance, when Captain Juan Francisco de Ochoa invaded lands belonging to *ayllu* Collatia in Quiquijana, the people described themselves as "poor, defenseless, pusillanimous Indians" who needed the land, and the animals they raised on the land, to pay their tribute. They also pointed out that when deprived of their own lands, community members went to live with Spaniards who readily received these Indians "*con todo gusto.*" The *ayllu* maintained that local Spaniards worked against their efforts to have people return to their villages, which had a very negative impact on the communities. They argued that hacienda Indians did not "pay attention to their caciques saying that they do not live or eat on community lands, but on those of Spaniards. And because of this they and their children do not fill their personal service or tribute nor do they respond to the Christian doctrine and the burden of not having . . . [these] Indians means that more burden falls on those in the community."[2]

Such clever defenses often won cases, but not all land usurpations could be contested in the courts. Powerful individuals, or those with powerful friends, appear to have used their influence to prevent matters from coming before legal authorities or to influence those authorities when possible. Costs also could restrict the effectiveness of the legal system, because although initial court costs were nil or relatively low, long and complicated legal battles had a way of becoming expensive. Influence, or the wealth to retain a lawyer with good knowledge of colonial procedures, allowed more well-to-do Spaniards to make legal battles lengthy and costly, sometimes discouraging communities from pursuing their interests and just causes. In 1763 a *curaca* in San Pablo de Cacha lamented that the same thing was happening to his community that so often "happened in legal battles over lands with Spaniards, generally the unfortunate Indians lose their just claims because they do not have the wherewithal to support the expenses of lawyers and others."³ Thus, while legal decisions most often favored the *naturales,* other disputes may have been prevented from reaching the legal system or were discouraged or dropped due to costs. However, in eighteenth-century Canas y Canchis and Quispicanchis the usurpation of communal lands by Europeans was not common.

For the communities there was nothing more vital than the land that guaranteed their social and biological reproduction. Attachment to communal lands provided a sense of identity. Family access to land, usually through the rights of the adult male tributary, was the right that most clearly defined membership in the community. Because mountains, rocks, bodies of water, and other natural objects were often sacred, even one's relationship to the religious forces that influenced life had geographic specificity. A *natural* moving to a distant location would encounter sacred places with attributes similar to those he had known before. The new places or objects of veneration, however, would not necessarily come to have the same depth of meaning that was incumbent in a knowledge and faith developed in familiar surroundings and nourished from childhood through adulthood.

Europeans did not covet all lands with the same intensity. The fertile river valley lands between Urcos (Quispicanchis) and the Quispicanchis-Cuzco border were the most highly prized. Lower and less frigid than Canas y Canchis and most of Quispicanchis, this region was excellent for cultivating the Europeans' prized grain—wheat—and its irrigation systems enhanced productive potential. It was here that many distinguished residents of Cuzco had their haciendas with gardens, orchards, and *"hermosas casas de recreo"* or "beautiful vacation homes."⁴

There were many regions that the elite found less appealing but nonetheless were desired by other Europeans. The lower zones of Quispicanchis were centers of coca production, a lucrative enterprise for the *hacendados* if often deadly for the workers. Other zones produced wheat, corn, and fruit, while intermediate and the higher zones were suited to varieties of sweet and bitter potatoes, barley, *ha-*

bas or fava beans, and Andean grains such as quinua and *kañiwa*. Livestock *estancias* or haciendas were also attractive enterprises for Europeans, and the higher zones of Quispicanchis and Canas y Canchis provided pasture.

The vertical topography combined with specific local conditions, such as rivers or lakes that tempered the cold—including the lakes near Langui or Pomacanchi—formed microclimates. These ecologic niches allowed for varied agricultural production in zones where otherwise only hardy crops could be grown. Thus, variations in European and indigenous production and settlement had bases in factors as diverse as climate, topography, natural resources, and proximity to Cuzco. Europeans preferred properties in the rich, mild valley lands close to Cuzco. This meant that much friction over land between *naturales* and Europeans was centered in the Vilcanota valley floor of Quispicanchis and along the small Huatanay river that flows down from Cuzco through Quispicanchis and into the Vilcanota and in this zone the Europeans tended to be people of power and influence.

Until the eighteenth century relatively few Europeans lived in the higher regions of the two provinces, Sicuani and mining centers such as Condoroma being exceptions. Parish priests in Canas y Canchis attested that few Spaniards lived among an overwhelmingly Indian population. The priest of Checacupe and Pitumarca noted that there were only three Spaniards in the parish with "three poor haciendas." Spaniards held neither haciendas nor *estancias* in San Pedro or San Pablo de Cacha, although five Spaniards lived in San Pedro and two Spanish women resided in San Pablo. Likewise, in Coporaque and Pichigua there were neither Spanish haciendas nor *estancias* and just a few "poor Spaniards" as residents. The community of Yanaoca contained one *estancia* belonging to mestizos, and four married mestizos, described as "poor," lived in the community.[5]

With the *revisitas* and sale of communal lands in the wake of the devastating epidemic of 1720, wholesale "transfers" of land from indigenous to European society ceased.[6] By the second quarter of the eighteenth century Europeans had acquired most of the land they were to acquire in Quispicanchis and Canas y Canchis during the colonial period. However, important individual and community struggles between *naturales* and Europeans over land persisted throughout the eighteenth century.

After the defeat of Tawantinsuyu the Spanish crown asserted its legal claim to all lands and began to reward or pay individuals with land grants and to sell properties defined as vacant. Under the onslaught of a host of European pathogens such as measles, mumps, smallpox, and the plague, the majority of *naturales* disappeared from the face of the earth. This meant that communities often lacked the people to work more marginal lands, and these areas fell into disuse. Even good lands could not always be worked, and under colonial law these fields and pastures were susceptible to being declared vacant and sold. Vacant lands also tempted Spaniards or other *naturales* to invade.

Most lands were lost to Europeans during the sixteenth and seventeenth centuries. In the Andahuaylillas region of Quispicanchis "there was a clear pattern of progressive alienation of communal land beginning at least as early as the Toledan *reducciones* and enduring into the twentieth century. The high water marks for the loss of indigenous lands may have been the Toledan *reducciones*."[7] The reduction system of Toledo concentrated people and shrank their land holdings, freeing lands to be purchased by, or granted to, Europeans. The peoples of rural Cuzco, particularly Canas y Canchis, slowly but persistently resisted and undermined the reduction system (see chapter 1). Through quiet but determined reoccupation of lands that had not been effectively alienated *naturales* reestablished older and more dispersed settlement patterns. As late as the 1790s the community of Andahuaylillas still had members living as far as twenty-two leagues from the parish center, a distance far greater than the one league in which Indians were supposed to live. It is unclear, however, if this Andahuaylillas *ayllu* had traditionally occupied this territory or had expanded into it during the colonial period. However, the concentration or reduction of communities sometimes meant the loss of, or separation of ties with, more distant *ayllus* that had been part of an integrated resource system—the vertical system of holdings to which

John Murra drew attention (although holdings could be horizontal as well as vertical). Other communities succeeded in maintaining at least some of their prereduction character: "The *ayllu* Incacuna, which had settlements in San Blas in Cuzco and in Andahuaylillas, is an example of an *ayllu* which succeeded in maintaining its preconquest dual location. The *ayllu* Sailla, reduced into the parish of San Jeronimo near Cuzco, is another example. Sailla maintained ten *topos* of land in Guaraypata in the areas called Guaina-Carisno and Apo-Carisno in the town of Quiquijana."[8]

In the late sixteenth century the Spanish crown initiated a policy that increased pressure on community lands. Declaring that lands held without just title would become crown property and be available for sale, King Phillip II embarked on a process of title clearance known as *composición* (*de tierra*). Compositions were yet another source of revenues for the crown: a government official inspected titles and granted clear ownership for a sum determined by the inspector. Conducted in conjunction with land inspections (*visitas de tierras*), there were four major periods of inspection and composition of titles in Peru—1590 to 1596, 1615 to 1622, 1665, and 1722 to 1725.[9] Although individual communities may not have been affected by all these inspections, many were touched by at least one. Other inspections and title clearance procedures were frequently conducted on a local level, especially at the request of Spaniards who desired to legitimize de facto possession of lands. *Naturales* who had acquired private lands, as well as communities, also used composition to ensure their titles. Most often, however, the *visitas* and *composiciones de tierras* meant a reduction of village property.

In Canas y Canchis and other Andean regions with a strong herding tradition based on llamas and alpacas, and with it dependence on broad expanses of pasture, *naturales* maintained greater control of their lands than indigenous peoples in other regions. They also more readily integrated European livestock into their way of life. Cattle and, especially, sheep reinforced indigenous traditions and did not leave much unoccupied space for Europeans. Thus, the importance of herding, developed out of the blessings of nature and human ingenuity, proved vital to indigenous retention of their lands and culture (see chapter 1).[10]

Most indigenous lands lost to Europeans were transferred through the aegis of the colonial regime. Reductions, compositions, and land grants effectively and "legally" removed lands from *naturales*, putting them into the hands of Spaniards. Colonial demands also forced communities to rent, and sometimes to sell, lands to meet state impositions. In this way even tribute became an effective, if unintended, means of transferring lands to Europeans. Tribute led the people of *ayllu* Vicho to sell communal holdings when the population fell below the number on which the community's tribute was based and there was no recount or lowering of exactions. To meet demands the *ayllu* rented out forty-one *topos* of land for 133 pesos—the amount of their tribute—but one year an irresponsible community official spent the money "without delivering said tribute." To avoid such calamities the cacique, *ayllu* members, and the *protector de los naturales* all agreed that it would be wise to sell the lands when the Spaniard who had been renting them made what was considered to be a generous offer. *Ayllu* Vicho was to receive payments of 133 pesos a year, paid directly to the corregidor, to cover tribute and 5 percent interest on the principal.[11] Insecurity over the ability to comply with tribute led the people of Vicho to part with lands in exchange for security.

Similarly, when the *encomendero* Pablo de Caravajal left land to *naturales* in Ocangate (apparently those in his *encomienda*) they decided to sell the land, in part, to help with their tribute payments. The property, located among the coca plantations of the valley of Cucho'a, was twenty-two leagues distant. In justifying the sale the Indians argued that this was too far. In addition, the bequeathed property was in the "*andes*" (a semitropical zone known to be unhealthy to sierra Indians), and it was "contiguous to infidel Indians," the chunchos. Assured tribute payment was more attractive to these *naturales* than owning a coca plantation in the *andes* among Spaniards, and living under the threat of attack by "*yndios infielez*," their *encomendero*'s gift of lands was converted into tribute relief.[12]

Similar to communities in most regions of the New World, the villages of rural Cuzco had to meet obligations to the church. To comply with the demands of their parish, the *curaca* of *ayllu* Marcaconga in Sangarará petitioned the state for the right to sell communal lands described as rocky, barren, and distant. The cacique also argued that service in the Potosi *mita* had left the pueblo "very dissipated and lacking Indians." Unable to make beneficial use of these marginal lands, the *ayllu* decided to sell them to lessen the weight of yet another obligation.[13]

Individuals and communities were willing to part with lands for ends they believed worthwhile. In the late eighteenth century a Spaniard was allowed to purchase property in *ayllu* Mohina (Oropesa), apparently the first time lands within the *ayllu* had been obtained by an outsider. Even though the sale was not for the community, there was no objection raised by the *naturales*. A well-to-do indigenous noble woman had willed a house and alfalfa fields in Mohina worth over a thousand pesos, as well as other houses in Mohina and Cuzco, to her family. Her nephew, Justo Sawaxaura, inherited dwellings in the *ayllu*. As Sawaxaura matured it was decided that he should attend the *Real Colegio de San Bernardo,* and the properties were sold to support his education. *Ayllu* Mohina raised no objection to a Spaniard buying property in their *ayllu* when it went to support the education of an indigenous noble.[14] Two Sicuani *ayllus* also agreed to give up control of lands to a Spaniard but not for money. They traded one precious resource—land—for another—water, the Spaniard being obliged to construct an irrigation canal in exchange for use of land.[15]

In the wake of the 1719–1720 epidemic a series of *revisitas* were conducted in Canas y Canchis and Quispicanchis to bring exactions in accord with the diminished population. Lands determined to be in excess of communal needs were sold by the government. However, unprecedented population growth caused the need for land to quickly surpass communal reserves, and within two or three decades communities such as Andahuaylillas, fully supported by the corregidor, demanded that the colonial state return the desperately needed lands.[16] Spanish policy, in keeping with indigenous tradition, had taken future needs into consideration, but it had not foreseen the exceptional growth. Having reduced the resources of communities such as Andahuaylillas, the government inadvertently initiated a period of heightened tensions and land-related conflicts as communities struggled to guarantee their future.

Communal lands determined to be unused or unneeded were declared vacant. Once verified as vacant, land could be purchased by making an offer not to the community, but to the government. The crown, constantly scrambling for revenues, usually accepted such bids. When Ylario Yañes, a Spaniard from Quiquijana, denounced property as vacant he offered to pay two-thirds the value. With no objection being raised by the community, colonial officials agreed to the sale. Why the *naturales* did not object is unclear. Perhaps some agreement had been worked out between them and the buyer, or perhaps the lands were truly vacant.[17] Likewise, when a Spaniard denounced lands near Acomayo as vacant, several Spaniards, but no community members, testified that the land had not been planted for seven years, with only some corrals and a few head of livestock being seen during that period. However, potato fields were sometimes fallowed for periods up to seven years during which time animals were grazed on the lands. Such lands were certainly not considered vacant by indigenous standards. Why did the people of Acomayo not object to, or support, the Spanish acquisition of these lands? Unfortunately the documents do not reveal if the Spaniard somehow prevented the people of Acomayo from resisting the sale, if an informal agreement had been reached, or if the villagers truly did not care.[18]

As we have seen, communities rented out lands to obtain funds for tribute or to meet other needs. As did other landlords, they sometimes got new renters when they were not pleased with the old. In 1776 the *naturales* of Yanaoca, being dissatisfied with the previous arrangement, changed renters and guarantors of the rental contract. The four caciques of Yanaoca, including a Spaniard who was married to one of the other *curacas*, an indigenous woman of royal lineage named Doña Catalina de Salas Pachacuti, agreed to be the guarantors of a rental contract with Joseph Becerra. The people of Yanaoca rented *estancia* Pullapulla to Becerra for a period of three years at 145 pesos per year. Every six months, the period separating tribute payments, 72 pesos 4 reals were to be paid to the community. In addition, the *naturales* had 397 head of cattle and 1,267 sheep grazing on the land that were also part of the agreement. There had been problems with the previous renter over the wages of communal members working as shepherds, and the people of Yanaoca made it very clear that "under no pretext would [the renter] ask said caciques for the five *septimas* (forced laborers) or other workers . . . [without assuring] payment of the daily wage." As in other cases involving married women, Catalina de Salas Pachacuti, the female *curaca*, was interrogated to assure that she agreed to the obligation and had not been forced into it by her husband. According to the document, such had been the law since the times of the emperor Justinian and the Roman senate.[19] Likewise, Phelipa and Josepha Puyucagua, being married women, were interrogated in a similar manner (including attributions to Justinian and the Roman senate) when they and their brothers Thomas and Joseph Puyucagua rented out family lands near Pampamarca to a Spaniard for 100 pesos a year.[20]

Not all land rental was by Europeans from *naturales*, as sometimes communities or individual *naturales* rented from Spaniards. In the mid–seventeenth century, caciques in Urcos and Andahuaylillas rented the local inn or *tambo* from Agustín Jara (de la Cerda) for a period of four years at 150 pesos per year. When Jara brought the matter before the government, the caciques had been in control of the *tambo* for some time but had not paid the Spaniard 230 pesos they owed.[21] Spaniards were not the only ones who could try to get the best of a deal.

Colonial land laws were structurally, though perhaps not consciously, weighted in the long-term favor of European land acquisitions. This dynamic was further enhanced, on occasion, by the prejudicial actions of certain colonial officials who favored Spaniards over Indians. In eighteenth-century Quispicanchis and Canas y Canchis this type of behavior does not appear to have been common, and the law did not direct colonial officials to support European interests over those of the *naturales*. However, friendship, kinship, business relationships, or racial identification led some officials to favor Spaniards over Indians.[22] The *naturales* of San Francisco Guayqui complained that Spaniards had usurped communal property. Unable to get justice through their corregidor, the *naturales* took the case to Lima. Authorities in Lima ruled in their favor, ordering the corregidor to support Guayqui so that "they would not have necessity to appear before the Royal Government over this matter again." Despite the threat of a five-hundred-peso fine, the corregidor of Quispicanchis either did not enforce or did not persist in enforcing the order. Four years later Don Mateo Parco Gualpa, the *curaca* of Guayqui, again complained that Gregorio de Olarte, Maria (Marcela) de Tapia, and Maria Ramirez harassed the Indians and had dispossessed them of two *fanegas* of cultivated fields as well as pasture lands. Gualpa protested that the Spaniards were "possessing and procuring the fruits [of the land] and availing themselves of everything in grave detriment to the Indians" who planted to pay their tribute and other obligations. Neighboring *curacas* confirmed the same, adding that Olarte, who had been involved in the earlier case, had driven off livestock and stopped people from planting their potatoes. Gualpa bitterly commented that Spaniards enter the community and "order the miserable Indians around as if they were their slaves" while prohibiting them from crossing over Spanish-owned property that would greatly facilitate the passage from one parcel of communal lands to another. The court again ordered Guayqui be put in possession of their lands, and this time the order was enforced. Under the protection of a Spanish official, community *curacas* walked over the contested property throwing rocks and conducting other symbolic acts of ownership. However, the arrogance of certain Spaniards, and the noncompliance of the corregidor, had led to renewed occupation of lands and racial harassment despite orders from higher crown officials.[23]

In 1765 when Sebastian Fuentes Pongo Yupanqui's lands in Acomayo were invaded by a Spaniard named Thomas de Tharraga, the corregidor did not come to the Indian's support. This *natural* also took his case all the way to Lima demanding that his lands be returned and that Tharraga pay rent for their use because he needed them "for the number of children he has to maintain." He argued that the corregidor did not come to his aid "due to the great friendship he has with said Don Thomas de T(h)arraga."[24]

Likewise, Jose Vilca, the cacique of Marangani, complained in the name of the people of *ayllu* Luracachi that the official who measured property boundaries (*medidor de tierras*) "dispossessed us with . . . violence" by remeasuring and selling to a European lands that the community had "possessed and enjoyed" at least since 1608. Despite the actions of the *medidor de tierra* and the sale of the land, all was not lost for *ayllu* Luracachi. A Spaniard from Marangani supported the Luracachi claims stating that the *naturales* had held the land from time immemorial and that they had titles. An official asked that the titles of both the community and the Spaniard who had purchased the land be presented for review.[25] The ultimate resolution is unknown, but this case, as so many others, created ambiguity for Indians. Government officials were the source of both the *naturales'* despair and their hope. One Spaniard, probably in association with the *medidor*, bought their improperly alienated lands while another Spaniard supported the *naturales'* claims and testified on behalf of the community. In the long run Europeans gained control of a sizable portion of indigenous property, particularly in or near larger urban settlements. However, the process was uneven and the tenacious commitment of indigenous peoples to their lands, their deep awareness of what was and had been theirs, as well as the possession of land titles from the early colonial period helped *naturales* hold on to fields and pastures, but each generation had to confront slightly altered circumstances—"*lo andino*" was not stagnant.

Although colonial law, corrupt officials, and population decline, among other factors, led to the alienation of indigenous holdings, the process was not quick enough or thorough enough for some Europeans. Force and a variety of illegal techniques were also used to take lands from the *ayllus*. Cattle and other livestock were used to trample, eat, and otherwise destroy crops to usurp lands or acquire labor.

Irrigation systems were tampered with, and water supplies were cut. Europeans even used indigenous surrogates—*forasteros* and hacienda residents—to invade, hold, and work communal lands. Violence and threats were employed to drive people from their lands, some Spaniards making life so difficult that *naturales* opted to sell their lands rather than confront day-to-day, year in year out harassment.

The simplest method of usurpation was to occupy and plant fallow or vacant lands and then wait to see what objections or resistance would be mounted by the community. If strong resistance was not forthcoming, the lands fell under the de facto control of the usurper with future possibilities of obtaining legal control through fraud or arguing that the lands were not needed or used by the *naturales*. For instance, when a local official illegally occupied communal lands belonging to Oropesa other Spaniards were emboldened to take urban plots. However, in this instance the official's status protected neither him nor the other Spaniards. Higher authorities, responding to the complaints of the *naturales* who rushed to challenge the usurpations, restored all lands to the people of Oropesa.[26]

Having sufficient lands, the people of *ayllu* Huayrachapi in Acomayo had not immediately protested when an hacendado made a minor incursion onto communal property. As time passed, however, the hacendado encroached even further. Lamenting that "with the passage of time he [the hacendado] has been introducing himself more and more" and that they, the "*miserables yndios*," no longer had sufficient lands, *ayllu* Huayrachapi desperately turned to the state for help.[27] Toleration had proven to be an invitation to further abuse rather than a means to avoid conflict.

Muscling land away from villagers began early in the colonial period, and one of the most contested zones was along the Vilcanota near the community of Quiquijana. In 1606 Francisco Huaman Sauñi and Pedro Ninaronto, *curacas* of *ayllu* Saiba in Quiquijana, complained "in the name of the Indians of the *ayllu* subject to them ... that we have had and possessed since the time of the *ynga* twenty-five *topos* of land named Guaguaconga and Cochapata where corn, wheat, and other vegetables are grown." A mother and son, Doña

Casilda de Anaya Maldonado and Lorenco Bezerra, had invaded their lands by "force and against our will" running cattle over the fields to drive the people off. Caciques from several local *ayllus* testified that *ayllu* Saiba had possessed the land for at least sixty years and that it had been conferred on them by Spanish officials. One elderly man over eighty years of age stated that he and others, his elders, knew that the "Indians and *curacas* of *ayllu* Saiba had always possessed Guaguaconga and Cochapata." After almost two years of claims and counterclaims, the corregidor, noting that the Spanish litigants had never presented a title to the land, ordered that the people of Saiba be restored their lands. On February 24, 1608, a crown official "took don Pedro Ninaronto and don Francisco Huaman Sauñi by the hand and put them on said lands and, in compliance with true tradition and possession they picked up clumps of earth, pulled weeds and uprooted bushes that were on said land and they went from one place to another passing over all of said land."[28] It took nearly two years for the *naturales* of *ayllu* Saiba to win their case. If their need for land had been more pressing, the impact of this invasion could have had severe ramifications.

Livestock, hacienda Indians, false testimony, and questionable legal practices were the tactics employed by a Spanish miner to force other Quiquijana people from their land that he had acquired. The miner told royal officials that he needed the property for a grinding mill and as a source of wood for his mining and refining operations. The Spaniard argued that he had no malicious intentions and that he would increase the royal treasury through payment of the tax (quinto) on precious metals. Even before he was granted legal title, however, the *naturales* of Quiquijana brought action against the miner asserting that he had "with a powerful hand, and of his own authority, violently entered" their lands. Once in possession of the contested property, he ordered Indians residing on his hacienda to occupy and prepare it for planting, and he pastured some two thousand sheep and goats and over sixty head of cattle and mules there. These animals damaged the *naturales*' corn, potatoes, and other crops. During the dispute the community water supply had been cut several times, and hacienda Indians and the overseer had "violently" taken calves and eaten them. In compensation the people of Quiquijana had received half or less of the value of the animals, sometimes nothing, and had been subjected to verbal abuse. The *protector de naturales* contested the awarding of the lands to the Spaniard and pressed the *ayllu*'s claims for justice arguing that the order granting the land to the Spaniard should be voided and the lands restored to the *naturales*, because it went against the common good of the Indians. He also reminded colonial officials that he, the *protector*, should have been consulted before any action was taken that affected Indians. "According to established law and custom in this realm in favor of *los naturales*, being privileged minors, . . . it is very clear that their defense was taken from them."

The *protector* also called attention to the fact that while the Spaniard owned a mine, he also owned an *obraje* in Guaro. What he really intended to do, according to the Indians and the *protector*, was to build another *obraje*. The mine was a considerable distance from Quiquijana, and the *protector* inquired as to why he did not refine the ore near his mine where there were good sites and sufficient resources, as well as space for his animals, without harming anyone. Instead, the Spaniard wanted arable communal fields. In closing his argument the *protector* also reminded crown officials that the steady income from tribute was worth more than the doubtful income the miner might produce, and that if the Indians' situation was not alleviated they would leave their communities and the crown would lose their tribute. There was no final ruling in the case. However, by using force, destroying crops, and occupying lands with hacienda Indians, this miner had successfully wrested the property from the *naturales*. Having forcefully gained de facto possession, he sought de jure confirmation of his prize and won it, at least initially. At the same time the people of Quiquijana, aided by the government's *protector*, put up a very strong defense, making the type of appeals and arguments that were often heard with favor.[29]

Given the importance of land, property disputes could go on for decades, and conflicts were not always over rich agricultural land.

Sheep, llamas, alpacas, cattle, horses, and mules all needed pasture. *Puna* grasslands, unsuited for most crops, were seasonally used for grazing. In 1690 Agustin Gualpa, along with other Urcos *curacas,* complained that Andres del Campo "criminally and without fear of God or royal justice did them notable harm." Campo, with a "powerful hand," had moved boundary markers, appropriated livestock, and taken their *punas.* The *curacas* stated that Campo unjustly impeded "the *indios* that are in our *punas* complying with their community obligation" and that he was slaughtering animals and committing "many other notable offenses." Four decades earlier, in 1652, Viceroy Salvatierra had written that the Indians of Urcos received many "vexations and harm from . . . Spaniards, and in particular Pedro de Campo and Joan de Contreras, who have violently dispossessed the community of the use and benefit of their lands." The viceroy ordered Pedro de Campo off the lands and the Indians put back in possession of their field and *punas.* Pedro was the father of Andres. Some forty years later the son was attempting to accomplish what his father had failed to do.[30]

Lands near provincial borders, particularly in isolated regions where authority and jurisdiction were unclear, were often at the center of conflicts. In 1718 Juan and Felipe Choque, speaking in the name of *ayllu* Chachaca of Acopia, informed officials that Doña Ursula Belasquez, one of the many hacendadas who demonstrated that mistreatment of Indians knew no gender bounds, had violently taken their lands. These were repartition lands granted to the *ayllu* by the crown and had belonged to them since time immemorial. The hacienda of Belasquez was in Canas y Canchis, and the disputed lands, though in Quispicanchis, were near her hacienda. A neighboring cacique testified that the property in question, which bordered the fields of his *ayllu,* belonged to the people of Chachaca, and he had known this "since he was old enough to know such things." Joseph de Abarca, a Spaniard, also testified for the Indians. He had lived in Checacupe for fifty years, and the Indians were his lifelong neighbors. He knew that although the fields in question were close to those of Belasquez, they belonged to Chachaca. On November 24 a crown official heard the case, and the following day the *ayllu* was put in possession of the land without contestation.[31]

Water rights, as important as the land itself, were another fountain of contention. Without life-giving water, or in insufficient quantities, young and weak plants wilted and died while older and hardier plants failed to mature or yielded a reduced harvest. Spaniards and Indians alike were dependent on precious rains and irrigation; however, living closer to subsistence indigenous peoples were especially susceptible to water shortages. A drought could mean disaster. Production might not be sufficient to meet both consumption needs and tribute. Although the colonial government, understanding the limits of authority and acceptable behavior, sometimes reduced or forgave economic obligations for a brief period after a natural disaster, such relief was not guaranteed. Colonial officials, hard pressed by their superiors to increase treasury revenues, with economic interests of their own, or doubting the veracity of testimony, could deny or delay relief from natural calamities. This, in turn, caused desperation and provoked resistance and fleeing.

When the parched earth of a particularly dry year yielded greatly reduced harvests, Don Bernabe Gualpa, a *curaca* in Mohina, sought to alter his *ayllu's* tradition of paying tribute in kind. Gualpa requested that instead of delivering wheat and corn, the *ayllu* be allowed to meet its tribute obligation in silver. The representative of the royal treasury argued against any such change maintaining, contrary to all evidence, that it had been such a good year that the haciendas could not even sell their harvests. Most likely eyeing the inflated prices that scarce agricultural produce would bring, this official hoped to hear additional silver jingling in his own or other pockets. However, other Spaniards, including the corregidor of Quispicanchis, testified that the harvest was only one-third that of normal years. The local priest also affirmed the shortage and asked that the *naturales* be allowed to pay their tribute in silver and not in wheat or corn "*pues no tienen.*" Despite the arguments of the treasury official, the crown waived payment in kind and warned caciques and tax collectors not to overcharge the tributaries.[32] Under circumstances that threatened the *ayllu*'s ability to survive, the government, influenced by both indigenous and Spanish testimony, ignored the treasury official and permitted a solution that maintained community integrity, lessened the likelihood of violent protest, and at the same time assured continued tribute payment to the crown.

In those relatively few places where the valley floor broadened and waters from rivers such as the Vilcanota or Huatanay and the smaller streams that flowed down side canyons could be used to irrigate, the lands were coveted by both Indians and Europeans. Good bottom lands and a water supply translated into high productivity, security, and profits. However, these same factors led to conflict. This was especially true for the region of Quispicanchis closest to Cuzco, where, as Cosme Bueno noted, "many distinguished *vecinos* from Cuzco and members of religious orders have haciendas."[33]

To advance their own interests certain Spaniards disrupted communal irrigation to water their own fields or to damage the production of the *naturales*. In these situations the government almost invariably supported village water rights, but the enforcement of this policy was more problematic than its declaration. In 1696 Don Diego Quispehumpiri and Don Francisco Rimache, caciques of Urcos representing *ayllu* Mollebamba, filed yet another in a long series of complaints against Spaniards over their right to water from the Vilcanota river. As early as 1617 the community had turned to the colonial state when a Spaniard interfered with the irrigation of their fields. In 1638 they again sought the support of the corregidor who ordered that they be supplied the water they needed. In 1645 the hacendada Ana Gomes de Leon cut off their water, but when the government ordered her to stop, another hacendado took up where she left off until he too was ordered to desist. Thus, in 1645 the flow of water had been cut not once, but twice. One disruption lasted a month, a dangerously long time for crops to go without irrigation. In 1696 the Urcos caciques testified that Spaniards were "harassing, mistreating and threatening our Indians with sword and dagger" and "impeding the irrigation of our lands tyrannically taking the water that since God created the world is ours." The *ayllu* sought compensation, but the corregidor only ordered the individual most responsible to leave them in peace and allow them to irrigate their lands "without harm or violence" ("*agravio ni biolencia alguna*").[34]

Vicho, another *ayllu* in Urcos, also had its water supply cut. Its irrigation water flowed across the lands of Spaniards who took advantage of the situation to interrupt the supply. The *ayllu* had suffered crop damage or loss on several occasions, and when Vicho again complained in 1712 the government already had in place a fifty-peso fine for every interruption. To ensure these disruptions did not threaten government revenues, the fines were to be applied to the *ayllu's* tribute. Even the threat of fines did not completely solve the problem, and from time to time communities continued to suffer these man-made "droughts." The protective justice of the crown was limited.[35]

Over time complex irrigation agreements were worked out to assure that needs were met. In June of 1754 the head *curaca* of Oropesa complained that haciendas had not only taken community lands but had restricted their water supply. By agreement the community was to receive water Monday and Tuesday nights, but this was not enough to complete its irrigation. When brought to the attention of the government, their access time was increased. The villagers were to have water for their fields (*chacras*) and garden plots (*solares*) all day and night on Monday and Tuesday, and on Sunday night they were to water their *cofradía* lands. Hacendados had cut the daytime supply of water, and community members complained that they could not complete their irrigating nor did they have ample water for the chickens they raised as part of their tribute. The Marques of Casa Xara, a powerful local hacendado serving as corregidor, ordered the Spaniards to use the water only during the assigned times and reaffirmed the community's right to the water while imposing a twenty-five-peso fine for violations. The hacendados, however, ignored the order, which raised the ire of other Spaniards as well as that of the Indians. Thomas de Dueñas, a resident of Oropesa and a member of an old Spanish family, testified that the *ayllus* predated the haciendas and that the hacendados were cutting off the Indians' water. Another

Spaniard stated that certain individuals were taking the community's water in "grave detriment to the *yndios* and *cofradías*."[36] Neither the government nor the Spaniards who testified for the Indians supported the actions of the hacendados. The law and their interests or sympathies rested with the community's production, survival, and well-being, not with advantages gained by a few Spanish hacendados.

Although the system of justice functioned reasonably well, equitable justice (even within the limits of that term in a colonial system) was not always rendered. The complexity of interests and contradictory testimony—Indians and Spaniards often arguing on both sides of the same case—could make it difficult for even the most scrupulous officials to determine where justice rested when trying to render fair decisions. For instance, Francisco Xavier de Arrillaga, a cacique from *ayllu* Guasau near Oropesa, complained that in a recount of the population and redistribution of lands Agustin Calbo, the official who conducted the *revisita*, had improperly taken lands from his *ayllu*. The cacique stated that "false and sinister" testimony had been given. These lies led to the loss of their lands as other Indians were placed on their communal property. *Ayllu* Guasau was then designated "various arid and dry lands as far as three or four leagues from their homeland [*patriasuelo*]." In addition, the cacique of two nearby *ayllus*, Carlos Guanca, complained that his people desperately needed lands. Many people had already left due to land insufficiency, and communal property had been rented out to meet pressing tribute payments. The *ayllu* was short twenty tributaries due to death and fleeing and the state not having conducted a recount. Yet other lands had been "usurped by various hacendados." Guanca joined Xavier de Arrillaga in seeking government support in restoring lands to their *ayllus*. At the same time, however, caciques from *ayllus* Cuzcoparte, Collana, Marcacolla, and Urinsaya complained that Xavier de Arrillaga was after their lands on the pampa of Guasau. Their tributaries only had one *topo* of corn land when they should have had two, only *forasteros* and the unmarried or reserved being limited to one *topo*. They also lacked communal pasture and mountain lands for maintaining their livestock. These caciques complained that the official who carried out the redistribution not only made bad decisions but also had created turmoil by appointing caciques for each *ayllu* when they were accustomed to having only one ethnic lord. They complained of European intrusions, stating that "even though in the book of repartition it seems that there are abundant lands . . . today we do not enjoy them" because of the "introduction of the many haciendas." These caciques concluded by requesting that the colonial regime provide them with more lands "with which we maintain our poor women and children" and that rule by just one cacique be restored.[37]

Although the final disposition of the case was not recorded, the government notified the people that the redistribution of lands would be revised and that *ayllus* Cuzcoparte, Collana, Marcacolla, and Urinsaya would again be permitted to be under the leadership of a single ethnic lord. But could the truth be discovered, or justice ever be served, in such complicated situations? It is possible that the Spanish official in charge of the *revisita* made the "bad" distribution to aid indigenous or Spanish confederates, but he claimed that Calbo, who did the leg work for the *revisita,* had informed him that the *ayllu* had sufficient lands. Why were the people of *ayllu* Guasau awarded lands distant from the community, while the Indians of Cuzcoparte, Collana, Marcacolla, and Urinsaya were placed on Guasau's repartition lands? Were there hidden disputes or antagonisms between the *ayllus?* Were caciques serving as front men for Spaniards? Why had no action been taken against the hacendados whom the Indians claimed had taken their lands? Why had the structure of caciques been changed? Indians, Spaniards, and government officials could all have had legitimate concerns that needed to be addressed, but all were also capable of confusing, complicating, or deceiving to advance their own interests. In this milieu it was difficult for even the most scrupulous official to render justice.

The depth to which *naturales* had adopted the legal system as a weapon of defense and resistance is illustrated by a dispute between the priest of Pichigua, Joseph Martines, and the *naturales* of *ayllu* Charachapi in the parish of San Pedro de Cacha regarding forty *fanegadas* of land. Through most of the 1760s, and again in the 1770s, in hundreds of pages of testimony the priest and the *ayllu* wrangled over the land. The problem stemmed from confusion over titles created by one hand of the government not knowing what the other hand was doing. A century and a half earlier a crown representative had confirmed the sale of *ayllu* lands to a European, while yet another official awarded the *naturales* title to the same land. The people of Charachapi had possessed the land throughout most of the colonial period; indeed they claimed it was theirs since the time of the Inca. The priest, in turn, presented titles and records of payment going back to the sixteenth century. The priest also maintained that it was ridiculous for the *naturales* to claim ownership since the time of the Inca, because, according to his understanding of history, in that period just the royal family owned land. Others only had usufruct of determined parcels with which they maintained themselves and paid tribute. The deliberate functioning of the colonial legal system was made manifest by procedures in the case. When the *naturales* were to be made aware of the crown's course of action an official recorded that

> the high mass having ended and all Spanish and Indian people having left [the church] I gathered them near the house of the priest of said parish of Cacha and reading in loud and intelligible tones I notified Don Roque Guaita, Don Jazinto Cano and Don Matias Limas, *caziques principales* of Charachapi and likewise Don Melchor Suclla and Don Luiz Aucaguagui, caciques of the incas, *ayllu* Hanansaya, of said pueblo of San Pablo in person being together and congregated the other principals and Indians of the community in the presence of many Spaniards of the community and several ecclesiastics and having read and explained in their tongue they [the Indians] indicated that they had heard and understood.[38]

The conflict remained very civilized and legal. The most vitriolic the debate became was when the cacique Guayta stated that the claims of Martines were "sinister" and the priest, in turn, tried to persuade officials that the *ayllu*'s claims were an "obvious trap." The corregidor, apparently irritated by the priest's continued complaints after he ruled in favor of the *naturales,* commented that the priest's actions stemmed from the "malicious free-will and greediness of his character."

Explaining why they could not have sold the lands, the *naturales* cited as their seventh point, the other points being made in a similar fashion, "chapter and verse" (they cited Ordinance 5, title 7, book 2) from the law "in which it is ordered that without license of the Superior government [Indians] are not able to sell community lands. . . . I again ask Dr. Don Joseph Martines where is the license of the Viceroy for such a sale [that] he ought to present." Martines responded to each of the *naturales*' points in kind, but lost the first round in this legal fisticuffs. However, Martines was not the type of person who gave up easily. In 1777 he submitted more than two hundred pages of additional documents and testimony.

The title discrepancies that led to the dispute originated in 1622. A Spaniard named Juan de Salas complained that while he had been in Cuzco, Don Carlos Palomino, a cacique of *ayllu* Charachapi, along with other caciques and armed Indians of the *ayllu,* entered "a pig *estancia* I have named Supacolla . . . and with little fear of God and Justice tore down huts, corrals, and pigsties (*chiqueros*) . . . wanting to kill the Indians who were there, and likewise they tore down some large corrals that functioned as boundary markers since the time of my grandfather." At the time several *naturales* supported the Salas version including Matheo Chaco. Chaco, who appeared to be over eighty, was in his *guasi* ([*wasi*] house) when Palomino and other armed Indians tore down the huts, pigsties, and corrals, all this he "saw with his own eyes." Palomino and two other caciques were jailed on the basis of the collective testimony, and, after first denying the accusations, they admitted everything except the verbal and physical excesses of which they were accused. They maintained, however, that they had been within their rights. The caciques of Characahapi testified "in Spanish being *ladino* [Spanish speaking]" and "*de mucha razon,*" that they "did not beat the Indians nor did they say bad words

[107]

to them and the reason they tore down said huts and corrals was because they were on their land."[39] They also tore down boundary markers and constructed new ones on Salas's lands. All this was done to be able to cultivate their fields and remove the Indians Salas had used to invade and possess other communal properties.

Under the guidance of the state the boundaries were restored, and Salas and the *naturales* of Charachapi were put in possession of their lands "pacifically and without one or the other speaking against [the settlement]. . . . Each one entered his lands, uprooted *ichu*, threw rocks . . . and [agreed that] neither be dispossessed without first being heard and by '*fuero y derecho*' [law and right] convinced."[40] Out of this seventeenth-century confusion emerged the dispute and duplicate titles that 150 years later led Martines and *ayllu* Charachapi to engage in a decade and a half of legal struggles over lands that both truthfully seemed to have believed were theirs. Without a legal system in which both parties trusted it is hard to imagine such situations not deteriorating into the use of force or violence.

On rare occasion *naturales* reversed the more typical order by invading the lands of Spaniards. When the priest Antonio Chavez y Mendoza became bedridden, a local cacique, along with his sons and some people of his *ayllu,* invaded the rented hacienda and threatened the overseer's life with slings and clubs. Pasturing livestock on planted fields, the indigenous invaders destroyed the crops already sown. They then planted the most fertile lands that had been left to fallow for another year. The priest was not the only victim, however, the cacique having taken fields from Indians as well. According to indigenous testimony, various *ayllu* members had fled due to the "rude and bad treatment" they received at the hands of the cacique. The cacique's wife had even fled to Cuzco to avoid his excesses. The *ayllu* whose lands had been taken requested that the state restore their fields and assure that they be left in peace, the cacique acting like "an irrational beast."[41] Both Spaniard and *natural* suffered at the hands of this cacique, who abused his power and ran roughshod over those around him, forcing his victims to turn to the state for protection as happened with the worst of the Europeans.

Naturales from Acos also invaded Spanish-owned lands, but they were encouraged by their priest. The priest maintained that his parishioners used the lands for the *cofradías* dedicated to San Miguel and San Juan Baptista and that the lands had been used by the church for two hundred years. When the new owner denied them their traditional access and threatened them with "bullets and lashes," the *naturales,* supported by the priest, reasserted their claim to the lands.[42] In a reversal of normal roles, Juan de Dios Xara, a Spaniard, came to the cacique of Guaro asking that he be put in possession of lands he had inherited as a child. For the last twenty years an indigenous woman named Andrea Yancay had used the field, but there was no doubt about the titles. Even though the Indian woman needed the land, the cacique, on orders from the government, "took [the Spaniard] by the hand and gave him possession in the name of your Magesty."[43]

In conclusion, the loss of most indigenous lands to Europeans in Quispicanchis and Canas y Canchis occurred in the sixteenth and seventeenth centuries, as population decline left lands vacant and property formerly dedicated to the Inca state and religion fell under colonial jurisdiction. While Europeans dominated some of the richest lands in the Huatanay and Vilcanota river valleys closest to Cuzco, *naturales* maintained a great deal of the land in the temperate and colder zones throughout the colonial period. Much of the success in land retention was due to their herding tradition that required the utilization of broad expanses of pasture as well as agricultural lands. Unlike in Mexico, few uncontested open spaces existed on which European livestock haciendas could be established.

Except for haciendas near population centers such as Sicuani and in the coca-producing regions, or in especially productive zones like Quiquijana and the rich lands close to Cuzco, this was a largely indigenous world. The last major loss of land took place after the lowering of tribute and consequent sale of communal lands in the wake of the devastating epidemic of 1719–1720. Thus, the loss of most lands took place in a nonviolent manner under the cloak of colonial law and were, with significant exceptions, accepted by the *naturales.*

However, in the eighteenth century and earlier there were struggles between individual Europeans and native peoples, as Europeans tried to wrest resources away from communities for their personal aggrandizement. Communities resisted these usurpations tooth and nail. Although this resistance sometimes developed into direct confrontation, most often communities used the weapon of the weak provided by the state—the protective system of justice—to conduct their struggles. With the support of the state-appointed defender of Indians, *naturales* waged fierce legal battles against those who sought to seize their lands.

Some officials acted prejudicially in favor of Europeans, but for the most part—within the context of an exploitive colonial system— the state usually functioned impartially recognizing that its legitimacy was at stake and that it was in its own interest, as well as the interest of *naturales,* to preserve communal land holdings. Thus, in Quispicanchis and Canas y Canchis the colonial justice system was a reasonably effective tool in protecting villagers and lands from European predations.

In the long run the policies of the state led to the reduction of communal holdings, although this was not a conscious intent. However, people do not live in the long run. In day-to-day existence the state and individual Spaniards were sources of protection and support for indigenous communities as well as oppressors. In this situation friends and foes were determined not just by race, but by face-to-face relations. In their legal battles the peoples of rural Cuzco were often supported by the testimony of their Spanish neighbors. The ambiguities and contradictions inherent in such relationships guided indigenous actions and were only enhanced by the equally troubling conflicts between *naturales* over land.

5

Ethnic Land Conflict
and the State

Se han introducido barbechandolas intrepidamente violentando la
posecion antiguada de ciento setenta años. *Naturales* of Layo protesting a land invasion by people of Langui

IN 1714 the people of *ayllu* Machacamarca in Andahuaylillas turned
to colonial authorities to recover lands that had been invaded by *naturales* from Ccatcca, a community in the neighboring province of
Paucartambo. This was not the first time Ccatcca had invaded. Since
1576 Ccatcca had tried to wrest fields from Machacamarca at least
seven times, forcing the *ayllu* to seek help from the crown to protect
their patrimony. Despite the soils being *"flacas"* or "weak" and requiring years of fallowing between cultivations, Ccatcca wanted what
Machacamarca had.[1]

Communities and *ayllus* in Quispicanchis and Canas y Canchis
were often at odds with one another over the control of land. These
disputes had complex and diverse origins and roots of varying depth.
Some were anchored in the distant and unknown past—"time immemorial"—while others were more shallowly rooted in circumstances
of recent vintage. Traditional rivalries, colonial demands, gender divisions, and population growth were among the factors that led
people to divide over the issue of land as they sought to preserve
themselves and their way of life. The complexities and contradictions
stemming from these tensions, filled with the richness of human experience but defying easy theoretic explanations, were important in
the formation of the world view of *naturales* in rural Cuzco. This
chapter examines the heritage of these traditional conflicts and the

changes brought about by early colonial policies such as the Toledan reforms (see chapter 1) and also discusses eighteenth-century conflicts in their more immediate circumstances. This indigenous world, as we have seen, was not so easily divided along European-indigenous racial lines, and this was true even in interethnic or intracommunity conflict. In this mature colonial society the divide between Indian and Spaniard was very porous and was shaped by face-to-face relations and notions of good governance. In addition, despite some two centuries of Spanish control indigenous peoples still maintained many of their old rivalries—their old agendas—and new ones had been created. There was no "peaceable kingdom," and when colonial pressures heightened tensions villagers often manifested these pressures along lines of ethnic land conflict.

A Fractured Heritage

Although disputes between native peoples in Quispicanchis and Canas y Canchis were intense in the mid- to late eighteenth century, earlier conflicts had left an important stamp on the region. Long before Pizarro set foot in Tawantinsuyu, Canas y Canchis was a center of territorial disputes. The Collas, centered in the Lake Titicaca basin, and the Incas had bitterly contested the upper Vilcanota region, which was desirable not only as a strategic route for moving goods and people between Lake Titicaca and Cuzco, but it was also more fecund and temperate than the surrounding altiplano.

Before the arrival of Europeans, most people had lived in small, relatively dispersed settlements. The desire to organize native peoples for purposes of imposing demands, extracting labor, and bringing people into the European orbit led Spain to forcibly resettle people into larger communities or *reducciones*. Established by Viceroy Toledo in the early 1570s, these reductions eroded regional and ethnic identity, heightened fragmentation, and led to focusing identity at the community or *ayllu* level.[2]

When Toledo "reduced" the *naturales* of the upper Vilcanota he set in motion decades of wrangling between certain communities such as happened when he divided the people of Colcatona and merged them into two other communities. One hundred Colcatona tributaries were integrated into Combapata and sixty into Checacupe, which provoked conflict between these communities over what had been Colcatona's land.[3] The people of Colcatona testified that when they had been together they had got along well "being all related and of similar surnames." Even after they had been divided relations between them remained good, and they did not have "lawsuits nor differences between themselves, just as when they were together in the pueblo of Colcatona."[4] In 1643, in an attempt to alleviate these disputes, the corregidor ordered all the Colcatonas to be settled in Checacupe. However, some contested lands remained in Combapata's possession. This solution, flawed from the outset, was terminated by force in 1652 when Checacupe invaded the lands.[5] Thus, problems stemming from the Toledan reductions continued to divide people in rural Cuzco eighty years after they had been implemented.

Communities used the process of reduction to further their own interests. In 1572 when a crown representative in Canas y Canchis sought boundary information from *curacas* to make accurate (in keeping with traditional holdings) distributions of land, he was given "very complex and contradictory information." A decade later *curacas* were again consulted about their lands because of the squabbles that had resulted from the distribution based on the testimony in which they had sought to advance community interests. Once more the *curacas* could not agree on boundaries. The official in charge of the inquiry reported that tensions over limits existed between the communities of Coporaque and Yaure (Yauri), Pichigua and Checasupa, Checasupa and Yanaoca, Sicuana (Sicuani) and San Pablo and Checa, and Combapata and Pitumarca with Checacupe.[6]

Such conflicts existed throughout the colonial period as *naturales* contested the control of lands—river valley lands that were good for agriculture, mountain lands suited to the cultivation of crops such as barley and potatoes and for grazing animals. Conflicts, such as those between Checacupe and Pitumarca, even occurred over lands too frigid and barren for most uses but desired for vicuña hunting.[7]

Canas y Canchis was an important center of llama and alpaca production under the Inca, and the Spanish conquest brought with it a variety of animals, including cattle and sheep, that began to share the pastures with the cameloids. The alpine nature of the environment, with its seasonal and temperate changes in spite of the tropical latitude, was conducive to transhumance.[8] The movement of livestock from pasture to pasture led to inadvertent, as well as intentional, trespassing as animals under the watch of careless, overworked, or aggressive herders entered where they were not supposed to be, causing damage and provoking tensions. Likewise, changes in the animal-to-feed ratio due to factors such as increased flock size or droughts and freezes that affected pasture growth, could stir up emotions as desperate herders sought food for their animals. When livestock entered cultivated lands the consequences were even more serious. Such incidents created harsh feelings and provoked violence, as did the theft of animals, which was also a common activity in the region. Thus, the nature of the terrain and climate, as well as the economic importance of livestock, influenced land conflicts in rural Cuzco.

Settlement patterns and *ayllu* size may also have contributed to problems of fragmentation in Canas y Canchis. In the eighteenth century the people of Canas y Canchis were divided into living units, *ayllus*, of two hundred persons or fewer per *curaca*. Ratios such as these may have been due, in part, to the importance of herding, which requires extensive grazing lands and militates against dense concentrations of people and livestock.[9] The Spanish division of the region into parishes with the reduction communities, composed of *ayllus*, serving as the center of the parish (although smaller nearby communities—*anexos*—were sometimes part of the same parish) further compartmentalized people. These divisions worked against a larger sense of identity such as those based on regional or ethnonational awareness. Even in Quispicanchis where the average ratio of *naturales* per *curaca* was over one thousand to one, problems between *ayllus* and between communities were common.[10]

As the indigenous peoples of Canas y Canchis and Quispicanchis approached the eighteenth century a heritage and structure of ethnic land conflict was already in place. During that century disputes not only continued but were exacerbated, and land, fundamental to Andean peasant existence, was at the center of much of the conflict. The crops and animals produced on the land provided the food and the means of trade that sustained life. From the earth also came the wherewithal to meet tribute demands and other obligations imposed by the colonial state. By complying with state and community obligations, *originarios* secured their right to community lands. This, in turn, helped guarantee the social reproduction of the family and the community. Thus, access to land was not only important in assuring the perpetuation of life but the perpetuation of a way of life.

"Turf Wars" along the Vilcanota

Among the least complicated and potentially most violent land conflicts were those involving the destruction of crops caused by wandering livestock. For a society in which herding was important and animals were used in agricultural work, such incidents were relatively common, but most intrusions did not cause serious damage or lead to violence. However, despite the vast majority of incidents being accidental, when damage was done strong reactions could be triggered. In just a few minutes livestock, especially cattle, could trample, devour, and otherwise destroy the crops that maintained a family. The fact that the owner or herder of the animals was seldom far away meant that the person whose corn, potatoes, or quinua had been damaged might confront the responsible party at the point when emotions were at their highest.

Sometimes alcohol heightened people's response or even provoked problems, as otherwise responsible herders, when inebriated, allowed animals to wander where they did not belong. One Sunday in 1703 *naturales* of Guayqui were enjoying libations after the fiesta for their patron saint when Diego Tito's oxen strayed into Thomas Condori's field. A quarrel followed, and Condori punched Tito, causing blood to flow. Tito's brother then struck Condori in the head with a rock, and in the scuffle Tito's wife was also injured. Alcohol and unattended oxen had involved two families in a brawl over damage to lands and crops as the community honored its patron saint.[11] Such events did not always involve alcohol. In 1716 Pedro Tiraquimbo was threshing wheat for the church in Quiquijana when an ox got loose and wandered into the field of Mateo Guamán. Guamán verbally abused Tiraquimbo, as well as his father, and then beat him with a stick. When Tiraquimbo took legal action against his attacker he was still in bed "swollen and in fear of his life."[12]

As with other matters, community members frequently turned to colonial officials to seek recompense for the damages done by livestock. In 1777 an indigenous official in Yanaoca who described himself as a "poor, unfortunate Indian" complained that another *natural* "without fear of God or Royal justice did harm to him and his wife and children by letting cattle into his potato and quinua fields" and assaulted him despite the fact that he carried the royal staff of office. The accused was jailed for lack of respect and fined six pesos.[13]

By the late colonial period many Indians had acquired private property. Land problems involving these individuals did not necessarily draw the community into the dispute. However, to help their neighbors and kin, and to avoid further intrusions that might threaten communal lands, *naturales* normally testified on behalf of neighbors whose lands had been invaded. When disputes were between people in the same community, the situation had the potential for damaging internal solidarity. If the individuals were from different *ayllus*, loyalties tended to divided along these lines. If they were from the same *ayllu*, friendship or ties to one's immediate family or kin—fictive or real—might determine loyalties.

Both urban and rural properties were disputed, but conflicts over urban property were usually resolved without violence. The factors that led to the disagreement were usually well understood by the parties involved, emotions were less likely to get carried away, and authorities were nearby to help maintain order. Many of these disputes involved women, especially widows. Because the husband's status as an *originario* guaranteed access to land and because it was the male who normally represented the family to the community governing structure, certain individuals tried to take advantage of the relatively weaker position of a widow to usurp or question her right to property. On the other hand, widows also relied on sympathy for their situation to assure possession of property, and some widows used this sympathy to advance their own interests over the legitimate objections of others.

Typical of legal complaints filed by women against those who were trying to take their property was a 1737 case in Quiquijana. The widow of a *curaca* turned to the Spanish legal system asking to be put back in possession of her residence and a small piece of land that had been occupied by another Indian. She maintained that she was poor—despite having been married to a *curaca*—and a woman, and because of this a man had taken her house and would not leave. The widow and her family had been given the house years earlier by a female friend who no longer needed the residence, much of her family having died in an epidemic. The benefactor supported the widow's claim stating that she felt sorry for the woman because she was poor like her, and colonial authorities agreed, putting the widow back in control of the property.[14] In a similar case an Urcos tributary, with sons of tributary age, claimed the house of his deceased uncle. The house, however, was occupied by the uncle's stepdaughter, who stated the property had been given to her by her mother. The mother's will clearly indicated that the daughter was to inherit the house and that the stepfather had agreed to this provision, but the nephew, emphasizing his claim as a tributary, tried to wrest the property from her. If the inheritor had been male it is doubtful the nephew would have attempted such an action.[15]

In some communities everyone, *ayllu* members and Spaniards alike, were provided an urban lot (*solar*) to meet housing needs. In Pomacanche, for instance, the community did not sell *solares*, "always being accustomed to give them free to subjects, Spaniards as well as Indians, who want to build houses for their own habitation."[16] With houses and improvements, however, these urban properties developed a market value and were sometimes sold. Therefore, although original grants of urban property may have been free, some property

did become private, and people were willing to pay for it. These holdings could be very important assets. When a cacique in Sicuani fell
ill, he also fell behind in his tribute payments. Due to his tribute debt
he lost his position as cacique and ended up leaving the community,
but he was able to sell his property for seventy pesos and in this way
avoided being ordered to an *obraje* to work off the debt.[17] The value
of property, even when some property was free, was enough to make
it worth contesting.

The ownership of private property pitted individuals against their
own community as disputes developed between those who owned
property and community members who wanted these lands. Felix
Poco complained that he was suffering "*inquietudes y perjuicios*" at the
hands of his *ayllu*'s people. Taking advantage of the fact that he had
been away fulfilling his obligation in the Potosi *mita*, neighbors had
occupied lands that had belonged to the family since the time of his
grandparents. Poco sympathized with the people of his *ayllu*. He recognized that they did not have sufficient fields or pastures to meet
their needs, but he protested that he and his brother were also short
of land for their crops and sheep. The brothers argued to the state
that they could not afford to tolerate the invasion by their needy
neighbors and thus they sought help from the government to regain
control of their lands.[18]

Disputes over communal property did exist, in which one person
desired use of lands awarded to another. This was particularly true if
the communal status of the *naturales* involved was questionable or if
the *curaca* practiced favoritism in the distribution of lands. A woman
with two sons, both *originarios* of "about tribute age," complained
that a *forastero*, supported by the *curaca*, had taken her communal
lands. Colonial officials supported her, but the usurper did not relin-
quish the property. In bringing her case before officials a second time
she complained that the *forastero* and *curaca* treated her poorly because they were friends and due to her "being a woman alone." Once
again she won the case and was awarded possession of the lands, but
the *forastero* counterclaimed stating that he needed the lands for his
four sons and two other young men he had taken in, and that the

woman was not an Indian but a mestiza whose testimony was "sinister." He asked the state to return the land "with the same violence that was done to him." By claiming the other was a *forastero* or a mestiza each party hoped to strengthen its case.[19] Thus, both parties argued to colonial officials that the other's claim was not legitimate, because their adversary was not a community member.

More typical of land conflicts were those that involved people from one *ayllu* or community against those of another village. These disputes often were related to long-standing tensions between communities, but at times they reflected nothing more than the desire of a particular individual to control more land. Even the family of Thupa Amaro was involved in such disputes. In 1787, just a few years after the rebellion, lands that the Thupa Amaro family had controlled for many years were claimed by the community of San Juan Camayna. This was not the first time that San Juan Camayna had contested the land. This community claimed ownership since the late sixteenth century, but legal title had been in doubt since 1601 when ancestors of Thupa Amaro took possession of lands granted them by the viceroy. The status of the property during the seventeenth century is unknown, but in 1705 the people of San Juan Camayna, claiming to have been occupying and using the property some eighty years, won a case against Bartolomé Thupa Amaro and were awarded the lands. A few years later the widow of Bartolomé, Cathalina Quispe Sisa, backed by a local priest and the corregidor of Canas y Canchis, evicted the people of San Juan Camayna from the contested fields, even though they were in the neighboring *partido* of Quispicanchis. The community complained that the corregidor and Quispe Sisa arrived very early one morning without previous notice and "they took the . . . lands by force without consent of the community." Six tributaries, all named Quispe, were dispossessed, and some of them ended up abandoning their community "because they did not have the lands to maintain themselves." Subsequent to this confrontation the Thupa Amaros controlled the lands until the 1780 rebellion changed their fortunes. Among those who benefited from the usurpation were José Noguera and Marcos Thupa Amaro, uncles of the rebel leader, and José Gabriel Thupa Amaro himself. Differing claims, such as those in this case, make it difficult to determine right and wrong. However, the politically powerful Thupa Amaros prevailed and were able to control lands that previously had been determined to belong to the people of San Juan Camayna. The 1780 rebellion saw the family almost annihilated by Spanish reprisals. In this situation, with the Thupa Amaros discredited and nearly exterminated, the *naturales* of San Juan Camayna again sought legal possession of the lands from which they had been forcibly removed. This time they won.[20]

The ancestors of Thupa Amaro were not just aggressors in land disputes with other Indians. Early in the seventeenth century one of these ancestors, Diego Felipe Condorcanqui, "*gobernador y indio principal* of Hatun Surimana," won a case against the community of Yanaoca and their caciques for having invaded his property. With the support of the local corregidor Condorcanqui regained his lands.[21] These cases involving the Thupa Amaros demonstrate several realities. First, individuals—especially those with political clout—could successfully take lands from others (although, in the case involving San Juan Camayna there was real doubt over legal title). Second, even the lands of powerful families such as the Thupa Amaros were subject to invasion. Third, *naturales* frequently relied on the support of colonial authorities to resolve their problems or support their interests.

Although individuals did invade lands, the most serious cases involved the actions of entire *ayllus* or communities. In the mid- to late eighteenth century the number of these invasions increased as governmental demands and population growth pressed people even harder. In 1754, for example, the *reparto* (forced distribution or sale of goods), which had been functioning informally, was fully legalized. Instead of improving, or at least stabilizing, the condition of *naturales* by fixing limits on the amounts forcefully distributed, legalization made the situation worse as corregidores often "sold" goods far in excess of the legal limit.[22]

In 1776 the division of the viceroyalty of Peru and the formation of the new viceroyalty of Rio de la Plata also disrupted trading patterns and economic life in the Southern Andes. And in an effort to increase revenues the Spanish crown made tax and tribute collection more efficient and subjected Indians to taxes on items they produced that had previously been exempt. The sales tax was also raised.[23] These factors, along with demographic revitalization, contributed to a crisis in Indian society that was reflected in tensions over land. Though these pressures began to undermine indigenous confidence in the reciprocal relationship between them and the state, the short-term effect often found communities turning against one another as they sought additional lands to meet their needs and burdens.[24] Thus, tensions created by the state were frequently turned against neighboring communities rather than being directed against colonial rule. This functioned to delay and decrease conflict with imperial Spain, while increasing conflict between peoples in Quispicanchis and Canas y Canchis.

Many of the disputes between communities that erupted in the eighteenth century were rooted in the distant past. The dispute between *ayllu* Machacamarca and Ccatcca, as previously noted, was one such conflict. In 1714 Machacamarca complained that Indians from Ccatcca, along with some non-Indians, had once again entered their lands and moved their border markers (*mojones*) and that this action was taken with the support and approval of the corregidor of Paucartambo. Machacamarca argued that the Paucartambo corregidor had no legal jurisdiction in the case, because the contested lands were in Quispicanchis and officials from Quispicanchis agreed. They ordered the territory restored to the *ayllu*, the proper borders reestablished, and the border markers "left free and disencumbered [*desembarazada*]." The "*tierras flacas*" under dispute could only be worked every seven years, yet as early as 1576 the communities were fighting over these fields. In 1579 a judge made it clear that the contested lands, although near Ccatcca, belonged to the people of Machacamarca and awarded them possession of their fields. In 1595 it was necessary to repeat the process. In that year an official wrote, "I took don Carlos Yucra, *principal* of the Collas Indians [*ayllu* Machacamarca] by the hand and I put him in '*rreal, corporal,* [and] *actual*' possession" of the lands. In 1616 Machacamarca once more complained that Ccatcca had entered their lands. In 1692 there was yet another incident, but this time a non-Indian was also involved. Machacamarca won the case, and the *naturales* of Ccatcca left. However, the non-Indian, Andres Morales, ignored the order and held on to some "considerable pieces" of land. It took the additional threat of a two-hundred-peso fine by the state to remove Morales. In 1700 the cacique of Machacamarca once more informed authorities that people from Ccatcca, supported by Morales, were harassing their possession of the fields. Morales was threatened with punishment, and the people of Ccatcca were ordered off the land. Finally, after this incident Machacamarca appears to have worked their lands free from Ccatcca's interference, but the desire to control "*tierras flacas*" had led to over a century of conflict between these communities.[25]

The people of Ccatcca either did not recognize the legitimacy of Machacamarca's title or the proximity of the fields to Ccatcca, and their distance from Machacamarca—particularly because they were left fallow for such long periods—proved too tempting. The residents of Machacamarca, however, were referred to as Collas, people from the greater Lake Titicaca region. They may well have been *mitimaes* resettled in the region by the Incas as part of their program to ensure production and social control in the empire. After the Spanish conquest it is possible that the people of Ccatcca were emboldened to challenge the right of the Collas, still considered outsiders, to the lands.

Other communities experienced an increase in tensions over land under the heightening economic and demographic pressures. Layo (Layosupa) was one such community. Layo had been at odds with neighboring communities, particularly Pichigua, before the crisis of the late 1700s. However, during this crisis these conflicts assumed a frenetic level. As early as 1633 Diego Arqui of Pichigua complained that people from Layo had entered his property with a "powerful hand" pasturing their animals on lands that had belonged to Arqui's family from "*tiempo inmemorial.*" Arqui won the case testifying that he used these lands to "pasture my animals with which I pay my tribute and my Potosí '*entero*'" (a payment to purchase one's way out of labor service in the mines). The people of Layo were not only ordered to stay out of the lands of Arqui and his family but those of Pichigua as well. However, less than forty years later Diego Arqui's grandson was again before Spanish authorities complaining about a land invasion by Layo. In 1673 the corregidor once more affirmed the Arqui family's rights, ordering the grandson to be put in possession of the disputed territory.[26] Thus, the roots of conflict between Layo and Pichigua were deeply imbedded in the past.

By the 1780s economic demands and a resurging population were severely straining the resources of Layo, and the community was once again engaged in a struggle for land with Pichigua. However, Layo was also involved in disputes with three other communities. Two of the latter, Macari and Santa Rosa, had been part of Canas y Canchis in the past. By the eighteenth century, however, boundary changes had integrated them into a neighboring province. The disputes were over pasture lands distant from the communities. The cacique and *común* of Layo stated that the territories in question had been given them in a royal repartition and that they had purchased additional lands from the crown. Resolution of the cases was delayed, however, because Layo's land titles had already been sent to Cuzco as part of the dispute with Pichigua. At the same time these cases were being contested Layo complained that the neighboring community, Langui, had invaded lands that had been theirs for 170 years. Representatives of Layo argued that the *naturales* of Langui with "acrimony and hostilities . . . [were] limiting the pasturing of our animals, threatening our women and children . . . and preparing our land for planting."[27] In a struggle to ensure adequate resources as the pressures of demographic revitalization and colonial demands threatened their way of life, the people of Layo turned against neighbors and traditional rivals in an attempt to assure their survival.

Direct economic demands were just one way the government brought about, or exacerbated, conditions in which land conflict erupted between indigenous peoples. Colonial policies not directly related to economic demands, or economic demands that required personal service instead of payment, also provoked tensions. In many of these situations, however, responsibility rests heavily, if not over-whelmingly, with the indigenous communities themselves. As we have seen, the Toledan reductions of the late sixteenth century caused a great deal of turmoil and, in some instances, prolonged property disputes. In the eighteenth century, however, exceptions the Spanish had made to their sixteenth-century reduction policy stirred disputes such as that between Acopia and Pueblo Nuevo de San Juan de la Cruz de Papres (Pueblo Nuevo or Papres) over repartition lands belonging to Yanaoca. The state had designated to the people of Yanaoca lands distant from the community. These lands may have been one of the "vertical niches" the community controlled before the arrival of the Europeans. After the original grant the people of Yanaoca, except for the *ayllu* that resided there permanently, stopped using the property, because they had sufficient resources much nearer to their community. This, in turn, led to a loss of meaningful contact with the faraway *ayllu*. In 1707 Yanaoca, claiming they had "super abundant lands" closer to their community, sought permission to sell their distant holdings. After nine years permission was received, and in 1716 Yanaoca sold some "*punas y pasto* very distant from said com-munity" to Pueblo Nuevo, which had been renting the parcels. The only complication in the sale were the two remaining tributary fami-lies of the Yanaoca *ayllu* who lived on the property. They were offered fields in Yanaoca, but they did not accept. Preferring to stay where they were, the two families requested "a piece [of land] in order to be able to live and attend to the rest of the obligations they have." After property was allocated for the two tributaries, Pueblo Nuevo purchased the repartition lands "for themselves, their children and successors."

The nearby community of Acopia had not expressed interest in the fields when Yanaoca owned them, but they continuously chal-lenged Pueblo Nuevo's possession. In 1723 the cacique of Pueblo Nuevo complained that Acopia was disturbing his people and acting as if the lands were theirs. In 1730 *naturales* from Acopia harassed Pueblo Nuevo and destroyed their crops by running pigs on to lands that had been sown with potatoes. In 1740 Acopia, using "false documents" and a "sinister" testimony, temporarily gained possession of the contested territory. However, when the deceit was detected the land was promptly restored to Pueblo Nuevo. The community also complained that during the period of illegal possession people from Acopia had robbed them and physically mistreated them. In the presence of the cacique of Acopia, a Spanish official took the *curaca* from Pueblo Nuevo by the hand and "they passed over said lands throwing rocks, pulling up plants, building up border markers," and making other acts of possession. In 1760 Acopia inflamed tensions once again by taking the lands of the two Yanaoca *naturales*, both dead, and by incarcerating people from Pueblo Nuevo in an *obraje* for no other reason than their being from that community. In 1786 Acopia "usurped a considerable quantity of lands," and the state once more had to restore Pueblo Nuevo's legal possession. By this time crown officials had so tired of the bickering that they ordered Acopia to sell, and Pueblo Nuevo to buy, the only lands over which uncertainty existed—those of the two former tributaries of Yanaoca—"in order to avoid by this manner the difficulties that may result."[28]

Although altercations between these two communities after 1740 could well have been based on increased need for resources, conflict broke out in the 1720s, and Acopia had not interfered in Yanaoca's earlier possession of the territory. It was only when Pueblo Nuevo bought the lands that Acopia began to contest the property. In addition, in 1720 a severe epidemic swept the Andes, leaving most communities in Quispicanchis and Canas y Canchis with sufficient lands to meet their needs for at least two decades. Thus, it is unlikely that the tensions of the 1720s or early 1730s stemmed from necessity. They more likely came from an ongoing rivalry between Pueblo Nuevo and Acopia. Ironically, in this instance the colonial regime provided the basis for a future dispute by not reducing an *ayllu* of Yanaoca into the community. However, the peoples involved, especially those of Acopia, bear responsibility for inflaming the conflict.

One colonial demand that had a significant impact on land conflict was the Potosí *mita*. Of all the provinces required to fulfill labor obligations in Potosi, the peoples in Quispicanchis and Canas y Canchis had the longest distance to travel. Because the time of travel was so great, a tradition of two years service (instead of one) evolved in many of the communities of rural Cuzco. The problems created by such long absences were numerous. Hardships were inflicted on families, some people never returned, and disputes erupted over property and livestock left in the care of others. There were people who took advantage of a neighbor's service in Potosi to use or appropriate fields, animals, or other goods (see chapter 7). The exploitation of the colonial regime forced these villagers to labor in Potosi, but because of the perfidy of their fellow community members they had to look to the government for support against those who should have protected them.

Another source of tensions over property, perhaps the most serious and socially harmful one, stemmed from antagonisms between community leaders and the people they governed. Conflict between *curaca* and community was not new to the eighteenth century, but, similar to other land disputes, it was exacerbated at this time. Since the early colonial period some *curacas* had neglected their community obligations, even exploiting community land and labor for their own advantage.[29] By the middle of the eighteenth century crown officials increasingly sought to appoint people to this sensitive position who did not always have community interests in mind. Indians from other communities and even people of European descent were sometimes made *curacas*. This process, however, was less common in Quispicanchis and Canas y Canchis until after the Thupa Amaro rebellion when there were "discernible . . . caciques, many of whom were *forasteros* installed by corregidores or *subdelegados* to do their bidding," not the bidding of the community.[30]

In 1778 one Sicuani *ayllu* complained to the state that their *curaca*, who had been appointed by the state and who was not from their *ayllu*, had committed so many wrongs against them that "there was not time nor paper" enough to enumerate them all, but they tried. They claimed that the cacique "without the least scruple of conscience nor fear of punishment of God" had collected tribute before it was due and had taken livestock and land from them. He also treated them with cruelty, forced them to work without pay, and wanted to use their daughters as servants. They argued that their cacique was not conforming to the rules that they believed should guide *ayllu*-cacique relationships. They were being exploited and abused instead of helped and guided. The *ayllu* wanted a *curaca* in whom they could have confidence, or as they put it, a cacique of "our *ayllu*, . . . our blood." They desired a cacique, who because of his close relationship to them, "knows how to guide us with the love, affection, and esteem we need."[31]

When *curacas* appropriated additional community lands for themselves, or rented out needed communal lands for their own profit, the community either had to endure this internal exploitation, take direct action against the *curaca*, or seek aid from the colonial legal system. When a former cacique of an Acomayo *ayllu* appropriated communal lands for his own use, the *común*, knowing the type of appeal that was likely to get a favorable hearing from the colonial state, complained that there was little land on which to grow the corn that maintained the tributaries. The government restored the lands to the *común* with the stipulation that the former cacique be provided lands in the *ayllu*.[32]

Erosion of the internal relationship between the *curaca* and the community or *ayllu* was one of the most serious problems confronting indigenous society. As with other land conflicts, responsibility for tensions rested with both the Spanish government and the *naturales*. However, in the case of *curacas* the colonial government had relatively more responsibility. Colonial society created economic situations in which *curacas* not only could, but in many instances were almost compelled to participate in the colonial economy.[33] The wealth, power, and security these economic opportunities presented allowed some *curacas* to bolster their positions and that of the community, but it also led other *curacas* to neglect their communal duties and to exploit community labor and land. In addition, by making *curacas* responsible for community tribute they were put in an economically vulnerable position. Some exploitation was undoubtedly due to the *curacas'* desire to protect against tribute debts that could leave them broke or worse. But when the reciprocal bonds between community and *curaca* were abused or ruptured the ties that bound colonial society together were weakened.

In conclusion land, the basis of life for the indigenous peoples of rural Cuzco, was also a significant source of conflict among them. Some disputes were anchored in the pre-Columbian period while others evolved during the colonial era. The Spanish imperial regime was responsible, directly or indirectly, for many land conflicts. Ironically, the *naturales* of Quispicanchis and Canas y Canchis really had few alternatives but to turn to the state to seek resolutions to their problems. Although the colonial system created or fostered land disputes between communities and *ayllus,* the functioning justice system also restored lands, upheld titles, and in other ways preserved the communal holdings. Controlling the legal system and being the grantor and guarantor of the resource that assured communal and familial existence placed the government in a very powerful position. Dependence on, and the functioning of, the legal system helped preserve ties between indigenous subjects and the colonial state while at the same time creating powerful ambiguities over which the native peoples mulled.

In the eighteenth century, especially after 1750, increasing colonial demands and demographic revitalization led to the heightening of tensions between the peoples of Canas y Canchis and Quispicanchis. Seeking sufficient resources to meet their needs and to comply with the escalating demands of Bourbon monarchs and local corregidores, *naturales* in rural Cuzco invaded the lands of neighboring communities. Though some of these invasions were directed at the nearest or easiest targets, others were directed along lines of long existing rivalries. In the eighteenth century the past rested heavily on native peoples as they struggled to survive in an increasingly difficult situation.

1. Canas y Canchis (also called Tinta), 1786

Source: AGI, Sevilla

2. Quispicanchis, 1786

Source: AGI, Sevilla

3. Harvesting Potatoes

Source: Felipe Guaman Poma de Ayala,
Nueva Corónica y Buen Gobierno
(Paris: Institut d'Ethnologie, 1936)

573

4. Priest Forces Indigenous Couple to Marry
Source: Felipe Guaman Poma de Ayala,
Nueva Corónica y Buen Gobierno
(Paris: Institut d'Ethnologie, 1936)

TRAVAXO
ZARAPVCOI ZVVAMĀTA

5. Stealing Corn

Source: Felipe Guaman Poma de Ayala,

Nueva Corónica y Buen Gobierno

(Paris: Institut d'Ethnologie, 1936)

6. Cuzco to Potosi

Source: Lillian Estelle Fisher,
The Last Inca Revolt: 1780–1783
(Norman: University of Oklahoma
Press, 1966), 47

7. Thupa Amaro

Source: Mariella Corvetto

8. Modern Communal Labor

Source: Author

6

Labor in the
Spanish Realm

Mandan a los miserables yndios como si fuesen sus esclavos. MATEO
PARCO GUALPA, *principal* of Guaqui

THE SORE muscles and aching backs of *naturales* kept the wheels of
Spanish colonial society turning. The peoples of Quispicanchis and
Canas y Canchis wove cloth, carried wood, irrigated fields, rang
church bells, dug graves, planted wheat, husked corn, pastured livestock, washed clothes, prepared meals, transported goods, and labored at a myriad of other tasks that maintained the European sector. Behind most of this work was the compulsion, direct or indirect,
of the state. Without this coercion native peoples were reluctant to
labor outside their communities when not handsomely compensated.
From the time of the conquest onward Spanish officials, recognizing
this resistance to work at low wages, argued that indigenous people
must be compelled to work for the new lords of the land. To justify
this position many of these same officials reasoned that *naturales*
were lazy and that it was in the Indians' own best interest to work
outside their communities. They could be better watched, they would
have more contact with European ways, and besides, so the argument
went, it served the royal good and the interests of Europeans in
America. This chapter explores indigenous work for nonindigenous
people in a variety of circumstances, including labor in *obrajes*, on haciendas, in the transport of goods, and as shepherds. It also examines
ways in which *naturales* tried to "work the system to their minimum
disadvantage," the importance of face-to-face relations and villagers'
commitment to this work to maintain their community and way of

life, and in the process it also takes up the debate over debt and cash advances.

Tributary Labor and Colonial Compulsion

To be members of a community and have access to land, *originarios* were obliged to comply with the colonial government's allocation of their labor to others. If they did not comply with these labor drafts they were subject to prosecution, and the community might strip them of their lands. If they fled to avoid forced labor they relinquished their *originario* status and became part of the largely rootless Indian population that survived by laboring in Spanish society or by finding a means to survive as an outsider in an indigenous community.

Through the *mita* or *septima*—terms used for forced labor—the colonial government made indigenous workers (adult, tribute-paying men) available to Spanish enterprises and governmental projects. Haciendas, *obrajes*, mines, inns, the delivery of mail; the state forced communities to provide workers for all these activities and many more, usually at the request of those who were to receive the labor.

Not all indigenous labor for the Spanish sector was so directly co-erced. More subtle, but quite effective, means were employed to impel people to toil for Europeans. Through baptisms, marriages, funerals, and fiestas the state-church apparatus led native peoples to labor outside their communities just as effectively as with tribute and *reparto*. It was through work for the Spanish that *naturales* could most readily earn the silver necessary to meet obligations and desires that could not be fully, or perhaps as easily, met by labor on their own lands or in their own houses.

In 1689 the priest of Andahuaylillas recorded the tasks in which his parishioners labored to fulfill their obligations to the state and the community:

> Twenty-five of these Indians work in the *setimas* [*septimas*] of the haciendas [*de Panllevar*] which are in diverse parts. Of the remainder [*septimas*] some in the *chasquis* [mail service], and in the

inn. Others in the employment of the caciques, councilmen, and other offices of the community. Others in the repair of the cut-waters of a large River, that they call Vilcamaio, that runs through the confines and outskirts of the said pueblo, which, if not prevented with time and diligence, overflows into the fields and inundates the sown lands leaving them sterile and without fruit. Others [work] on the conservation of the bridge that is in the pueblo of Urcos on the said Vilcamaio River. . . . And others in the care of the roads.[1]

Almost all the communities of rural Cuzco had to provide similar labors to the private sector and the state as well as service to the church, which the priest of Andahuaylillas had failed to mention. For instance, the community of Papres sent seven *mitayos* to Potosi and five to the *obraje* of the Marques de Valle Umbroso. Papres also voluntarily provided eighteen choir members, twelve *mayordomos*, and two sextons for the church, while seven other *naturales* served in community offices. In Pomacanche the cacique distributed the tasks imposed by the colonial state according to *ayllus*. *Ayllu* Pomachapi was required to send two *mitayos* and a captain and *enterador* to the Potosi *mita*, and to their *encomendero* one *pongo* or house servant. To the church *ayllu* Pomachapi provided five choir members, six *mayordomos* of brotherhoods, and two sextons. Another villager served as *fiscal* of the community. Another *ayllu*, Canchichapi, sent three *mitayos* to Potosi, while seven more were obliged to pasture livestock, work in the *obraje*, and perform other tasks for the Conde de la Laguna. Twenty-one more served in the church and community. The nearby community of Santa Lucía was exempt from the Potosi *mita*, but it was required to provide two people to guard the cattle of a Jesuit hacienda near Cuzco, and another person served the Santa Catalina monastery in Cuzco. Six more were compelled to work on various haciendas. They also provided nine tributaries to serve in various church obligations and three more to fill community offices.[2] *Originarios*, through the direct and indirect compulsion of the crown, provided much of the labor that supported the church and state as well as the nonindigenous population in Quispicanchis and Canas y Canchis.

Most indigenous laborers working on Spanish enterprises in the upper Vilcanota were from local communities and found themselves in this employment for one of three reasons. They were ordered to work as *mitayos* or *septimas* by the colonial government. Their *curacas* sent them to work to earn money for the community. Or they contracted, as individuals, to work to meet needs or fulfill personal obligations. The reason most often given by *curacas* and community members for working in the European sector was the necessity of meeting tribute. Tribute, therefore, not only filled the royal coffers, but it assured a labor force for European endeavors.

If a community member was unable to pay his tribute the cacique might use community funds to cover the shortage, or if he were so disposed due to character, custom, kinship, or some other tie, he could meet the tributary's quota out of his own pocket. Either way the indebted tributary would need to find employment, usually in the European sector but perhaps working in some capacity for the *curaca*, in order to repay his debt. Personally advancing or paying tribute debt was a potentially dangerous practice for the cacique and one that could not be relied on often. Most *curacas* lacked resources to sustain this largesse on any scale without endangering their own well-being and freedom. For instance, in 1725 the cacique of Urcos fell some 2025 pesos behind in his tribute payments. The *curaca* did what he could to avoid the inevitable confrontation over tribute arrears. Whenever the *cobrador* came to collect the *curaca* had conveniently traveled to Cuzco, but finally colonial authorities put an end to such avoidance or resistance and ordered him jailed and his goods seized until the community's tribute was paid.[3]

For *curacas* one alternative to being personally jailed for tribute shortfalls was to detain delinquent tributaries until they met their obligation. This often involved having the state sentence the tributary to an *obraje* where he was forced to work until the debt was paid. The use of jail to force tribute payment, or to keep tributaries from fleeing their obligations, was reflected in the accusations against prisoners held in one Canas y Canchis jail. The prisoners, all *natu-*

rales, consisted of three thieves, one rapist, one who had a private debt, and ten who had not paid their tribute.[4] Even Eugenio Canatupa Sinanyuca, the respected Coporaque cacique of royal Inca blood, was threatened with punishment by corregidor Muñoz de Arjona when he was not able to deliver the entire tribute for which he was responsible. Sinanyuca was able to get more time to pay, however, because of his good reputation. The local priest swore that the *curaca* was not only honest, but provided Christian instruction to his people. Because he was such a trusted *curaca,* the priest argued Sinanyuca deserved more time to make the tribute payment. In this case Sinanyuca's personal reputation saved him from more serious problems with the state. Ironically, only nine years later, Sinanyuca's bad relationship with another priest led him to form a bond with a different corregidor who also had bad relations with the new priest. The new corregidor was Antonio de Arriaga, the corregidor against whom Thupa Amaro rebelled. In both circumstances face-to-face relations shaped Sinanyuca's loyalties.[5]

Hacienda Labor

The degree to which haciendas relied on the labor of *naturales* is exemplified in the account books of a hacienda in Andahuaylillas. In roughly one year, under the heading "Expenses on the Cultivation of the Lands," there were over 130 entries, almost all to indigenous workers paid at the traditional rate of two reals a day. For instance, two men irrigated hacienda lands for one day and earned four reals. The pay was the same for the four people who husked corn and earned one peso (eight reals). Many times Indians used their own oxen and plows, or other tools, while working for the Europeans, and for this they were also paid. Unfortunately not all entries in the hacienda account book gave the time worked. For instance, it remains uncertain if the four *naturales,* each with ox teams and plows, who broke the earth to prepare it for planting earning three pesos two reals worked one day or two. Another man with an ox team and harrow passed over fields and earned four and one-half reals for his work. It is unclear if there was a wage differential for the tasks performed by the men and by the animals, or if the unspecified times of labor were different, or both.[6]

When the community of Urcos was ordered to provide *mita* workers for a local mine, they argued for increased pay for performing certain jobs; four reals for digging the ore, three or three and one-half reals for carrying it to the surface depending on the depth of the mine, three for grinding ores, and the normal two reals for others who worked in construction, carried straw, or performed similar tasks. The *naturales*, pointing to the comparative difficulties of the tasks, reasoned that it was wrong that they receive only two reals a day, like hacienda Indians, when they were working "doubled over with the face almost in the dirt." Colonial officials did not concur with the people of Urcos in their concept of just wages. It was ordered that the *naturales* be paid "the two reals daily they are accustomed." To alter the payment, a government official argued, would be in "general detriment to the hacendados, and many harms would result to all of the Kingdom."[7] Thus, it was most unlikely that wage differentials existed for *naturales* who were forced to work on haciendas, but this does not eliminate such a possibility for those people who freely contracted their labor and the use of their tools and animals.

Resistance to and renegotiation of duties and obligations, similar to the effort to get higher wages in the mines, was an ongoing process that was part of the probing and testing imbedded in colonial relations. Native peoples typically sought to reduce or maintain older levels of burden, and Europeans most often tried to increase them. Deaths, changes in colonial government, abuses, excessive work, natural disasters, and epidemics were among the events and calamities that disrupted customary patterns and prompted efforts at renegotiation.

In the late sixteenth century, Jesuits in Quispicanchis requested the government provide them with *mitayos* to work their lands for, as the Jesuits handsomely put it, "otherwise they [the lands] are of no benefit." Viceroy Toledo responded by ordering the Jesuits be supplied with "all the Indians they need" to work their lands and guard their cattle. As a result, twenty-four men from local communities were ordered to work on the Jesuit hacienda. The obligated communities included Oropesa, Andahuaylillas, Guaro, and Urcos. Forty years later a dispute erupted between the cacique of Urcos and the Jesuits over the number of workers allocated. Citing a document that stipulated five people were to be sent from Urcos, the Jesuits demanded the assigned workers, but the cacique refused to supply more than the three *septimas* it was accustomed to providing. Upon this denial the Jesuits had the cacique jailed. The cacique pleaded that only sixty-six *originarios* remained in his *ayllu* and that his people were already providing the Spanish sector thirteen *mitayos*, three more than they should have been under the *septima* or one-seventh provision. Three went to individuals in Cuzco, six to Francisco de Loyasa, one to Francisco Peres, and three to the Jesuits, and now the Jesuits wanted two more, which the cacique argued would do "notorious harm" to his *ayllu*. When testimony ended the cacique had been languishing in jail for several months with the Jesuits agreeing to have him freed if they received their two *mitayos*. The cacique, wanting out of jail, tacitly agreed to the proposition but maintained that his *ayllu* should not have to supply the extra workers. Confronted with burdens in excess of the *septima*, this Urcos cacique did what he could to resist excessive colonial demands and call attention to the plight of his people, even sacrificing his own freedom until it became clear that he would not prevail.[8]

Communities became embroiled in power struggles with Spaniards over their *septima* workers just as Spaniards were at odds with one another over access to *septima* labor. In 1651 Captain Juan Roldan de Huerta petitioned the government for *mitayos* to work his lands and alfalfa fields. He was awarded the labor of four *mitayos*—two from Quiquijana, one from Urcos, and one from Andahuaylillas—for which the captain paid the government twenty pesos. Colonial authorities stipulated that the people were to work only on "your haciendas named Guanchaco . . . paying them in silver in their hands, . . . treating them well without giving them excessive work . . . nor working them on other jobs . . . under a penalty of 500 gold pesos for each one." By 1667 Captain Roldan had died, and his widow, Maria Marquez, complained that the *curacas* of Quiquijana refused to send her *mitayos* claiming that the corregidor told them they no longer had to honor that *mita*. Marquez lamented that her hacienda had fallen into disrepair due to the "lack of Indians" and that it was because she was "alone and a widow" that she was "vexed and bothered." She stated that the corregidor "continually takes Indians from Quiquijana and the rest of the province" to work on his own haciendas. The community of Quiquijana, most likely aided by the corregidor, also requested a series of "responses, recounts, and other procedures" to slow down and disrupt the widow's efforts to regain their labor. Finally, in 1669 an order came from Lima stating that Marquez was to be supplied the *mitayos*. However, the resistance of the *naturales* through nondelivery of their *septima* did not stop entirely. In 1684 Marquez once again was forced to plead her case outside the province, and, prevailing in her claim, she once more presented the corregidor with an order demanding the delivery of the *mitayos*.[9] But the corregidor and villagers had pursued their own interests, supporting one another, at the expense of the widow.

In addition to having labor extracted through direct state compulsion, tributaries worked on Spanish haciendas under orders from their *curacas* to earn tribute monies. Haciendas were dependent on this labor, which may help explain the relative rarity of complaints emanating from *naturales* employed by haciendas. There were exceptions, however, such as those encountered by *naturales* from Pomacanche. Sent by their cacique to earn silver for tribute, thirty-seven Pomacanche Indians worked on the hacienda Buenavista during the month of June earning a total of 140 pesos. In July twenty-one *naturales* from the village irrigated, fertilized, and did other tasks on the hacienda for which they were owed over 60 pesos. Having labored enough to earn 208 pesos 4 reals, the hacendado refused to pay despite his own *mayordomo* testifying that the workers of Pomacanche were owed the money. The hacendado maintained that the cacique was "unjust, wrong, and malicious," and that the hacienda actually belonged to his son-in-law, whom they needed to see about the debt. It is impossible to know whether this was a delaying tactic, an effort to avoid the debt, or the truth, but the cacique and tributaries were having to struggle to receive the just compensation for the work they had already performed. It was to avoid situations like this that customarily payment was ordered to be made "in the hand" after the work was performed.[10]

The refusal of communities to provide non-*mita* labor to haciendas, an expression of independence or a form of resistance infrequently employed, not only aroused the ire of Spaniards but threatened their economic well-being. Ramon Troconis, a "usually calm man," became very upset after the cacique *principal* of Andahuaylillas, Vicente Casimiro Choquecahua, denied even the priest's request to provide Troconis with the workers he needed to plant his fields. Without the labor of the *naturales* Troconis was in danger of losing his hacienda.[11] Choquecahua had been sympathetic to the Thupa Amaro rebellion, openly admitting he did not support the Spaniards. After the collapse of the uprising, it was reported that Choquecahua had people in his community refer to him as Inca and that he surrounded himself with the appropriate pomp. Spaniards complained that

> not only on Sundays, but also on certain local fiesta days, the Indians who live in his *parcialidad* come with their arches of branches and line up on either side of their cacique, Visente Choquecahua, who comes out of his house and goes among them dressed like a military man with his staff of command and his sword. As he takes his first step into the street they begin to play the drums and trumpets and to fire a salute. With this accompaniment they bring him to the church with his dancers and dances in front. They enter the church and after the mass the same Indians line up again with their arches and go to the door of his house. They again fire a salute and [the cacique] enters the house with the *principales* and *mosos* from his faction. They [then] let the day go by getting drunk. All his Indians call him by the title of Inka.[12]

When a local hacendado convinced two villagers to work for him, Choquecahua punished them and temporarily took away their lands. Using such tactics, Choquecahua was able to prevent community members from going against his orders and providing labor to Spaniards. However, it is clear that, at least publicly, Choquecahua had support. Spaniards complained that Choquecahua "in his maliciousness has ordered the Indians not to pay attention to Spaniards nor to any hacendado, not to work in their *chacras* even for money and with this attitude they all say that the Inka does not want them to work. . . . It's true that none of his Indians work on the haciendas of Spaniards, saying that their cacique has ordered them not to do any such thing. So, his Indians shout that they are especially distinguished by the respect deserved by their Inka."[13]

Needless to say, a variety of charges were brought against Choquecahua. For the hacendados it was bad enough that the cacique had himself referred to as Inca when the flames of the Thupa Amaro rebellion were just ceasing to smolder, but denying them access to labor was going too far. They clearly realized, as Europeans had all along, that without the labor of Indians there would be no Indies.

Yanaconas and Forasteros

Prior to the Europeans' arrival there were many people in the Inca empire who performed specialized tasks or who worked for others without ties to a community. One of these categories was the *yanacona*, who worked for or in service to others. In the colonial period the status of *yanacona* continued, but another important category—*forasteros*—also emerged. Having left their natal communities the *forasteros* were not subject to the services and obligations imposed on tributaries, but they also did not have their rights. Without guaranteed access to land *forasteros* often had to find the means to rent land, usually from indigenous communities, to have a place to live, grow their crops, and pasture their livestock. *Yanaconas* and *forasteros*, similar to individuals from communities, sought work in European society to meet their needs and survive. *Yanaconas*, however, without roots in or links to a community, depended on selling their labor and skills to maintain themselves. The conditions of these people varied according to the individual for whom they worked. Many lived a relatively free life, often with greater prosperity than *originarios*. However, fate also played a role. A truculent master could make life nearly intolerable, leaving little recourse but flight. Escape was made more difficult by the fact that *yanaconas* had to cut their hair to distinguish themselves from other *naturales*, but hair grows.

Naturales who became *yanaconas* due to adverse turns in their lives were more likely to end up laboring in difficult circumstances. However, because the supply of labor in the Spanish sector was almost always insufficient, *yanaconas* undoubtedly sought to attach themselves to persons of better reputation. *Yanacona*-master relations, though economically based, could be paternalistic. Likewise, though the status of *yanacona* was usually inherited, this was not always the case. The children of *yanacona*, however, had few realistic options to change status. In 1705 one such child tried to free himself, complaining to the bishop of Cuzco that "my employer has held me in his power and in servitude since my birth, more than twelve years ago, simply because my parents were his *yanaconas* and I was born on his hacienda."[14]

In urban areas such as Cuzco, many *yanaconas* were skilled artisans. Others were mainly servants, the term *yanacona* sometimes being translated as servant. The status of servants varied greatly, the relationship between servant and master being personal. While some were accorded good treatment, others were physically abused or regarded as mere work objects. Female servants sometimes were subjected to their master's sexual advances. Although the status of servant or *yanacona* had its advantages, it normally meant the end of communal life and the legal freedoms, such as they were, enjoyed by *originarios* and *forasteros*. Some *yanaconas* viewed themselves as better off than community members due to the lack of obligations, but those working as servants were often required to render a deference that other *naturales* did not necessarily have to give. The attachment to a master, and the sense of protection and independence that a servant or *yanacona* might develop could have dire consequences. When José Mateo, alias *el Viscayano*, ordered Juan, the servant (*criado*) of Captain Don Manuel Antuñano, to saddle his mule, Juan responded that he was not his *"criado."* Enraged by this response, the Spaniard drew his saber and stabbed Juan in the left side and leg. *El Viscayano* fled, and an order was put out for his arrest, but Juan ultimately bled to death for speaking with an independence that at least one Spaniard did not recognize.[15]

Yanaconas on haciendas often were compensated with land for subsistence crops, clothes, food, and other basic items depending on the nature of their work and life. The women, children, and elderly were not supposed to be forced to work, although they often did work, and religious instruction was to be provided for the salvation of their souls. *Yanacona agregados*, those living on haciendas, such as the four *yanaconas* that Juana de la Minera had living on her property near Urcos, were likely to be long term or permanent residents on the hacienda.[16]

Yanacona often have been associated with those who had abandoned their traditional community relations, but that was not always the case:

> Equating yanaconas and migrants is too simplistic an approach to the complex relationship of these two sectors. The reduced obligations of the yanaconas were a strong impetus for relocation and the growing number of Indians who illegally assumed yanacona status contained many migrants who had abandoned their reducciones. But to claim that yanaconas severed all linkages with their kurakas or ayllus is too strong; to insist on the physical separation, typical of the conquest era, rather than social or spiritual alienation, is to ignore the diversity of linkages within indigenous communities.[17]

For instance, in the mid–seventeenth century, of the fifteen *naturales* working on an estate near Quiquijana six were *yanaconas* and nine were *mitayos* from local *ayllus*. "Three of the yanaconas were from the city of Cuzco, two from the nearby town of Oropesa, and one from Quiquijana. All six of the yanaconas recognized the authority of kurakas from their home communities; the originario of Quiquijana clearly retained his ayllu identification and remained under the jurisdiction of the same kuraka who governed the mitayos from his kin-group."[18]

Although most *yanaconas* resided on a hacienda and were subject to the authority of the hacendado or mayordomo alone, this was not always the case. In the seventeenth and eighteenth century some *yanaconas* in rural Cuzco continued to live in or near their communities of origin with their kinship and social networks largely intact but with their rights, obligations, and status changed. In these situations becoming a *yanacona* was a strategy, an option, evolved by local peoples and accepted by the Spanish, that provided *naturales* with yet another way of coping with colonial demands and life as second-class subjects within that world. Ann Wightman states,

> Recognizing this type of yanacona status, some colonial authorities believed that the new yanaconas had altered little more than their physical appearance, "changing their traditional clothing and adopting that of the yanacona." Although the authorities failed to comprehend the significance of this transition from traditional to colonial culture, administrators were probably correct in assuming that some yanacona were living in the vicinity of their original reducciones. Rather than being simply the consequence of Indian migration, the growth of the yanacona sector must also be seen as an alternative to migration: a compromise which enabled originarios to maintain some linkages with their home ayllus while engaging in temporary wage-sector employment, or which allowed locally assimilated forasteros to accumulate cash to satisfy their adopted communities' demands.[19]

Perhaps it was this sort of arrangement that led to the problem between a *yanacona* named Lorenzo Quispe, resident in Cuzco but from Oropesa, and the cacique of Oropesa. Even though Quispe had been living in the *ayllu* of *yanaconas* in Cuzco for seven years, he was still on the Oropesa tribute list, and therefore the cacique continued to try to collect tribute from him until colonial officials freed Quispe of his communal obligations.[20]

Forasteros often sustained themselves by working for Spaniards, and the higher wages of mining centers made these places especially attractive. In the mid–seventeenth century the mines of Condoroma in Canas y Canchis contained 23 percent of the *forastero* population of the entire province. Another 15 percent—150 Indians—resided in Sicuani, a major population and trading center on the royal road.[21] Undoubtedly, many of these *forasteros* were employed by people of European and mixed descent and worked in the commercial sector to provide themselves with the necessities of life and meet their financial obligations. Though Condoroma and Sicuani, with nearly forty percent of the *forastero* population were the most significant concentrations of such migrants, *forasteros* were found throughout the province and represented about a quarter of the adult male population.

In the mid–seventeenth century, 18 percent of the total *forastero* population in Canas y Canchis came from within the province, while an additional 5 percent were from Quispicanchis.[22] As with the *yanacona*, becoming a *forastero* did not necessarily imply having moved to distant parts and having severed all ties with kin and the community of origin. Some of the *forasteros* even continued to pay partial, if not full, tribute to their home communities.[23]

References to *forasteros* of all ages in Quispicanchis and Canas y Canchis are common, such as that made by the priest of Sicuani in the late seventeenth century who listed 270 male *forasteros*, large and small, and 380 females, or *forasteras*. More rare, however, was this priest's reference to 15 *forasteros*, male and female, living on the *estancia* of Doña Bernarda Hurtado de Laguna.[24] Few records remain of the agricultural work *forasteros* performed on local Spanish haciendas except in coca-growing regions. Miguel Cano de Herrera, an hacendado in the coca-producing zone of Ocongate had numerous *forasteros* as well as *yanaconas* working on his hacienda.[25] In the insalubrious coca fields of Paucartambo and Quispicanchis *forasteros* found work, but diseases such as the dreaded *uta,* which ate away the flesh of its victims, were a part of life in these zones.

Even on the rich agricultural lands of Quispicanchis near Cuzco little mention was found of agricultural work performed by *forasteros.* In 1689 the priest of Andahuaylillas reported that 27 *forasteros* lived in the community, but he does not mention if they worked on haciendas or in *obrajes.* In nearby Oropesa over 1,000 *naturales,* male and female, lived on the twenty-two haciendas in the parish, and these people composed 78.5 percent of the *naturales* in the parish. Many of these, such as the 150 persons living on the hacienda of the Conde de la Laguna, were undoubtedly *forasteros,* but their status was not given.[26] Thus, the role of *forasteros* as laborers in the Spanish sectors of Quispicanchis and Canas y Canchis remains fairly vague, except for the mines of Condoroma. Some of this incertitude was likely due to the fact that it was often to the advantage of both *forasteros* and Spaniards, particularly after the 1720s when *forasteros* in this zone began to be consistently required to pay tribute (usually one-half that of an *originario*), to evade detection and enumeration by colonial authorities.

In the late eighteenth century Luis Farfan, the nonindigenous cacique of *ayllus* Urumarpa (Urumarca) and Ancamarpa (Ancamarca) in Acomayo, was accused of hiding tributaries and using them for his own interests. From *ayllu* Uramarpa alone he was reported to have hidden twenty-six *originarios* and eighteen *forasteros.* In addition, seven unregistered men were found on his hacienda, and another ten were encountered in nearby punas. Farfan also stood accused of having registered forty-five *originarios* as *forasteros*—the former paying a higher tribute than the latter—and of having hidden many others to keep them off the tribute lists altogether. It is unclear if the *naturales* conspired with Luis Farfan or just followed his orders. However, the accuser was not a royal authority or an abused Indian but a disgruntled relative named Geronimo Farfan.[27]

Although some *naturales* undoubtedly became *forasteros* for reasons emanating from their personal lives, the vast majority assumed this status to avoid tribute and other obligations demanded of them as *originarios*. In the wake of the crisis produced by the great epidemic of 1719–1720 *forasteros* in Quispicanchis and Canas y Canchis were forced to pay tribute, usually at half the rate of *originarios*. They were, however, still exempt from obligations of forced labor. The cacique of *ayllus* Pumamarca and Ayarmarca in Cuzco had nine *forasteros* living in his *ayllus*. Of these, three were from Quispicanchis and one from Canas y Canchis. Originally required to pay tribute of nine pesos a year, this was reduced to four because the *forasteros* lacked sufficient lands to meet the demands placed on them. Having difficulty meeting even the lowered demands, these *forasteros* apparently benefited little from having given up their status as *originarios*.[28]

Obrajes and *Chorillos*

Forced labor in an *obraje* was one of the most unpleasant tasks imposed on *naturales,* but despite their reputations as sweatshops *obrajes* were an important source of employment to free workers—villagers and especially *forasteros*—who needed money. However, though there were usually concentrations of *forasteros* in the vicinity of Quispicanchis textile factories, "few descriptions of *obrajes* specifically identified *forastero* workers."[29]

The supply of wool from regional flocks, the washing capacity and power provided by the Vilcanota river, and the numerous villages located along the river made Canas y Canchis and Quispicanchis important centers of colonial textile production. The cloth produced in these *chorillos* and *obrajes* was mainly of a rough weave destined for the indigenous clothing market, particularly mining centers such as Oruro and Potosi. The *obrajes* of Cuzco were considered to be among those that afforded the best treatment and highest wages in colonial Peru. Due to the rather dismal reputation of *obrajes* in general, what this implies is unclear. For instance, in the late eighteenth century, *obraje* workers near the city of Cuzco were sometimes deceived and not paid their wages, which perhaps helps explain why some of the workers developed a reputation as thieves: they robbed to survive.[30]

Likewise, the owner of an Urcos *obraje* wanted to move it, for the location was "unhealthy" and "the reason why some Indians died." This was "one of the most gloomy and uncomfortable *obrajes,* the heat, the bad ventilation, and the rains that were absorbed in the narrow patio made it a true dungeon of sufferings for the miserable workers who worked there, the consequence of which they became sick and died, only to be replaced by others who ended in analogous conditions."[31]

In the sixteenth century Viceroy Toledo obligated certain communities to provide workers for the textile mills as part of their *septima.* The independence brought by wool production in some communities had the impact of reducing the independence of others due to colonial demands. As with the Potosi *mita,* colonial policy toward forced *obraje* labor changed little despite repeated questioning of the system and horrific accounts of working conditions. Several seventeenth-century decrees ordered that *naturales* not be forced to labor in, or be confined in, *obrajes,* but such regulations met with little compliance. *Obrajes* continued to be granted *mitayos,* and sometimes these workers were held under lock and key just as if they had been convicted of some wrongdoing.

One of the first entreaties for *obraje* labor in Quispicanchis came in 1571 from Juan Alvarez Maldonado, who requested Toledo grant him forty workers. Toledo, stipulating that the workers be paid their wages "in their hands" and that much care be taken that "they may be taught . . . in the things of our holy Catholic faith," honored the request. The communities of Andahuaylillas, also known as the *villa deleitosa* (delightful villa), San Clemente de la Laguna (Urcos), and Quiguares were ordered to provide workers for the *obraje.* The caciques of Quiguares, informed that they were to send fourteen workers, refused the demand complaining that the *obraje* was too far away and they were already serving in an *encomienda.* Their refusal landed the caciques in jail, but after further consideration they were freed and their people exempted. Instead, colonial authorities decided that Andahuaylillas and Urcos, being closer and described as being only "two arquebus shots distant from the said *obraje,*" would contribute twenty-four and sixteen *mitayos*, respectively. This settlement remained in effect until 1642 when Andahuaylillas argued that they really should send only twenty. After some seventy years, the people of the *villa deleitosa* were apparently trying to readjust or improve their terms of service. Their *curacas* also claimed that the *mitayos* were owed more than a thousand pesos in back wages, and without these wages tribute could not be paid. Although these accusations may have been well grounded, the claims concerning the number of *mitayos* may also have been a ploy to draw governmental attention to force payment of wages. It is also possible that the issue of wages and tribute was brought up to initiate an inquiry into, and hopefully a lowering of, their *mita* service.[32] Either way, the strategy invoked by the *naturales* to accomplish their ends rested in the hands of the colonial legal system.

Besides providing labor for the Guaro *obraje*, the community of Andahuaylillas was only "two stone throws" away from another textile mill that adversely impacted their lives. In the late seventeenth century the priest of Andahuaylillas noted the environmental degradation caused by the *obraje* as well as the suffering, oppression, and damage done to people's health by the *obraje* and its owner, Antonio Becerra. "It is very harmful . . . because it has a fulling mill (*batán*), through whose currents the water is infested with much harm, and deterioration of the health of the people; treating the people badly by taking the water from their fields for said fulling mill, . . . having the Indians locked up in the cells of his (Becerra's) *obraje* with hardships and insufficient pay for their work, . . . for this reason [the Indians] had stopped sowing their fields and *chacras*, and remained without fruits and grains for their sustenance in some years."[33]

In the eighteenth century, *obrajes* and *chorillos* (small textile shops without a fulling mill) dotted the landscape of Quispicanchis and Canas y Canchis. Lucre, Quiquijana, Pomacanche, Oropesa, Guaro, and Andahuaylillas all had at least one *obraje*, while many more communities contained the smaller *chorillos*. A *chorillo* employed only a handful of workers, and the large *obraje* of the Marques de Valle Umbroso in Oropesa had some four hundred workers engaged in weaving, carding, spinning, separating wool according to quality, washing the wool, or one of the many other *obraje*-related tasks.

Workers were frequently held against their will and kept working after their period of service terminated. The political influence of *obraje* owners made it hard for *naturales* to get any action, let alone a favorable hearing, on accusations of abuse or mistreatment. This was especially true when very powerful Spaniards such as the Marques de Valle Umbroso were involved. Matheo Cusiguallpa and Pedro Carlos Inga, caciques from different communities, both complained that they had *indios de septima* in the Marques' *obraje* and that they could not get them out nor were they allowed to change them, as they should *septima* workers.[34]

A later Marques de Valle Umbroso, Diego de Esquivel y Navia, observed in his *Noticias Cronologicas de la Gran Ciudad Del Cuzco* how an even more influential colonial personage, the bishop of Cuzco, solved a labor shortage in the *obraje* of Andahuaylillas. While in the *villa deleitosa* on a tour of Quispicanchis parishes, the bishop had people incarcerated in the *obraje* "with the pretext that they did not know Christian doctrine."[35] The bishop's miter provided power enough to impose a temporary, if highly suspect, punishment on *naturales* in Andahuaylillas to the benefit of the *obraje*.

The owners of large textile mills were to settle accounts every six months in the corregidor's presence. When the owner of the Guaro *obraje* failed to pay the *naturales* on schedule in 1700, the corregidor forced payment of wages and the adjusting of accounts. Out of over 330 indigenous workers, however, only 56 were owed back wages, a total of 1,129 pesos. The remainder of the workers were indebted to the *obraje*, the vast majority of these for under 20 pesos. Though debt was used to bind people to their work, in this *obraje* very few of the 277 workers were so deeply in arrears to make it likely that their debts were designed to hold them on any long-term basis. Only 4 owed more than 60 pesos, and 118 workers owed under 9. The larger and medium-range debts may also have been the result of cash advances sought by the workers to meet some immediate need or crisis.[36] In this situation debt, instead of being a burden, represented security against the unknown, which was made possible by employment. In other words, these could have been paternalistic relations instead of oppressive control.

In the Guaro *obraje* most *naturales* were engaged in piece work. The weaver Thomas Pinto had woven a dozen stockings at two pesos each for a total of twenty-four pesos. He also had woven fifty other items worth one real each. His total earnings for the term between the settling of accounts were thirty pesos and two reals. However, he had a debt of sixty-eight pesos two reals. Thus, after being compensated, on paper only, Pinto still owed thirty-four pesos. There were some 260 other Indians, including 59 women, working along with Pinto in the *obraje,* and only one was owed money by the *obraje.* No woman had a debt over twenty-five pesos, most female debt being under nine pesos. The debt structure of the Guaro *obraje* in 1705 was very similar to what it had been five years earlier, but there were a few more workers—7—indebted far beyond what one could expect to earn, that is to say far beyond what was necessary to hold a worker if debt was used strictly to provide a legal basis for restricting a worker's freedom. These large sums were either cash advances provided skilled workers to "encourage" them to stay, or they represented the cost of materials advanced to workers—debt—which they had to work off.[37]

The gender differentiation in amounts owed and jobs held indicates that men far outnumbered women in the *obraje,* they were employed in the most lucrative positions, and they were most likely to have large debts. When workers in *obraje* Marabamba in Andahuaylillas were paid, they were divided into five categories; weavers, nappers, carders, spinners, and women. The weavers were the worker elite. Of fifteen weavers, only three had no debt, and four had debts of over 100 pesos, one owing 193 pesos and one-half real. Of nineteen nappers twelve had no debts, and the others owed sums ranging from 9 to 55 pesos. The *obraje* employed eight carders, and though only one carder had no debt, the highest debt among these workers was 19 pesos 6 reals, and five were in arrears for sums under 5 pesos. Out of twenty-two spinners, ten had no debt, the obligations of the others ranging between 27 and 47 pesos. Eighteen women were on the list of *obraje* workers, of which these fifteen had no debt. No woman owed over 3 pesos 6 reals. If the weavers were clearly the worker elite, women were employed in the lowest paid and least skilled positions and they were almost debt free.[38] If debt was being used to retain workers it was used predominantly for the most skilled male workers.

The status and relations of noncommunity *obraje* workers in the villages in which they lived are far from clear. In the late seventeenth century the *obraje* in Guaro, one of the oldest in Quispicanchis, was owned by two Spanish women—Louisa de Vera and Magdalena de Abendaño—and had some 400 workers. The indigenous population of Guaro was 1060 people. Over 600 of these were *originarios* and *forasteros,* but the remainder were *obraje* workers. The fact that they were discussed separately from the *originarios* and *forasteros* indicates that while they lived in Guaro, they were not part of the *ayllu* and community structure. At least in this case, the *obraje* workers, like *naturales* resident on haciendas, were an entity unto themselves.[39] These people were most likely *forasteros,* but they may have differed from other *forasteros* in that their employment meant that they did not need lands—other than a house and garden plot—unlike other *forasteros* who grew crops or pastured livestock.

Likewise, most of the workers in *obraje* Marabamba were not part of the *ayllus* of Andahuaylillas. Instead, they lived in a *ranchería* "six stone throws" distant from the community on land that was part of hacienda Marabamba. These workers, living on the *obraje* owner's lands, were not fully a part of either the European world or the indigenous world. They comprised a separate unit, a separate people, within this colonial world.[40]

Most *naturales* who contracted to work in local *obrajes* left their homes every morning and returned home every night. Those serving sentences or paying off debts were supposed to be freed once their time was served or their debt paid. However, various machinations were used to hold workers who had their liberty restored only with the greatest reluctance, and then often only after the state threatened to impose sanctions.

In some instances debt was clearly a means—an insurance policy for *obraje* owners—that secured at least part of the work force. José Quispe Tito was one of the *naturales* who found himself a virtual prisoner in a textile mill. Eight years had passed since Tomas Quispe Tito and his son, José, had a falling out, but finally the nearly blind father went looking for his son. After leaving home, José had found work in *obraje* Quispicanchis owned by the Marques de Valle Umbroso, and that is where the elder Quispe Tito found his son. The *obraje* manager would not even examine the son's account to see how much, if any, was owed, and the young man certainly would not be freed. Turning to the government, the father asked for help so that his "unhappy [son] may have his liberty restored" and so that he could help his "poor and mendicant" father. Under governmental pressure, the *obraje* managers responded that the son was in debt. He had been advanced ninety-nine pesos, six and one-half reals and had earned sixty-eight pesos, six reals, leaving him with a debt of over thirty pesos to work off. Such a debt may have been difficult to retire, but without the father's persistence the son may have been further indebted without realizing it was possible to once again be free.[41]

The competition for *obraje* labor was stiff and led to deceitful practices, disputes, and even better working conditions, as *obrajes* sought to attract and hold laborers. Due to bad treatment and the difficulty of life, Matias Tito, an *originario* from Oropesa, left the textile mill in Lucre when his debts were paid. With his family, Tito traveled to the province of Abancay where he readily found work in another *obraje*. Being an *originario* in Oropesa, however, he continued to pay tribute there. Life improved for Tito and his family in their new surroundings. They were assigned lands, had a house, and caused no problems. Tito noted, "we behave according to my class and we attend catechism, mass . . . and [do] other Christian acts." Indeed, the local priest testified that Tito was a good Christian. However, he had not returned to Oropesa to pay his tribute, and the *cobrador* of his *ayllu* sought to incarcerate Tito in Lucre. Tito, supported by the priest and *obraje* owner in his new home, claimed that what the *cobrador* really wanted was "to enslave me, and all of my family, in the . . . *obraje*." Indeed, Tito claimed that he had not returned to pay his tribute out of his fear of being "enslaved" in Lucre. He could pay tribute, a commitment guaranteed by his new boss. Agreeing to honor his contribution, colonial authorities allowed Tito to remain in Abancay rather than being returned to where he had been an indebted worker.[42]

In a similar case a young girl, Yldefonsa Umpiri, stated that she and her grandmother were being held in an Abancay *chorillo* against their will. Yldefonsa claimed that they and the other workers were forced to sleep at the *chorillo* "in order that . . . they may not leave without adjusting their accounts." Wanting out of the situation the girl fled to her mother in Acos (Quispicanchis). At first the mother was reluctant to get involved, but with the help of the textile mill owner in Acos she finally filed a legal complaint. The owner of the Abancay *chorillo* argued that the charges were false, that Yldefonsa and her grandmother were not imprisoned. He also demanded that the owner of the Acos mill return two workers, a father and son, who had left his *chorillo* and found work in Acos while still owing twenty pesos. These two men were the grandfather and either the father or uncle of Yldefonsa. The owner of the Acos *obraje* showed baptismal and tribute records to prove the men were from Acos, not Abancay, and he cited a royal decree stating that Indians should be returned to their community of origin.

Treatment in the Abancay *chorillo* may well have been as bad as claimed, but it also appears that the family used the labor shortage to reconstitute itself in Acos. Knowing the need for labor, this family was able to get Spaniards to contest one another for their work and in the process be supported in their familial reconstitution. The more powerful *obraje* owner apparently prevailed over the owner of a *chorillo*. The defender of the *naturales* argued in favor of Yldefonsa and her grandmother, and, although there was no final ruling, testimony ended with the Acos mill owner refusing to return the two men, stating that he supported them "not for the personal interest of having the Indians in my house . . . but to look after these unhappy ones [Indians] whom he [the Abancay *chorillo* owner] wants to obstruct in what they do and make them do what they do not want to do."[43]

Though the selflessness of the *obraje* owner is highly suspect, his influence was positive for this family. Wanting workers, and perhaps being a decent human being, he helped them deal with a difficult situation from which both he and the family would benefit at the expense of another Spaniard.

Communities and *curacas* also owned *chorillos* in which *naturales* labored. Canas y Canchis, its herds of sheep and alpaca providing the raw materials for textiles, contained numerous *chorillos* that produced rough woolen cloth. In addition to the *chorillos,* individuals also had looms on which they wove to meet familial needs and to earn silver for necessities and obligations. Near the end of the eighteenth century officials in Quispicanchis enumerated *chorillos* and looms belonging to tributaries for purposes of taxation and registered a total of 135 looms. Spaniards and "other castes" paid a four peso tax per loom from which *naturales* were exempt. In 1765 a similar debate had arisen, but at that time the colonial official decided that Indians should continue to be exempt from taxes on goods "that come from their own industry and work." As the century closed yet another official was facing the same dilemma of deciding between enforcing a regulation that required taxes be paid on weavings and another that exempted *naturales* from such payments. Some argued that indigenous looms should be assessed at only half the rate of what others paid, while many, including the *Protector de Naturales,* argued that they should remain exempt. No sooner had the process begun than requests for exemptions started to be filed. Favian Amau of Acos, Andrea Colla of Guaro, and Ysidro Hancho of Oropesa and the entire community of Sangarará were among those who asked for special consideration. Confronted with an increasingly complicated situation, the official—like his predecessor a few decades earlier—ruled that *naturales* were to remain exempt because "of the difficulty there is in verifying the exaction, and in consideration of these being a poor people who have no other assistance for the payment of their tribute than the support of the little work in which they are occupied, and because being divided in villages and estancias . . . the collecting creates great difficulty."[44]

Thus, the same laws that oppressed them and made them second-class citizens also provided *naturales* a small breathing space from time to time. Although indigenous weavers and those they supported may have been very concerned, even outraged, that such a tax might again be considered, the exemption provided reason for them to continue working within the system, working it to their minimum disadvantage, to resolve problems.

Pastors, Packers, and Producers

Livestock was vital to economic life in Quispicanchis and, especially, Canas y Canchis for both Europeans and Andean villagers, because the wool, leather, food, and transportation provided by the livestock helped maintain people and were a major source of income. Those who tended these animals were also important, though not prominent, members of the regional workforce. Many were quite young, as boys and girls were often the guardians of livestock. Other shepherds lived apart from their *ayllus* and families for periods of time as they tended flocks on higher summer pasture.

Pastors were compensated for their services primarily in two ways. Some received coins, goods, and a ration of animals. Others were remunerated through a share of the natural increase of the herds they watched. Both methods of pay had their risks. Sick, diseased, or undernourished animals meant a low survival rate, making the earnings of the shepherd based on natural increase low. Likewise, drought and excessive cold affected the growth of pasture and the health of the livestock, both of which impacted the earnings of the pastor. If the natural increase was not as great as the owner expected, the shepherd might be accused of hiding, stealing, or eating animals, or of being insufficiently attentive in their care and supervision.

Manuel Cabrera, a tributary from Ocongate, had been sent by his cacique to guard forty-eight head of cattle on the hacienda of Ylario Perez. For his service Perez agreed to pay Cabrera's tribute as well as provide him with clothes and other items he needed to maintain himself. However, in the more than two years the pastor worked he received only one basket of coca. His tribute had not been paid, he was not allowed to graze his own animals, and he was not provided with salt for the cattle. During the time four animals had died, but Cabrera claimed they had been skinny to begin with. The increase in the herd was also less than Perez had expected. Because of the "shortage" of cattle, Perez confiscated 317 of the cacique's ewes. The cacique complained that the sheep were the "only resource with which I . . . maintain my large family, and the delivery of my obligation [tribute]." The pastor, cacique, and hacendado were all discontented with the situation. The hacendado certainly had not lived up to his commitment to the pastor. He, in turn, claimed the work performed had been inadequate. The Spaniard had forcibly "compensated" himself for his losses, although the cacique was taking legal recourse against the hacendado to regain his sheep and for the bad treatment accorded the pastor. Was this simply the case of an abusive, arrogant European trying to take advantage of *naturales,* or had the shepherd "appropriated" calves when the hacendado did not live up to his part of the bargain? Abusive treatment may have been countered by quiet, but determined, resistance.[45]

The number of animals watched and, consequently, the responsibility of pastors varied significantly. While Cabrera had been pasturing less than 50 head of cattle, five Indians on a hacienda in a nearby province were responsible for 429 cattle, and another eleven shepherds watched over 5,427 sheep.[46] In any case, the position of pastor was one of responsibility, and most *naturales* did their work very competently, just as most employers compensated herders according to agreements and did not question their work. For instance, when the Spaniard in charge of a Coporaque hacienda left on the long trip to Tucumán to buy mules for the great livestock auction in Coporaque, Nicolas Caricachuta was employed to tend 300 sheep, 20 cows with calves, 1 bull, and 2 steers. For his labor Caricachuta was to receive forty pesos and a supply of *chuño* each year, and every month he was to get 1 sheep and two reals worth of coca. In the almost three years the sheep were in Caricachuta's care the flock had not grown. Pasture had been in short supply due to the weather. The sheep were skinny, and 66 ewes died, Caricachuta having saved the skins. In such circumstances there was no disagreement, and no mention was made of the lack of natural increase.[47]

It was not just Spaniards who had need of pastors, well-to-do Indians also employed people to care for their flocks. Sometimes the animals were their own, other times they were rented. Churches and brotherhoods owned considerable livestock, usually sheep, and these animals were rented to Indians as well as to Spaniards. Pedro Aragon, an affluent *natural* from Sicuani with houses and *chorillos*, rented 850 sheep from the church and hired Ventura Pisco to pasture the flock. When Aragon died a cacique sought to take over the rental of the sheep, arguing that Aragon's son, Sebastian, was too young and the family now too poor to afford to rent the flock and therefore the flock would suffer. But Fernando Aragon, described as a clothing merchant and apparently a relative, put up a bond for Sebastian, and he was able to continue renting the sheep while hiring a pastor to watch over them.[48]

Prior to the arrival of Spaniards, llamas had been the only pack animals in the Andes, although humans also carried goods. In the colonial period the llamas that were bred and tended by the peoples of the upper Vilcanota remained a central force in colonial transportation and marketing. This llama-herding tradition and being on the royal road near both Cuzco and the coca-growing regions of Quispicanchis and Paucartambo had led to a specialization by people in Canas y Canchis in *trajines* or the transport of goods. By the late seventeenth century indigenous dominance of transport was threatened, however, as mules became more common. As early as 1615 the viceroy Marques de Montesclaros tried to protect Indian interests by ordering that "the *trajín* of this herb [coca] to Potosi be only on llamas and not on mules."[49] But by 1678, when caciques of Canas y Canchis sought to protect the llama pack trains, the situation had deteriorated and mules were becoming more and more dominant to the detriment of Canas y Canchis villagers who had come to depend on *trajines* to meet their needs and the colonial demands placed on them:

Your Excellency the Caciques of the Province of Canas Y Canches
say that in it, [and] in that of Lampa and Cailloma in times past
there had been a great number of Spanish *carnereros* [llama pack-
ers] who in order to make their trips in said *ganado de la tierra*
[llamas] solicited Indians from the corregidores of this Province of
Canas, thus those that lived in it like those of Lampa and Cailloma, worked transporting coca, wine, flour, corn and the rest sup-
plying the other Provinces and mining centers as far as Potosi and
by means of these *trajines* they delivered the Royal Tributes using
Indians because since time immemorial it is established in the said
province that the Indians work with their llamas for the delivery of
the tributes and for some years in this region they have ceased to
do it not having *tragin* of llamas caused by the introduction of too
many [*trajines*] of mules.[50]

Even though mules and nonindigenous muleteers eroded the *naturales'* dominance of the transportation sector, by no means were the
people of rural Cuzco eliminated from this important role in the colonial economy. Many began using mules to remain competitive in
the business. Even after the rebellion of 1780 people from Canas y
Canchis continued to transport goods throughout the region stretch-
ing from Lima to Potosi. Cloth from local *obrajes* and *chorillos*, as well
as coca, sugar, and *ají*, were among the items frequently carried.
Though the names of prominent *naturales* appear in *trajín* records,
much less is known about ordinary workers. One such worker was
Luis Xavier. In 1766 Pedro de la Llana had been asked to get help
taking goods to Potosi. Sitting in jail he found Xavier, an Indian from
Yanaoca, who was incarcerated for a debt owed to a priest. His obligations were paid, and he was put to work in a *trajín*, but Xavier was
not as dependable as most and he fled abandoning the goods and
mules.[51] The son of Eugenio Sinanyuca, the *curaca* of Coporaque,
tried to take advantage of the mule trade centered in his community
to make money, but apparently the business had its risks. He and his
partner lost their shirts dealing with mule traders and ended up
owing more than eight hundred pesos.[52] Perhaps colonial Peru's most

famous muleteer was Thupa Amaro. His *trajines* stretched throughout much of Peru, including the silver mines of Potosi. For instance, in 1775 "Josef Tupamaro" contracted to haul six *pearas* (sixty mules' loads) of *obraje* clothing and four of sugar to Potosi.[53]

By the eighteenth century Potosi was not the incredibly lucrative market it had been earlier, but it still was dynamic enough to be the most frequent destination of pack trains from Cuzco to Upper Peru. For example, when the corregidor of Quispicanchis died in 1730 he had some fourteen thousand pesos worth of goods, mainly clothes woven in local *obrajes*, in Potosi.[54] The continuing importance of the market in the "*tierra arriba*" or Upper Peru, especially Potosi, is further illustrated by the destination of the merchandise, mainly clothing, being shipped out of Lucre where one of the most important *obrajes* of Quispicanchis was located. In 1775 of the twelve recorded pack trains that left Lucre all were carrying "*ropa de la tierra*" (one also had sugar), and all were headed for Upper Peru.[55]

Thus, the peoples of the upper Vilcanota region were intimately involved in the colonial economy as pack train workers and owners, as breeders of llamas, as shepherds, and as producers of wool, meat, and leather. These activities associated with livestock were yet another way in which the peoples of rural Cuzco maintained themselves and their way of life while complying with colonial demands.

Priests, Parishioners, and Labor

Communities often were required to provide, and provided out of tradition and respect, people to work for the parish priest. These *naturales*, separate from official church business, cooked the priest's meals, worked his fields, ran his errands, and helped in innumerable other ways. Some of this labor was compensated, and some was donated by the community, the actual accommodations varying from parish to parish and priest to priest.

Relations between a community and its priest were as complex as the personalities involved and even more highly charged than other Indian-European relations due to spiritual and temporal authority of the priest. Some priests were exceptionally thoughtful of their parishioners. Most seem to have performed their services in a manner satisfactory to the *naturales,* but others abused and exploited their spiritual flock.

In his will the grateful priest of Checacupe left cattle and mules to the two *naturales* who had worked as his servants.[56] The priest of Tinta and Combapata even willed his hacienda to the Indians of his parish. He stipulated that revenues from the hacienda be used to pay the contribution of Indians, alive and dead, that supported the "war against the infidels," and that each of the living was to receive the contribution in his or her own hand in the churches. The priest also owned considerable sheep, and although some of these were to be used to cover the aforementioned contributions, some went to support the hospital for *naturales* in Cuzco. In addition, sixty *fanegas* (1.6 bushels per *fanega*) of wheat were to be provided to the *naturales* of his parish, and 150 pesos were to be divided evenly between the five *ayllus.* After this was done, any remaining funds were to go into the community chest to help his parishioners through leaner times. The priest's generosity was threatened, however, by the priests who followed him. The *naturales* of Combapata and Tinta complained that the new priests, "without legitimate title," were enjoying "the fruits and rents of the haciendas" that had been given to them by their former priest. The contrast between the priest who willed his property to his indigenous parishioners and those priests who were usurping what now rightfully belonged to the communities reflected the complexities inherent in priest-community relations. However, the differences stemmed from the character of the individuals involved, not from any institutional relationship between communities, priests, and the church.[57]

Everyday acts of kindness by priests, as by anyone in colonial society, seldom found their way into the historical record except in wills. More frequent were the complaints against priests who were not living in accordance with their position, or who were abusing members of their parish. In 1740 the caciques of Layo complained to the bishop of Cuzco that their priest did not compensate them for their work. He also physically abused them and overcharged them for burials. Without an excessively high funeral payment, he would not perform "the sacred burial and the cadaver goes twelve or fifteen days without burial." The Layo caciques, reflecting on the proper behavior of a priest as opposed to the treatment they were receiving, asked that another priest be appointed, stating, "the priest has so little caring, he does not look on his sheep (parishioners) with the affection that he ought."[58]

Naturales in Pitumarca suffered under some particularly bad priests. Two women who worked as servants for the priest fled after he "seduced them in their innocence . . . under the promise of marriage."[59] The people of Pitumarca and Checacupe complained that they were "treated as slaves" by another priest. The *cura* beat and whipped them, not even community officeholders being exempt from such abuse. The priest forced them to work in his house, sow his fields, build his fences, carry *guano*, haul earth for bricks "and a thousand other services all free, and if something is lacking . . . [he uses] the lash." The *naturales* lamented that even with all this work the priest still "treats us bad [which] is a very grievous thing." Petitioning the government for relief from their suffering, the peoples of Checacupe and Pitumarca argued that "we are poor Indians loaded down with difficult duties" who are being forced to "maintain the luxury of the priest." Did the priest have the right to whip them, beat them, and use them in his private business without paying them, the *naturales* inquired? They then pleaded, "we ask and supplicate . . . in the name of the King, Our Lord, . . . that he support and protect us miserable defenseless Indians, defending us from such cruelty and work." In this case, however, royal justice did not provide relief. Perhaps due to fear of reprisal, perhaps out of ignorance, or perhaps due to internal divisions, no individual from either community signed his name to the document as required by law. Without a signature the colonial official who received the complaint recommended that "they proceed with great prudence," meaning nothing was done.[60]

There were limits to what *naturales* would endure even from a priest, and alcohol sometimes lowered both inhibitions and the threshold of violence. An Indian couple, Diego Leon and Rosa Canche, had been drinking when an argument erupted between them and the priest of Combapata over eight reals that the priest maintained they owed him. In the heat of the argument the woman verbally abused the priest, scratched him, and finally bit him, drawing blood.[61]

Villagers in rural Cuzco typically respected the church and the office of priest, but they expected the priest to behave in a manner appropriate to his position. A community might provide a certain amount of labor free to a good priest while making labor available to him at the going rate of two reals for other jobs. However, when priestly demands were excessive or the behavior not appropriate the community withheld labor, demanded their wages, protested their situation, and sought redress as they did with others who transgressed their sense of right and wrong.

In conclusion, through systems of forced labor and direct and indirect economic coercion *naturales* were compelled to labor in European society. Although conflict developed between individual Spaniards and peoples in the communities over labor, what is more remarkable in Quispicanchis and Canas y Canchis is the relative rarity of such disputes. The state created a situation in which community members had to seek work in the European sector, but even in the late eighteenth century with the rapid population growth there was never such an excess of laborers that Europeans on a broad scale were tempted to systematically erode working conditions, which could heighten tensions and provoke resistance such as refusal to work. However, individuals, families, and even communities relied on this need for labor to maintain or better their situation, often with the help of a Spaniard who wanted their labor. Thus, within the coercive confines of colonial society indigenous peoples were often able to "adjust," if not set, their terms of service. The nature of agricultural production with its demands for labor at crucial times kept most local Europeans on a reasonable course of behavior, although they seemed inclined to get along with their indigenous neighbors in any case. The Spaniards needed the Indians, and the state made sure that the Indians needed the Spaniards. Without doubt the *naturales* of Canas y Canchis and Quispicanchis, along with other indigenous peoples, were the shoulders on which the Spanish colonial empire rested. This was evident in the fields, *obrajes,* and houses of Europeans, but nowhere was it clearer than in the silver mines of Potosi.

7

Community, Identity,
and the Potosi *Mita*

Although this kingdom is delightful and fertile with all the fruits that
nature brings, it would enjoy very little esteem if it lacked Gold and
Silver: their presence was one of the incentives for its Conquest, and
the reason for its permanence. VICEROY AMAT

... pueblos muy fallidos, y dicipados, por los aprietos de Corregidores,
y principalmente la mita de Potosi, donde cada año se despachan de
cada Doctrina mas de veinte Indios, que son familias enteras porq'
cada uno ba con hijos y mujer, los quales se mueren alla, y los que no,
jamas buelven a sus Pueblos, y si algunos lo hasen, es al cavo de muchos años, y estos tan viejos que no sirven ya de nada en sus Pueblos.
PRIEST of San Pablo de Cacha and San Pedro de Cacha, 1689

BY THE eighteenth century the very name Potosi had long jingled
with silver and been synonymous with untold riches and the power of
Spain, but the "king of all mountains, the envy of all kings" was a
mere shadow of its former self.[1] Many communities were also mere
shadows of their former selves, however, and much of their decline
was due to the system of forced labor for the mines—the *mita*—to
which they were subject. The silver flowing from the veins of Potosi,
first in a torrent and later in a stream, led imperial Spain to turn a
blind eye to the persistent pleas of its indigenous subjects to end the
mita that ravaged their communities as thoroughly as the periodic
epidemics. Numerous colonial officials anguished over the reports
they read and the abuses they observed, but the *quinto*, or royal fifth,
of the processed ore that the state received and the impact of silver on
the viceregal economy led them to the almost inevitable, if sometimes
hand-wringing, decision that the Potosi *mita* must be maintained.[2]

Viceroy Borja, noting the importance of Potosi silver, and indirectly of the *mitayos* or *cédulas* (*mita* workers), to the Peruvian economy quipped "estriba esta maquina" (it rests upon this machine).[3] Thus, while the debate over the *mita*, which the colonial jurist Solórzano y Perei(y)ra reflected "was not less deep than the mines themselves," persisted, so did the system of forced labor.[4] For over two centuries imperial Spain demanded that *naturales* from Quispicanchis and Canas y Canchis, the only two provinces of Cuzco subject to the Potosi *mita*, and thousands upon thousands of people from communities in other provinces lend their muscle and sweat, and all too often their blood and their lives, to keep silver flowing from Potosi's veins. The *mitayos* and their communities not only drove the colonial economy but were a major force in sustaining the Spanish empire and in helping forge the modern world's dominant economic system.

Mita service was so onerous that virtually all peoples subject to the labor draft, regardless of ethnicity or class, wished to see it terminated. Thus, at the macro level there existed an "ideological" commitment to ending the *mita* even though there was no coherent panindigenous movement or identity. At the same time, however, the *mita* severely strained the bonds that linked community, *curaca*, and the state, and which were primary ingredients in the social glue that kept colonial society from coming apart. To avoid descending into the bowels of the "*cerro rico*" and to escape such horrors as laboring over mercury vapors, many people permanently fled their communities, giving up the status of *originarios* and becoming *forasteros*. In this way the *mita*, one of the few forces that had the potential to unite peoples, so fractured them in their day-to-day lives that it severely strained communal solidarity.

Fleeing and reluctance to work in Potosi made it difficult for communities to meet their *mita* and tribute obligations, but failure to comply with these demands put both the community and the *curaca* in danger of state reprisals. Faced with these problems, villages developed strategies to ameliorate their *mita* burden and ensure the compliance of community members with colonial demands. In evolving these strategies peoples such as those in rural Cuzco sought

[163]

to enforce communal solidarity and in this way safeguard their social reproduction, their survival as a people. This chapter explores the impact of the *mita* on the communities as well as the strategies developed by indigenous peoples to maintain their communal structure and way of life while complying with imperial demands that in their eyes guaranteed their right to exist. The chapter also follows Cuzco *mitayos* to Potosi to examine their lives in the Villa Imperial and the community that developed there. The *mita* destructured communities at one level, but at another level it not only provided the impetus to reinforce communal solidarity in Canas y Canchis and Quispicanchis but enforced these local and regional identities in Potosi through policies of segregation and separation. Thus, the *mita*, perhaps the most destructuring force in the Southern Andes next to epidemics, also maintained structures of identity.

Mitayos, Free Workers, and the World beyond Peru

After the fall of Tawantinsuyu, Europeans quickly spread out over the remains of the Inca empire in search of the sources of gold and silver that dazzled Pizarro and his men, when Atahualpa, true to his word, filled a room with objects made of the precious ores. In 1545 this search was rewarded when an Indian named Hualpa, working for a Spaniard, discovered what soon became the world's greatest silver mine. The Spaniard registered the first claim at Potosi and was among the first to be enriched by its ore. Like later *mitayos,* neither Hualpa nor his grandchildren, who petitioned the crown for rights and exemptions in compensation for the service their grandfather had rendered Spain, benefited from the discovery.[5]

Word of the precious ore spread like wildfire, and Potosi, despite its location in a cold, sterile, windswept, and sparsely inhabited region of the Andes some four thousand meters above sea level, sprang into existence overnight. Both Spaniards and Indians rushed to the *cerro rico* with dreams of becoming filthy rich. When Pedro de Cieza de Leon arrived in Potosi in 1549 he reported that "so many people came to work the mines, that the place appeared like a great city."[6] By

1610 Potosi had some 160,000 residents, including 76,000 Indians and some 6,000 people of partial or full African heritage.[7] Father Joseph de Acosta wryly observed that the, "force of silver, which drawes unto it the desire of all thinges, hath peopled this mountaine more then [*sic*] any other place in all these Kingdomes," but as silver production fell so did the population.[8] By 1719, with an epidemic in Potosi, the Villa Imperial had shrunk to 60,000, and as the eighteenth century closed the number of residents was estimated at 24,500.[9]

In the first years after discovery the amount of ore extracted from Potosi was truly fantastic. Cieza de Leon observed that every week after the silver was smelted and the *quinto* removed "there came to his Majesty thirty thousand or twenty-five thousand pesos, and sometimes forty thousand," and he believed much silver illegally avoided the royal fifth.[10] The richest surface ores were quickly exploited and production fell, but prosperity returned to Potosi when the amalgamation process, which used mercury to refine low-grade ores, was introduced in the 1570s. Processing large quantities of lower-grade ore meant that massive numbers of workers were needed. Because free labor was not attracted to the more difficult and less rewarding tasks, Viceroy Francisco de Toledo imposed the *mita* on indigenous communities in the surrounding highland provinces to secure not only a labor supply for the mines but wages below that of free laborers. After its introduction this *mita* subsidy drove the mining industry and maintained Potosi's economic prominence. The dual impact of amalgamation and forced labor was dramatic. The sixteenth-century miner and author Luis Capoche gave an indication of this change through his figures on the royal fifth in the years immediately preceding and following the arrival of the first *mitayos* in 1574. In 1571 the *quinto* was 167,864 pesos. By 1577 it was already at 475,483, and by 1581 the crown received 802,923 pesos from the royal fifth.[11]

Eventually even the low-grade ores began to give out, and Potosi went into a period of decline from about the middle of the seventeenth century through the first quarter of the eighteenth century, followed by a partial recovery in the late colonial period. However, even with the decline in 1776 the *cerro rico* alone still accounted for 325,000 out of 800,000 marks of silver (40.6 percent) produced in the viceroyalty of Peru.[12]

Rich deposits of ores were discovered in New Spain at about the same time that the *cerro rico*'s treasures became known, but it was Potosi that became synonymous with wealth in the European mind. Following the introduction of the amalgamation process "Peru accounted for 65 per cent of all American silver shipped to Seville."[13] Thus, in the early colonial period Potosi overshadowed Mexican mines and earned for the city the motto:

> I am rich Potosi,
> Treasure of the world,
> The king of all mountains,
> and the envy of all kings.

The mining complex of Potosi was held to paying the full *quinto* much longer than were the mines of New Spain and even longer than other regions in Peru. It was not until 1736 that Potosi had its royal fifth lowered to a tenth, the standard "*quinto*" of the mining industry. Almost one hundred years earlier some mining centers in Peru were paying a tenth, while in New Spain many miners had paid 10 percent since 1548, and by the 1660s "only insignificant quantities of silver [were] paying the fifth."[14] In addition to the *quinto* on silver, the Spanish crown had a monopoly on the mercury trade and took a fifth from the production of mercury at the Huancavelica mercury mine in Peru before selling the quicksilver to miners. The government also taxed the minting of the silver and the assay of the ore, not to mention all the sales taxes coming into the treasury due to the lucrative trade. Thus, in the last half of the sixteenth century through the early seventeenth century, a crucial period for Spain, the major source of bullion for the crown was Potosi. This fixed the lion's share of Spain's attention on the *cerro rico* and ensured that Potosi miners could count on Spain to maintain the forced labor regime of *naturales* on whose backs Spanish wealth rested.

Though much of this wealth was sent back to Spain, the majority remained in the orbit of Potosi. The flush nature of this silver-laden market made Potosi the focus of merchants and traders not only in the Andes but throughout the colonial world. Goods flowed to the *cerro rico* from places as distant as Salta, Tucumán, and the central valley of Chile to the south, and from as far north as Ecuador and Mexico. Indians in Cajamarca, Quito, and even Mexico labored in fields and *obrajes* to provide goods for the Potosi market. In the early seventeenth century the cloth that came to Potosi from the Guánuco region of Mexico alone was reported to have a value of one hundred thousand pesos. Grapes came from Arica; apples, preserves, coca, and other products from Cuzco; hams, bacon, tongues, and other meats from Tarija and Paria; and fish from the sea and from Lake Titicaca.[15] The extent of trade between New Spain and Peru was so great that it has been argued that in the sixteenth century Mexico "behaved towards Peru as a metropole toward its colony."[16]

High profits drew provisions and trade not only from the Americas but from throughout the world, as the prodigal habits of the Potosino elite grew in fame. So great was the pull of this market, it has been suggested that in its prime "for a brief moment Potosi acted as the magnet for the entire Atlantic economy."[17] Galleons arrived from Manila with treasures from the Pacific and Asia, and the fleet from Europe carried goods from all corners of the globe. Soon precious stones from Ceylon, silks from China, linens from the Low Countries, rugs from the Near East, perfumes from Arabia, and woolens from England adorned the bodies and houses of those who had grown rich in the Villa Imperial.[18]

The very name Potosi took on almost supernatural qualities in European minds as not only the Spanish crown, but merchants and bankers from Antwerp to Genoa anxiously awaited the arrival of the silver fleets. Potosi's wealth was "the envy of all kings," and it also drew the attention of queens and their advisers. Francis Drake was knighted by Queen Elizabeth after capturing a Peruvian treasure ship. As early as 1584 Richard Hakluyt wrote that with all the unemployed youths and knowledgeable shipbuilders in England it would be easy "to spoil Phillipps Indian navye, and to deprive him of yerely passage of his Treasure into Europe, and consequently to abate the pride of the Antechriste of Rome, and to pull him downe in equalitie to his neighbor princes, and consequently to cutt of the common mischefes that comes to all Europe by the peculiar aboundance of his Indian Treasure."[19]

In the distant and struggling colony of Virginia, John Smith compared the "good hap" of the Spanish to the misfortune of the English. Encouraging the people of Virginia to develop the local fishing industry, Smith told the colonists "let not the meanesse of the word fish distaye you, for it will afford as good . . . gold as the mines of Guiana or Potassie. . . . "[20] In Flanders one sees the impact of New World silver in the painting of Pieter Bruegel. The Duke of Alba, pictured in the *Massacre of the Innocents* (c. 1566; Vienna, Kunsthistorisches Museum), most likely would not have been in the Netherlands trying to maintain the empire if the promise of American treasure had not loosened the purse strings of money lenders.

The Spanish crown, proud of its colony, did not discourage lavish descriptions of the mountain of silver "who the four parts of the world know by the experience of their goods."[21] Antonio de Leon Pinelo, an "able and prolific official of the Council of the Indies," produced a book entitled *Paraíso en el Nuevo Mundo*. Wildly exaggerating, he wrote that the ore extracted from the *cerro rico* would be sufficient for a bridge or road of silver from Potosi to Madrid 2071 leagues long, 4 fingers thick, and 14 *varas* wide. No wonder he located Paradise not far from the *cerro rico!* And in the Spanish-speaking world if one wanted to describe how precious something was they may well have said "*vale un Potosi.*"[22]

The influx of silver proved to be a mixed blessing for Spain. The bullion allowed Emperor Charles V to pursue "fantastically expensive foreign policies."[23] Much of the precious metal went into the struggle for dominance in Europe and into the effort to control the spread of Protestantism. Father Acosta knew this when he wrote in his *Natural & Moral History of the Indies* that, "We ought . . . humbly pray that He [God] will be pleased to favor the pious zeal of the Catholic

King, giving him prosperous success and victory against the enemies of the holy faith. In this cause he spends the treasure of the Indies which have been given to him, and he needs much more."[24]

Her external power reduced by lavish and optimistic policies, Spain's internal structure was weakened as well. Problems of empire led to the neglect of the internal economy and state structure. Foreign merchants and bankers gained control of large segments of the economy, and much of Spain's wealth ended up in other lands. In 1600 Gonzalez de Cellorigo admonished his country saying, "our Spain has concentrated on the trade of the Indies, and has neglected trade with neighbouring kingdoms. If all the gold and silver that has been and is being found there were to flow into it, it would still not be so rich or so powerful as it would be without them."[25] Suárez de Figueroa summed up Spain's situation in another way, "our Spain is the Indies of the Genoese."[26]

The significance of Potosi silver extends far beyond the fate of Spanish monarchs and their rivals. Potosi's riches played a significant role in the inflationary spiral known as the "Price Revolution" that was germane to the development of the capitalistic economic system. Adam Smith believed that the New World silver was "the sole cause of this diminution [between 1570 and 1640] in the value of silver in proportion to that of corn."[27] This quantity theory was refined by Earl Hamilton, who stated that "pouring into Europe in a mammoth stream, American gold and silver precipitated the Price Revolution, which in turn played a significant role in the transformation of social and economic institutions in the first two centuries of the modern era."[28]

Attacks on the "quantity school" come from several directions, but even some of these attacks also are based on the importance of New World silver. Fernand Braudel and Frank Spooner argue that it was not the quantity of bullion that caused the inflation but the social circumstances that caused the money to circulate at a high velocity: "The moment a silver fleet arrived from America, one money market after another in Europe experienced successively 'largesse' or easy money conditions. . . . Thus the money from Seville circulated from one money market to another, in settlement of commercial and financial transactions often to a value of ten or a hundred times its own value, and then passed on to the next money market for a fresh period of cash advances and trading settlements. Whether as coin or as bills of exchange, money cascaded from person to person."[29]

Europe had been experiencing a quickening of exchange and a slight inflation before treasure began to arrive from America. The vitality of capitalism in these early years certainly cannot be attributed to American silver alone, but the inflation that spread out from Seville, northern Italy, and the Netherlands contributed to the Price Revolution and capital accumulation. "The rich tended to grow richer and the poor poorer," and the nascent capitalist system was sustained. It was the toil of men such as Eugenio Mamani, a *mitayo* from Canas y Canchis who died in Potosí at age twenty, that helped spur the economic development of Europe and in this way contributed to the formation of the economic system that still dominates much of the earth.[30]

Life and Labor in Potosí

If the name Potosí became synonymous with riches, it also became synonymous with colonial exploitation. The forced migration, the separation from family and community, the disintegration and depopulation of communities, the generation of a large and rootless *forastero* population, the harsh work and death in the mines and refining industry, the imposition of higher state demands: these were the underside of what made Potosí "the king of all mountains, the envy of all kings."

In the early years the rich ores of Potosí were near the surface, and the conical shape of the *cerro rico* made it easier to find and exploit deposits that would otherwise have been buried under hundreds of feet of earth. Drawn to the *cerro rico* by high wages and stories of veins bursting with silver, "Indians came from all parts to extract silver from the hill."[31] *Encomenderos* ordered those entrusted to them to go to Potosí to work.[32] *Yanaconas* were ordered by their masters to find employment in the mining or support industries of the burgeoning city. *Curacas* sent their subjects to the *cerro rico* to earn tribute monies, or to fill *curacas'* pockets. But even with the high earnings and forced and free or *minga* labor (in Potosi the term *minga* was used for those who freely contracted their labor and thus was different than the traditional Andean use of the term), the supply of workers was never adequate to the miners' desires. The Spanish crown and mine owners were constantly looking for additional sources of labor, such as Indians captured in frontier wars who could legally be enslaved. As early as 1559 Viceroy Hurtado de Mendoza ordered that *naturales* condemned to death or exile have their sentences commuted to work in the mines of Potosi.[33] By 1574, the same time the *mita* was being implemented, an ordinance "required that ten per cent of all Indians belonging to *repartimientos* whose masters had died, or gone away, be sent to complete their service in the mines."[34] Black slavery was another remedy considered, but slavery never proved to be a viable solution to the labor shortages. The high cost of slaves made them too valuable to risk in such difficult and hazardous work.[35] Though these attempts reflected the demand for labor, they contributed little to the workforce.

Some of the first *naturales* from Canas y Canchis sent to Potosi labored not for a Spaniard but for an upper-class Indian. Don Carlos Inca, the heir to the Inca throne and the Spanish puppet ruler, had been granted an *encomienda* in Canas y Canchis, and he owned mines in Potosi. In 1566 Don Carlos empowered Pedro de la Torre "to sell the silver mines I have in *la villa de Potosi* and in other parts [and] to have care and administration [of] the Indians that I have and had in said *villa*." The Canas y Canchis people laboring for the Inca heir were also among the first to complain of having been sent to toil in Potosi.[36]

It was not through mine work but the transport of goods to the *cerro rico* that most communities of the upper Vilcanota first began their relationship with Potosi. Luis Miguel Glave uncovered twenty-four contracts to carry coca from Paucartambo, a province of Cuzco bordering Quispicanchis, to Potosi between the years 1560 and 1575.

Fourteen of these contracts were from Canas y Canchis, leading Glave to state that there was "a labor specialization of the Canas in the transport of coca."[37] The *trajines* or transport of goods remained a very important activity in Canas y Canchis throughout the colonial period, but once instituted it was the *mita* that took most Cuzco *naturales* to distant Potosi.

By 1560 the richest, most accessible ores had been mined, and returns were starting to diminish. Free Indians and Spaniards, along with their *yanacona*, drifted away as the mines got deeper, the work harder, and the rewards less. The shortage of labor became a serious concern for miners and the crown. *Encomenderos* and caciques no longer sent Indians to the mines in such large numbers, and the *naturales* left the mines "for the valleys of Chuquisaca (Charcas) and temperate lands, and thus each day there were fewer."[38] Low earnings and arduous work held as little attraction for indigenous workers as for anyone else.

Faced with declining *quintos* and a scarcity of labor, the Spanish crown decided changes had to be made. The royal bureaucracy could not afford to allow Indians, or those who controlled their labor, the choice of not working in the mines. To solve the problem Francisco de Toledo was sent to Peru. Toledo, influenced by the work of Juan de Matienzo, wanted *naturales* protected from abuses, but he also believed that it was right and proper that they serve the Spanish. Matienzo had even gone so far as to argue that the Indians were "enemies of work, friends of laziness and of drinking and getting drunk" and therefore must be forced to work.[39] Matienzo and Toledo ignored the fact that when earnings had been high labor had been available.

Arriving in Peru on 30 November 1569, Toledo surveyed the situation and decided on three major changes that would have a profound impact on Potosi and much of the indigenous population of the viceroyalty. First, the native peoples, who often lived in small groups or *ayllus*, were to be congregated or "reduced" into communities. This not only would make it easier to govern and Christianize the *naturales* but to enforce state demands such as tribute and labor exaction. Second, the amalgamation process, using mercury to process low-grade silver ores, was to be introduced to revitalize production. Third, because the amalgamation process was much more labor intensive than older methods of mining and smelting had been—large quantities of low-grade ores had to be mined, transported, crushed, ground, mixed, squeezed, and heated; and the refining mills, crushing stamps, and systems of water power had to be built and operated—Toledo imposed the *mita* on subject indigenous peoples. By 1574 the new system was in place, and the first *mitayos* arrived in Potosi.

For imperial Spain the Toledan reforms were an overnight success. Silver production and royal *quintos* skyrocketed. For *naturales* employed in the revitalized free wage sector, the combination of mercury and *mita* generated some well-paying jobs, but Toledo fixed the wages of *mitayos* at about one-third to one-half those of free workers. Because *mitayo* earnings were low they had to sell their labor in the "free" market during what were supposed to be their weeks of rest in order to survive, and this served as a control on the wages of free laborers. Thus, by imposing the *mita* the crown provided the mining sector with cheap, reliable, forced labor and an increased supply of free workers. For the crown and the miners this was good business. For *mitayos* such as those from Canas y Canchis and Quispicanchis, the new Toledan order became a harsh, disruptive force in their lives.

The *mita* stretched over a vast region of the southern Andean highlands from southern Bolivia to as far north as Canas y Canchis and Quispicanchis. Most of the subject regions were around 3,500 meters in altitude, and Quispicanchis and Canas y Canchis were calculated by the crown as being 180 leagues—some 450 miles—from Potosi (see plate 6).[40]

Only males between the ages of eighteen and fifty were legally subject to the labor draft, and when first put into effect, the base *mita* population in the subject provinces was 91,000. By law no more than one-seventh of these men were to serve each year. Ideally, a tributary would serve no more than four or five times in his life. This one-seventh or *septima* was referred to as the *mita gruesa* and totaled 13,500 in the first few years.

Theoretically, *mitayos* worked one week and had two weeks free so only 4,500 people—the *mita ordinaria*—were supposed to be toiling at any one moment. In reality *mitayos* had to sell their labor in the free wage sector for most, if not all, of their "rest periods." Such was the impact of the *mita* and disease, that a little over a century later, in 1688, from the original *mitayo* population of 91,000 only 33,423 remained, the *mita ordinaria* declining to 1,674. Canas y Canchis reflected this decline, as the *originario* or tributary population in the province fell from 6,023 in 1575 to 3,683 in 1684 and to 1,755 in 1728.[41]

Long delays in adjusting the *mita* to the dwindling population placed additional burdens on the communities. In 1617 the *mita gruesa* from Canas y Canchis numbered 754. By 1733 it had fallen to 318 and about 1780 there were only 269 *mitayos* in the province. At the village level in 1575 the *mita gruesa* for Sicuani and Pichigua was 52 and 128, respectively, but by 1733 these figures had dropped to 30 and 65. In 1692 the Quispicanchis *mita gruesa* was 111, but by the 1780s only 44 *mitayos* were sent.[42]

In the late sixteenth century Luis Capoche calculated that some 13,000 *mitayos,* along with their wives and children, came to Potosi, raising the total number of migrants to around forty thousand. As Capoche put it, "the roads were covered and it seemed that the whole kingdom moved."[43] Departure for the *mita* was a sad occasion. Families were separated, and the *mitayos* and their kin and friends had learned from experience that some would not return. In 1792 the *Mercurio Peruano* described one such unhappy occasion:

> The Indians that go to Potosi and its refining mills leave their homeland with very much mournfulness. . . . The day of their departure is very sad. . . . [After mass] they pay [the priest] in order to entreat from the Allpowerful the success of their journey. Then they leave for the plaza accompanied by their parents, relatives and friends; and hugging each other with many tears and sobs, they say

goodbye and followed by their children and wife, they take to the road preoccupied with their suffering and depression. The doleful and melancholy nature of this scene is augmented by the drums and the bells that begin to signal supplications.[44]

The migratory process began in earnest when the corregidor or his representative notified the community and their *curaca* of their obligation to serve in the Villa Imperial and the date they had to depart. In 1655 the crown representative in Quispicanchis informed the villagers of Pomachape that "they ought and they are obliged to dispatch '*yndios*' to the Potosi *mita*." He also notified the *curaca*, Bartolome Choque Fonsa, of his responsibilities. He was to bring his people to the nearby plaza of Pomacanche "with their llamas and all provision in the form as is accustomed" under penalty of two hundred lashes and four years in an *obraje*.[45] The process was similar in the neighboring community of Papres some thirty years later. The corregidor ordered villagers to gather in the plaza, and through an interpreter he informed them of their *mita* obligation while warning their cacique that the *mitayos* must be present and ready on the appropriate day with their supplies, coca, llamas, and other things they would need so that they could leave for Potosi without delay.[46]

Communities often tried to lessen the burden by providing those going to Potosi with supplies. Variations in the goods that families of equal size had on their llamas as they started down the royal road toward Potosi suggests, however, differing levels of support. No matter what the supplement, the primary burden was borne by those selected to serve. Many *mitayos* transported large loads of coca not only to avoid purchasing the precious leaf in the inflated market of Potosi but to sell to help maintain themselves.

In 1770 a Potosi official observed that the leaders of *mita* contingents and their helpers brought goods to sell in Potosi, especially to the Indian merchants. Among the items loaded on their llamas were clothes, coca, and the Peruvian chili or *ají*.[47] Though not revealing if the goods were personal or communal, a list or *cédula* (the term was also used to describe the workers on it) of *mitayos* and their wives from Pomachape details the supplies taken to Potosi, which included *chuño*, corn, coca, wheat, and a shelter. This list represents just one small portion of the wealth, human and otherwise, that the *mita* transferred out of indigenous communities and into the nonsubsistence colonial economy.[48]

Many Quispicanchis *mitayos* departed from the pampa of Antucota. In 1644 don Juan Laymichape, a cacique from Marcaconga, left from there as the *enterador* of his *ayllu* with a contingent that included himself and sixteen *mitayos* and their families along with their llamas, coca, *chuño*, and corn. Thirty years later, in 1674, Laymichape was still a *curaca* in Marcaconga, but when he saw his people off to the Villa Imperial the contingent numbered only seven. In three decades his community's *mita* had plummeted to less than one-half of what it had been.[49] What must have gone through the mind of Laymichape as he watched his people depart from Antucota fully realizing that, if the present were like the past, some would not return?

TABLE 3. Goods Taken to Potosi by Indians of Pomachape

Name	Goods Taken to Potosi
1. Joseph Lope, capitán de *mita* y Josepha Asensia	6 llamas loaded with *chuño*, wheat, corn, coca, and shelter (*toldo*)
2. Joan Vilca Poma, *enterador*	3 llamas loaded with corn, *chuño*, wheat; a *burrico* with coca and shelter
3. Martin Choque, *cédula* and Josepha Malque	6 llamas loaded with corn, *chuño*, wheat, coca, and shelter
4. Joseph Alvarado, *cédula* and Teresa Sisa	4 llamas loaded with corn *chuño*, wheat, coca and shelter
5. Joan de Mendoza, *cédula* and Jacoba Poco	5 llamas loaded with corn, *chuño*, wheat, coca, and shelter

Source: ADC. Corrg. Prov. Leg. 61, 1679–1705. 1690. Mita.

In 1690 *mitayos* not only still left from Antucota pampa, but "an arbour [had been] built for the purpose of the despatch of the *mita*."[50] Despite the sharp decline in population the *mita*, as symbolized by the construction of the arbour or *ramada*, was as strong as ever. For over a century more the peoples of Quispicanchis and Canas y Canchis watched their loved ones, friends, and fellow community members disappear down the royal road for the mines and refining mills of Potosi.

One of the most serious consequences of the *mita* was the separation of families. Children from rural Cuzco most often accompanied their parents to Potosi, but this was not always the case. When the contingent from Papres departed in 1687 many *mitayo* couples left their children behind. Agustin Quispe and his wife bid farewell to three children. Mateo Masi and Isabel Poco had to leave "one young [*tierno*] son," while Melchor Canaya, who had been selected to go as a backup worker or *remuda*, and his wife, Juana Caya, left two "hijos tiernos."[51] Both communities and parents had different customs. Some took their children, others did not. Likewise, certain colonial officials included children in the record, while others recorded only adults. For instance, a list of *mitayos* from Papres does not mention children being left or going. In the same year twenty-one *mitayos* from Acopia showed no children accompanying their parents to Potosi, but the same document recorded that couples from Pomacanche had children with them. Pedro Chuchocane and his wife, Juana Micayla, took their two sons, aged seven and nine, while Gabriel Quispe and Ysabel Ticlla took one child.[52] In a 1689 survey of parishes in Quispicanchis and Canas y Canchis some priests mentioned the Potosi *mita*, and others did not. Almost all of those who did, such as those of Sicuani, Langui, Layo, San Pedro de Cacha, and San Pablo de Cacha, noted that the families accompanied the men.[53] *Mitayos* from Cuzco almost never went alone. Thus, the *mita* was in reality a family *mita*. If there was no spouse someone else went. When Diego Choque left Pomacanche for the *cerro rico* his mother went with him, and when Juan Pacha departed from Sangarará the eight-year-old daughter of Aria Rrosa was sent along to assist him.[54]

The trek across the altiplano was long and difficult, with cold temperatures and rain adding to the hazards. For some three months Cuzco *mitayos* walked and camped their way through the Andes to the *cerro rico* under the guidance and supervision of the *enterador* or captain of the *mita*. For those with small children the journey must have been especially arduous. Perhaps this is why some couples made what must have been the very difficult decision not to take their children with them, which, in turn, certainly provided incentive to return.

The *mitayos* were to be paid for their travel to and from Potosí, but the payment or *leguaje* was a matter of continual contention not only between *mitayos* and miners but also between the crown and the mining sector. Despite repeated royal orders, colonial officials lacked the will, or perhaps the power, to enforce payment. Because it was against the crown's interests to suspend the *mita* if the *leguaje* was not paid, the position of those authorities inclined to enforce payment was weakened. Thus, *leguaje*, instituted to help *mitayos* and those left behind to survive, was nonexistent or inconsistent for most of the colonial period. For Cuzqueño *mitayos* this meant one-half year of service, three months each way, with only partial compensation, if at all. As late as 1729 villages in Canas y Canchis were still demanding the payment, and they implied that if the *leguaje* was not paid their tribute would not be forthcoming.[55]

In addition to the other difficulties, the sheer distance to Potosí was also a significant problem. A Sicuani priest reported that the number of community members continued to decline, "it is rare that [the *mitayos* and their families] return for lack of provisions and for the very great distance that they are from Potosí and because the Royal ordinances are not complied with."[56] *Mitayos* were supposed to serve one year in Potosí, but the great distance and time of travel led the communities of Canas y Canchis and some other distant regions to develop a policy of two years' service. The burdens and separations forced on peoples who came from villages in these provinces were even greater than for those who lived closer to the *cerro rico*. A Canas y Canchis priest, sensitive to the impact of colonial exactions and abuses, complained the communities were "dissipated" due to pressures from corregidores "and principally the *mita* of Potosi, where each two years they despatch from each parish more than twenty Indians, that are entire families."[57]

Upon arrival in Potosi *mitayos* were assigned their various tasks, some being sent into the mines while others were ordered to the refining mills. From the very onset of the *mita* there was a consistency to these assignments, communities being placed with the same miners and refiners year after year. Death, decline in population, sale of mines, and alteration in assignments sometimes disrupted the consistency, but for the most part *mitayos* had knowledge, either personal or by word of mouth, of the people for whom they worked in Potosi. For instance, in 1692 officials allocated to Miguel de Gamberete two different groups of eighty *mitayos* each for his mines and refineries. In one group twenty-five *mitayos* were from Pichigua and thirteen from the Cachas (San Pedro and San Pablo). The other group contained twelve *mitayos* from three communities in Canas y Canchis and thirty from five different Quispicanchis communities. In 1736 *mitayos* from Pichigua were still being assigned to one Francisco Gamberete, but the number had been reduced from twenty-five to eighteen.[58]

If the mine owner had a reputation for abuse, the prospect of descending into the mines or laboring in the choking dust and poisonous mercury fumes of the refineries was even more repugnant. On the other hand, if *mitayos* were treated reasonably, albeit within the context of exploitative forced labor, the service might be somewhat more readily tolerated. These face-to-face relationships influenced behavior and compliance with, or resistance to, the *mita*.

Few Cuzco *mitayos* had the resources to purchase their way out of service as did many *naturales* in regions closer to the Potosi market. This practice, known as *faltriquera,* was not widespread in rural Cuzco. *Mita* captains from Canas y Canchis testified that there were few *indios de faltriquera,* or *colquehaques* as they were also called, in their province, "because those [Indians] that there are, are few and poor." Likewise, when asked if there were *colquehaques* in their province, the captains from Quispicanchis answered no, "because they are few and all come in person to serve their *mita*."[59]

Those with the wherewithal made arrangements to pay for a substitute. This was an expensive process, because no one wished to go to Potosí without substantial compensation.[60] When Mateo Gamarra was assigned to Langui's *mita* he purchased a substitute, because his wife was ill and could not make the hard journey. He hired Fernando Gamarra, perhaps a relative, for 179 pesos only to have Fernando flee, leaving Mateo broke and pursued by the people in Potosí who had received neither the *mitayo* nor the money due them.[61] Two centuries earlier Luis Capoche had observed that desperate *naturales* would give fifteen or twenty head of livestock "that is all their wealth" to avoid the *mita,* and that was exactly what Mateo Gamarra had done. Few could purchase their way out of the *mita* repeatedly, and Gamarra was no exception. He had sold goods, food, and animals, and used what silver he had to hire a replacement to be with his sick wife. When he was again selected for the *mita,* because, in reality, his earlier obligation had not been filled, there was nothing left. Gamarra pursued the only option left open to him: he appealed to colonial officials for exemption from the *mita.* Besides having tried to comply with his obligation the year before, he argued that he was "of advanced age, as his grey hair showed, [and with] the habitual illnesses of deafness and the swelling of one leg." He also argued that it was unjust that the community had selected him as captain of the *mita* after what he had been through "wanting me to sacrifice to the death."[62] The community had asked too much. This *natural* had to protect himself, so he sought relief from state-imposed demands, but the process put him at odds with his community rather than with the colonial regime.

Others purchased their way out of service, such as Diego Arqui of Pichigua, who said that he used his lands to pay his obligations, including his Potosí *entero* or payment.[63] In reality *faltriquera* was nothing more than a cash subsidy to miners and refiners who, especially in periods of low productivity, preferred cash, although they also made money illegally renting out the *mita* labor provided by the state. For more wealthy *naturales* and those with ready access to lucrative labor or commodity markets, *faltriquera* was an option that allowed them to avoid the rigors of forced labor. For the poorer members of the community it was a glaring reminder of the class differentiation that existed within communities.

Quispicanchis and Canas y Canchis were known for their consistent delivery of *mitayos*. A seventeenth-century document that stipulates which communities the government considered *buenos, medianos, o malos* (good, average, or bad) in their *mita* compliance has "*bueno*" behind most Cuzco communities. This was not the case for all regions. The province of Chuquito near Lake Titicaca did not have such a reputation.[64]

The high level of *mita* compliance in Quispicanchis and Canas y Canchis was reflected in the increasing percentage of all *mitayos* who were from rural Cuzco, especially Canas y Canchis. When the *mita* was first established, Canas y Canchis contained 5.9 percent of the total number of *mitayos*. By 1692 this percentage had increased to 11.9, making it the province that supplied the highest percentage of *mitayos*.[65] By fulfilling their *mita* obligations the communities of rural Cuzco maintained their good standing, their right to exist, with the crown. *Mita* service for the Spanish monarch was understood, as it had been with the Inca, as establishing a special bond of reciprocity between subjects and ruler.[66] However, the villages of Cuzco paid a heavy price for their strict compliance with the *mita*, for many *mitayo* families remained in Potosi or became *forasteros* in provinces near the *cerro rico*.[67]

As the eighteenth century neared, colonial officials recognized that the failure of *mitayos* to return home was devastating the provinces. Viceroy de la Palata's census revealed that since Toledo established the *mita* a little more than a century earlier there were 58,092 fewer tributaries, over half the original total, living in the communities subject to the *mita* and that 5,557 *originarios* were living in Potosi. He ordered these people returned to their communities and excused them from tribute for one year, but as was often the case the order was not enforced. In 1692 Viceroy Monclova found 6,084 *originarios* still living in Potosi. While Quispicanchis had only 143 *originarios* resident in the Villa Imperial, Canas y Canchis had 999, more

TABLE 4. Reputation for *Mita* Delivery in Cuzco and Chuquito

Community and Province	Mita Ordinaria	Buenos, Medianos, Malos
Canas del Cuzco		
Siquane	19	buenos
Singa y Lurucache	15	buenos
Marangani	5	buenos
Coporaque	11	buenos
Yaure	31	medianos
Checasupa	15	buenos
Layosupa	11	buenos
Pichigua	43	medianos
Cacha	17	buenos
Charrachape	2	buenos
Ancocaba	1	bueno
Llanguisupa	12	buenos
	185*	
Tinta Canches		
Checacupi	21	buenos
Cangalla	5	buenos
Tinta Canches	24	buenos
Combapata	7	buenos
Combapata de D. Ant.	5	buenos
Yanaoca	29	buenos
	91	
Canches Quispillactas (Quispicanchis)		
Pomacanche de Rios	19	medianos
Pomacanche de P. Arias	6	buenos
Sangarará	13	buenos
Collopata	8	buenos
Acopia	7	buenos
	53	

Table 4 (*cont.*)

Community and Province	Mita Ordinaria	Buenos, Medianos, Malos
Chuquito		
Chuquitos	116	medianos
Acora	90	buenos
Hilave	83	medianos
Jule	105	medianos
Pomata	93	malos
Yunguyo	61	malos
Cepita	70	malos
	618	

*Addition error in total is from the original.

Source: AGN. B. A. Sala 9, 6–25, 22. Meml de las Provincias y Pueblos qe estan obligados a enuiar yndios para la mita.

than any other province. The neighboring province of Azangaro was fourth on the list with 623 resident tributaries, but this was only two-thirds of the Canas y Canchis total. Included in the list were only those adult males born in their provinces who had come to Potosi, not those born in Potosi and referred to as "*criollos*" in parish records.[68] These *originarios* composed a significant segment of what should have been the Canas y Canchis population, considering that the entire population of the province—men and women, young and old, *originarios* and *forasteros,* Indians and non-Indians—was 14,200 in 1689–1690.[69] When their families are included in the total, a quarter to a third of what should have been the Canas y Canchis population lived in or near Potosi. Forced labor in the *cerro rico* indeed drained life out of the upper Vilcanota basin.

In 1754 *originarios* were once again ordered to return to their provinces, and 1756 figures indicate that the *originarios* living in Potosi had dropped from over 6,000 to 2,969. However, though the *mitayos* may have left Potosi, they did not necessarily return to their *ayllus*. Corregidors in the *mita* provinces complained that because of desertion, moving to other regions, or not being well guarded by the captain of the *mita*—"for one of these same causes"—there was lack of *cédulas* to fill the quotas. Orellana, a crown official involved in the mid–eighteenth century controversy over *originarios* resident in Potosi, confronted the same dilemma that others before him had faced. He clearly recognized the needs of the crown and noted that years earlier the government had suggested having people settle near Potosi. The *originarios*, he argued, were voluntarily fulfilling this crown desire. He also noted, ironically if not hypocritically, that "it is not a crime in the Indians having sought their liberty [from their communities] . . . imitating all other men prone to leave subjugation." Orellana recognized, however, the problem this presented to the communities and commented that the difficulty was an old one with "pernicious results in the destruction of these pueblos and principally those of greatest distance." He added "that continuing the bleeding of these pueblos will shortly make them cadavers." In the end, Orellana recommended that the government ought to proceed gently in any changes, which usually meant that nothing would be done.[70]

Originarios from Canas y Canchis and Quispicanchis who remained at the *cerro rico* sometimes continued to pay tribute and serve in the *mita*. In this way they maintained communal rights and preserved the possibility of returning to their natal community. Perhaps these were people who had fallen into debt and had to remain, or they had found lucrative work that allowed them to accumulate funds to live on after returning home. The priest of San Pablo and San Pedro de Cacha noted these long absences, stating that if the *mitayos* and their families returned from the *mita* "it is after many years, and these so old that they do not serve for anything in their Pueblos."[71] Undoubtedly many *originarios* in the Villa Imperial hoped to avoid the *mita* and tribute; however, *curacas* were dogged in their pursuit of community members residing in Potosi. *Mita* captains from Quispicanchis maintained that while their *curacas* did not know where most absent Indians were, "that only in this *villa* (Potosi) are there some from whom they collect the *tasa* or tribute."[72]

The *curaca* or his agent, often the captain or *enterador* of the *mita*, tried to force those who had fled to serve. In 1643,

the *gobernador* of Santiago de Yanaoca [Canas y Canchis], Fernando Surco, accused Pedro Alata Arusi of changing his name to Pedro Gualpa and his place of origin to Oruro to evade *mita* service. Surco chased Pedro down after he fled from Potosi after only a few days working in the *cerro*, and had him jailed pending a decision by the *Audiencia de Charcas*. Pedro said that he had been born in Oruro and later moved to the *estancia* of González Picón at the age of seven, after his parents had died. Evidence on both sides of the dispute showed that he had then been entrusted to Domingo Arusi and raised along with his three sons. Arusi was originally from Santiago de Yanaoca, and served in the *mita* from the *estancia*; when his sons came of age they too traveled to Potosi from there. Pedro fled from Potosi after his first taste of *mita* service, and when he was captured by Surco he challenged the legal basis for his obligation. Despite serious questions concerning his true origin—he changed his birthplace to Arequipa during the course of the litigation—the *Audiencia* ruled that his adoption by Domingo Arusi did not oblige him to serve in the *mita*.[73]

The *enteradores* from Acopia had better luck in forcing Baltasar and Agustin Ramos to serve in the *mita* after they fled. The *Defensor de los Naturales* argued for the community, stating that it was important to have those serve who ought to serve, because it increased royal fifths, served the public good "and because the said Provinces and pueblos . . . are deteriorated of people." The father of these brothers had died, and for many years they had lived in the province of Porco near Potosi. However, when the baptismal record was presented and Agustin's godmother confirmed his birth, that was enough for the court, which ordered that they ought "to be restored to their pueblo and Province of origin in order . . . [that] they may have recourse to *mita* service from which depends the conservation of the Royal treasury and the public good."[74]

Most people who fled their communities were not found. By the late seventeenth century 12.5 percent of the *forastero* population of Chayanta, a province close to Potosi, was composed of people from Canas y Canchis. Having either escaped *mita* service or having decided not to return home after completing their turn, these folk ceased to be a part of their communities in rural Cuzco. Such *forasteros* found places where they could rent or gain access to land, or they congregated where employment could be found, such as the mining center of Cabanillas where several *forasteros* from Canas y Canchis resided.[75]

Months of backbreaking, dangerous work often led to flight. Even among the Spaniards who argued that *naturales* were lazy and must be forced to work there were few who maintained that *mita* work was easy. In the sixteenth century, when the mines were not yet so deep, Father Acosta provided this description of mine work:

> They must descend [great depths] to labour in the mine . . . They labour in these mines in continuall darkness and obscuritie, without knowledge of day or night. And forasmuch as those places are never visited with the Sunne, there is not onely a continual darkness, but also an extreme colde, with so grosse an aire contrary to the disposition of man, so as such as newly enter are sicke as they at sea. The which happened to me in one of these mines, where I felt paine at the heart, and beating of the stomach. Those that labour therein use candles to light them, dividing their work in such sort, as they work in the day rest by the night, and so they change. The mettall is commonly hard, and therefore they break it with hammers, splitting and hewing it by force as if they were flintes. After, they carry up this mettall upon their shoulders, by ladders of three branches made of neates lether twisted like peeces of wood, which are crossed with staves of wood, so as by every one of these ladders they mount and discent together. They are ten *estados* [an *estado* is 2.17 yards] long a peece, and at the end of one, beginnes another of the same length, every ladder beginning and ending at platforms of wood, where there are seates to rest them like unto galleries, for that there are many of these ladders to mount by one

at the end of the other. A man carries ordinarily the weight of two *arrobas* [an *arroba* is 11.5 kg or about 25 lbs.] of mettall upon his shoulders, tied together in a cloth in the manner of a skippe, and so mount they three and three. He that goes before carries a candle tied to his thumb, for as it is said, they have no light from heaven, and so go they up the ladder holding it with both their handes; to mount so great a height which commonly is above a hundred and fiftie *estados*, a fearful thing and which breeds amazement to thinke upon it, so great is the desire of silver, that for the gaine thereof men indure any paines.[76]

Acosta might have added that *mitayos* did not have a choice. They were forced to "indure [*sic*] any paines." Vicente Cañete y Dominguez, a late eighteenth-century defender and reformer of the *mita*, was horrified by labor conditions. He also noted that workers were carrying loads twice the weight that Acosta mentioned and noted that "one bad night can break the most robust and well nourished man. For these unhappy ones all nights are very bad. They climb and descend overloaded with four *arrobas* [100 lbs.] of weight, through caverns filled with horror and risk, that seem like habitations of devils."[77]

Toledo had sought to assure that *mita* work would not be overly arduous by limiting workers to carrying no more than two loads a day, or what was easily done in one day, out of the mines. However, formal regulations gave way to quota systems that not only demanded much more work but imposed penalties for not meeting the quota.[78] Under such conditions the already risky and arduous labor became even more of a nightmare. *Mitayos* were supposed to enter and leave the mines every day, but this quickly gave way to week-long shifts.[79] The workers entered the mines on Monday, and on Saturday afternoon they were led back down the mountain where they were counted and paid. In the mid–seventeenth century Acarete du Biscay gave this account of their return from the mines: "After six days of constant work, the conductor brings 'em back the Saturday following to the same place, there the Corregidor causes a review to be made of 'em, to make the owners of the mines give 'em the wages that are appointed 'em, and to see how many of 'em are dead, that the couraces [*curacas*] may be olig'd to supply the number that is wanting: for there's no week passes but some of 'em die, either by divers accidents that occur, as the tumbling down of great quantities of earth, and falling of stones, or by sickness and other casualties. They are sometimes very much incommoded by winds that are shut up in the mines."[80]

Deaths were all too frequent. One mine owner had been ordered to suspend operations because his mine was in need of repair, but he ignored the order. Two days later the mine collapsed, killing twenty-eight Indians. Upon learning of the tragedy, the grief-stricken wives, children, and parents "broke the heavens with their cries."[81] To avoid the perils of exposure, some refinery workers who handled mercury sought to protect themselves "by swallowing a double duckat of gold roled up; the which being in the stomacke, drawes unto it all the quicke-silver that enters in fume by the eares, eyes, nostrilles, and mouth, and by this meanes freed themselves from the danger of quicke-silver, which gold gathered in the stomacke, and after cast out by the excrements: a thing truly worthy of admiration."[82]

The *mitayos* of Quispicanchis and Canas y Canchis, as other *mitayos*, were overwhelmingly concentrated in the hazardous and difficult jobs of climbing the leather ladders and carrying the ore out of the mines (*apiri[e]s*) or breaking the ore loose in the mines (*barreteros*).[83]

Parish death records in Potosi do not specify the cause of death, or whether or not the deceased was a *mitayo*. It is impossible to know if Joseph Ninachi from Lurucachi, who was married to Martina Colquema and who died on 28 October 1750, at age forty, was a *mitayo* and, if so, if he died of work-related causes. But the death registries from parishes where the people from Quispicanchis and Canas y Canchis lived are strewn with entries such as that of Ninachi, and hundreds more for their wives and children.[84]

The many thousands of indigenous workers in Potosi needed coca to dull the pain and allow them to endure the harsh labor, high altitudes, and inadequate nutrition that were part of life in the mines. Luis Capoche observed that *naturales* would pay any price to get coca and without it would not work. Mine owners used coca as an inducement to free laborers who went with "more disposition . . . to work" if they received a coca ration. Although Capoche believed that coca was just a "superstitious vice," he recognized that people would not work without it and concluded that "there would not be a Potosi longer than the coca lasted."[85] The eighteenth-century Potosi historian Bartolomé Arzáns de Orsúa y Vela was forced to chew coca, which made his tongue grow "so thick that there was no room for it in my mouth," before entering the mines, because besides suppressing appetite and increasing vigor the workers claimed the "richness of the metal will be lost" if someone entered the mines without chewing coca.[86]

To supply this lucrative market, other *naturales* worked, and all too often died, in the hotter, damper, lower altitudes where coca was grown and where diseases such as "*mal de los Andes*" consumed them in a manner "that leaves them [the Indians] no more than bones, and skin full of sores."[87] For the people of rural Cuzco, however, especially those of Canas y Canchis who had access to nearby coca-growing regions and who used their llamas to transport goods, the demand for coca in Potosi and other markets provided a means to earn silver. Thus, the exploitation of some lessened the burden on others.

Potosi, not a residentially integrated city, was physically divided by a stream that ran through it, which provided water for power and washing ores to the refineries. From the earliest days indigenous peoples lived on the side of the stream closest to the *cerro rico*. Toledo merely reinforced this tradition when he ordered the *naturales*, in keeping with the notion of two republics (one Indian and one Spanish), to live on the opposite bank from the Europeans. The residences of the indigenous barrio reflected the differences in standards of living in this segregated world. In contrast to the Spanish neighborhoods, the "houses of the Indians were small and little more than huts or *chozas* where they lived in very crowded conditions."[88] The indigenous barrio was further divided into settlements or *rancherías* that corresponded to the *mitayos'* communities and provinces of origin. State-church policy perpetuated communal and ethnic ties by organizing people into barrios and parishes based on their home provinces and communities. In this way the colonial migrants, like many of their modern counterparts, often maintained their regional and ethnic identities, and the "destructuring" *mita* also became a force for maintaining older structures or "restructuring."

Even in matters of faith native people were kept separate from the Spanish community and, to a fair degree, from other Andean indigenous peoples. People from Quispicanchis were incorporated into the parishes of Santa Barbara, San Sevastian, and San Pedro. *Mitayos* and others from Canas y Canchis lived in the parishes of San Pedro, San Pablo, San Juan, Concepción, Copacavana, Santiago, and Sta. Bunvana (Santa Buenaventura?).[89] *Mitayos,* and sometimes the *criollos,* were also required to support a church and a priest in Potosi based on their villages of origin. Not only were *naturales* from the same region concentrated in the same part of the city, but they were often in the same parishes and attended the same masses. For instance, the three communities over which Thupa Amaro was *curaca*—Pampamarca, Su(o)rimana, and Tungasuca—were all in the parish of Santiago.

Community members even remained united in death. Those few parish death registers that specify if the deceased was born in rural Cuzco or in Potosi indicate that about half the deaths recorded from rural Cuzco were actually people born in the Villa Imperial who were referred to as *criollos* (not to be confused with people of European descent born in the New World, the more common usage of the term). Even though many of these *indios criollos* from Cuzco no longer had lands or possessions in the *ayllus* from which their families had come, they continued to have contact with people from their villages and were identified with those people by church and state. For instance, when Roque, the legitimate child of Martin Vilcay and Maria Poma, both *criollos* of Potosi, died in 1761 at one year of age, his passing was recorded, along with the deaths of others from Coporaque, in the parish of Concepción. Even though both parents had been born in

Potosí, he was identified with the community from which his fore-
bears had migrated. Likewise, Ysidora, the child of Manuel Humachi and Alfonza Chequa—both *criollos* of Potosí—died after one day
on this earth. Four days later the mother joined her baby, apparently
of complications resulting from childbirth. The mother was at least a
second generation *criolla*, both of her parents having also been *criollos*. Mother and child, however, were recorded in the death register
under Sicuani, the family's ancestral home.[90]

Just as in their villages, some priests were good, but others were
tyrannical and venal. Complaints against Potosí priests for abuses
and excessive charges for funerals, weddings, and baptisms were numerous. In 1770 *enteradores* noted the "extortions and bad treatment"
their people suffered at the hands of the religious, and in 1772 priests
in the Villa Imperial were admonished not to use violence to "uproot
idolatry."[91]

Despite these problems, it was in the parishes that the *naturales*
conducted their lives. It was here that they went to hear mass and to
pray for aid and understanding in facing the crises and suffering that
life, and the colonial order, presented. It was also here that they married and had their newborn consecrated with holy water. It was here,
and in the mines and markets, that they went about the business of
life and made their way in the world of Potosí.

It was also in the parishes, *rancherías*, and markets that they
bought and sold goods and enjoyed what leisure time they had. The
Indians purchased some of the 1,600,000 *botijas* (earthen jars) of *chicha* that were drunk every year during the heyday of Potosí, as *naturales* sought relief from their aches and miseries and celebrated their
rituals and fiestas.[92] Racially discriminatory laws were instituted to
control the drinking and rowdiness of the *naturales* in Potosí. It was
illegal, although not necessarily enforced, for Indians to overindulge
during the normal work week. Due to the realities of the work regime, as well as the law, most drinking was done after mass on Sun-
days. To further control the situation, a law was passed that sought to
dampen indigenous revelry by prohibiting *naturales* from beating
their drums while drinking. The drumming of inebriated Indians

disturbed the Spaniards, who described the sounds emanating from the indigenous *barrios* as "bien indecente y mal sonante." It was most likely also on Sunday that indigenous prostitutes were kept busiest with their "ejercicio amoroso."⁹³

The lives of *mitayos* and others in Potosi were subject to the whims of man and nature. Arbitrary violence was common. Catalina Caña and her two grandchildren were awarded 150 pesos by authorities when the person in charge of a llama pack train threw a rock that hit her son, a *mitayo* from Canas y Canchis, in the head and killed him.⁹⁴ Drought meant that water wheels could not turn and ores could not be ground or washed. Without the processing of the ores, miners could not pay their workers. Without pay *mitayos* and free laborers found themselves in dire circumstances and often deserted Potosi. No wonder that during one drought the town council ordered Potosinos to make "sacrifices, supplications, prayers and processions" to bring rain.⁹⁵

Epidemic diseases also left their deadly mark. Early on Cieza de Leon commented that "the climate of Potosi is healthy, especially for the Indians, for few fall ill there."⁹⁶ This normally astute chronicler could not have been more mistaken. Brought to the Villa Imperial by *mitayos*, traders, and an array of others who passed through the city, European diseases such as smallpox, measles, plague, mumps, and influenza ravaged the *rancherías* and then were carried back out to the provinces to infect or reinfect victims. Potosi laborers became unwitting vectors of death.⁹⁷

In 1719–1720 an especially deadly pandemic struck Potosi and wrought havoc throughout the Andes. During one sixty-day period 2,500 people died, 2,140 of them being *naturales*. According to Potosino historian Arzáns, the total number of dead during the pestilence was 22,000; and another 10,000, mainly Indians, died in the nearby environs. Deeply affected by the death and suffering he witnessed, this historian wondered if the maladies were due to the "forgetfulness of God" and "the bad influence of the stars that presided this year of 1719."⁹⁸ Refining nearly came to a standstill, because "all of the *mita* Indians perished" as did many of the free wage laborers. Those free workers who did survive, recognizing the opportunity created by scarcity, demanded double their normal wages.[99]

The 1719 pandemic carried away numerous Cuzco *naturales* residing in the Villa Imperial, including twelve people from Pomacanchis, twenty-three from Coporaque, and thirteen from Pueblo Nuevo, which was three to six times the death rate these communities had experienced over the preceding decade. Families were decimated or wiped out: for instance, Pablo Luntu and his wife, Nicolasa Casa; Francisco Cayagua, age thirteen, followed shortly his father and mother; and Maria Colquema and her son, Melchor.[100] Confronted with massive death and with no end of the epidemic in sight, *mita* captains and *enteradores* asked that the *mita* be suspended until the epidemic ceased. Ever mindful of their home communities, these indigenous officials warned that if this was not done before the new *mita,* people would flee and the communities would be ruined. Soberly reflecting on the devastation, these *naturales* noted that already "innumerable *mita* Indians from all regions may be dead with the pestilence."[101]

Rural Cuzco and the *Mita* in the Eighteenth Century

The devastation of 1719–1720 disrupted compliance with the *mita* by communities in Canas y Canchis and Quispicanchis for several years, the longest known interruption of the colonial period. In 1727 the colonial official Felipe de Santisteban was ordered to recount tributaries in the provinces of Lampa, Azangaro, and Canas y Canchis to reestablish tribute payments and the Potosi *mita.* In the six years since the epidemic the communities of Sicuani, Marangani, Lurucachi, Checacupa, and Pitumarca had not delivered *mitayos* to the Villa Imperial. Though these communities may have sent *mitayos* to Potosi after 1727, the fact that new *mita* numerations were conducted in 1733 for Quispicanchis and Canas y Canchis and again in 1736 for Canas y Canchis suggests ongoing instability in *mita* compliance in the wake of the devastation. Authorities couldn't even agree on the number of *mitayos* the Cuzco communities were obligated to send,

two 1733 lists of *mitayos*—one from Lima and the other from Potosi—providing differing *mita* quotas. Not surprisingly the list from
Potosi, where demand for workers was ever pressing, ordered a significantly greater number of *mitayos*—453—to the mines than that
from Lima—318.[102] It is unlikely that such numerations would have
been conducted on the heels of one another had the *mita* been reim-
posed smoothly, and villagers no doubt did what they could to avoid
reestablishing this dreaded service that bled them of their neighbors
and provoked internal discord.

In addition to the harsh work in Potosi, *mitayos* faced other problems. Who would take care of their children, fields, and animals?
Would fellow villagers act in good faith and protect their interests?
The relative infrequency of complaints by returning *mitayos* suggests
that their interests were, for the most part, well protected during
their long service in Potosi. There were, however, exceptions. When
Diego Merma, a tributary from Yauri, was ordered to Potosi he had
to arrange care of his 120 sheep. He rented the flock under the normal terms—one-half the natural increase—to Mateo Lima who, in
turn, contracted the sheep to Thomas Pallani and Bernabe Cabana.
Upon his return Merma went to reclaim his flock, but was refused.
Instead, Lima offered him a *reparto* mule, three mares, and seventeen
sheep. Even though he really wanted his sheep, Merma took the
mule as partial payment of what was owed him. However, the cacique soon came looking for him, demanding thirty-five pesos, the
reparto price of the mule, and Pallani refused to return his sheep.
Merma took his complaint before Corregidor Reparaz, stating that
Pallani and Cabana were "indios ricos" and were the source of many
problems and complaints in Yauri. The "indios ricos" maintained that
the sheep had been full of worms, and many of them, and their
young, had died. The corregidor ordered Pallani to return one hundred sheep to Merma, but the process had been divisive. Merma did
not get back as many sheep as he had rented out, let alone the increase. Having complied with his *mita* service, he was left poorer
than before. Fellow community members had taken advantage of
him.[103]

TABLE 5. 1733 Tributary and *Mita* Populations of Quispicanchis and Canas y Canchis (Lima)

Community	Tributary	Originarios	Forasteros	Service to Church and State	Mita Gruesa	Ordinaria
Quispicanchis						
Cullupates	160	127(142?)	18	15	18*	6
Papres	93	83	10	13	10	3
Pomacanchi	240	74	166	28	6	2
Guayqui	53	46	7	12	4	1
				Totals	38	12
Canas y Canchis						
Sicuani	288	272	56	14	30	10
Senca	250	167	83	7	22	7
Lurucachi & Marangani	115	74	51	25	5	1
Coporaque	168	101	67	16	12	4
Ancocava	97	46	51	25	5	1
Yauri	252	153	99	26	18	6
Checacupa	250	84	166	26	8	2
Layosupa	166	136	30	26	15	5
Languisupa	186	169	17	17	21	7
Pichigua	531	490	41	33	65	21
Checacupi	227	121	106	15	15	5
Pitumarca & Cangalla	29	27	2	6	3	1
Cacha	176	93	83	27	9	3
Charrachape	76	34	42	12	3	1
Tinta & Tungasuca, Sumimana, Pampamarca & Urinocas	—	405	—	34	53	17
Combapata	190	152	38	19	19	6
				Totals	318	102

*2 extra or *remuda* go with the *mita*.
? There appears to have been a mistake made by the person who composed the document.
Source: ANP. L.10 C.234. 1727 Diligencias que se actuaron en orden a la revista y numeracion . . . Lampa, Azangaro, Canas y Canchis.

Lucas Chancayarni of Pichigua also suffered a loss of animals due, in part, to the *mita*. Shortly before departing for Potosi, someone stole ninety sheep from Chancayarni. He complained that the *mita* "obligation has prejudiced me considerably because it has not given me opportunity to look for . . . [the sheep] robbed from me."[104]

Absence in the *mita* also led to disputes over property. In 1780 Domingo Hanco, the cacique of *ayllu* Chiguaro in Sicuani, claimed that Pasqual Quispe had left for Potosi owing him twenty-eight pesos that he needed for tribute payment. The cacique sought to collect the supposed debt from Quispe's goods. Quispe and his wife, Lucía, had entrusted their possessions to a friend who denied the cacique's claim and strongly defended their interests.[105] A few years earlier members of the Hanco family had been on the other side of a property dispute. Antonio Hanco's father had been awarded an urban plot before leaving for the *mita*, but the property was occupied while he was away. Fifteen years later Antonio brought the case before Corregidor Reparaz, who awarded him the contested real estate despite the long period of possession by others.[106] Likewise, when two brothers from Lurucachi were serving their turn in Potosi, individuals from their community began using their private lands without permission. The brothers complained that they had been complying with their communal obligations, and now they scarcely had lands "to plant or maintain the few sheep that we have." In addition, the villager who had taken their property already had enough for ten tributaries and had thrown rocks at them. Colonial officials put the brothers back in possession of their fields.[107]

Because of the *mita*, the people of Marcaconga even experienced a change in the line of *curaca* families, which, in turn, evolved into a communal rift. In 1705 Juan Tanqui petitioned the government to be installed as *curaca* of Marcaconga. Tanqui was of "the blood of *curacas*" but had been in Potosi serving as *mita* captain when his relative, the *curaca*, died. In this situation another *curaca* was selected, but Tanqui, supported by community elders who wanted him back in power, turned to the state to install him as the rightful community leader.[108]

One of the greatest problems confronted by the *ayllus* was depopulation due to flight and disease. Although *mita* obligations were supposed to be adjusted to population fluctuations, such adjustments or *revisitas* were less frequent than their need. And because, until the mid–eighteenth century, the population usually declined, remaining community members were encumbered with even heavier burdens. Those who fled sometimes improved their situation, integrating into new communities; for example, some individuals from Quiquijana, Pichigua, Yauri, Langui, and Sicuani married people in the Colca valley.[109] Others did not fare so well, however. Sebastian and Diego Palli, from Marangani but living as *forasteros* in the province of Larecaja, did not adapt well to their new surroundings. They defied obligations imposed in the community where they relocated, they spoke badly of the priest, stole from the church, and attempted to start an uprising. Sebastian died, but Diego was convicted of sedition, given one hundred lashes, and sentenced to an *obraje* where he was to receive no wage because of "the gravity of his crimes."[110]

Forasteros from other provinces also sought refuge in Canas y Canchis and Quispicanchis. Some of these people settled in the larger towns or found work on haciendas, in mines such as that at Condoroma, or in coca production.[111] *Forasteros* were reasonably well received by the communities of Canas y Canchis for much of the colonial period. With the population declining and tribute and *mita* demands pressing ever harder, renting land to *forasteros* was a ready source of revenue for the community or *curaca*.

Many of these migrants, or their children, married into the local community and in this way gained access to land, sometimes being referred to as *sobrinos* or nephews.[112] *Forasteros* were not normally rented the better fields, although this did happen, but as the situation changed and per capita resources diminished, renting any fields to *forasteros* frequently irritated needy *originarios*. Such was the case when the people of Checacupe and Pitumarca complained to royal authorities that lands allocated to the community and needed by the *originarios* were being rented out by the cacique.[113] In this situation *forasteros* were not always so welcome. Diego Sunca, a *forastero* from a nearby province, had come to Marangani with his entire family to escape the Potosi *mita*. Sunca had lived in Marangani for one and a half years, and the cacique assessed Sunca ten pesos "tribute" every *tercio*, or twice a year. As tribute was once again being collected there had been drinking, customary at such events, and an argument erupted. The *forastero* complained that the tribute demanded of him was too high. Sunca never made it home. He was found dead in a creek with a cut on his forehead. Well-off for a *forastero*, Sunca owned considerable personal items in addition to some 200 llamas, 125 *pacochas* or alpacas, and 700 sheep. After Sunca's death indigenous officials in Marangani took 160 of his sheep, which the state ordered returned to the family. When asked why they had taken the sheep they answered simply that Sunca was "comfortable and a *forastero*."[114]

Communities, caciques, and provincial corregidors were under constant pressure from officials and mine owners in Potosi to maintain *mita* deliveries. If the pressure from Potosi was constant however, so was the resistance by those who were obligated by the *mita*. Corregidores and other Spaniards from rural Cuzco had no inherent interest, other than to avoid trouble with colonial authorities, in having the *naturales* on whom they relied for labor, production, and as a market going off to Potosi. Likewise, *curacas* saw the *mita*, and flight from the *mita*, as a threat to communal and their own well-being. Accusations of hiding men and using them for private purposes were frequent. In the 1720s a crown representative conducted a *revisita* in Canas y Canchis and regions near Lake Titicaca, but Potosi miners distrusted his figures because he was the corregidor of Canas y Canchis and his brother was a priest near Lake Titicaca. The Potosinos instinctively suspected that there were *naturales* who had not gone on official lists because the brothers or their associates wanted to pocket their tribute or use them in their own businesses.[115] Similar arguments had been made since the initiation of the *mita*. Corregidors who did not force compliance with the *mita* were threatened with suspension, while miners and government officials also blamed *curacas* and hacendados who gladly received those who fled the *mita* for the decline in their labor supply. It was argued that corregidores "occupied [Indians] in their businesses, *tragines*, and marketing," and they and other Spaniards in the provinces were accused of "excesses and frauds" in lowering the *mita*.[116] Thus, on the issue of the *mita* the people in the provinces—rich and powerful, poor and weak, indigenous and Spanish—shared a common ground, but the influence of Potosi silver usually outweighed local concerns.

Community members did not always share the *mita* burden equally. Differences in wealth, influence, and *ayllu* affiliation created tensions and discontent, as some *originarios* were forced to serve in the *mita* more often than others. A Combapata tributary testified that it was the poor and those without means who were sent to Potosi.[117] Not all of those who avoided the *mita*, however, purchased a replacement. Some tried more devious means. When José Chaco, a Coporaque *cobrador*, fled with the tribute it was discovered that he had accepted bribes from those seeking to avoid the *cerro rico*. Mateo Arpi had paid fifty pesos, much less than the cost of a substitute, while Melchor Umidiauri had "bought" a position serving the priest to free himself from the *mita*.[118] Those without means, or without special attachments to the *curaca*, resented practices such as these that placed an unfair burden on the poorer, less well-connected, members of the community. The *mita* captain of Yanaoca complained that the same people were repeatedly sent to Potosi "without giving them the rest disposed by ordinances." At the same time the Combapata captain maintained that such mistreatment of poor community members was among the reasons that many *mitayos* remained in Potosi.[119]

In the upper Vilcanota *naturales* helped meet their needs and comply with colonial exactions through the production and transport of goods to Potosi and other markets. The *trajines* or hauling of merchandise was especially important here. In this way the continued economic importance of Potosi and other mining centers in *Alto Peru* created an ironic situation for the peoples of Quispicanchis and Canas y Canchis. Their forced labor in the mines produced the wealth that spurred the colonial economy and created markets that needed to be supplied. Through their work in *trajines*, agriculture, and *obrajes* they earned silver and supplied the markets that they helped create. This made it possible for them to meet levels of demands that could not have been sustained without these earnings. The *mitayos'* work in Potosi made possible increased state exploitation, which the *naturales* were able to meet by working to supply Potosi and other markets where demand would have been much weaker without their *mita* labor.

Naturales in Quispicanchis and Canas y Canchis developed strategies to preserve their communities and minimize the damage of the *mita* while forcing people to render this obligation to the crown. The degree to which they succeeded is evidence not only of their tremendous will to maintain their communal way of life but of their ingenuity. As with other matters, the colonial legal system was one of the first lines of defense employed, although it never brought the total relief so desired. Although the crown pressed enforcement of the *mita,* it occasionally lowered or relieved this burden when formally requested and when to do otherwise would well have strained relations and undermined colonial legitimacy. For instance, during and after epidemics, such as that of 1719–1720, the *mita* was not always enforced. Likewise, during times of drought *mitayos* were not pursued, apparently, when they returned home. Some government officials used incentives and their legal powers to foster *mita* compliance. Corregidor Don Gregorio de Viana of Canas y Canchis encouraged compliance, and the return of *mitayos* to their community, by ordering caciques in Sicuani to distribute vacant urban plots "to the Indians that go to the *mita* . . . of the Villa de Potosi."[120] By this gesture Viana, in a small but direct way, acted to maintain the community, and his own and the crown's interests.

Through the legal system the *naturales* denounced abusive treatment in Potosi and attempted to abolish *mita* service entirely, often with the support of Spaniards. When the caciques of Tinta petitioned the government to abolish the *mita* in 1789, the priests of the province provided written support for the abolition. The priest from Langui and Layo wrote that due to forced labor in Potosi "these poor *mitayos* suffer such calamities in their leaving, stay and return that they cannot explain it without making the heart cry blood." The priest argued that in the mines they contracted diseases that are "very grave for the fatigue of the chest and lungs of which they suffer, that while they do not die they are unfit for all species of work: he who suffers most from this disease, for which there has not been a remedy, hardly lives a year; in the present [year] fourteen have died vomiting blood from the mouth."[121] The priest of Yanaoca argued the case against the *mita* more succinctly, "Your Excellency the state in which these miserable Indians are found most probably [is] caused by said *mita.*"[122]

Complaints by Canas y Canchis caciques against the *mita* in the 1700s mirrored those made two centuries earlier. The travel stipend or *leguaje* was not being paid. People had to sell many of their goods just to provision themselves for the journey. When they returned to their communities nothing awaited them—"their houses [were] destroyed, their fields . . . [were] uncultivated"—except the "payment of five or six *tercios* [tribute for two and one-half or three years] that they have fallen behind during their absence in Potosi." The caciques continued to be charged tribute, and one of them argued, "[as] we caciques do not have the means to replace this money. It is necessary to charge them [the *mitayos*] upon their return. This is the cause why more do not return to their Pueblos remaining vagabonds." Such situations hardly enhanced communal solidarity or good will for the corregidor; however, it was good for the state's treasury. In addition to tribute problems, *curacas*, like the priests, complained that those *mitayos* who did come home often suffered with pain, lung problems, injured chests, were unfit for work, and often died within a short time.[123]

The caciques of Canas y Canchis summed up their despair over the *mita*, and their desire for government help in changing policies, in the first few lines of their petition when they wrote, "The caciques of the entire province of Tinta in voice and name of our respective communities . . . say that when evils frequently become insupportable, hope has no other asylum than the recourse, and the humble representation of them, to our superiors."[124]

Although individual colonial officials sympathized with the *naturales,* or supported them for their own reasons, crown policy maintained the *mita* throughout the colonial period. In 1791 the people of Tinta, having once again sought to abolish the *mita,* received a reply to their request. The subdelegate of Canas y Canchis was "to proceed with the greatest wisdom and prudence in order that the Indians do not go away angered." *Mitayos* were to be paid their *leguaje,* the *mita* was not to exceed the one-seventh limit, no people were to remain in Potosí after completing their service, and they were to be accompanied home, but the *mita* was to be maintained![125] This response, similar to the petition for abolition, could have been written two hundred years earlier. And like previous pronouncements, this one seems to have had little impact, for the communities of rural Cuzco continued to complain about the *mita* until it was finally abolished amid the turmoil of colonial rebellion in 1812.

To ensure compliance with the *mita* and other governmental demands under these difficult circumstances the *naturales* of *ayllu* Suio in Sicuani developed a strategy and order that governed their communal lives. They stated,

> That being the ancient and established custom we gather every year in a certain place that we are accustomed, in the semester of San Juan, in order to deal with the things pertaining to the Service of God, of the King, and the public good, and on the same day we elect from one year to another the officials of *Alcalde,* Seconds, Captain *enterador, cédulas,* and the other obligations. . . . [In the *mita*] we are subject to go first as *cédulas,* [and then as] *enteradores,* this is after serving the personal obligations and menial positions [*serviles*] of Second, local *mita* service, mail carrier . . . and the rest . . . all of these obligations serve as steps for us . . . [and those who complete them can then fill] the honorific posts that distinguish loyal and true subjects of Your Majesty.[126]

Thus, *ayllu* Suio used the Potosí *mita* and other demands that threatened community solidarity to enforce that solidarity by making compliance steps on a ladder that led to positions of honor within the community. By so doing Suio protected its social reproduction and safeguarded its compact with the king and state through internal and agreed on means.[127]

Despite efforts to ensure that the *mita* rotation was completed, *mitayos* sometimes fled Potosi and returned home. Such action may be viewed as a form of resistance, but the premature return of *mitayos*, especially when not justified by community standards, put the *curaca* and community in a difficult position. In these instances unprovoked fleeing was not viewed by villagers as resistance to colonial authority, but as a challenge and threat to the community.

When Lucas Cano, the *enterador* from Layo, and his son Juan, a *cédula*, slipped away from Potosi before finishing their service, community officials had their goods, including over seven hundred sheep, twenty cows, and some seventy-five llamas, embargoed. Then Lucas, his wife, and two of his sons were jailed. In spite of Cano's accounts of abuse, community officials argued that Cano had "abandoned the people that were his responsibility whom he ought to have restored to the pueblo and from whose abandonment new responsibility and delay in the collection of tributes can result, inasmuch as those dispersed Indians perhaps may not return to their pueblo. Cano is accustomed to fleeing the Potosi *mita* as he did now some years ago, that when named *cédula* he fled without completing his time."[128]

With a history of fleeing, Cano's tale of abuse was not believed. Cano and members of his family escaped from jail twice. The first time they not only put up resistance but were aided by members of the neighboring community of Langui. The peoples of Langui and Layo were often at odds with one another, so it was not surprising that they might help someone avoid the "justice" of Layo. It was somewhat ironic, however, because just a year earlier the people of Langui had brought charges against one of their *enteradores*, Matias Aquino, for fleeing Potosi with all but one of the *mitayos* under his supervision. Aquino claimed that he and the others had fled due to excessively harsh labor demands and difficult conditions. Aquino declared that it was "too much work that caused us to give up, as we did not rest, not even an instant, even though working with our wives and children while not completing [the quota] of our day's work and recently we found ourselves in a state of perishing without having anything to eat."[129] Juan Apasa, the *mitayo* who remained in Potosi, claimed that Aquino had acted in bad faith as *enterador*, while others testified that Aquino had influenced people to leave. Another *enterador* who served after Aquino stated that he and the *mitayos* had been well treated and had been paid their travel monies. Others maintained that they had always been treated "with the utmost humanity and consideration" in the De La Cuesta refinery. Not only were they paid their *leguaje*, but they even had money advanced to them when needed by the operators of De La Cuesta.[130] It appears that Aquino and most of those under his supervision attempted to take advantage of the bad reputation of Potosi to cover their desire not to serve. The people of Langui disliked *mita* service, but they realized the necessity of fulfilling their obligation to the crown to maintain the community. Trusting their own face-to-face experience, their personal relations, they did not support what they considered to be the unwarranted complaints by those who wished to avoid what they all wished to avoid, but could not. By fleeing when conditions did not warrant such resistance, Aquino and the others had violated norms of conduct and placed an economic burden on the community. To keep the community out of difficulties with colonial authorities, the community brought charges against Aquino to force payment of the 378 pesos he and the others owed, which otherwise might fall on the community.[131]

In 1775 an *enterador* and *mitayos* from Coporaque also abandoned Potosi and returned to their community. Due to their good reputation, however, these *naturales* were treated quite differently by their *curacas*, Eugenio Sinanyuca and Roque Mollo. Two days before Christmas the *curacas* wrote to the corregidor that Bartolomé Garcia, *enterador*, and Gregorio Choquecota, *cédula*, had returned from Potosi without fulfilling their obligations and that they had been detained. When asked why they had fled, the *curacas* noted, they had experienced very bad whippings and affronts on the part of the head carpenter and other administrators of the refinery of Dn. Bernardo Zenda and that not being possible for them to endure such inhumane treatment they returned, obliged by the conservation of their lives to seek refuge, abandoning their pack llamas, their sleeping gear and their prebend of food; that a few days earlier for the same reason two other *cédulas* of the said *mita* did the same abandoning their wives and children: that when the women with their weeping [asked] said administrators not to mistreat thusly their husbands, they also mistreated them with blows, afterward locking them in a chapel, and that lately the cruelty of said administrators is so great that . . . they have forced the wives of these Indians to work in place of their husbands. The two aforementioned Indians, especially the *enterador*, are known in these *ayllus* for being of very good repute, for which reason we cannot presume that they have come back fleeing, but obliged by grave motives. . . . We assure Your Magesty that we received continual complaints . . . for some years from the captain *enteradores* and *cédulas* that return from said *mita* [and] they do not pay the *leguaje*, nor justly [pay] the daily wages and that they oblige them to work more than physically possible and as a result many Indians return with chest injuries and they die here then asthmatics, for this reason everyone has the greatest horror of said *mita*. Although we have tried to persuade the two Indians to return to complete their *mita* time they absolutely resist and we do not have [means] to remit them by force a distance of more than two hundred leagues. . . . Captains have also complained on other occasions of violence. . . . We implore Your Magesty . . . for a remedy of the referred excesses that we bear and for which we ask justice. . . .[132]

Like the people in Langui, the caciques of Coporaque trusted in their own and the community's face-to-face experiences. On this occasion, however, the community supported the assertions of their neighbors who were of good repute, especially because they had previous knowledge of the abusive treatment meted out by those to whom village *mitayos* were assigned. Corregidor Reparaz, known for his fair treatment of the *naturales*, asked officials in Potosi to end the abuses the *mitayos* suffered at the hands of those in the refinery of Bernardo Zenda, and he ordered Bartolomé Garcia and Gregorio Choquecota freed on bail.[133] Reparaz trusted the word of Sinanyuca and Molle, just as Sinanyuca and Molle trusted the word of their people. Because their face-to-face dealings created trust, the corregidor, *curacas*, and community member were able to work together to alleviate a difficult situation.

When such understanding relations did not exist, which was much of the time, the result of such conflicts could be very different. The "cacique of Surimana from 1750–1766, was bankrupted by the seizure of a train of mules and a hundred pesos' worth of goods because his *mita* quota was one man short."[134] The nephew of this unfortunate cacique, himself a *curaca*, sought to put an end to the *mita* that had so affected his uncle and the people he governed. The uncle was Marcos Thupa Amaro, and the nephew was José Gabriel Condorcanqui, better known as Thupa Amaro.

8

Rebellion, Cultural Redemption, and Thupa Amaro

Cuando los incendios no se apagan en los principios, suelen sus llamas consumir lo más distante. CORREGIDOR ANTONIO DE ARRIAGA

The tradition of all the dead generations weighs like a nightmare on the brain of the living. And just when they seem engaged in revolutionizing themselves and things, in creating something that has never yet existed, precisely in such periods of revolutionary crisis they anxiously conjure up the spirits of the past to their service and borrow from them the names, battle cries and costumes in order to present the new scene of world history in this time-honoured disguise and this borrowed language. KARL MARX, *The Eighteenth Brumaire of Louis Bonaparte*

HAVING determined that corregidor Antonio de Arriaga should be hanged, José Gabriel Thupa Amaro called on Antonio Lopez de Sosa, a trusted old friend and the *criollo* priest of Pampamarca, to inform the corregidor of his fate. Handing Arriaga a picture of Christ, the priest conveyed the sentence of death. On 10 November 1780, Arriaga, dressed in a penitential habit, was led to the gallows in Tungasuca. The corregidor asked Thupa Amaro's pardon for once having called him a "fraudulent Indian." Then Antonio Oblitas, a shoemaker and former slave of the corregidor who had been selected to be the executioner, carried out the Inca's order and hanged Arriaga.

The indigenous residents of Tungasuca looked on in near disbelief as the corregidor was executed and the insurrection made public. The use of a penitential habit and the presence of priests added to the formality and "legality" of the situation, as Arriaga was shorn of the symbols of power and the rebels then dressed Arriaga "in sackcloth and ashes and as [in?] the penitential habit of the Franciscans, [which] was a visible effort to gain the support of the people also." The hanging only enhanced Thupa Amaro's already considerable authority and mystique among those who witnessed the ceremony and execution.[1]

The capture and execution of Antonio de Arriaga was the opening salvo of the Thupa Amaro rebellion that swept like wildfire across the southern Andes in late 1780. Although not openly separatist, Thupa Amaro envisioned broad changes and reforms that he must have known would be unacceptable to viceregal officials. The colonial government might tolerate the execution of a corregidor, particularly one such as Arriaga who had been abusive and excessive, without resorting to reprisals. However, it would never accept the appropriation of the 22,000 pesos of tribute—the sweat and toil of Indians—that Thupa Amaro had taken from the Canas y Canchis treasury to initially fund the rebellion. Yet, at least publicly, Thupa Amaro took his actions in the name of the Spanish crown (see plate 7).

Even though *naturales* were experiencing increasing tensions, they were not necessarily disposed to rebel, or, if they rose up, to reject the king who was viewed as the ultimate arbiter of justice and as above the fray. Recognizing the strength of the ties between indigenous peoples and the Spanish monarch, Thupa Amaro launched his rebellion in the name of King Charles III to rid themselves, and the crown, of bad government. He sought to win support from those who would have hesitated or shied away had they seen their actions as part of an open rebellion against the king rather than against unjust authorities and laws. Even to the condemned Arriaga, the Inca claimed to have received royal orders for his execution.[2]

This chapter explores indigenous perceptions of the ties and reciprocal obligations that linked them to the state and their expectations of good governance in the context of escalating demands and tensions. It focuses on the erosion of legitimacy, especially at the face-to-face level. Behind these realities are the cultural efforts to assure the perpetuation of a way of life and their moral economy, which was being severely strained, and the rebirth of alternative cultural visions to guide their lives as colonial legitimacy withered.

One of the leading scholars of eighteenth-century rebellion in Peru, Scarlett O'Phelan Godoy, argues that the insurrection erupted in the southern Andes, because it was precisely in this region where "the colonial contradictions accumulated."[3] In Canas y Canchis and Quispicanchis indigenous traditions, though altered, still functioned to preserve strong communal identity. By the late eighteenth century, however, demographic revitalization, economic demands, and shortages of land had begun to erode the *naturales'* security. With their future uncertain, the contradictions of being both Indian and subjects of Spanish colonial rule were exacerbated. However, there were considerable obstacles to a united challenge to the escalating demands and increasingly difficult conditions of eighteenth century colonialism. Indigenous peoples were separated not only by their own cultures and ethnicities and by differences in regional economic and political circumstances but by language. The people near Cuzco were Quechua speakers, while those in the rebellious zones of Bolivia often spoke Aymara.

The execution of Arriaga, though it was Thupa Amaro's entrance onto the revolutionary stage, was not the first Andean upheaval of 1780. There were actually several uprisings that year, Thupa Amaro and his followers constituting the largest and most successful rebellious force. The movements that have been subsumed under the name of the Thupa Amaro rebellion were complex. They shared some characteristics, but their participants also had different agendas. In the province of Chayanta in upper Peru, fighting had broken out in August and September of 1780, a few months before the Cuzco insurrection, under the leadership of Tomás Catari. By January of 1781 he had been captured and executed. His brothers, Dámaso and Nicolás, assumed control of the rebellion, but they shortly met their brother's fate.

Even though the Chayanta and Thupa Amaro revolts had several factors in common, they differed significantly. Leon Campbell argues that there were "profound differences between neo-Inca nationalism as it was expounded by the elitist Túpac Amarus of Cuzco, whose purpose was to unite everyone who was not a Spaniard, and the radical, populist, and separatist views held by the commoner, indigenous Kataris of Upper Peru, whose ideas were shaped by the strong presence of native community leadership."[4]

Thupa Amaro sought to incorporate *criollos* to a much greater degree than did the movements in Upper Peru. The Chayanta rebels more often turned against their own *curacas* as well as the Spanish, and what resulted was an inner civil war as well as a rebellion against colonial rule. *Forasteros* added to the complexity of the ethnic composition of the Chayanta region and provided a basis of conflict with *originarios*. Spaniards also controlled considerable lands, in contrast to the home provinces of Thupa Amaro where there were relatively few *forasteros* or Spaniards, except in mines and the region of Quispicanchis closest to the city of Cuzco. After the defeat of the Catari brothers, Julián Apasa, better known as Túpac Catari (borrowing names from Túpac Amaru and Tomás Catari), emerged as the leader of indigenous rebel forces in the Aymara-speaking regions of upper Peru. Túpac Catari, though acting with a great deal of independence, accepted the Thupa Amaro family as leaders of the rebellion. However, by November of 1781 he too had met his end at the hands of colonial justice, and many of his followers had grown wary or tired of the movement.

Operating out of Quispicanchis and Canas y Canchis, Thupa Amaro barely survived seven months after initiating the rebellion. He, his wife, and other family members and rebels were executed in a most brutal fashion in the plaza of Cuzco on 18 May 1781. Parts of their bodies were sent throughout the region to serve as grim reminders of the consequences of rebellion to others who might consider rising against Europeans. But the insurrection did not die with its leader, as the rebellious forces continued the struggle under the control of the Inca's cousin, Diego Cristóbal Thupa Amaro. The rebels fought on, but as the situation grew more desperate they eventually accepted the viceroy's offer of pardon. By early 1782 the reins of empire were firmly back in Spanish hands; thousands had died, however, and the viceroyalty had been shaken to its foundations.

During the rebellion many of the more alienated or radicalized *naturales,* a distinct minority in the Cuzco region but somewhat more prevalent in Chayanta- and Aymara-speaking zones, wanted to rid the Andes of all peoples who were not indigenous. Europeans and Africans as well as those of mixed descent were to be driven out or exterminated. They wanted an indigenous world with indigenous rulers who would follow "indigenous" ways. There were to be no more *puka kunka* or "red necks," as the Spanish derisively were known. In addition to the demonization of Spaniards, much hate was also evidenced toward blacks, who, though often slaves, were many times in positions of power over *naturales* as servants and overseers of Europeans.[5] Mestizos and Indians living as non-Indians—*cholos*—were also looked on disdainfully by those who wanted to return to an indigenous world.

Other *naturales* may have harbored certain sentiments or prejudices of these more alienated Indians. However, most had a much less radical vision in mind and acted with greater moderation toward the "other." They did not seek to drive from their world everyone who was not Indian. Thupa Amaro, though a descendant of the Incas, was a mestizo with many mestizo and *criollo* friends. He did not share the intense prejudices against non-Indians of the more radicalized *naturales.* He had his own vision of the world to be created, and it included people other than *naturales.* However, the times in which he lived meant that even his moderate vision threatened to turn this world upside down.

Over the course of the eighteenth century the Bourbon monarchs of Spain, like other European colonial rulers, sought to exert greater control over their colonies and to make the colonies yield increased revenues. Indigenous peoples had long been subject to a variety of exactions such as tribute and forced labor. However, in the quarter century or so preceding 1780 new demands were added to the older burdens. The communities of Quispicanchis and Canas y Canchis were hard hit by imperial policies. Tax collection was made more efficient, and the *reparto* (forced distribution and sale of goods by the corregidor to Indians, and sometimes to Spaniards and mestizos) was legalized. The situation was further complicated in 1776 with the division of the viceroyalty of Peru and the creation of the new viceroy-alty of Río de la Plata, which disrupted trading patterns and economic life in the southern Andes. Tensions also increased when the *alcabala*, or sales tax, was raised and a number of items *naturales* produced became subject to the tax for the first time. These changes, added to traditional demands such as the Potosi *mita* and tribute and made even more acute by demographic resurgence, weakened the social glue that secured the relationship of the *naturales* to colonial society. As the situation deteriorated increasing numbers of indigenous peoples, and some Europeans, began to question the legitimacy of those who governed.

None of the economic factors was significant enough on its own to incite rebellion, but forming a conjuncture they created the basis of a growing crisis that affected the colonial economy and the indigenous communities. O'Phelan refers to these economic changes and demands as "the feather that broke the camel's back," arguing that "if the Bourbon fiscal reforms had not been applied with such rigor in this region, the great rebellion probably would not have broken out, or, in any case, it would not have manifested itself with the same intensity."[6]

Repartos, Revolts, and Moral Reckonings

There were indications that the changing conditions were having an impact. The number of violent incidents between colonial officials and communities grew rapidly in the mid–eighteenth century and peaked in the decade before Arriaga was hanged. These outbreaks took two forms: revolts and rebellions. Rebellions normally encompassed larger regions and had internal organization or planning. They lasted for days, weeks, or even months. The state or church—the system of rule—as well as individuals were attacked. Many non-Indians participated, particularly in leadership roles. And the punishment of leaders tended to be harsh and extensive. Smaller, more constrained incidents, commonly referred to as the revolts or tumults, were quite different. As those William Taylor studied in Mex-

ico, they tended to be local in character, spontaneous, of short duration, directed against individuals, and sought to maintain or restore
an existing order or end abusive treatment. They were the form of
violence *naturales* engaged in most typically, and the participants
were usually not punished harshly.[7]

Like a fire bell in the night, the growing levels of violent protest
should have alerted colonial officials with access to information from
all parts of Peru that exactions were amiss and needed to be changed,
but this was not the case. Escalating protests triggered relatively
little response at the macro level among elite viceregal authorities,
and demands continued to escalate or were enforced with increasing
efficiency. Viceroy Manuel de Amat y Juniet was an exception. He
warned that if the harsh policies of debt collection continued it
would not be "possible to maintain order in the pueblos."[8] He was
joined by *visitador* Antonio de Areche, who understood the potential
for social disorder stemming from excessive or abusive behavior. He
was, however, all too aware of the state's need for increased revenues.
While in Peru, Areche wrote to an associate in Mexico, "In Mexico
there is usually justice; here tyranny is common. . . . Peru is being ruined by the lack of honest judges, forced Indian labour and the forced
trade conducted by the district officers. The corregidores are concerned solely with their own interests. . . . Oh dear friend! how close
we are to losing everything here, unless these disgusting abuses are
corrected, because they have already continued far too long, and a
tragic end can be foreseen if a remedy is not provided. Here everything is private interest, nothing public good."

Areche saw the corruption in the system and understood that
people were being pressed too hard, but with imperial interests in
mind he too enhanced that pressure without correcting the ills. After
the rebellion the intendant of Cuzco, Benito Mata Linares, wrote that
"although many reasons had [been] given in an attempt to explain the
unrest in these provinces, he [Linares] shared the view which attributed it to the new taxes that Visitor Areche had tried to impose."[9]

Did the increased pressures and growing number of confrontations create a "climate of violence" in the communities? What was

the meaning of this increase in protest? The viceroyalty of Peru was divided into more than seventy provinces or *partidos*. Revolts were not distributed evenly throughout the realm; some provinces experienced a few incidents, but others had none. These protests were widely scattered.[10] Even at their peak an average of less than one violent incident per *partido* per decade occurred. For instance, in the decade that began in 1730 there were ten violent outbreaks, while in the decade of the 1760s there were twenty, and in the decade just before the rebellion there were sixty-six.[11] Quispicanchis and Canas y Canchis had less than ten such incidents in the eighteenth century prior to 1780. Even though my research has uncovered incidents not previously tabulated, viewed from the community level such violence was not common.[12] To understand the potential for a tumult or revolt, one might consider that in the provinces of Quispicanchis and Canas y Canchis there were twenty-one *doctrinas*, or parishes, not to mention related communities (*anexos*). Most *doctrinas*, in turn, had several *ayllus* from which tribute or *reparto* payments were collected. Tribute alone was collected twice a year. Add to these figures other demands, such as those for labor and personal service, as well as chance encounters or confrontation that might result in tensions, and then multiply these combined figures by ten for each decade. When looked at from this perspective, though the frequency of violence was increasing it certainly was not commonplace. In addition, while news of violence spread to nearby communities, the relative isolation of many of the communities, and the highly specific nature of the immediate causes that underlay many of the revolts, lessened the regional impact of, and the potential for broader collective action from, these protests.

When a tumult that stemmed from abusive or excessive behavior occurred in Quispicanchis or Canas y Canchis, the state usually sought to extinguish the conflict in a way that would not cause it to grow and become more dangerous. The justice system did not typically inflict harsh punishments on those who killed or attacked abusive officials. Brutal or excessive behavior by authorities threatened the existing order by bringing into question the protective justice and the legitimacy of the crown. When a cruel overlord was assaulted, the relatively light punishment often meted out to the assailants was one way viceregal authorities tried to preserve the colonial order, and, perhaps, indirectly warn lower officials to curb their excesses.

The revolts that rocked communities in Quispicanchis and Canas y Canchis prior to 1780 stemmed from a variety of causes but were almost always sparked by some precipitating incident rather than being planned. Hence, instead of constituting a climate of violence it is more appropriate to speak of a climate in which violent protests were more likely to occur—a significant difference. The *reparto* was a factor in some revolts, but the distribution of goods and the collection of *reparto* debt was often carried out in conjunction with the collection of tribute or with other festivities, making it unclear as to what degree the *reparto* was the principal factor in such violence or complaints against officials or the state.

Stolen *reparto* goods were sometimes encountered in markets as thieves tried to sell their booty, indicating that the informal market was not saturated with *reparto* items, at least at non-*reparto* prices. Likewise, more luxurious *reparto* goods, such as silk and fine European cloth items, were passed on in wills, particularly of richer Indian women. Of the few cases encountered with specific complaints about the *reparto*, two involved "Don Joseph Thumpa (Thupa) Amaro," *cacique principal y governador del Pueblo de Pampamarca*. A *cobrador* for Corregidor Gregorio de Viana had, as part of the *reparto*, charged the future rebel leader fifty pesos six reals for two and a half *arrobas* of iron, but Thupa Amaro complained that he never received the iron. In another incident Corregidor Pedro Muñoz de Arjona jailed the *curaca* for twelve days due to a *reparto* dispute.[13] Thus, the future rebel leader may have had even stronger animosity against the *reparto* than most.

The *reparto* then, though resented, was not necessarily the direct cause of widespread violence in the upper Vilcanota, but it was a contributing factor to a general heightening of tensions for several reasons. The *reparto* was not new when it was legalized in the mid–eighteenth century. In 1689 the priest of Quiquijana wrote that the corregidors of Quispicanchis were "distributing by force, with all violence, mules, and clothes—from Castile as well as local—at exorbitant and excessive prices; proceeding in their collection with great pressure, and rigor, and for this reason they [the Indians] are destroyed, poor, and reduced to nothing, without having anything to eat, nor with which to be able to sustain themselves."[14]

After 1720 the *reparto* system "appears to have been expanding."[15] By the time of its legalization in the 1750s it was already a well-known, if disliked, institution. The *reparto* rates for the *naturales* in Quispicanchis and Canas y Canchis were, however, among some of the lowest in the Andes (5.1 to 10 pesos per capita), other provinces being subjected to *repartos* 50 to 100 percent higher.[16] *Reparto* prices were, nonetheless, often double or triple the market price. For instance, Castillian cloth that had a market price of five pesos had a list (*arancel*) price of seven pesos four reals and a *reparto* price of sixteen pesos. A basket of coca went respectively—market, list, *reparto*—for four pesos, eight pesos four reals, and twelve pesos, while mules had a market price of eleven pesos and a list and *reparto* price of thirty-five pesos.[17] Items such as coca, iron, and certain domestic and imported cloth were useful but certainly not desired at *reparto* prices.

Mules were a major *reparto* item, Canas y Canchis and Quispicanchis being forced to receive 2,000 and 2,500 mules, respectively, in every *reparto*.[18] Other items, such as razors, books, and fine cloth were of questionable, if any, use to most people. Thupa Amaro complained that a knife of inferior quality that normally cost one real sold for a peso in the *reparto*.[19]

Each corregidor was allowed to make one distribution of goods worth a total fixed value during his five-year term of office, but many conducted multiple *repartos* at values far in excess of the established schedule. A Quispicanchis priest gave this account of the *reparto* in his community:

Right after the corregidors arrive in any town of their province, they send their servants to the *alcaldes* and *alguaciles* so that they will, from house to house and hacienda to hacienda, notify Spaniards and Indians [of whom they have a list] to come and present themselves in front of them to get the *repartimiento*, and their cashiers distribute them not the items that they have asked for but whatever they want to give them, without even telling them nor negotiating the prices with them, they give them the bundles and write down the amounts owed. They [corregidors] break the tariffs set by law, that having been told that [the *repartimiento*] should not be more than a hundred forty thousand pesos, mules and clothes included, in this province of Quispicanche during their five years in office, it is well known that one distributed more than three hundred thousand pesos, and that this could not have been possible without excessively charging provincial Indians and Spaniards. The source of this is that the tariff is assigned by province and then nobody knows how much each of the villages in the *repartimiento* have to be allocated.[20]

In 1766 the priest of Checa and Canas y Canchis likewise argued that the corregidor had distributed some 300,000 pesos worth of goods, even though the *arancel* was 112,500 pesos.[21] Corregidor Arriaga, accused by Thupa Amaro of making three *repartos* instead of the one permitted and of collecting a total of some 300,000 pesos instead of the assigned *arancel*, certainly was not the first corregidor of Canas y Canchis to distribute goods far in excess of the legal limit.[22] Arriaga's fate, however, was sealed more by his own character and by the fact that in 1780 conditions were worse and the *naturales* were harder pressed.

These harsher conditions led tolerable but difficult (and sometimes illegal) demands to be increasingly perceived as excessive and intolerable. As changing circumstances made it more difficult for *naturales* to meet exactions, the state officials who enforced the demands were increasingly perceived as excessive and abusive. Indeed, *abusos y excesos* was the term used in legal documents to describe the actions of individuals who exceeded the understood cultural and legal limits that guided acceptable behavior.

When the degree of *abusos y excesos* was severe enough to not only transgress the *naturales'* sense of justice but their limits of tolerance, the legitimacy that a state representative enjoyed was stripped away, leaving the offending individual subject to attack. The personal fortunes of the corregidor were linked to the *reparto*, for profits went to him and his backers, not to the state. Therefore, there was very strong incentive for the corregidor to make sure the *reparto*, legal and illegal, was strictly enforced. In this situation the harsher character of some individuals may have led to attacks on their person, while others who were enforcing similar demands and confronting similar problems were not assaulted.

The collection of *reparto* debts was a factor in several violent outbursts in Cuzco, including deaths of officials in Pomacanchis, Cacha, and Quiquijana.[23] The case of a *cobrador* in Cusipata (near Quiquijana), who was killed after trying to collect tribute, at first glance appears to be an attack or protest against tribute, but when looked at carefully the incident seems less a protest against colonial demands than a lashing out against an especially abusive official.

In 1774 don Carlos Ochoa, a mestizo *cobrador*, went to collect the tribute owed by Lucas Poma Inga, the cacique of Cusipata. Ochoa, along with his brother and several associates, arrived at the house of Poma Inga and confronted the cacique. Poma Inga could only pay sixty pesos of the tribute owed and offered the *cobrador* a note for the remainder. Though Poma Inga was known for being reliable in meeting his obligations, this was not good enough for Ochoa, who had a reputation for ferocity. The *cobrador* and his friends hauled Poma Inga from his home, tied him up, beat him with a whip, and took him to Ochoa's home where the cacique was again beaten and then locked in a storage room. Those who saw the cacique said he had been severely abused, and a doctor and a scribe later testified that he was "very badly beaten over all of his body, the head, and stomach by fists, clubs, and kicks with spurs." Caciques from Quiquijana also confirmed this description.

In desperation Poma Inga's wife, whom the *cobrador* had also assaulted, asked the priest to intervene on her husband's behalf. The priest told her that Ochoa was "a very fearsome man and that he was not able to intervene with him," but after a second request from the desperate woman the priest wrote a note to Ochoa. The *cobrador* not only ignored the message but verbally abused the person who delivered it. Seeing that their cacique was in very bad shape and fearing for his life, the people of Poma Inga's *ayllu* decided to rescue him "for the great love [they had] for their cacique." At night they broke into Ochoa's house, removed Poma Inga, and killed Ochoa for having treated their cacique badly and with "ignominy." Antonio Acuña, a tributary who served the priest, stated that at about eight in the evening there had been a great disturbance in the street, and the priest had ordered the door of the church to be closed and barred. He and the priest passed a restless night in the church, and in the morning they opened a window and received the news that Ochoa had been killed. Acuña and the priest went to the *cobrador*'s house and found his body on the floor "amid many stones."

After the incident the priest cared for Poma Inga, who was "almost without movement," in the church and later testified both to his good character and to the bad character of the *cobrador*. Other people of European descent also supported the actions of the community. Pascual Antonio de Loayza, a muleteer returning from the Coporaque livestock auction, stated that he knew Poma Inga well, considered him a friend, and also knew that he was well respected by his *ayllu*. He had seen Ochoa and his associates beating the *curaca* and had observed Poma Inga's condition while locked up. Andres de Acosta, another Spanish muleteer, testified similarly. It was also reported that Poma Inga, even after being beaten, told his people "not to riot and to try to calm themselves."

The corregidor also summoned caciques from Quiquijana and took testimony, but no action was taken by the state or any of its representatives against those involved in Ochoa's death. In view of the excesses committed, the incident was either viewed as a provocation by the *cobrador*, or it was deemed unwise to punish community members given the circumstances.

Although Ochoa was a *cobrador*, the people of Poma Inga's *ayllu* killed him not because of this but because he was abusive. His abuses delegitimized his authority. They went beyond the bounds that gov-

erned Indian-Spanish relations in the colonial world. Neither the
naturales nor the Europeans saw the killing as a challenge to colonial
authority as a system. Violence was not directed at other representatives of the state or at Europeans in general, and it did not go beyond
the borders of the community. After the incident Cusipata settled
into its former routine, its moral economy restored.[24]

As the case of Ochoa indicates, at the local level *naturales* perceived and acted on differences in the behavior of individuals. Face-
to-face relations were important in determining the course of events.
For instance, Juan Antonio Reparaz, a corregidor of Canas y Canchis, dealt fairly with the *naturales* he governed in the day-to-day
matters that came before him. He even donated thirteen thousand
pesos out of his own funds to build bridges for certain communities,
including Tinta, the provincial capital of Canas y Canchis where Arriaga was executed, after his term as corregidor ended. This was done
"to facilitate safe transit," according to indigenous leaders of Tinta
who urged the completion of the project after its disruption by the
rebellion, because people often drowned and goods were lost while
fording the river.[25] It does not follow that the system Reparaz was
enforcing was just. Indeed, his contribution toward the bridge most
likely came from his profits in the *reparto*. His treatment of the
people of Canas y Canchis, however, was perceived as fair within the
context of an increasingly exploitative system.[26] Thus, the colonial
norms of behavior and understanding—the groundwork of the moral
economy—were maintained, making violent confrontation between
naturales and Reparaz unlikely.

The majority of corregidors in Quispicanchis and Canas y Canchis were not as considerate as Reparaz. Excessive or new demands,
violations of traditional arrangements, or treatment that transgressed
normative behavior strained or ruptured Indian-corregidor relations.
In 1767 Corregidor Muñoz de Arjona worsened the conditions of villagers in Pichigua and Yauri when he ordered them to transport
dried llama dung to the silver mines of Condoroma. Several of the
people obliged to serve this *mita* had previously hauled llama dung,
burnt in the refining process, to the mines and had also transported

metals from the mines to earn money, some of which undoubtedly was used to meet state demands. However, under the corregidor's new orders the burden on the *naturales* was increased, and community members were no longer free to decide if they wished to earn money transporting dung up to the cold and windswept mines of Condoroma. Moreover, mine owners now compensated these forced laborers with coca, clothes, food, and silver, but not exclusively with the much needed silver as previously had been the case. This made it more difficult for people in Pichigua and Yauri to meet other state exactions. It should come as no surprise that Muñoz de Arjona had business dealings with Condoroma miners (although so did Thupa Amaro). It was in his own interest to assure the supply of llama dung and a flexible system of payment.[27]

Differences between colonial officials, the ways they were perceived, and the responses they evoked were apparent in Thupa Amaro's attitude toward the last four corregidors who governed Canas y Canchis prior to the rebellion. While he grew increasingly impatient with the system the corregidors enforced, he clearly recognized differences between individual corregidors. Of these four men Thupa Amaro disliked two, had mixed feelings about one, and "got along well" with the other. Corregidor Gregorio de Viana "harassed him greatly with the *repartimiento*" and treated him badly in business dealings. The next corregidor, Muñoz de Arjona, confirmed him as *curaca* of Pampamarca, Surimana, and Tungasuca, something that Viana had not done. Muñoz de Arjona and Thupa Amaro coexisted in harmony for a while, but when the corregidor jailed the *curaca* over a dispute with a *cobrador*, the relationship soured. Thupa Amaro "got along well" with the next corregidor, Reparaz. In commenting on how the actions of Reparaz influenced him, the rebel leader informed captors that "the rebellion had been thought of for many years, but he had not determined to rebel because Corregidor Reparaz, Arriaga's predecessor, had treated him very well and looked on the Indians with compassion."[28] Thupa Amaro had been swayed by the actions of an individual corregidor to set aside the idea of rebellion against the colonial state. Personal relations and behavior had made a difference. However, Thupa Amaro did not hold a similar opinion of the next corregidor, Arriaga.

Although efforts to end abusive treatment and restore less exploitative relations explain much of the violence that dotted the social landscape of rural Peru, the causes of such events were complex. Those in power sometimes found themselves in danger for reasons not directly related to their own actions, as misinterpretations, quick tempers, and fears led to confrontational situations. Officials also took advantage of fiestas to inform communities of demands, to distribute *reparto* merchandise, or to collect debts. Such actions provided a provocation at a time of community solidarity and sometimes triggered violent responses.

The proclivity to violence in these situations was increased by the consumption, often ritual, of alcohol. In Quispicanchis and Canas y Canchis *chicha* and *aguardiente* lessened inhibitions and allowed anger and aggravations to surface that otherwise might have remained repressed.[29] Though such violence was usually spontaneous, the relationship of alcohol to violence was not always innocent. Alcohol was sometimes used to encourage and provoke extreme conduct, such as when in 1765 workers in the *obraje* of Pichichuro (*partido* of Abancay, Cuzco) testified that they had planned an uprising in the *obraje*. The extent of the plan appears to have been to ask for their corn ration in advance so they could sell it and use the earnings to buy *chicha* to give them courage for the rebellion.[30]

In 1768 alcohol was also involved in a disturbance in Coporaque when the corregidor tried to replace one cacique, don Cristóbal Sinanyuca, with another, Eugenio Sinanyuca. The *naturales* of *ayllu* Collana, who had been under the guidance of don Cristóbal, refused to allow the formal investiture of Eugenio and instead, shouting and using their slings, disrupted the ceremony and attacked those who were preparing to offer Mass as part of Eugenio's installation. Those who participated in these actions, not all of the *ayllu* by any means, had been drinking *chicha* and *aguardiente* and chewing coca at the house of don Cristóbal for at least three days prior to the violence.

The cacique provided them with most of the alcohol they drank and the coca they chewed and had encouraged resisting the investiture of his successor. Under the influence of alcohol and chewing coca, which promoted ritual group solidarity and was encouraged by don Cristóbal—himself notorious for his "public and continual drunkenness"—some community members reacted with violence.

Don Cristóbal had previously abandoned the community and had only returned a few days before the new cacique was to take office. It was because of his absence, his frequent inebriation, and his neglect of duty that he had been removed from office. Some people of *ayllu* Collana feared that don Eugenio, who was described by a member of another *ayllu* as having a character admirable in its "formalidad, onra y juicio," who was known never to get drunk (not drink sufficiently in times of ritual?), and who got along well with Spaniards, would try to collect the back tribute (*rezagos*).

Inebriated and uncertain about the new cacique, some *ayllu* members tried to prevent don Eugenio from assuming office. The violence quickly subsided, and Eugenio was installed as *curaca*. Although several community members active in the tumult were identified, the government only brought charges against the former cacique and two others. Once the new cacique was in office his presence was not a source of problems in the community. In fact, don Eugenio became one of the more active *curacas* from the region in protesting the *mita* and its abuses, and he had some success in protecting his people. Perhaps it was partly for this reason that when the Thupa Amaro rebellion broke out and Eugenio Sinanyuca remained loyal to the crown, so did most of the people under his rule.[31]

Even though these provincial revolts were not directed at the colonial system and did not in and of themselves create a climate of violence, they heralded the coming Thupa Amaro rebellion. They reflected the increasing stress communities were experiencing. The threshold of aggravation lowered as *naturales* became ever more desperate in their effort to preserve their way of life. Nevertheless, to the extent that the pre-1780 revolts remained indigenous in character, they sought more to restore or maintain a disintegrating order than to destroy the colonial system itself. Until the *naturales* believed their social reproduction was threatened, open rebellion was unlikely. [32]

A Conjuncture of Crises

To observant high-level authorities the protests and tumults of the late 1770s must have appeared to be hydra-headed. No sooner was one situation dealt with than another appeared. However, the authorities focused much of their attention on urban turmoil rather than on the countryside. Many of these tensions were rooted in the crown's efforts to increase colonial revenues. In 1772 the sales tax (*alcabala*) was increased from two to four percent, and in 1774 *aduanas* or custom houses were established in the Cochabamba region.[33] Compliance with the new *alcabala* was uneven, but in Cochabamba rioting caused enforcement of the new tax to be halted. The Cochabamba disturbances were the first major Andean response to the economic policies initiated in the 1770s that would later cause rioting or conflict in many places, including La Paz, Arequipa, and Cuzco.

Despite resistance to the 1772 increase, four years later the crown once again raised the sales tax, this time to six percent. To put teeth into this and other new measures, José Antonio de Areche was named *visitador general* (visitor general). In July of 1776, the same month that the *alcabala* was increased a second time, an *aduana* was ordered to be constructed in La Paz. Shortly thereafter Upper Peru was transferred out of the viceroyalty of Peru and incorporated into the new viceroyalty of Río de La Plata. Thus, "1776 was . . . a crucial year in the growth of social unrest which reached its climax in 1780."[34]

The 1776 *alcabala* affected items produced by *naturales* that had previously been exempt from the taxation—*chuño, charqui* (dried meat), *ají,* and cloth woven in indigenous *chorillos* for example—as well as other goods such as grains, leather, cotton, tobacco, sugar, and *aguardiente.* In 1779 even coca was subjected to the tax. These new charges impacted a wider segment of the indigenous population than was readily apparent, for after the *reparto* was legalized in the 1750s indigenous "trading of local products such as coca, textiles, cotton, chili and other items" increased to meet the new demands.[35] These changes were also felt by muleteers such as Thupa Amaro or Julián Apasa (Túpac Catari), many of whom were *naturales* or who employed *naturales*.

Just months before Arriaga was executed royal authorities discovered sedition in Cuzco—the Farfán or Silversmith conspiracy. One of the plotters indicated that "Cuzco was in such a state of unrest mainly because of the *Aduana*, and that many *chapetón* [Spaniard] gentlemen and lawyers [clerks?] were planning to revolt . . . and were assembling in order to prevent the establishment of a Custom House and the collection of new taxes."[36] Demonstrating their awareness of regional events, the conspirators argued that "if the *Aduana* were abolished, all the unrest would cease, as it had in Arequipa." Thupa Amaro was certainly sympathetic to these concerns. Just prior to the insurrection he was being pressed by customs officials for a debt of some three hundred pesos stemming from his business activities.[37]

The Farfán conspirators were, for the most part, *criollos*. However, they recognized the need for additional support, including that of *naturales* and Bernardo Tambohuacso Pumayali, a cacique from Pisac who was implicated in the conspiracy. Having agreed that an alliance was needed to challenge royal authority, the Farfán conspirators advocated a variety of reforms. For the *naturales* tribute and the *reparto* would be terminated, and for others the *aduana* and the 6 percent sales tax would be eliminated. Farfán had doubts about the participation of *naturales* in the rebellion, especially if *criollos* were not fully committed, but Tambohuacso argued that he could supply people "who would be eager to fight under his command . . . and that other caciques were equally willing to participate." The plot was discovered, and Farfán and the others, including Tambohuacso, were hanged. Upon learning the cacique's fate, Thupa Amaro was reported to have commented that "he did not understand how the Indians could have let it happen."[38]

The Farfán plot shook the sleep from the eyes of colonial authorities. One of them observed that "since Cuzco was the capital of the

Viceroyalty[?], the heart of the noble Indians' settlement, and refuge for numerous common people, it could be the province most likely to act as a model for others to follow, and therefore, if Cuzco was not effectively crushed, there could be little doubt that general unrest would spread uncontrolled."[39]

Such sentiments were late in coming. The Bourbon reforms had disaffected a wide segment of colonial society, including *criollos*, mestizos, Indians, and even some people of African ancestry. This was particularly true of those involved in trade, such as merchants, hacendados, and muleteers. Thupa Amaro, after all, was an *arriero* with some 350 mules. In the course of his work he became familiar with regions and peoples as distant as Potosí and Lima. Among those who joined the Inca in rebellion were several fellow muleteers and traders from the Canas y Canchis region, some of whom were also relatives as well as colleagues such as Pedro Mendigure of Pomacanchis, Francisco Noguera and Francisco Túpac Amaru of Surimana, and Juan Túpac Amaru of Tungasuca.[40]

Once the insurrection was ignited, Thupa Amaro staffed his command with many creoles and mestizos: "Of the forty-two persons holding the most important military titles, sixteen were designated as *españoles*, a social classification including both Spaniards and Creoles; seventeen were mestizos; and nine were considered Indians. Clearly, the Túpac Amaru rebellion was not directed by a network of loyal caciques, since only six caciques, four of whom were mestizos, including Túpac Amaru, were in the military high command."[41]

Despite a leadership structure that was largely nonindigenous, *naturales* adhered to the rebellion. Thupa Amaro and his family were at the very head of the movement. Though mestizos by birth, they were viewed by their neighbors as indigenous because of the Inca heritage. Who, after all, could be more Indian than the Inca and his family! Relying on his stature as an Inca, Thupa Amaro was able to mobilize *naturales* not only in Canas y Canchis and Quispicanchis but in more distant regions where the return of the Inca awakened powerful sentiments. It was precisely his ability to appeal to different segments of society, wearing different hats for each one, that made it possible for Thupa Amaro to bring together disparate forces that had little more in common than their antipathy toward the burdens of colonial rule. Tensions within this fragile coalition quickly came to the fore, as the spectre of race war emerged from the revolutionary violence. Many *criollos* were ready to question royal authority, but they shied away when indigenous rebels vented their anger by slaughtering people of European descent.[42]

Not just *criollos* and mestizos remained cool to the rebellion. Many *naturales* remained neutral or even fought for the crown. Royal exactions may have been increasingly excessive, but when confronted with the insurrection a large percentage of the indigenous population hesitated in making common cause. Even in other Cuzco provinces, few *naturales* were willing to risk their lives taking up arms against royal officials and colonial society, let alone the king.

The Colonial Glue Comes Unstuck

Governmental exactions and stricter enforcement of policies contributed to a growing indigenous malaise that weakened the ties between *naturales* and the colonial order. These tensions, however, in combination with demographic resurgence, also produced fissures between indigenous peoples and communities.

In 1719–1720 the pandemic that swept the Andes worked to its deadly conclusion in rural Cuzco. Between 1682 and 1702 deaths in Ccatcca, a community near the Paucartambo-Quispicanchis border, averaged between 20 and 25 per year. In 1720, between June and August, 469 people died. After this nobody recorded the mortalities, because the priest and those in charge of the major *cofradías* had died.[43] The community of Quiquijana suffered similar devastation. The epidemic raged for nearly half a year, after which it was reported that "there are very few people in the pueblo, for which cause all the plantings of maize and wheat, potatoes, and other vegetables have been lost, not having people to harvest them. They have also lost the royal tributes because of the death of the Indians and . . . caciques."[44]

In the wake of this devastation, communities often rented out or sold off land, because they needed silver to meet colonial demands or they lacked sufficient human resources to work their fields. Other communities had their lands sold by the state after *originarios* were recounted to update tribute and labor quotas, as the government looked to profit from holdings deemed to be in excess of communal needs. The government, keeping village needs in mind, reserved what were considered to be sufficient lands for the tributaries, the old, the children, the handicapped, the *cofradías*, and other community needs including natural growth. However, the communities and the government were unprepared for the unprecedented population revitalization following the eighteenth-century pandemic. The birth records of Ccatcca give an indication of the skyrocketing growth, births rising from twenty in 1731 to being consistently over one hundred by the 1740s.[45]

The alienation of lands and increasing numbers of villagers meant that by midcentury some communities were already desperately short of lands. In 1745 the *naturales* of Andahuaylillas, one of the communities whose holdings had been reduced by governmental sale after the pandemic and recount, turned to the colonial courts for help. Supported by their corregidor, they demanded the return of their property. What had been thought to be sufficient lands for long into the future were no longer adequate to meet communal needs.[46]

From 1689 to 1786 population growth in Quispicanchis was 53.3 percent (16,700/25,931), while Canas y Canchis experienced a 103.4 percent (14,200/28,885) increase.[47] This resurgence is particularly significant coming on the heels of a disastrous epidemic and two centuries of little, or negative, population change. With the population burgeoning, Andahuaylillas was not alone in its need for more lands. Other communities—such as Layo, Langui, Marangani, and San Pedro de Cacha—also had been decimated by the 1719–1720 pandemic only to be gripped in the vise of population revitalization and state demands a few decades later.

These were not the only stresses that stemmed, at least in part, from population fluctuation. One of the most important aspects of a community's internal functioning was its reciprocal relationship with

TABLE 6. Population of Canas y Canchis in Late Colonial Period:
Originarios (O) and *Forasteros* (F)

	1728		1785		1796		1812	
Community	O	F	O	F	O	F	O	F
Sicuani	232	56	1003	95	1148	182	1162	446
Lurucache	167	83	175	1	193	22	179	29
Marangani	64	51	168	2	162	10	200	—
Cacha	93	83	430	1	541	5	445	1
Charrachapi	34	42	114	2	115	2	129	1
Tinta	149	—	371	4	409	2	441	10
Pampamarca	182	74	235	12	209	40	207	38
Combapata	152	38	196	—	218	4	241	16
Checacupe	121	106	135	67	235	1	211	3
Cangalla	27	2	368	2	497	3	368	22
Yanaoca	144	50	227	44	456	130	350	101
Coporaque	111	67	453	31	489	33	393	29
Ancocahva	47	51	222	16	271	16	172	14
Yauri	153	99	700	45	790	182	51	530
Pichigua	492	41	552	12	616	40	510	46
Checasupa	179	153	494	—	599	3	515	4
Languisupa	169	17	198	18	188	35	157	40
Layosupa	136	30	270	19	365	23	239	99
Canchis	1221	535	3195	186	3727	271	3583	566
Canas	1431	508	3116	185	3774	462	2987	683
Province	2652	1043	6311	371	7501	733	6570	1249
Total O & F	3695		6682		8234		7819	

Source: Luis Miguel Glave, *Vida símbolos y batallas. Creación y recreación de la communidad indígena. Cusco, siglos XVI–XX* (Lima, 1992), Cuadro 12, 110–111.

its *curaca*. In the Cuzco region many *naturales* of noble birth continued to exercise authority as ethnic lords late in the colonial period,
even if the "ethnicity" had been reduced to the community level.
These community leaders, like everyone else, were hit hard by the
plagues of 1719–1720. In Quiquijana almost all the officeholders died.
One witness reported to the corregidor that,

> don Francisco Niño, don Martin Tiraquimbo, don Melchor Gua-
> mansauni, don Thomas Ramos, and don Alonso Orcoguarana
> who were *caciques principales* and *governadores* of this pueblo are
> dead, they died in *la peste* . . . and of the same fate have died all the
> *segundos* and *mandones* like Francisco de Estrada who died without
> one member of his family remaining, and in the same manner
> Matheo Pichu with all his family, don Gavriel Cusigualpa, Agus-
> tín de Rado, don Ygenio Ninamalco and others, and don Blas
> Chinche who was *alcalde* with the said don Melchor Guaman-
> sauni, and those that were placed after by your mercy, Señor Cor-
> regidor, they also died, as did all the *regidores* and *ministros de jus-
> ticia*, and the only *mandones* that remain alive are don Miguel
> Quera and don Fernando Vitorino.[48]

The epidemic meant that the ranks of the traditional *curacas* were
diminished, leaving positions to be filled by family members or even
by people who were not from *curaca* families or even from the community.

Throughout the colonial period, as the economy and society
changed, so did the role and actions of curacas. Many became involved in trade and business. In rural Cuzco, as elsewhere, new situations tempted some caciques to abuse their position.[49] However,
traditional ties remained vitally important for most Cuzco indigenous leaders. Thupa Amaro was a prime example of a *curaca* who
functioned both as a regional trader and a protector of the people in
his *curacazgo*. Nonetheless, by the mid-eighteenth century there were
several cases in which the relationship between *curacas* and their
communities had soured to the point that community members

turned to the state to alleviate their problem. At the same time corre-gidors increasingly sought to replace ethnic leaders with *naturales* friendly to their interests, and in the wake of the epidemic there were divisions that could be exploited. In these situations community support could be very important in helping a *curaca* maintain his of-fice, another reason for the *curaca* to preserve good relations with his community.

One cacique who abused the people under his control was Santos Mamani of *ayllu* Lurucache. Even prior to being elevated to the po-sition of *curaca*, Mamani had been accused of mistreating people, and after being appointed over two dozen *naturales* signed a formal com-plaint protesting the abuse they received at the hands of the *curaca*. Not all community members opposed Mamani, but those who did argued that Mamani was not really one of them but "a *cholo*" whose parents were *forasteros*. A Spaniard testified to the same but stated that Mamani's father had also been a cacique, even though he should not have held the position due to being a *forastero*. The situation be-came further confused when another witness testified that Mamani's mother had been the daughter of a cacique, which could have served as the basis for his claim to the position. *Ayllu* members also denied Mamani's right to be cacique on the basis of not having served in of-fices that made him eligible for such a high position. They argued that Mamani never went as a "*cédula* to the Potosi mita [this] being a custom among us," nor did he fulfill other communal obligations. The *ayllu* complained that Mamani has "done us much harm [and] does not treat us as God orders":

> He tries to martyr us with whips, rocks, and clubs beating widows and married women like men. He encourages his wife, mother and son to kill us. To even say *buenos días* to him, it is necessary for one to approach him with *aguardiente*. . . . He takes the bread from out of our mouths. . . . Regarding the distribution of lands, we do not know if we have land to work or not. Whoever has sufficient *aguardiente* is owner of the lands, . . . his accountant . . . is a boy who knows nothing . . . and treats older men with disrespect. To

remedy this situation, we ask the great favor of Our Magesty that Don Juan Paulino de Andia be our *Casique Y Governador* in order that he put us all in peace and quietude and that we may not be like cats and dogs in one single *ayllu*.[50]

Mamani had been elevated to the position of *curaca* by Lima officials when he presented papers, claimed by the community to be false, supporting his right to be *curaca* during the absence of the *cacique principal*, Miguel Copa, who was in Potosi serving as the *mita* captain. Reparaz, the normally judicious corregidor of Canas y Canchis, was in office when Mamani presented his claim. Copa argued that Reparaz favored his rival who Copa referred to as this "*cholo baca* (*vaca* [cow]) Mamani." This dispute continued after Arriaga became corregidor. Lima officials, despite the irregularities and reports of beatings and assaults, upheld Mamani as *curaca*. Arriaga, however, sided with Lurucache against Mamani. Less than half a year before he was hanged, Arriaga informed his superiors that it was "necessary to apply opportune measures for the public tranquility because the community resists Mamani." To accomplish this Arriaga undermined Mamani's power by appointing two *ayllu* members trusted by the people of Lurucache, both from the Copa family, to serve as tax collectors.

After the 1780 rebellion the government replaced Mamani with a Spaniard named Francisco Martinez. Under Martinez, Mamani was given a dose of his own medicine. He was imprisoned and "slapped down" by Martinez for owing five reals and for being arrogant, having insisted that Martinez refer to him as king. However, the Spanish cacique did not limit his brutality to the unpopular Mamani, and when "Lorenzo Copa, a former cacique who was generally beloved in the community, attempted to defend an innocent man from the two hundred lashes ordered for him by Martinez. Martinez beat Copa so severely that he became paralyzed and later died. Many others were beaten . . . or whipped by Martinez and his subordinates."[51]

The people of Lurucache had not been allowed to select their own *curaca*. Instead, the state had appointed caciques, one Indian and one

Spanish, who were not community members. In the tensions that followed, the community divided, and even corregidors took opposite sides. Governmental meddling had created a complex and devisive situation, as neither of the appointed *curacas* treated *ayllu* members as they believed a *curaca* should treat his people or, as the people of Lurucache put it, "as God orders."

Conflicts between community and *curaca* were more frequent after the Thupa Amaro rebellion. *Curacas* who had strongly supported the rebellion were, not surprisingly, no longer in place. And the role of the indigenous nobility in the uprising caused authorities to look warily at the appointment of *curacas* who claimed Inca heritage. These were the very people who had previously commanded the most respect in the communities. Increasingly, non-Indians, as well as *naturales* from outside the community, were placed in vacant positions.[52]

The increase in colonial exactions before the uprising also put more pressure on *curacas,* because they could be held personally responsible for community debts. When vacancies occurred some of those who normally would have been selected as cacique found the position less attractive than might previously have been the case, while others were attracted to it for the wrong reasons.[53]

Therefore, the relationship between *curaca* and community was increasingly a point of tension in many communities. More villagers had to struggle to ensure that they had a *curaca* who treated them with the respect and concern that "God orders." However, while conflicts did exist between people and their *curacas* in Quispicanchis and Canas y Canchis, the problem was not as severe as in other regions. When problems did develop the people of the upper Vilcanota did not easily accept the deterioration of this linchpin position in their culture that was vital in assuring their way of life. When necessary they even turned to the state for help in preserving their reciprocal relationship with their *curaca,* and for the most part they were successful.

To divisions resulting from *curaca*-community tensions must be added still other causes of internal discord. *Originarios* were often at odds with *forasteros* who lived in their communities. Although there were fewer *forasteros* in Quispicanchis and Canas y Canchis than in many other regions of the Andes, they were still an important group. In the wake of the 1719–1720 pandemic, *forasteros,* who often rented lands from communities, were obliged to pay tribute. The rental of lands helped communities meet their own obligations, but as the population grew and land became more scarce, complaints about land rentals to *forasteros* increased. Likewise, with their new tribute burden, *forasteros* found it more difficult to meet community demands. As we have seen, tensions between *forasteros* and *originarios* were sometimes reflected in the less than cordial treatment afforded some *forasteros* who broke laws or offended communal values.

Intracommunity conflicts, involving different *ayllus* and *moieties* (halves—in the Andes these halves were *hanansaya* [upper] and *hurinsaya* [lower]), were also very much a part of life in the late eighteenth century. Sometimes these were ritualized conflicts such as the *tink(c)u* battles. However, in certain circumstances, such as those surrounding the death of Esteban Alfaro in Langui, ritual battle may have been used to settle personal grievances between individuals from different *ayllus*. Several *naturales* named Guaguamamani were implicated in the death of Esteban, and just the year before another Guaguamamani was involved in a death during a *tinku* battle.[54]

Further tensions developed between *hanansaya* and *hurinsaya,* and between *ayllus,* when the head *curaca* favored one group, particularly his *ayllu, moiety,* or family over others. Such favoritism was resented. Relatively common was the complaint of a Pomacanchi villager who noted that the oppression of the *curaca* had caused many people to flee the community, "in particular those of [his] *ayllu*."[55]

Tensions such as those relating to *curacas, forasteros, ayllus,* and *moieties* did not exist everywhere, at least at an intense level, yet they were fairly common. Often with deep roots and reinforced through daily experience, they led to serious rifts within communities. In this situation many of the internal tensions created by state demands were expressed along lines of internal division—inward—rather than against the state.

When communities did look outward, they frequently focused their attentions not on the state but on the lands of neighboring communities. In an effort to increase their resource base and comply with state demands, *naturales* invaded the fields and pastures of other communities. However, as we have seen, it was not just state policies but also rapid population growth that lay at the heart of land conflict in Quispicanchis and Canas y Canchis.

No wonder the worldview of villagers in Quispicanchis and Canas y Canchis was complex and contradictory. Demographic revitalization eroded their per capita resource base at the same time that state economic demands pressed them even more. When mid–eighteenth-century changes in political administration and economic policy were added to longer-term and structural changes, a conjuncture was produced in which the relations and assumptions that collectively guaranteed the existence of communities and *ayllus* came increasingly under doubt. By 1780 colonial policies that for more than two centuries had functioned to restrict the scope of ethnic identity, and which in the process exacerbated local and internal divisions within Indian society, had been so effective that some *naturales*, even in zones as traditional as Quispicanchis and Canas y Canchis, questioned their ability to culturally survive.

In this situation the power of the *curaca* and community opinion were not always strong enough to control the antisocial behavior of individuals such as Lucas Cahua of Coporaque. Cahua, an elderly Indian reserved from obligations, unilaterally extended his reservation to his son. When the cacique assigned Cahua's offspring to serve in Potosi, the son not only refused to go, but the cacique's house mysteriously burned. In addition, the elderly Cahua beat other community members, did not go to Mass, and threw rocks at other people's livestock and used his dogs to herd them, apparently with the idea of stealing the animals. The cacique summed up his attitude toward Cahua when he said he was an "indio de mal corazon" (a bad-hearted Indian).[56] It may well be that the *curaca* or the community had done something to alienate Cahua, or it could be that he just was an ornery man distanced from the others for no reason other than his own character. Alone, he was who he was—an eccentric old man—but Lucas Cahua was not alone. He was one of a small, but growing number of *naturales* who were part of a community, yet not a part of it. By not behaving within community norms and by treating community members as he did, Cahua was part of the internal transition that could lead down the road from *indio* to *campesino*. Cahua may have been a product of colonial society, but to others in the community he, and those like him, were "de mal corazon." They threatened, and reflected a deterioration in, communal relations.

The Indigenous Glue Hardens

Similar ideas and circumstances often produced different, if not opposite, tendencies in individuals as well as in communities. Identification with the Incan heritage resonated with some indigenous peoples but not all. Longing for the return of the Incas was not new in the eighteenth century, but it reverberated with increasing strength. The desperate present made the rebirth of the past a source of hope as well as provided an alternative vision to the Spanish-dominated world. Throughout the colonial period there were those who believed in *Gran Paitití,* an Inca society in the jungle where survivors of Cuzco had fled and rebuilt after the Spanish conquest. A millenarian belief, that of *Inkarrí,* also grew after the collapse of Tawantinsuyu. According to *Inkarrí,* the Inca would return and bring order and justice to the world. In the late colonial period many *naturales* were attracted to the cultural renewal and identity offered by *Gran Paitití* and *Inkarrí.* However, as Alberto Flores Galindo warned, one should not see in *Inkarrí* and *Gran Paitití* "a mechanical response to colonial domination." Flores Galindo also noted that although in the eighteenth century such ideas were widespread, they were not continuous and were probably best thought of as "small islands and archipelagos."[57]

Identification of the Incan past as a more harmonious world stirred pride in some of the indigenous nobility. This is reflected in the colonial portraits of Inca nobles who chose to have themselves painted not in Spanish clothes, their everyday dress, but as Inca royalty. During the rebellion Thupa Amaro not only donned Incan apparel and symbols, such as a gold sun, but he and his wife, Micaela Bastidas, had themselves painted as an Inca royal couple.[58]

The collective memory of the Incan empire and its glories was enhanced, perhaps created, through the reading of Garcilaso de la Vega's *Royal Commentaries*. Indigenous nobles and peoples of European or mixed heritage pored over the work of this first generation mestizo who sought to redeem his mother's people. Again Flores Galindo informs us:

> *Comentarios Reales,* that book of Renaissance history, came to be read much as a pamphlet by figures such as Túpac Amaru, who took as emphatic denunciation the comparison of the Incas and the Romans, the criticisms of Viceroy Toledo, the veiled suggestion that a just and equitable empire ought to be reconstructed. Garcilaso turned the Inca era, Tawantinsuyo, into a golden age. The Inca believed the past could fill a moralizing function by offering models for the present: his historical conception was infected by utopia in the strictest European sense of the word. He was a Platonic historian. The eighteenth-century indigenous elite, which had easy access to Spanish language and to the printed word, understood this inner message of the book; they in turn, transported it orally to other social sectors. We know "a work by Garcilaso" accompanied Túpac Amaru in his travels.[59]

Though this growing consciousness or "Inca nationalism" was important, it is necessary "to maintain a clear distinction between the mass of the tributary population and the aristocracy of the caciques; both groups served part of the old tradition, but a different part."[60] However, even if the concern with Incan heritage was not *the* unifying factor for consciousness, it was important in the larger awareness that developed among certain *naturales*.

The Juan Santos Atahualpa rebellion in the central *montaña* region of Peru during the 1740s and early 1750s was strengthened by the belief that its leader was the returning Inca. Juan Santos claimed descent from the Inca Atahualpa, and, armed with a Jesuit education, he struggled to restore the Inca kingdom and to remove Europeans from the realm he and his followers controlled. When Juan Santos and his troops marched on the community of Andamarca, "the defense preparations organized by Andamarca's respectable 'citizens' fell apart. Only two shots were fired before an Indian voice shouted: 'This is our Inca, come over here.' Juan Santos then peacefully entered, marched toward the plaza, and accepted the homage of his new vassals. As a horrified eyewitness later recalled, the Indians and mestizos who betrayed Andamarca's defense 'kissed the Rebel's hands and feet.'"[61] The meaning of an Inca and acceptance of an Inca ruler had cultural resonance for the people of Andamarca.

Thupa Amaro sought to capitalize on the prestige of the Inca by being officially recognized as heir to his namesake who had been executed by Viceroy Toledo in 1572. Traveling to Lima, Thupa Amaro presented baptismal and marriage records to the *audiencia,* but the high court never ruled on the *curaca's* claim. While in Lima Thupa Amaro also sought exemption from the *mita* for the people in his *curacazgo* and for other Canas y Canchis communities. Despite the failure of his mission, *naturales* in his province began to view Thupa Amaro as special. A former priest of Langui and Layo later noted that "when Túpac Amaru came back from this capital [i.e., Lima] to his ancient home . . . I noted the Indians looked at him with veneration, and not only in this village but even outside the province of Tinta; the province, proud with his protection, imagined itself free from the mita obligation."[62]

During a growing belief in the imminent return of the Incas, presaged by Juan Santos Atahualpa, and the expanding belief in *Inkarrí* and *Gran Paitití,* Thupa Amaro moved toward what he considered to be his destiny. At his home the Quechua play "*Ollantay,*" portraying Inca characters, became a popular entertainment, and he read Garcilaso de la Vega. Thupa Amaro, born heir to the Inca throne, transformed himself into the Inca.

The Inca had been a religious as well as temporal leader. In the late colonial period, however, being religious meant, for most *natu-*

rales, being Christian while also maintaining Andean religious beliefs. This syncretism ran deep. Even in Cuzco, a center of Andean Christianity, Christian symbols were often arrayed in Incan clothing during fiestas, and Incan symbols such as the Sun God were included in public celebrations. The Bishop of Cuzco noted that the Indians "convince us that they adore the true God only when they see Him dressed like the Incas, whom they believed to be deities."[63]

It was Thupa Amaro's good fortune that circumstances in Canas y Canchis aided the *naturales'* perception of him not only as Incan but as a defender of the Christian faith. The bishop of Cuzco, Juan Manuel Moscoso y Peralta, was quite friendly with Thupa Amaro. However, bad blood existed between the bishop and Corregidor Arriaga, just as it did between Arriaga and Thupa Amaro. The bishop and corregidor had first clashed while both were serving in the distant province of Tucumán (Río de la Plata), but when they were transferred to Cuzco their dispute became public and reached crisis proportions. Priests and civil officials took one side or another in the dispute. What should have been personal problems ended up taking on larger meaning due to this church-state conflict. Such was the case in San Pablo de Cacha.[64]

As Epiphany approached in January of 1780, the *naturales* of San Pablo de Cacha desired to bring their nativity scene from its chapel to the church. However, they had not met the priest's pecuniary expectations, the gift or *don* that priests often received, and their request was refused. Their religious festivities dashed, the community raised a tumult against the priest and did the same again on the first of February. The next month, Francisco, the priest's slave, struck fear into the hearts of the villagers when he fabricated a story in which the corregidor was plotting to kill them in retaliation for their commotions against the priest. According to Francisco, Arriaga was sending four hundred soldiers to "pasarlos a cuchillo" ("to put them to the knife)." Panic-stricken, people fled to the surrounding countryside. In the flight one person fell from a bridge, drowned, and was secretly buried. Arriaga, learning of the incident, had Francisco detained and then expelled from the province, stating that law "prohibits that seditious and prejudicial blacks live among the *naturales* of these kingdoms." However, fear of Arriaga had been created, through no fault of his own, which augmented the low opinion some already held of him. Writing to the priest, Arriaga, concerned about the impact of the incident, reflected that "when fires are not promptly extinguished, their flames usually consume the most distant." These were especially prophetic words, for just nine months later Arriaga was the kindling from which the flames of the Thupa Amaro rebellion grew.[65]

The personal authority of the Canas y Canchis corregidor was further eroded when Arriaga became involved in a jurisdictional fight between parish priests and Bishop Moscoso over control of church property. Arriaga sided with Joseph and Justo Martinez, the priests of Pichigua and Yauri, respectively. Two Yauri *curacas,* Diego José de Meza and Francisco Guambo Tapa, had rented church lands from Justo Martinez. The bishop insisted the Yauri priest comply with his orders, giving him say over church property, but neither the *curacas* nor the priest wanted the bishop interfering in his affairs. The bishop sent the mulatto priest of Coporaque, Vicente de la Puente, to Yauri to enforce his wishes. De la Puente, already at odds with the people of Coporaque, did not improve his reputation in Yauri. It was bad enough when he embargoed the priest's goods, but he went too far when he had an aide break down the door to Justo Martinez's house. The *curaca* and community members confronted the aide and drove him out in a minor tumult. After receiving this news the bishop ordered de la Puente to return to Yauri to arrest the priest, but de la Puente's arrival was preceded by rumors, including, once again, one that warned that Indians would be killed. Unlike the people of San Pedro de Cacha, the people of Yauri did not flee. De la Puente arrived with armed support, but the community was prepared, and a fight ensued in which several people were injured. Among those named as responsible for the tumult were Meza and a *curaca* from Coporaque, Eugenio Sinanyuca. When representatives of the bishop injured an indigenous parishioner, Arriaga intervened in the case at the community's request and, most likely, because he was a friend of

Justo Martinez. Arriaga was excommunicated by the bishop "for protecting sacrilegious natives," although his dispute with the prelate was undoubtedly the real cause.[66] It was the bishop's representative, not the corregidor, who had the priest and people of Yauri. It was Arriaga, however, who publicly fell afoul of the church, having sought to protect a *natural* and a priest from abusive church officials.

Although Arriaga is often portrayed as being alienated from the church, he was really at odds with the bishop and those priests who supported the Cuzco prelate. Arriaga was not alienated from all local priests. Joseph, Justo, and Antonio Martinez, priests in Pichigua, Yauri, and Sicuani, respectively, were friends of the corregidor. They were also on generally good terms with their parishioners. For instance, it was to the church of Joseph Martinez that Doña Maria Hincho and Don Mariano Puma (see chapter 2) had donated their hacienda. However, due to personal conflicts and defiance, Moscoso undermined the power of these priests, which further eroded Arriaga's support in Canas y Canchis religious circles.

The animosity between the bishop and Arriaga contributed to the erosion of the authority of the corregidor. Arriaga had been excommunicated and portrayed as the *bête noire* behind a proposed massacre. In addition, local priests friendly to Arriaga were removed from their parishes. Being blamed for abuses that in actuality rested on the shoulders of the bishop, Arriaga's own economic abuses seemed even more excessive and made him increasingly vulnerable. Perhaps it was because of the corregidor's problems with the church that the priests who had the opportunity to intervene to save his life were more disposed to confess him and watch him hanged.

Once the rebellion was initiated, Bishop Moscoso, no matter what his earlier relationship to Thupa Amaro had been, brought the weight of Christian opprobrium down on the Inca and the movement he led. Following the attack on Sangarará in which royalists took refuge in the church that was then set ablaze and they were burned to death, Moscoso excommunicated Thupa Amaro.[67] While this action may have dissuaded some *naturales* from joining the rebellion and encouraged others to take up arms against the rebels, it had little effect on those people who were already in the Thupa Amaro camp.

After the excommunication there were still over twenty priests and other religious personnel who supported the rebel leader.[68] Gregorio de Yepes, the priest of Pomacanchi, tended to the rebel's religious needs. Yepes even compared Thupa Amaro to David, who would slay the Spanish Goliath. The priest proclaimed that the Inca was an "instrument of the Lord . . . for the correction of many wrongs and abuses."[69] The priest of Pampamarca, Antonio Lopez de Sosa, had been close to Thupa Amaro since he was a child. In the absence of Thupa Amaro's father, the priest had been, in effect, a surrogate parent to the young José Gabriel. He was also Thupa Amaro's first teacher. It was most likely Lopez de Sosa who backed Thupa Amaro's entrance into the school for the *curacas'* sons in Cuzco. He also performed the marriage ceremony joining the Inca heir to Micaela Bastidas. Relatives of Thupa Amaro claimed that it was Lopez de Sosa who encouraged him to rebel by reading him his family tree and telling him not to tolerate bad treatment by corregidors. One of the relatives even declared that "the entire affair was the priest's fault, and that he should be punished for his sins." Indeed, the priest of Tinta may have written some of the rebel proclamations.[70] Having these Christian priests within the movement lent further credibility and sacredness to Thupa Amaro and the insurgency.

During the rebellion Thupa Amaro portrayed himself not only as a cleansing arm of the Spanish king but as a divine Inca and a representative of the Christian God. This imbued Thupa Amaro with authority, with majesty, and it gave his followers deeper faith in the righteousness of their leader and their cause. Though Thupa Amaro and most of his followers thought of themselves as Christian, not all the rebels shared these convictions. Elements within the insurrection committed acts designed either to offend Christian sensibilities or demonstrate the weakness of Christian divinities. In Calca rebels gave no quarter to men, women, or children of European descent. One mestizo rebel killed a European woman, her husband, and her children in the church. Having finished with the slaughter, the mestizo, still in the church, violated the woman's corpse. The location and brutality of these acts was apparently a deliberate challenge to, or defiance of, European Christian authority. Also in Calca two Spanish brothers "were killed, their blood and hearts were consumed, their tongues cut off and their eyes pierced," such mutilations being in keeping with Andean ritual. In other instances enemies were ritually mutilated. Some were beheaded, their blood drunk, their hearts removed, or their bodies dismembered. In the community of Juli located on the shores of Lake Titicaca royalist forces encountered numerous dead, including the bodies of two caciques, "their heads in gallows and their hearts extracted," while "the corpse of a cacique's wife was without blood, supposedly drunk by the rebels."[71] Whether these were acts of syncretic Christians against those determined to be un-Christian or whether they were assertions of Andean religious authority over Christians or defeated enemies is unclear, but they were, at least in part, religious acts. Likewise, rebels in Caylloma challenged Christian power by killing Spaniards who had taken refuge in a church and cried out that the "time of mercy is finished, there are no Sacraments nor God with any power."[72]

In Cuzco, as well as regions to the south where Túpac Catari led the insurrection, rebels determined that certain Spaniards and Indians were outside the Andean (syncretic) Christian fold. As representatives of the anti-Christ, these people were open to attack. In the Lake Titicaca community of Copacabana, royalist Spaniards killed in the hostilities were said to be "excommunicated" or "demons." These dead, in keeping with Andean tradition for those who violated standards of conduct such as criminals, were not interred. The unburied dead could not regenerate or be reborn. The offending Spaniards would never return.[73]

In the first weeks of the rebellion a faction of the insurgent army questioned Thupa Amaro on the need for Christian priests. They told the Inca, "Thou art our God and Master and we beg thee that there be no [Catholic] priests from now on, molesting us." The Inca responded that this was not possible for "who would absolve us in the matter of death." For Thupa Amaro, a Christian priest was needed for the sacred duty of seeing people into the world beyond life.[74] At times, however, the rebel's syncretic Catholicism seemed to go against the most basic of Christian beliefs while still maintaining a Catholic form. Thupa Amaro was reported to have informed his troops on the eve of battle that only those who did not invoke the name of Jesus or confess would be resurrected after three days.[75]

Thupa Amaro's legitimacy rested to a large degree on his religious authority. He sought to enhance this authority before and during the rebellion. He and other rebel leaders, such as his cousin Diego Cristóbal Thupa Amaro, presented themselves and their followers as the true Christians. The Inca, hinting at an afterlife, indicated that his followers "would have their reward." They, in turn, imbued him with "the power to raise the dead."[76] In the Quispicanchis community of Guaro, Thupa Amaro informed his army and the community that until then "they had not known God, nor had they understood who He is, because they have respected as God the corregidores, thieves, and the priests, but he was going to remedy this."[77]

Rebel leaders, however, also appealed to Andean religious traditions. To convey their messages and arouse their followers they sometimes chose to speak at *huacas*—Andean religious shrines. When he could, such as after capturing the *obraje* in Pomacanchis, Thupa Amaro, in accordance with Inca tradition, distributed cloth. The syncretic nature of belief also manifested itself in the use of cemeteries—of both Christian and Andean importance—to persuade people to join the rebellion out of obligation to their ancestors, ancestor worship being a significant aspect in Inca religion.[78] Thupa Amaro, therefore, invoked both Andean and Christian belief systems and the syncretic mixture of these systems to strengthen his position as leader.

However, those *naturales* who opposed Thupa Amaro certainly did not view him as a Christian leader, nor was the rebel army seen as tramping out the vintage of the Christian God. The bishop of Cuzco even reported that among Indians loyal to the crown there were those who did not loot the battlefield after an engagement, for the rebels were excommunicated, outside the Christian fold, and their possessions were believed to be of the same status as their owners.[79] Nonetheless, both insurgents and royalists considered their work to be the work of God. This meant that to a certain extent "the war between the Inca and his enemies was a war among Christians who accused one another of heresy and rebellion."[80]

The Thupa Amaro Family

While he relied heavily on his religious-cultural authority and business associates to ignite and spread the rebellion, Thupa Amaro depended most on his family. Kinship was very important to indigenous people, and for that matter to non-Indians. When the rebel leader needed people he could trust implicitly he looked to his family. Some of his relatives were fellow muleteers and shared Thupa Amaro's knowledge of places and people beyond Quispicanchis and Canas y Canchis, but with or without this knowledge the innermost circle of advisers and confidants were family members, not specialized military or political strategists.

The authority of these people was enhanced by their being related to the Inca, their being part of the royal family. Diego Cristóbal Thupa Amaro, who assumed leadership after the Inca's capture, proclaimed that he loved Thupa Amaro like a father and that the Inca "called me son, and as such he always treated me."[81] The oldest son of Thupa Amaro, Hipólito, was also in the inner circle, but the most important person in this group was the rebel's wife. Micaela Bastidas enjoyed respect and a position of leadership within the movement, man and wife being a unit and complementing one another. Her status was not just ascribed; it was also achieved. Her competency further expanded her role. She shared many of her husband's responsibilities and exercised sweeping authority on her own. Bastidas collected and distributed supplies, engaged in propaganda efforts, dealt with prisoners, issued orders, and even advised on military policy. When Thupa Amaro was slow to lay siege to Cuzco, she cautioned him "that the soldiers did not have enough food, and although they were still receiving a salary, that money would last only a short time after which they would desert." She also reminded her husband that "you will have noticed they [the rebel soldiers] act mainly out of self interest, and they are more frightened now that . . . rumours that the troops from Lampa and Arequipa have united and soon will surround you."[82]

Spanish authorities clearly recognized the importance of the kinship network—the royal family—in the rebellion. The Thupa Amaro family was nearly annihilated in public and brutal executions that made manifest the consequences for those who attacked the colonial system. However, on 16 May, two days before the executions, the Inca, his family, and others who were to be executed were allowed back in the Christian fold, their excommunication being absolved.

The cruel sentences were to be carried out on May 18, after the prisoners confessed, heard mass, and took the last communion. When the day came, the city militiamen, armed with daggers and side arms, surrounded the large plaza; and the four sides of the gallows were circled by a body of mulattoes and soldiers from Huamanga, all having guns and fixed bayonets. Nine persons were to be put to death on that day: José Berdejo, a Spaniard and son-in-law of Francisco Noguera, the Inca's commander; Andrés Castelo, a captain; Antonio Oblitas, the Zambo who hanged Corregidor Arriaga in Tinta; Antonio Bastidas, a brother-in-law of Túpac Amaru; Francisco Túpac Amaru, an uncle; Hipólito Túpac Amaru, the twenty-year-old son of the Inca; Tomasa Titu Condemayta; Micaela Bastidas, the Inca's wife; and José Gabriel Túpac Amaru himself.

All the prisoners wore handcuffs and fetters and came out at one time, one behind the other. They were put in sacks and dragged along the ground tied to the tails of horses. All were heavily guarded and accompanied by priests, who comforted them as they approached the foot of the gallows, where two executioners awaited them. Berdejo, Castelo, Oblitas and Bastidas were simply hanged. Francisco Túpac Amaru, a man almost eighty years old, and Hipólito had their tongues cut out before being hanged. The Indian woman Tomasa was garroted. . . . The Inca and his wife had to witness all these executions, and finally that of their oldest son. Then the Inca's wife, Micaela, dressed in the habit of the Order of Mercy, mounted the platform. Her tongue was to be cut out, but she refused to let the executioner do it; and so it was taken out after her death. She was also subjected to the garrote, but because she had a very small neck, the screw caused intense suffering without strangling her. The executioner then put a lasso around her neck and pulled it one way and another, all the while repeatedly striking her, until she died.

José Gabriel was then brought out to the center of the plaza. There the executioner cut out his tongue and threw him on the ground face down. He tied his hands and feet with four cords, fastened these to the girths of four horses, which four mestizos then drove in the four directions. Either the horses were weak or the Inca unusually strong, for he was not immediately torn to pieces, but remained suspended in mid-air, spider-like, for some time while the horses strained to pull him apart. The hard-hearted visitador [Areche] finally ordered the Inca's head cut off. At the same time he arrested the corregidor of Cuzco and another official for not providing suitable horses. The Inca's body was dismembered, as were the bodies of his wife, son, and uncle. Only the heads were removed from the bodies of the remaining victims. . . .

The Inca's youngest son, Fernando, a nine-year-old child, was exempted from capital punishment. With a chain on his foot and guarded by four soldiers, he was taken to the foot of the gallows and forced to witness the cruel deaths of his parents. His heart-rending shrieks resounded for a long time in the ears of the people who heard them.[83]

To make clear what had transpired, and what would happen to others who rebelled, body parts of the executed were displayed throughout the region: "The trunks of the mutilated bodies of the Inca and his wife were taken to the height of Picchu [mountain above Cuzco]. There they were thrown into a bonfire and reduced to ashes, which were scattered into the air and cast into the Huatanay River. The rest of the gruesome sentence was carried out to the letter.

Hipólito's head was sent to Tungasuca, and his limbs were scattered in different places. Francisco's head was taken to Pilpinto, one leg to Carabaya, the other to Puno, and an arm to Paruro."[84]

Thupa Amaro had known his fate since the day his sentence had been handed down: "His head was to be sent to Tinta and kept on a gallows for three days and then put on a post at the entrance of the town. The same thing was to be done with one of his arms in Tungasuca, and the other arm would be exhibited in the province of Carabaya. One leg was to be sent to Livitaca in the province of Chumbivilcas, and the other to Santa Rosa in the province of Lampa. His houses were to be demolished completely and the sites publicly salted."[85]

In 1783 Diego Cristóbal Thupa Amaro and his family, after having been pardoned, fell afoul of Spanish justice and met similar fates. His mother was sentenced to be hanged, quartered, and burnt before his eyes. Diego himself had "pieces of his flesh torn off with red hot tongs" before being killed. To further disperse and weaken the family some ninety kin were taken to Lima in chains, and many were then sent off for Spain only to be shipwrecked. One colonial official commented that "[n]either the King nor the state thought it fitting that a seed or branch of the family should remain, or the commotion and impression that the wicked name of Túpac Amaru caused among the natives."[86]

In this manner the Spanish attested that they fully understood the importance of family in Andean society, particularly the family of the Inca. And, indeed, Thupa Amaro's family had been important in garnering support for the rebellion. In Quispicanchis, for example, rebel leaders included Patricio Noguera, son of Antonia Túpac Amaru, who was married to a woman from Acomayo; Antonio Bastidas, José Gabriel's brother-in-law, who lived in Urcos; and Pedro Mendigure, a muleteer from Pomacanchis, married to Cecilia Túpac Amaru; and Francisco Túpac Amaru, who was also a muleteer and whose wife came from Pomacanchis.[87]

Curacas, Rebels, and Royalists

One of Thupa Amaro's most important attributes in gaining the adherence of the *naturales* of Canas y Canchis and Quispicanchis to the insurrection was his relationship with other local *curacas*. With few exceptions people in the Cuzco region, in contrast to Catarista regions, followed the lead of their *curacas* in supporting or opposing the rebellion. More caciques in the Catarista zone of operations seem to have abused their ties with their communities, making them, as well as Spaniards, the focus of rebel violence.[88] In Cuzco, with many *curacas* of Inca blood still in authority and setting the example for *curaca* behavior, this was not the case. With few exceptions, the *ayllus* followed the lead of their *curacas*. One such exception occurred in Quiquijana, where the cacique at first supported Thupa Amaro, but when his support faltered the people drove him out of the community.[89] The possibility of such actions by the *ayllus*, not to mention the presence of a rebel army, may have helped sway certain *curacas* in favor of the movement.

Thupa Amaro was generally well thought of as a *curaca*, and his stature had been enhanced with both *curacas* and tributaries as a result of his efforts to abolish the *mita*. When he initiated the rebellion, however, Thupa Amaro's hold on his position as *curaca* was in some doubt. On 14 August 1780, Melchor Choquecondori petitioned Lima authorities to be installed as *curaca* in Pampamarca, Thupa Amaro's *curacazgo*. Choquecondori informed Lima officials that he could not submit all his papers, because they were in the hands of the parish priest, Antonio Lopez de Sosa. Choquecondori knew that the priest was his enemy, "because he unjustly favors a friend of his who he calls, even though he is not, Don José Tupa Amaro."[90] Whether this challenge came strictly from Choquecondori's own volition, or was encouraged by others, is unknown. In any case, it meant trouble for Thupa Amaro and may have been another factor that contributed to the timing of the rebellion. For the most part, however, the Inca's relations with local *curacas* were good, although not always strong enough to overcome particular concerns of individual caciques.

Out of twenty-five regional *curacas* who supported the rebellion, twelve were from Canas y Canchis and another five from Quispicanchis.[91] Because their relationships with their *ayllus* were strong, the *curacas* were able to command the respect and support of their people. When the *curacas* decided to follow Thupa Amaro this translated into a swelling of the rebel ranks. Among these *curacas* were some we have come to know. Puma Inga, the *curaca* who was badly beaten by a *cobrador,* served as head justice for Thupa Amaro and paid for his actions with his life, executed by having his body cut to pieces with swords.[92] Ramón Moscoso, the Spanish *curaca* from Yanaoca who served as guarantor of community land rental, fought with Thupa Amaro. Catalina Salas Pachacuti, a *cacica* of royal Inca blood and the wife of Ramón Moscoso, worked closely with Micaela Bastidas during the rebellion. Guamba Tupa, who had been outraged by Bishop Moscoso's actions in Yauri, also joined the rebellion. Despite Thupa Amaro's links to the bishop, Guamba Tupa supported the Inca, because he represented the traditional rights and the supremacy of Inca royal authority. During the conflict with the bishop, Guamba Tupa commented that "we Incas ought to be supported, protected and defended and we ought to be honored."[93] Diego Meza, the other *curaca* from Yauri who had opposed the bishop, also joined the rebellion. One of the two female *curacas* to join Thupa Amaro, Tomasa Titu Condemayta of Acos, was a person of high standing in Cuzco rural society. Bishop Moscoso commented that except for Titu Condemayta, no cacique of honor rebelled. She apparently decided to join the insurrection on her own before being contacted by rebel forces, and she was of such stature that she dealt directly with both Thupa Amaro and Micaela Bastidas. The Spanish recognized Titu Condemayta's importance by hanging her the same day as the royal couple and displaying her head in Acos.[94] The *curacas* from Quispicanchis and Canas y Canchis were key in gaining initial support for the rebellion.

In the province of Cuzco, not including the city and surrounding zone (the *cercado*), it has been calculated that out of a total population of 174,623 people some 28,495 were aligned with rebel *curacas*, and some 36,775 followed loyalist caciques. The overwhelming bulk of rebel support came from Thupa Amaro's home province and from neighboring Quispicanchis. These provinces contributed approximately 85 percent of the rebels, while the other Cuzco provinces contributed the remaining 15 percent of the rebel forces.[95]

The percentage of *naturales* under loyalist *curacas* in Canas y Canchis and Quispicanchis was 24.7 and 10.9 percent, respectively, some 64.4 percent coming from the other *partidos*. These figures, inevitably not as precise as they seem, do give an indication of Thupa Amaro's strengths and weaknesses in Cuzco.[96] The powerful, well-to-do, noble *curaca* of Azángaro, Diego Choqueguanca, fought against Thupa Amaro. Rebel forces, in turn, burned haciendas and killed people in the zone controlled by Choqueguanca.[97] From Chinchero, to the north of Cuzco, another powerful *curaca*, Mateo Pumacahua, led his people into battle against the Thupa Amaro army and was instrumental in the royalist defense of Cuzco. The depth of the differences between the two *curacas* was symbolized in a painting that Pumacahua commissioned after Thupa Amaro's capture. The painting "depicted a puma [Pumacahua] defeating a snake [Amaru] beneath the benevolent gaze of the *Virgen of Monserrat*, Chinchero's patron saint. In the background stood Pumacahua and his wife, both dressed in Spanish garb, affirming their territorial sovereignty. Beneath the painting was inscribed Ceasar's dictum: *Veni, Vidi, Vici,* commemorating the defeat of this rival faction, an action which brought the house of Pumacahua renewed respect."[98]

Not all royalist *curacas* were of such high standing. Santos Mamani, the abusive cacique of *ayllu* Lurucache in Marangani who had been opposed by many of his people, battled for the crown. In 1787, however, Mamani was accused of having been a rebel, a powerful accusation in the post-Thupa Amaro era. Various royalists, including Pumacahua, testified on his behalf, stating that Mamani and people from Marangani had served the crown's forces well in May and June of 1781. Mamani had been in charge of guarding the royalists' sheep, and Pumacahua testified that in the battle for mount Condorcuyo, Mamani and his people "demonstrated . . . valor and loyalty." Mamani even had been rewarded for his service with a rebel flag captured in the engagement.[99] In Quispicanchis, *curacas* in the region closest to Cuzco where Spanish presence was strong also remained loyal to the crown.

The situation surrounding the decision of Eugenio Sinanyuca, the *curaca* of Coporaque, to not join the rebellion reflects the complexity of life in rural Cuzco and makes apparent the importance of personal considerations and face-to-face relations in determining perceptions and consequent loyalties. Sinanyuca and the *naturales* of Coporaque were at loggerheads with their parish priest, Vicente de la Puente. When the Coporaque priest did the bishop's bidding in the Yauri conflict, Sinanyuca defied the priest. Tensions were such that the *curaca* publicly refused, during Mass, to supply a worker for the church as was the tradition. Sinanyuca did this on Corpus Christi of 1780, "repeating the preponderance of ritual in the most important social actions of these [Canas] communities."[100]

De la Puente initiated legal action against Sinanyuca, but with the exception of two communal officials, the powerful *naturales* and the *común* of Coporaque allied themselves with their *curaca*. Sinanyuca also served as Arriaga's *cobrador* and was on good terms with the ill-fated corregidor. De la Puente, certainly backed by Bishop Moscoso, brought ecclesiastical charges against Sinanyuca. In this way the priest sought to avoid the civil authority of Sinanyuca's supporter, Arriaga, while enhancing the influence of his supporter and Arriaga's enemy, Bishop Moscoso. The *curaca,* on the other hand, turned to the corregidor for help. In May of 1780 de la Puente also brought charges against Sinanyuca for events that had happened over a year earlier. After Mass at the beginning of *carnestolendas* in the previous year, the people of Coporaque conducted their own rituals, including offerings to the earth of the hearts of sacrificed animals and the smearing of corral fences with a mixture of blood and colored earth. The Coporaque priest claimed that acts were committed against his person and the "sacred order." The troubles between priest and community obviously had been brewing for some time. In the ensuing year Coporaque, under the guidance of Sinanyuca, denied the priest traditional "gifts" and did not fill voluntary, but expected, labor services. Even *Visitador* Areche entered the fray, arguing that Sinanyuca should be removed from his position as *cobrador*. Areche saw an opportunity to implement his plan to remove caciques from the tribute process and leave tribute collection in community hands. Although this might weaken the power of exploitative *curacas,* it would also alter the relationship between *curacas* and community. Areche's plan may have aroused the concern or ire of other *curacas* in Canas y Canchis and in this way contributed to their support of the rebellion. Certainly Sinanyuca realized that if de la Puente, Moscoso, and Areche had their way his authority might be weakened or worse.[101]

The charges against Sinanyuca, instead of having a "chilling effect," spread tensions to the surrounding region. When the bishop ordered de la Puente and other church officials to enforce orders against Sinanyuca they were threatened. The priest claimed that the community was "entirely stirred up" due to Sinanyuca and Arriaga's aide, Francisco Cisneros. Observing piles of rocks in the plaza that had been placed there for use in a confrontation, the religious forces retired from Coporaque. When yet another Moscoso representative sought to remove Sinanyuca from the community, the *curaca* appeared before the residence of the priest in the company of some five hundred villagers and in a loud voice informed the official that he would not leave. Later the *naturales* destroyed a church jail and rooms in the priest's house, while accusing de la Puente of having stolen from the church and *cofradía.*[102]

De la Puente, backed by armed guards, once again tried to reestablish church authority in the community. Counting on the element of surprise by arriving early in the morning, de la Puente underestimated his foe. Sinanyuca and the villagers were waiting for him. Using the church bells, Sinanyuca had summoned a thousand *naturales* who menaced the priest and his forces. The women were especially hostile. In the confrontation two of the priest's aides were stoned, and one was "dragged from the patio of the [priest's] house to the jail, with such horrible blows that they left him for dead bathed in blood and the face like a swollen monster."[103] The tumult lasted over four hours, community members parading in front of the priest's house carrying a coffin and singing an Inca war song, "We will drink from the skull of the traitor, we will use his teeth as a necklace, from his bones we will make flutes, from his skin a drum, afterwards we will dance."[104]

The priest and what remained of his guard and staff fled, while the people continued to dance and sing. After this incident the entire community of Coporaque, not just Sinanyuca, was threatened with excommunication. Later they, and other communities hostile to the bishop, were excommunicated. Arriaga, whose excommunication had been lifted, came to the defense of Coporaque and began legal proceedings against local priests, which he promised to send to the viceroy or Areche in November, a proposition with which his hanging made it impossible for him to comply.

The entire zone—Pichigua, Yauri, and Coporaque—had been upset by these conflicts between Bishop Moscoso, Corregidor Arriaga, and the priests and *curacas* of these communities. In light of this struggle with the priest and bishop it is less puzzling why Sinanyuca and his people, who had been supported by Arriaga and excommunicated by the church, remained aloof from Thupa Amaro, who was a friend of the bishop and who executed the corregidor, while priests such as his friend Lopez de Sosa watched.

Sinanyuca and the people of Coporaque, and others like them, were not behaving in a manner contradictory to their interests. They acted out of their own circumstances, their own experience, their own self-interest. They were not a generic Indian mass. They were not united with other communities or regions just because they were of the same race. They were the people of the *ayllus* of Coporaque, and their leader was Eugenio Sinanyuca. In these very personal matters they did not share Thupa Amaro's experiences or interests. Out of reasons grounded in their own personal experience many of them distanced themselves from the rebellion.

Conclusion

Cultural tradition, communal solidarity, and hope for a more just order under an Inca led *naturales* to follow their *curacas* in joining the insurrection, but few would have followed if community-*curaca* ties had not been strong. The length of the conflict, the misfortunes of war, and personal concerns, however, ultimately meant that both Indians and non-Indians reevaluated their commitments. Micaela Bastidas noted the fragile adherence to the movement when she commented that the rebel troops might begin to desert, because "they act mainly out of self-interest."[105]

Such personal convictions and self-interests were powerful motivating factors for rebels and loyalists alike, but they had their consequences as well. Esteban Castro, an *arriero*, joined the rebel ranks because of the commitment to eliminate "corregidors, *repartos*, *aduana* or sales tax." Left to serve as a sentinel in the heights above Quiquijana because his mules were tired and, according to Castro, because the others did not think much of him, he was supposed to capture Spaniards who passed by. No Spaniards passed, at least not until two days before Christmas of 1780 when the *arriero* was himself captured. Later the same day he suffered the consequences of his decision; he was hanged and quartered.[106] Brigida Guaman of Acomayo took a different decision. Disguising herself as a man, she spied on the Thupa Amaro forces until she was discovered and driven away by the rocks from rebel slings.[107] Likewise, Maria Herrera, the wife of the Sicuani *curaca* Simon Callo, did not support the rebellion. In subsequent years Herrera was reminded of her decision by a former associate who had supported Thupa Amaro and now treated her as a "whore."[108] Even Thupa Amaro fell into royalist hands due, in part, to personal motives. A woman from the Canas y Canchis community of Langui, who held Thupa Amaro responsible for the deaths of loved ones to the forces of Thupa Amaro in the rebellion, helped capture the rebel leader. In turn, *naturales* in Langui later killed the woman. They held her responsible for the capture of their Inca.[109]

There would be no *pachacuti*—no cataclysm—no just, new order reborn of the dead generations. The traditions of the past had been awakened and had taken on similar, but new, forms in their new setting. However, in making their own history the peoples of Canas y Canchis and Quispicanchis were far too varied, their experiences and heritages too rich, to act with only one vision. For a brief moment in the late eighteenth century, seeing their way of life being eroded, these diverse peoples came closer to functioning as one than they may ever have done before and certainly than they have done since.

9

Más Allá

THE REBELLION produced neither a cataclysmic *pachacuti* nor an Andean reordering under Inca rule, but the shaking of this world had a lasting impact and pushed some relatively rapid reforms. In the late 1780s an *audiencia* or high court was established in Cuzco that could give indigenous complaints a quicker hearing as Thupa Amaro had demanded. The *reparto* was abolished, although in Canas y Canchis and Quispicanchis complaints continued to be filed indicating that distance still existed between formal codes and the informal reality. The office of corregidor was done away with, but in the upper Vilcanota this did not bring great changes, for under the intendants who took their place it was pretty much business as usual. Cuzco *obraje* workers continued to clean, card, and spin fleece and then weave wool into profits for their bosses; the local industry even underwent a resurgence before its eventual decline. *Arrieros* still loaded this cloth, *ají*, and coca on their mules and llamas to sell in distant markets. In other words, *naturales* still provided the muscle and much of the production that made nonindigenous society possible. The Potosi *mita* also persisted. It was not until the smoke and shot of the independence wars were in the air and the *mita* was unenforceable that Spain finally saw fit to remove this yoke from indigenous necks. Thupa Amaro's noble heritage caused the crown to look warily at those who came from similar backgrounds or were of traditional *curaca* families. In the villages and *ayllus* the state increasingly sought to appoint or confirm *curacas* who were not from such backgrounds or with whom they could do "business." And the office often became elective instead of inherited, a significant restructuring.

The engagement of indigenous and nonindigenous peoples discussed in this work, and which Alberto Flores Galindo saw as increasingly common in the eighteenth century prior to 1780, became less vital, although it did not disappear, in the wake of the rebellion.[1] There indeed had been growing interaction between the indigenous and Spanish realms in late colonial Canas y Canchis and Quispicanchis, as the mature indigenous colonial society recuperated from the enduring traumas of conquest and epidemics and began to more fully interact with and engage Europeans. Some of the changes that early on had seemed so destructuring had served in the long run as focal points of unity or restructuring. In their daily lives villagers dealt with the Europeans on a face-to-face level, understanding that they could work with some people and not others. Likewise, the nonindigenous population often interacted with their indigenous neighbors on a similar basis, even supporting them in court cases over other Europeans.

It was this cultural confidence, reflected in the demographic resurgence, and cooperation that made it possible for *naturales* to rise up against colonial exploitation in the late eighteenth century when the Bourbon regime and its agents pressed them ever harder. They first addressed the legal system and then protested what they perceived as abuses. When these actions did not bring the desired result they took the next step—rebellion. Flores Galindo writes,

> it seems that the return of the Inca, as an alternative to colonial oppression, was born of the approximation of the Indian and Spanish republics, those seemingly impassable worlds. A plain biological fact: the increase of mestizos [22 percent of the population] over the course of the century. Andean culture moved from repression and clandestinity to tolerance and into public ambits. . . .
>
> But this process of convergence was to be interrupted by the social conflicts which broke loose between 1780 and 1824. The wars of independence over, the shared traditions of the country were superseded by social and ethnic divisions. In what remained of the nineteenth century, the Andean utopia would become a peasant utopia destined to remain confined to rural environs.[2]

The fear and doubt instilled in *criollos* and mestizos by the rebellion also went a long way toward assuring there would be few ideologic efforts to involve *naturales* in the wars of independence or in nascent national politics. However, vision of an Inca monarchy once again briefly bloomed in Cuzco in the first years of the nineteenth century, and Thupa Amaro's old nemesis, Mateo Pumacahua, became an early martyr of the independence movement.[3]

In 1790 Benito de Mata Linares, the governmental official who had spread around the blame in the wake of the insurrection, noted that since the upheaval one could notice in indigenous people a "pride, insolence, and laziness" that had not existed before and that they had lost the "terror" or "servile fear" that before had gripped them with just the "name of Spanish."[4] The fact that he had not noticed the growing "pride" or changes in relations that he interpreted as insolence or laziness had been one of the problems. The Thupa Amaro rebellion did not change indigenous peoples as much as it changed nonindigenous perceptions of them. Most *naturales,* after all, had remained neutral or were even royalists, but they, like the rebels, had experienced the changing realities of the eighteenth century. While indigenous voices were rarely reflected, the nonindigenous world sensed or feared what for many of them appeared to be a new reality. Thus, after three centuries of domination many people of European heritage were once again (some still) viewing their indigenous neighbors through cultural lenses that mirrored those through which the first Spanish had observed New World peoples when they initially arrived. With roots at least as deep as Aristotle, these perceptions of the "other"—uncivilized, dangerous, and powerful—were deeply ingrained in Western tradition, and the fire of the Thupa Amaro rebellion rekindled these views.[5] The degree to which people such as the villagers of Quispicanchis and Canas y Canchis were still seen as not conforming to Eurocentric views of cultured or civilized beings was used against them and, indeed, continues to be used against them. It was the baggage, the inheritance, of Spanish and European pride and ethnocentrism.

These "sentiments," especially at an ideological level, were focuses of debate in late colonial and early republican society that sought, once again, to determine what role indigenous people ought to have in the new political arrangements and what the state's indigenous policy should be. The *naturales'* own pride, self-defense, and ethnocentrism did not make coexistence with the nonindigenous world any easier, but it did help preserve their identity as distinct peoples and cultures. These low-intensity cultural wars continue to mark relations between Peruvians. Reflective of the rhetoric among people of European heritage was the comment by one colonial observer who admitted the Europeans also had vices but argued that *naturales* had "acquired our [European] vices without adopting any of our virtues."[6]

At the local level, people continued living their lives and dealing with one another in the matters of day-to-day existence much as they always had. As in most realities, many people lived lives that had little to do with the dominant discourse of their times, although they themselves were often imbued with this rhetoric. There were contrary voices even in the drawing rooms and governmental offices of Lima, though precious few Euro-Peruvians thought indigenous peoples and their cultures worthy of respect. Even those sympathetic to indigenous people, who pointed to exploitation as a cause of "their" situation, still advocated, at best, assimilationist policies that sought to Europeanize and thereby get rid of native peoples. They were, after all, people of their own times, and it would be asking too much to expect more.

The specter of race war that gripped Euro-Peruvian society after the Thupa Amaro insurrection tore down cultural bridges and opened and maintained a gulf between indigenous peoples and the new Peruvian rulers. National dialogue that concerned indigenous policy or indigenous political rights was normally conducted in the absence of indigenous voices. However, economic and social realities also had to be dealt with in this highly articulated world. Though independence brought the legal end of the colonial justice system that had been one of the most effective means of communal defense, indigenous people were often able to take advantage of nonindigenous needs to maneuver the new nations into recognizing that the easiest way to get what they wanted was to work within indigenous notions of just reciprocal relations that in large part derived from colonial experiences. Economic realities played a large role in this process. Though the Peruvian state was committed to ending tribute, which was seen as a vestige of colonialism, the distancing from colonial practices could only go so far. After an initial attempt to do away with the race-based head tax, Peru, as other Andean nations, fell back on an indigenous "contribution" that to a large degree propped up the state until the guano boom finally provided the wealth to compensate slave owners and relieve the race tax on villagers. The Peruvian treasury's dependency on the indigenous head tax provided breathing room for the communities in that the colonial "arrangement"—taxes and work for land and survival—was altered in word but perpetuated in deed, which allowed *naturales* more time to make their adjustments to the new situation as they had learned to do so well and so often. Peru still owes a large and unpaid debt to its indigenous citizens not just for the work they have done and the exploitation they have suffered but for providing the means for the new nation to survive economically when those who benefited the most from new arrangements were reluctant to tax themselves as needed.

Eventually the Peruvian state whittled away at many of the reciprocal relations that provided protection to the villages, but even into the twentieth century, communities still focused arguments and expected results that were in accord with colonial practices. Thus, the men, women, and children—the *ayllus* and communities—of Quispicanchis and Canas y Canchis entered the republican period shaken but viable. In their long colonial experience they had learned painful lessons that helped them cope with new situations. They survived (see plate 8).

As for the Thupa Amaros, their saga continued in tragedy. One group of important prisoners of the insurrection was first taken to Lima, and then some of them were shipped off to Spain aboard the *San Pedro Alcántara* on a voyage that symbolized not only their sad and difficult state but also the decline of Spain.

The *San Pedro Alcántara*, in addition to its passengers, carried over 7,500,000 pesos in gold and silver. Its initial departure from Callao delayed due to overloading by a captain who was trying to make his pockets bulge with coin, the ship finally set sail in April of 1784. Once under way smallpox broke out. Leaking badly after an arduous rounding of the horn, the ship had to dock at Rio de Janeiro before setting out for the Atlantic crossing. As it finally approached the European coast, its crew apparently believed they were near Cadiz, and the ship went aground and sank north of Lisbon. Goya's painting *El naufragio* (1793; Madrid, Oquendo Collection) has passed this tragedy on to popular history. Of the 152 people who died, 16 were Thupa Amaro family members or rebels. Miraculously, one of the survivors was Fernando, the son of Michaela Bastidas and Thupa Amaro, whose screams had echoed through the central plaza in Cuzco as he was forced to witness the execution of his mother and father. Fernando and the other surviving rebels never made it back to the Andes. They died in Spain far from their fields, mountain gods, friends, and natal communities.[7] But the actions of Fernando's parents, relatives, fellow villagers, and neighbors did not die or disappear from history. They lived on in oral traditions and archival documents. From these sources their lives, their deeds, their humanity (and those of their European and mestizo neighbors as well) have been reconstructed and our understanding of their world made fuller and richer. Indeed, far more than most people of their era, they have lived on because of what they did. Thupa Amaro and the villagers of Quispicanchis and Canas y Canchis became sources of pride and hope, of dreams of justice and a better life for some, and of fear for others. In recent times the images of Thupa Amaro and the people whose struggles he represented have become so potent that the Peruvian government used his likeness to represent its efforts in a program that had as its stated aim the improvement of the lot of Peru's poor. The struggles of the peoples of Quispicanchis and Canas y Canchis, as represented in the image and name of Thupa Amaro, have become symbolic, even synonymous, in the minds of a great many Peruvians, with the struggle for social justice in the Andes.

Glossary

aduana. Custom house.

aguardiente. Distilled spirit, usually of sugar cane.

ají. Hot, flavorful Peruvian pepper.

alcabala. Sales tax.

alcalde. Mayor.

altiplano. High, broad plane between ridges of the Andean sierra.

alguacil. Constable.

anexo. A community that is part of a parish, but not the center of the parish.

apiri. Worker who carried ore out of mines.

arancel. List of fees.

arriero. Muleteer.

arroba. Weight of about 25 pounds.

ausente. Absent or missing tributary.

audiencia. High court of appeal and its jurisdiction.

ayllu. Primary living or identity unit of Indian peoples based on kinship or access to land. Usually there were several *ayllus* in a community.

azogue. Mercury.

azoguero. Owner of an amalgamation mill (mercury process) and silver mines; person who mixes mercury with ores.

barratero. Worker who broke ore from walls of mines with iron bars.

batan. Fulling mill.

bayeta. Rough, woolen cloth.

botija. Earthenware container used to transport liquids such as wine.

cabildo. Town council.

cacique. Community or *ayllu* leader, often hereditary and of noble birth. The same as *curaca*.

caja de comunidad. Community chest in which tribute monies, documents, and other valuables were stored.

cantor. Choir leader or member.

carga. Bulk measure of about 6 bushels.

carnero de la tierra. Llama.

carnestolendas. Period from Sunday before Ash Wednesday to Ash Wednesday itself.

catarista. Follower of Tomás Catari and his brothers or Túpac Catari (Julián Apasa).

cédula. Term applied to those who served in the Potosi *mita* by Royal decree.

cerro rico. The silver bearing mountain in Potosi.

chacra. Small farm.

charqui. Dried or jerked meat.

chicha. Andean alcoholic beverage usually, but not always, made of corn. Also known as *aka* or *aswa*.

cholo. Indigenous person who dresses as a European or who doesn't live under community guidance.

chorillo. Small textile mill.

chuño. Bitter potatoes preserved and made edible by alternative freezing, squeezing, and exposure to sun. Can be stored.

cobrador. Person who collected tribute and other colonial exactions.

coca. Plant whose leaves were chewed to help provide endurance and cut appetite. Also chewed socially and in rituals.

cofradía. Lay religious association or brotherhood.

compadrazgo. System of ritual or fictive kin.

composición. Inspection and legalization of land titles through payment to the crown of a sum determined by the crown.

comunidad. Indigenous community.

corregidor de indios. Provincial magistrate of a province who also received tribute payment and distributed the *reparto.*

criollo (indio criollo). White born in the New World (indigenous persons born and living in Potosi were known as *criollos*).

cura. Parish priest.

curaca. Andean term for cacique.

defensor de los indios. Same as *Protector de los naturales.* Person entrusted to prepare and argue Indian legal cases.

doctrina. Parish.

don. Traditional gift or offering. Honorary form of address for male.

efectos de castilla. European imported goods, mainly from Spain.

efectos de la tierra. Goods produced in the colonies, usually by indigenous people.

encomienda. Grant of indigenous labor by the crown. The person who has an *encomienda* is an *encomendero.*

enterador. Community member who delivered *mita* contingent to Potosi.

entero. Another term for *faltriquera* or cash payment in lieu of service in the Potosi *mita.*

estancia. Property dedicated primarily, although not necessarily exclusively, to livestock raising or grazing.

faltriquera. The practice of sending money to hire a replacement rather than serving in the Potosi *mita* in person. Those who did this were known as *indios de faltriquera* or *colquehaques.*

fanega or *fanegada.* Variable quantity of land depending on type of soil, usually refers to amount of land needed to sow about 1.5 bushels of seed. A *fanega* is also a dry measurement equivalent to about 1.5 bushels.

fiador. Guarantor of a loan, investment, or some other business activity.

fianza. Security bond. What a *fiador* provides.

forastero. Indigenous person who left his community of origin and no longer had the rights, especially access to land, and obligations of a community member. Subject to tribute in Cuzco region starting in 1720s.

ganado mayor. Large livestock such as cattle and horses.

ganado menor. Smaller livestock such as pigs, sheep, and goats.

gremio. Guild, such as the miners' guild in Potosi.

hacienda. Agricultural or livestock estate; treasury.

hacienda de pan llevar. Food-producing hacienda.

hanansaya. Upper moiety or half of a community. In the colonial period sometimes an *ayllu* name. See *hurinsaya.*

hatun runa. Adult *male* Indian.

huaca. Sacred place or object.

huayra. Oven used by Indians to smelt silver in Potosi.

hurinsaya. Lower moiety or half of a community. In the colonial period sometimes an *ayllu* name. See *hanansaya.*

ichu. Andean bunchgrass that grows at high altitudes.

jornal. Daily wage.

ladino. Indigenous person who speaks Spanish. Also an Indian who has adopted Spanish manners or dress.

legua. Measure of distance equivalent to about 2 1/2 miles in Spanish America.

leguaje. Travel compensation for the Potosi *mitayos.*

mayordomo. Overseer.

mestizo. Person of mixed Indian and European ancestry.

minga. Term for free labor in the Potosi mines. Otherwise a form of labor exchange.

mita. System of forced labor for Indians. A turn.

mitayo. Person serving his *mita.* The terms *cédula* and *septima* were also used for such workers.

mitimaes. Indians used by Incas to colonize conquered territories or assure control of a people.

moiety. Half of a community—*hanansaya* or *hurinsaya.* See *parcialidad.*

mojón. Border marker.

natural. Colonial term for indigenous person.

obraje. Textile mill.

oidor. Audiencia judge.

ordenanza. Ordinance.

originario. Person who lived in a community and had access to land and other rights and was required to meet colonial obligations in exchange for these rights.

parcialidad. Moiety of indigenous community. Most communities were divided into two sections or *parcialidades,* *(h)anansaya* and *(h)urinsaya,* which in turn were composed of *ayllus.*

parroquia. Parish. Term was used in Potosi for indigenous living districts, and in this sense it is the same as a *ranchería.*

peara. Measure of volume equivalent to load carried by ten mules.

peso. Coin of account or circulation. The common *peso* consisted of eight reals. The *peso ensayado* was 12 1/2 reals.

principal. Person of standing in Indian community, often hereditary.

protector de naturales. The person entrusted to bring and argue cases before the court or appropriate legal authority on behalf of the Indians. See *defensor.*

puka kunka. Derisive Quechua term for Spaniards. Literally, "red neck."

puna. High, cold region suited mainly for grazing, although at lower levels some bitter potatoes are also cultivated.

quinto. One fifth. The share of silver production that went to the crown.

ranchería. Small settlement. In Potosi same as *parroquia.*

real. One-eighth of a peso. A bit.

reducción. Resettlement of native peoples into Spanish-style communities. The resettled community.

regidor. Councilman.

repartimiento. Allocation of indigenous labor by the state. Also a district. Sometimes used as *reparto.*

reparto or *repartimiento de mercancías.* Compulsory distribution of goods to indigenous tributaries by the corregidor.

residencia. Judicial examination of a corregidor or other official after his term of service.

revisita. Reinspection or recount of a province to determine tribute and number of tributaries.

rezago. Debt owed from earlier obligations that were not met.

Glossary

ropa de tierra. Rough cloth or clothes produced in colonial *obrajes* and *chorillos.*

sacristán. Sexton.

septima. One seventh. Term used for *mita* or forced labor, because only one-seventh of tributaries were to be forced to provide service at one time.

sínodo. Payment to local priest, often coming out of tribute.

solar. Town lot.

subdelegado. Highest appointed official in a rural district under the Intendant system. Replaced *corregidors.*

tambo. Inn.

tincu. Ritual battles, usually conducted during *carnestolendas.*

tocuyo. Rough cotton cloth.

topo. Measure of land, which varies from region to region. Sometimes standardized as the land needed to sow 1 1/2 fanegas of seed.

trajín. Transport of goods.

trajinante. One who works in a *trajín.* A packer.

troje. Granary, barn, storage area.

vara. Approximately 33 inches.

vara de justicia. Staff of office carried by authorities such as *curacas.*

visita. Tour of inspection. One who conducts such an inspection is a *visitador.*

yanacona. Indigenous person in service to an individual or the crown. Sometimes defined as serf or servant.

zambo (sambo). Person of mixed Black and Indian ancestry.

Notes

Introduction

1. Wachtel, *Vision of the Vanquished.*

2. For example see Stern, *Peru's Indian Peoples.*

3. There are various spellings of the name of the rebel leader. The most common—Túpac Amaru—was that preferred by the Spanish. In this work I will use the form most frequently used—Thupa Amaro—by the rebel leader himself. For a discussion of the issue of the name see Rowe, "Thupa Amaro," 6–9.

4. Scott, *Weapons of the Weak,* xviii.

5. For the difficulties of this process see Mallon, "Promise and Dilemma," especially 1507, 1511.

6. Tedlock, "From Participant Observation," 69–94; Gossen, "The Other in Chamula Tzotzil," 443–75.

7. Polanyi, *Great Transformation,* 46.

8. See E. P. Thompson's discussion of the work of Paul Greenough on Bengal in "Moral Economy Reviewed," in *Customs in Common.*

9. Geertz, *Interpretation of Cultures,* 18.

10. Guha, "Prose of Counter-Insurgency," 84.

11. Thompson, "Moral Economy Reviewed," 344.

12. Thompson, "Moral Economy of the English Crowd." For a more updated view of Thompson's thoughts on moral economy as it has come to be used in other fields, especially peasant studies, see "Moral Economy Reviewed," especially pages 339–51. Much of this discussion is drawn from an article of mine in the *Hispanic American Historical Review* (Stavig, "Ethnic Conflict, Moral Economy." A conversation with Brooke Larson at the 1986 CLASCO conference in Lima and the paper she presented, "'Exploitation' and 'Moral Economy' in the Southern Andes: A Critical Reconsideration," were helpful to me. Also on the Andes, see Platt, *Estado boliviano y ayllu andino*; and Langer, "Labor Strikes and Reciprocity," 2. In Mexico see Gosner, *Soldiers of the Virgin.* Also see Scott, *Moral Economy* and *Weapons of the Weak.* Thompson has been criticized for not differentiating between sectors of the "community," a differentiation that is fundamental to my argument. For such a critique see Desan, "Uses and Abuses of 'Community.'"

13. For the use of history in the Andes see Patterson, "Inca Empire," 6–7; Scott, *Weapons of the Weak,* 336. Scott states that "the claims of the poor derive their normative force and strategic value from the fact that lip service is still being paid to them by the locally dominant elite."

14. For example, see Reddy, *Rise of Market Culture,* 331–34.

15. Larson, "Exploitation and Moral Economy," 27.

16. De Certeau, *Practice of Everyday Life,* 31–32.

17. For a discussion of the notion of a "rational peasant" see Popkin, *Rational Peasant.*

18. For further discussion see Scott, *Weapons of the Weak.*

19. Bloch, *French Rural History,* as cited in Scott, *Weapons of the Weak,* 28.

20. Barrington Moore Jr., *Injustice,* 18, 506.

21. Mallon, "Promise and Dilemma," 1500.

22. Hobsbawm, "Peasants and Politics," 3–22; Scott, *Weapons of the Weak*, xv.

23. On uneven exchange and class differences in indigenous communities, see Wolf, "Vicissitudes of the Closed Corporate Peasant Community," 327; Orlove, "Inequality among Peasants," 201–14; and Spalding, "Kurakas and Commerce," 592.

24. Scott, *Moral Economy*, 7.

25. Scott, *Moral Economy*, 9.

26. For such abuse in the late seventeenth century, see Sánchez-Albornoz, *Indios y tributos*, 91–110, 142–49.

27. Spalding, "Kurakas and Commerce," 592.

28. Spalding, "Kurakas and Commerce," 594–99. While I have not completed the analysis of my Potosi research, it is clear that tensions between *curacas* and *ayllus* were greater than in the zone of Cuzco I studied.

29. Indians who moved from their community of origin to another community were known as *forasteros*. Their descendants maintained this designation. *Forasteros* were exempted from certain obligations, such as service in the Potosi *mita* and part or all of the tribute payment. Indians who remained in their communities of origin and met their obligations were known as *originarios*.

30. *Ayllus* were subdivisions of the community that originally were based on kinship or territorial claims. *Ayllus* were organized into moieties or halves. The two moieties were *hanansaya* and *hurinsaya*.

31. The classic discussion of familial self-exploitation to meet the burdens of life is found in Chayanov, *Theory of Peasant Economy*.

1. Nature, Society, and Imperial Heritages

1. Betanzos, "El Dios Viracocha y Los Canas," 62; Betanzos, *Narrative of the Incas*, 10.

2. Garcilaso de la Vega, *Royal Commentaries*, vol. 2, pt. 16:104 and pt. 18:108.

3. Cieza de Leon, *Señorío de los Incas*, 142–44 (chap. 42).

4. Cobo, *History of the Inca Empire*, 131–32. Others maintain that the Canas and Canchis were brought into the empire only after the death of Viracocha

when his son, Pachacutec, assumed the royal fringe and that this transition came about peacefully, the Canas and Canchis having fought as Incan allies in the wars against the Chancas. See, for example, Aparaicio, "Historia de la Provincia de Canchis," 88–89.

5. Julien, *Inca Administration*, 35.

6. Glave, *Vida Símbolos y Batallas*, chap. 1, especially 27.

7. Glave, *Vida Símbolos y Batallas*, chap. 1.

8. Glave, *Vida Símbolos y Batallas*, 38; Aparicio, "Historia de la Provincia de Canchis," 85–92. He cites Aguero, *Historia de el Peru*, 115; and Valcarcel, *Estado Imperial de los Incas*, 145.

9. Gorbak, Lischetti, Muñoz, "Batallas Rituales," 246, 250.

10. ADC. Corrg. Prov. Leg. 61, 1697–1705. 1697. Sangarara. Cristobal Quispe indio prisionero.

11. ADC. Corrg. Prov. Leg. 79, 1745–73. 1772. Langui. Criminal contra Faustino Guagua Mamani sobre la muerte que susedio . . . a Sebastina Lazo; see also Hopkins, "Juego de enemigos," 168–69.

12. Bertonio, *Vocabulario de la lengua aymara* (republished from the original: Guamán Poma de Ayala, *El primer nueva corónica*, 1:89–92).

13. In northern Peru this process seems to have begun a few years sooner. See Ramirez, *World Upside Down*.

14. Gade and Escobar, "Village Settlement," 441.

15. Gade and Escobar, "Village Settlement," 441.

16. Glave, *Vida Símbolos y Batallas*, 67–68, 88.

17. Stavig, "Ethnic Conflict," 766.

18. Rasnake, *Kurahkuna of Yura*, 187–88.

19. Aparicio, "Historia de la Provincia de Canchis," 95; Hemming, *Conquest of the Incas*, 257–58.

20. Bueno, *Jerarquia Eclesiastica peruana*, unpag.

21. Cieza de Leon, *Travels*, 355–57.

22. Guamán Poma, *Primer Nueva Corónica*, 845.

23. "Descripción Corográfica," 75–76.

24. Cieza de Leon, *Travels*, 354.

25. Yamamoto, "Papa, Llama y Chaquitaclla."

26. Jacobsen, "Livestock Complexes," 117–22.

27. Esquivel y Navia, *Noticias Cronologicas*, 363–80.

28. ADC. Corrg. Prov. Leg. 60, 1601–77. 1662. Don Bernabe Gualpa, cacique de Moina reducido in Oropesa.

29. AAC. 28.3 LXI, 3, 47. Pleitos. Autos sobre arrendamiento de una estancia perteneciente a la Iglesia de Marangani a D. Andres Garcia.

30. ADC. Intend. Ord. Leg. 21, 1790. El Señor Yntendte del Cuzco acompañado testimonio de la sentencia de deposecion.

31. Guamán Poma, *Primer Nueva Corónica*, 1027; lectures of Ramiro Ortega (visiting scholar from San Antonio Abad in Cuzco) at the University of California, Davis, 1990.

32. Scott, *Moral Economy*, 2, 5.

33. Ortega, lectures at U.C. Davis, 1990.

34. Pizzaro, "Descubrimiento y Conquista del Perú," 104.

35. Aparicio, "Historia de la Provincia de Canchis," 95.

36. Tandeter, *Coercion and Market*, 19.

37. Gade and Escobar, "Village Settlement," 432.

38. Cobo, *Inca Religion and Customs*, 3.

39. Cobo, *Inca Religion and Customs*, 3.

40. Griffiths, *Cross and the Serpent*, 263.

2. Sexual Values and Marital Life in the Colonial Crucible

1. AAC. LXXVI, 2, 26, fol. 18, 2–15–9.3–26 Capellanías, 1759. Títulos de la hacienda Pumahincho . . . de la iglesia de Santa Lucía de Pichigua.

2. The literature on syncretism and religious resistance is extensive. One might begin by looking at articles in two issues of the journal *Allpanchis*, vol. 16, no. 19 (*El Cristianismo Colonial*), and vol. 17, no. 20 (*Religion, Mito y Ritual en el Peru*); MacCormack, *Religion in the Andes*, see especially chap. 6; MacCormack, "Pachacuti," 960–1006; Spalding, *Huarochirí*, see especially chap. 8; Arriaga, *Extirpation of Idolatry in Peru*.

3. Kinsey, *Sexual Behavior in the Human Male*; Kinsey et al., *Sexual Behavior in the Human Female*; Masters, Johnson, and Kolodny, *Human Sexuality*.

4. Boyer, "Women, *La Mala Vida*," 279.

5. Stavig, "Violencia cotidiana de los naturales," 460–61. I am referring to crimes found in the archives, which I realize are an incomplete record. Violence was not always criminal, and communities resolved many violent disputes without going to outside authorities.

6. Gruzinski, "Individualization and Acculturation," 96–117; Harrison, "Theology of Concupiscence," 135–50.

7. Lavrin, "Sexuality in Colonial Mexico," 48–49.

8. Harrison, "Theology of Concupiscence," 139.

9. Harrison, "Theology of Concupiscence," 148.

10. Lavrin, "Sexuality in Colonial Mexico," 74; Harrison, "Theology of Concupiscence," 142.

11. Harrison, "Theology of Concupiscence," 142–49.

12. Lavrin, "Sexuality in Colonial Mexico," 48–49; see also Twinam, "Honor, Sexuality, and Illegitimacy," 123–24.

13. Gruzinski, "Individualization and Acculturation," 103–4.

14. Confessional materials were revealed in some instances related to insurrection.

15. ADC. Corrg. Prov. Leg. 70, 1776–79. 1777. Don Lorenzo Leon de Aragon, vecino de Sicuani sobre unas tierras en el Ayllo Quehuar que defiende el actual cacique. . . .

16. ADC. Corrg. Prov. Crim. Leg. 79, 1745–73. 1772. Criminal contra Pasqual Quelca, yndio del pueblo Quehue sobre la muerte que se la acumuló de su mujer Maria Puma, yndia del mismo pueblo. Love is an abstract concept and its meaning in this context could be quite different from modern western concepts of love.

17. ADC. Corrg. Prov. Leg. 61, 1679–1705. 1704. Causa criminal . . . contra Gregorio Leon, indio por aver estrupado Petronia Turuco muchacha de edad de 9. . . .

18. Guamán Poma, *Primer Nueva Corónica*, 501.

19. ANP. Leg. 35, C. 103, 400, 1670. Juicios de Residencias. Incidente de car-

ácter penal dentro del juicio de residencia . . . contra el Capitan Dn. Pedro de Roda. It is possible that rape was defined differently by Cuzco villagers, but I came across no evidence to suggest this.

20. For references to premarital sex see Bolton, "Qolla Marriage Process"; and Carter, "Trial Marriage." See also Harris, "Power of Signs"; and Price, "Trial Marriage."

21. *Tincu* battles sometimes involved the capture of women where sex was assumed to be a right of capture. For a modern view of peasant courtship and sex in another Andean region see Izko, "Condores y Mast'akus."

22. Harrison, "Theology of Concupiscence," 143.

23. ADC. Corrg. Crim. Leg. 77, 1769–70. 1770. Criminal contra Pedro Rodriguez vezino del Pueblo de San Pedro de Checa sobre el rrapto que executo en Agueda Aguilar vezina y niña de siete años; ADC. Corrg. Prov. Leg. 61, 1679–1705. Aío 1704. Causa criminal . . . contra Gregorio Leon.

24. Guamán Poma, *Primer Nueva Corónica*, 163; Cobo, *Historia del Nuevo Mundo*, 103–7.

25. ADC. Inten. Prov. Crim. Leg. 120, 1758–88. 1785. Criminal contra Blas Conde por la muerte que executó en Rafael Conde . . . ambos naturales de la doctrina de Langui. Although corporal punishment was common, most criminals were sentenced to labor.

26. AAC. 29.1, XII, 1, 16. Quejas. 1752. Queja de Miguel Lloclla maestro cantor de la iglesia de Pomacanchi, contra el curaca Juan Esteban Pacheco, por atropellos.

27. Guamán Poma, *Primer Nueva Corónica*, 164.

28. Guerra, *Pre-Columbian Mind*, 220. Guerra's comments are based on the *Recopilación de Leyes*, 1581 edition, vol. 2, book 8, title 20, law 7; Carter, "Trial Marriage"; Bolton, "Qolla Marriage Process," 226; Zuidema, "Inca Kinship System."

29. Harrison, "Theology of Concupiscence," 144.

30. Harrison, "Theology of Concupiscence," 144.

31. AAC. 28.1–21.2. XLVII, 3, 53, Pleitos. 1795. Margarita Arias, mujer legítima de Diego Montesinos vecinos del pueblo de San Pablo de Cacha, partido de Tinta, contra su marido, por incestar con una hija que tiene de adulterio. Sleeping in the same bed may not have been uncommon.

32. ADC. Inten. Prov. Crim. Leg. 125, 1800–24. 1802. Autos criminales seguidos de oficio de la Rl. justicia . . . ayllo Anza.

33. Carter, "Trial Marriage," especially 210–12 for "process"; Bolton, "Qolla Marriage Process," 217–39; Price, "Trial Marriage"; Romero, "Tincunakuspa," 83–91; on the concept of "marriageways" see McCaa, "Marriageways in Mexico and Spain," 12–13.

34. Socolow, "Acceptable Partners," 234.

35. I came across no cases in which high-status indigenous men were living with indigenous or nonindigenous women of lower status in a situation in which they could be married. Thus, it was not possible to determine if they received the same deference as well-to-do Spaniards.

36. Guamán Poma, *Primer Nueva Corónica*, 283. For a discussion of why Guamán Poma might have idealized or created archetypes see Adorno, "Language of History," and Guamán Poma, *Writing and Resistance in Colonial Peru*.

37. Pizarro, *Relation of the Discovery*, 408–9; Father Martin Murúa supports Guamán Poma's statements about punishment for premarital relations, but he also contradicts his own comments and says that such relations were sanctioned. Murúa, *Historia del origen*, 310–11; on the *acllas* see Silverblatt, *Moon, Sun, and Witches*, 82–85, 101–3.

38. Price, "Trial Marriage," 311; Pizarro, *Relation of the Discovery*, Vol. 1, 408–9.

39. Socolow, "Acceptable Partners," 226; Twinam, "Honor, Sexuality, and Illegitimacy," 124; Lavrin, "Introduction," 10–11.

40. Lavrin, "Introduction," 10; for a modern view of attitudes toward virginity in the Andes see Izko, "Condores y Mast'akus," 60. Izko writes, "La virginidad no es valorada por sí misma; constituye simplemente un estado biológico que debe desembocar en la etapa fecunda, destino de toda mujer."

41. Pizarro, "Relación del descubrimiento," 579; de Acosta, *Historia natural*, 603; Silverblatt, *Moon, Sun, and Witches*, 101–8.

42. Arriaga, *Extirpation of Idolatry in Peru*, 55.

43. Izko, "Condores y Mast'akus," 60. Izko states that in the region of Bolivia he studied young indigenous people engage in sexual relations before the process of marriage has begun "como siempre han sucedido."

44. ADC. Corrg. Prov. Crim. Leg. 79, 1745–73. 1766. Criminales contra Diego Quispe, sobre la muerte de Visente Leon.

45. ADC. Inten. Prov. Crim. Leg. 124, 1792–99. 1798. Pomacanche. Expediente criminal iniciado pr Clemente Rayme, y su hija Santusa contra Pasqual Colque Alcde Ordo del Pueblo de Pomacanche sobre barios excesos.

46. Twinam, "Honor, Sexuality, and Illegitimacy," 123–25. For present sexual attitudes see Harris, "Power of Signs."

47. Various words are used to describe trial marriage. The two most common today are *sirvinacuy* and *tincunacuy*. *Sirvinacuy* is a Quechua term taken from the Spanish word for service, *servir*. *Tincunacuspa,* coming from *tincunacuy,* expresses the action and effect of two persons intimately meeting or joining. Early in the colonial period *pantanacuy* was another term applied. See Maclean y Estenos, "Sirvinacuy o tincunacuspa," 4–12; Carter, "Trial Marriage," 178–79; Price, "Trial Marriage," 311–16; Romero, "Tincunakuspa," 85–87. Romero says the word comes from Quechua of Ancash *tincuna cushga* (*unirse, aliarse*).

48. Romero, "Tincunakuspa," 85–86.

49. De Toledo, "Ordenanza VIII," 177; Romero, "Tincunakuspa," 88–89.

50. Romero, "Tincunakuspa," 86–88. See also Price, "Trial Marriage," 311.

51. Lavrin, "Introduction," 6; Socolow, "Acceptable Partners," 226–27; Twinam, "Honor, Sexuality, and Illegitimacy," 125–42.

52. Twinam, "Honor, Sexuality, and Illegitimacy," 142. Also see pages 118–23, 125–34.

53. Modern Andean peoples have knowledge of herbs and drinks that are used as contraceptives or to induce abortion. While people most likely had this knowledge during the colonial period I found no confirmation of this in the region under investigation; Carter, "Trial Marriage," 180; Izko, "Condores y Mast'akus," 100–103.

54. Price, "Trial Marriage," 310–13. Price gives references to the contradictory information on relationship formation. The process of relationship formation remains murky due largely to the paucity of data and differences in class; Silverblatt, *Moon, Sun, and Witches,* 8, 87–94; documentation in Cuzco leans toward mutual attraction, although no document spells out exactly how or why the relationship began.

55. McCaa, "Marriageways," 13–14. McCaa draws attention to matchmakers

and the elderly in relationship formation in colonial Mexico and notes the apparent absence of parents, relatives, and authorities, whereas in the preconquest era a variety of people were involved; for an arranged indigenous marriage in Mexico that did not work see Boyer, "Women, *La Mala Vida*," 271.

56. Bolton, "Qolla Marriage," 230; Izko, "Condores y Mast'akus," 59–65. Izko implies that mutual attraction is the basis of relationships.

57. Romero, "Tincunakuspa," 86.

58. Cobo, *Historia del Nuevo Mundo*, 38; Price, "Trial Marriage," 311.

59. Romero, "Tincunakuspa," 86–87.

60. Lavrin, "Introduction," 9.

61. Socolow, "Acceptable Partners," 210; Lavrin, "Introduction," 7.

62. AAC. 27–29.1, XII, 1, 14. Pareceres, Peticiones, Solicitud. 1786. Información recibida por Don Manuel de Tonnegra, subdelegado de Tinta, contra el licenciado Ildefonso Loaiza. On forced marriage in an earlier period see Guamán Poma, *Primer Nueva Corónica*, 542; and Silverblatt, *Moon, Sun, and Witches*, 138–47.

63. ADC. Inten. Ord. Leg. 48. 1800. El comun de los Pueblos de Checacupi y Pitumarca puesto a los pies de V.S. . . . qe nro. cura el D.D. Jose Loaisa nos tiene en estado de un total desesperación. While such actions may well have taken place, native peoples did exaggerate at times to make an effective case.

64. ADC. Intend. Crim. Leg. 107, 1792–94. Expediente relativo a la queja por el subdelegado del partido de Tinta, y otros contra el cura ynter . . . de la Doctrina de Yanaoca sobre excesos.

65. Harrison, "Theology of Concupiscence," 147. Questions about sex with priests was one of the questions in the confession manual.

66. AAC. 28.1–29.1, LXXIV, 1, 10.f.10. Pleitos. 1794. Causa de varios capitulos criminales que Francisco Quispe, Jacinto Quispe y otros, sacristanes y alcaldes ordinarios de la Doctrina de Checacupe y Pitumarca le ponen a su cura propio Don Jose Maria Loaisa.

67. AAC. 27–29.1, XI, 3, 5, 50.f.10. Pareceres, Peticiones, Solicitud. 1758. Sumaria información por el Obispo acerca de vida y costumbres de Juan de la Fuente y Centeno, cura propio de la Doctrina de Quiquijana. . . .; Twinam, "Honor, Sexuality, and Illegitimacy," 119. She indicates that the word for children of priests was "*espurios*" (illegitimate, bastard)."

68. Silverblatt, *Moon, Sun, and Witches*, 8.

69. Silverblatt, *Moon, Sun, and Witches*, 15; on a similar ideal regarding Spanish marriage see Boyer, "Women, *La Mala Vida*," 256–58.

70. Silverblatt, *Moon, Sun, and Witches*, 15. Silverblatt states that while there was equality in the rites of marriage "men and not women represented the household to the imperial administration." It is impossible to determine the degree of influence women had over the public actions of men. In a personal conversation (1986), the Peruvian anthropologist Ella Schmidt noted that in the Cuzco regions where she worked, men were the public spokespeople, but wives were consulted before decisions were made.

71. ADC. Inten. Ord. Leg. 18, 1789. Sicuani. Cathalina Sisa viuda vesina del pueblo de Sicuani . . . estoy padeciendo en esta carcel; on complementarity see Isbell, "La otra mitad esencial"; Harris, "Complementarity and Conflict"; for women and tribute in colonial Peru, see Silverblatt, "Universe Has Turned Inside Out," 168.

72. ADC. Inten. Crim. Leg. 105, 1789–90. 1790. Checacupi. Criminal contra el casiq. D. Julian Vargas sobre agravios q. representan los yndios de los ayllos del pueblo de Checacupi.

73. Stavig, "Violencia cotidiana," 460–61; For jealousy and responses to adultery in colonial Mexico see Taylor, *Drinking, Homicide, and Rebellion*, 83–97.

74. ADC. Corrg. Prov. Leg. 81, 1776–84. 1777. Sicuani. Criminal contra Melchor Cansaya, indio del ayllo de Chumo del pueblo de Sicuani por la muerte q. dio a Philipe Apacyupa indio de la Prov. de Calca; Harris, "Condor and Bull," 40–65; Twinam, "Honor, Sexuality, and Illegitimacy," 123–24.

75. Lavrin, "Sexuality in Colonial Mexico," 68–69. Lavrin states that "violent revenge for adultery does not appear to have been common." Taylor, *Drinking, Homicide, and Rebellion*, 85, writes that adultery and jealousy in indigenous villages "appear to be fundamental sources of violent conflict."

76. ADC. Corrg. Prov. Crim. Leg. 121, 1789–90. 1789. Criminal contra Javier Rafael e Ygnacio Rafael yndios del pueblo Pitumarca sobre la muerte ejecutada en Ventura Cusimayta, soltero yndio del mismo pueblo.

77. ADC. Corrg. Prov. Leg. 61, 1679–1705. 1703. Urcos. Catalina Malqui y cuñado Juan Humpiri. It was usually the elder brother who protected female relatives from their husbands, and this could be a comparable situation, yet

the lack of the husband's involvement is peculiar. Harris, "Condor and Bull," 44–49; Harris, "Complementarity and Conflict," 35.

78. ADC. Corrg. Prov. Leg. 62, 1706–18. 1706. Ocongate, estancia de Toctopata. Contra Bartolomé Mamani por la muerte de Ynes Sisa su mujer.

79. The term "useless" was used by both men and women to describe mates they wished to have killed; supporting material has shed no light on the meaning of this term.

80. ADC. Corrg. Prov. Crim. Leg. 79, 1745–73. 1773. Marangani. Criminal contra Agustin Masa, yndio del pueblo de Marangani y Maria Cama viuda yndia del pueblo de Nuñoa por la muerte de Maria Mamani Sisa y Salvador Masa . . . mujer y hijo de dicho Agustin Masa.

81. ADC. Inten. Prov. Ord. Leg. 91, 1788–90. 1790. Oropesa. Auto criminal que sigue de oficio de la R. Justicia contra Domingo Udco reo de causa crimen pr el beneno que dio a su muger Marsela Paez en el ayllo Choquepata terminos de este pueblo de Oropesa. Documentation ended without determination of responsibility, but only the spouse was accused of the poisoning, not the lover. There was no accusation of witchcraft or sorcery either. For witchcraft in the colonial world, see Behar, "Sexual Witchcraft, Colonialism, and Women's Powers," 178–206.

82. ADC. Inten. Prov. Crim. Leg. 124, 1792–99. 1799. San Pablo de Cacha. Expediente promovido contra los reos Blas Condori y Cruz Mamani sobre el omecidio que estas executaron en la persona de Tomas Mendoza yndio originario del ayllo Charachapi Urinsaya en el pueblo de Sn Pablo de Cacha a instancia de su muger lexitima Esperanza Malqui.

83. Stavig, "Violencia cotidiana," 460; Taylor, *Drinking, Homicide, and Rebellion*; on Guamán Poma see Silverblatt, *Moon, Sun, and Witches*, 145.

84. For Spanish attitudes toward violence see Boyer, "Women, *La Mala Vida*," 256; Harris, "Condor and Bull," see section on wife beating. Harris cites an expression "of course he beats me, that's how husbands are," 48. There is an expression in modern Peru that perhaps reflects and seeks to justify some of the spousal violence, "Cuanto más me pegas, más te quiero." For a discussion of spousal violence in modern rural Cuzco, see Harvey, "Domestic Violence in the Andes."

85. ADC. Corrg. Prov. Crim. Leg. 79, 1745–73. 1749. Pichigua. Contra Bentura Laguna, yndio del pueblo de Pichigua por la muerte de su mujer, Esperanza Choque.

86. ADC. Corrg. Prov. Crim. Leg. 79, 1745–73. 1771 Pichigua. Criminal contra Blas Rodriguez, mestizo, del pueblo de Pichigua por la muerte de Martina Calle yndia su mujer. For wife abuse while drinking in the modern era see Harris, "Complementarity and Conflict," 34–35.

87. ADC. Corrg. Prov. Leg. 61, 1679–1705. 1691. Quiquijana. La muerte de Francisca Poca.

88. For a discussion of the brother's role in protecting the sister in modern Andean society see Harris, "Condor and Bull" and "Complementarity and Conflict," 35.

89. ADC. Corrg. Prov. Crim. Leg. 81, 1776–84. 1779. Coporaque. Criminal contra Pasqual Paucara y Faviana Paucara pr la muerte violenta q. ejecutaron en Pablo Guana yndio del pueblo de Coporaque.

90. On a similar case in Mexico see Boyer, "Women, *La Mala Vida*," 271.

91. ADC. Corrg. Prov. Leg. 68, 1770–72. 1771. Varios papeles que se interceptaron a Dn. Eugenio Sinanyuca. Señor Vicario.

92. ADC. Corrg. Prov. Leg. 68, 1770–72. 1771. On spousal abuse and solutions in Spanish society see Boyer, "Women, *La Mala Vida*," 252–86, especially 264.

93. ADC. Inten. Crim. Leg. 109, 1797–99. 1799. Siquani. Expedte. iniciado pr el Dr. Dn. Grego ... Sanchez cura de Siquani contra Mariano Maruri y otros sobre excesos y escandolos. In one of the cases it is clear that the spouse had urged the cura to take such action.

94. Lavrin, "Introduction," 27; Da Silva, "Divorce in Colonial Brazil," 313–14.

95. Lavallé, "Divorcio," 427–64; Boyer, "Women, *La Mala Vida*," 258–81. Boyer points to cases in Mexico where men took action (274–77). Separations were not necessarily permanent; Da Silva, "Divorce in Colonial Brazil," 317–26.

96. AAC. 22.2–29.2–21.2 XLIX, 2, 40, 1671. Miserables-Población Indigena. El protector de naturales, a nombre de Joana Inquillay, mujer y conjunta persona de Domingo Lopez, pone demanda de divorcio contra su marido.

97. For a study of bigamy in nonindigenous colonial society see Boyer, *Lives of the Bigamists*.

98. AAC. 21.2 LXXV, 2, 30, f.33. Liturgia. Auto, cabeza de proceso y comision contra una india nombrada Teresa Sisa, casada dos veces, en Urcos y Guanta causa promovida por el licenciado Dn. Diego Felipe de Albarca, Presbitero.

1698. Documentation ended after she had been whipped; on bigamy see Boyer, "Women, *La Mala Vida,*" 258–59.

3. Robbers, Rustlers, and Highwaymen

1. ADC. Corrg. Prov. Crim. Leg. 79, 1745–73. 1773. Dn. Tomas Rado y Dn. Francisco Guamantilla contra el yndio Andres Quispe por robo de bacas y otros excesos.

2. ADC. Corrg. Prov. Crim. Leg. 79, 1745–73. 1771. Criminal contra Andres Quecaño indio del Pueblo de Checasupa.

3. For similar situations in which Indian-state relations were strengthened and weakened see Stavig, "Ethnic Conflict," 743, 746–48, 754–62.

4. Stavig, "Ethnic Conflict," 760.

5. Nothing suggests that the attitude toward a crime by a non–Indian was any different than toward an Indian, although blacks and mestizos were often held in disregard by *naturales.* For one Andean Indian's attitude toward blacks see Guamán Poma, *Primer Nueva Corónica,* 664.

6. All debate stems from the seminal works of Hobsbawm, *Primitive Rebels* and *Bandits;* see also Slatta, *Bandidos;* Flores Galindo, "Los rostros de la plebe"; and Aguirre and Walker, *Bandoleros.*

7. Scott, "Resistance without Protest," 419, 450; and *Weapons of the Weak,* chap. 7. Only if all theft is viewed as social banditry because it involves social interaction—a pitfall I believe it is important to avoid—can the state be held directly accountable for most such crimes involving *naturales.*

8. Crimes of passion, often involving the consumption of alcohol, were the leading causes of murder in Quispicanchis and Canas y Canchis. With the exception of the Thupa Amaro rebellion, political crimes such as the murder or beating of a public official or an attack on crown property were infrequent. See Stavig, "Violencia cotidiana" and "Ethnic Conflict."

9. Morner, *Perfil de la sociedad rural,* 19, 118; Stavig, "Ethnic Conflict," 738. There is a significant increase in recorded criminal activity in the decade before the Thupa Amaro rebellion, but there are other periods, earlier and later, in which increases in criminal activity were also recorded. Recording of cases and preservation of documents, however, were not consistent throughout time. Thus, one cannot ascertain the real increase in crime, and it would be

inappropriate to view it as a crime wave. In addition, some cases make general reference to multiple thefts by a criminal but list only one specific accusation. Other cases list several crimes by the same person, which can create misleading perceptions. Rather than generating statistical tables and using specific figures that create the illusion of precision where such exactness cannot exist, I have chosen to avoid illusory precision.

10. Scott, *Weapons of the Weak*, 265; see also Scott, *Moral Economy*.

11. For a later period, but a similar conclusion see Langer, "Andean Banditry"; in colonial Mexico see Taylor, *Drinking, Homicide, and Rebellion*. Although not parallel, the work done on slavery in the United States is useful in examining questions of resistance and making a life within an oppressive system. See, for example, Genovese, *Roll, Jordan, Roll*.

12. Scott, "Resistance without Protest," 419.

13. Borah, "Spanish and Indian Law," 276–77.

14. Kellogg, *Law and the Transformation of Aztec Culture*, xix–xx.

15. ADC. Intend. Prov. Crim. Leg. 121, 1789–90. 1789. Expediente sobre las muertes executadas en las fronteras de partido de Quispicanchis por los indios infieles chunchos de aquellas valles y montañas.

16. Stavig, "Ethnic Conflict," 766–67; Rasnake, "Kurakuna of Yura," 187–88.

17. Guamán Poma, *Primer Nueva Corónica*, 1, 162–63, and for crop theft see 3, 114 [115], 1038–39. For a discussion of Guamán Poma and his work see Adorno, "Language of History," 151–90 (as cited in Guerra 34–37). On robbery the *Relación* states, "XXIII. Who robbed something to eat or dress, or silver or gold, to be questioned, if the theft was forced by need and poverty, and if it was found that was the case, the thief not to be punished, but the one who has the office of purveyor." On laziness, "XXIV. In every town to have a judge against idlers and lazy people, to punish them and make them work."

18. ADC. Corrg. Prov. Leg. 65, 1738–50. 1747. Indio forastero de Guaro . . . robo en Yanaoca.

19. ADC. Inten. Prov. Crim. Leg. 125, 1800–24. 1804. Criminal contra Javier Quispetuma.

20. ADC. Corrg. Prov. Crim. Leg. 79, 1745–73. 1747. Criminales contra Juan Julio y Estevan de Cazeres por el robo de un blandon de la iglesia de Coporaque, y otros.

21. ADC. Inten. Crim. Leg. 109, 1797–99. 1798. Autos en que los yndios de Si-quani se quejan contra los carniceros de S. Geronimo por la extorcion q. les infiere.

22. ADC. Corrg. Prov. Leg. 79, 1745–73. 1768. Destierro a . . . indio Gregorio Mamani al obraje de Lucre.

23. ADC. Corrg. Prov. Crim. Leg. 81, 1776–84. 1780. Criminal contra Simon Gamarra y Thomas Condori, sobre varios robos que se les imputan.

24. Borah, "Spanish and Indian Law," 276.

25. ADC. Corrg. Prov. Crim. Leg. 80, 1773–75. 1774. Criminal contra Pedro y Felipe Cansaya, yndios del pueblo de Quehue por varios robos.

26. ADC. Corrg. Prov. Crim. Leg. 63, 1719–22. 1722. Thomasa Sisa india contra Nicolas Quispe natural de Guaro.

27. ADC. Corrg. Prov. Crim. Leg. 79, 1745–73. 1773. Criminal contra Matias Usca indio del pueblo de Yauri y Juan Paucara yndio del de Coporaque por la muerte que se egecutó en Miguel Macarco, assi mismo yndio del referido pueblo de Coporaque.

28. ADC. Corrg. Prov. Crim. Leg. 79, 1745–73. 1748. Criminal contra Joseph Guamani y Agustin Guanco yndios del pueblo de Yauri . . . por la muerte que dieron a Pablo Lopez español forastero.

29. ADC. Corrg. Prov. Crim. Leg. 81, 1776–84. 1784. Criminal contra Ylde-fonso Mamani yndio del pueblo de Checa de esta provincia sobre la muerte que executó en . . . Doña Angela Castro, española de Layo.

30. Borah, "Spanish and Indian Law," 276–77.

31. Stavig, "Violencia cotidiana," 459.

32. ADC. Corrg. Prov. Crim. Leg. 74, 1741–59, 1751. Ygnacio de Aparicio becino del pue. de Urcos y rresidente de la hacienda de Mollebamba . . . me querello civil y criminalmente contra un yndio del collao llamado Matheo Cohacalla.

33. ADC. Corrg. Prov. Crim. Leg. 81, 1776–84, 1777. Dn. Eugenio Sinanyuca vezino del Pueblo de Coporaque contra Agustin Gonzalez sobre robo de mulas y caballos.

34. ADC. Intend. Prov. Crim. Leg. 125, 1800–1824. 1806. Criminal contra Man-uel Arizapana seguido pr Buenava. Vilca pr muerte que perpetró en Eululia Arizapana.

Notes to Pages 76–80

35. ADC. Intend. Prov. Crim. Leg. 124, 1792–99. 1794. Criminal contra Estanislao Marroquin, Juan Tito vecinos del Partido de Lampa ladrones.

36. ADC. Corrg. Prov. Crim. Leg. 81, 1776–84. 1780. Criminal contra Simon Gamarra y Thomas Condori, sobre varios robos que se les imputan.

37. ADC. Intend. Prov. Ord. Leg. 96, 1802–3. Lucas Chancaiari contra Luis Acsana. Pichigua.

38. For discussions of regional economy see Assadourian, *Sistema de la economía colonial* and *Participación indígena*.

39. ADC. Intend. Prov. Crim. Leg. 124, 1792–99. 1795. Autos criminales seguidos de oficio de la Rl Justicia a representación del Alcalde Mr de Acomaio contra Miguel Balderrama y Fermin de la Torre por los crimines hechos.

40. ADC. Corrg. Prov. Leg. 61, 1679–1705. 1705. Thomas Ramos Tito contra Francisco Pichacani.

41. ADC. Corrg. Prov. Crim. Leg. 80, 1773–75. 1773. Criminal Contra Diego Cajia y Sebastian Olguno yndios . . . de Yauri por la muerte . . . [de] muchacho indio llamado M. Colque del mismo pueblo.

42. ADC. Intend. Prov. Crim. Leg. 125, 1800–1824. 1802. Autos criminales seguidos de oficio de la Real Justicia contra los reos Francisco Chahuara indio natural de Pichigua y vecino de Santiago de Pupuja, y Melchor Pacco vecino de Ayavire, por la muerte que executaron en la person de Pasqual Chulluncuya indio de Pichihua.

43. ADC. Corrg. Prov. Leg. 79, 1745–73. 1768. Destierro a el indio Gregorio Mamani al obraje de Lucre.

44. ADC. Corrg. Prov. Crim. Leg. 80, 1773–75. 1774. Criminal contra Pedro y Felipe Cansaya, yndios del Pueblo de Quehue por varios robos de que fueron acusados.

45. ADC. Corrg. Prov. Crim. Leg. 81, 1776–84. 1777. Criminal contra Josef Lerma y su muger por barios robos . . . quebrantando el destierro.

46. Stavig, "Violencia cotidiana," 460–61.

47. ADC. Corrg. Prov. Crim. Leg. 81, 1776–84. 1777. Eugenio Pilpinto y Pascual Tomayconsa yndios del Pueblo de Pampamarca contra Juan de Dios Melgar sobre robo de algunos piezas de plata egecutado en la casa del cura del referido pueblo.

48. ADC. Corrg. Prov. Leg. 62, 1706–18. 1706. Juan de Buenaño y Bartolome de Contreras por robo de Doña Juana de Aguirre.

49. *Cuzco 1689*, 247–48.

50. ADC. Corrg. Prov. Crim. Leg. 81, 1776–84. 1780. Criminal contra Diego Mamani y Mateo Caucata Guanca yndios por el robo que hicieron a Francisco Guanca yndio. Reparto demands in Canas y Canchis and Quispicanchis were not high compared to other regions. See Golte, *Repartos y rebeliones*, 95.

51. ADC. Corrg. Prov. Crim. Leg. 81, 1776–84. 1779. Criminal contra Pasqual Villegas y Roque Taco vecino el primero del Pueblo de Yauri y el segundo de Coporaque por varios robos en que fueron aprehendidos.

52. Stavig, "Ethnic Conflict," 767–70.

53. Hobsbawm, "Peasants and Politics," 13.

4. Indigenous-Spanish Struggles Over Land

1. ANP. D. I., L.1, C. 72, 1571. Testimonio de los autos que siguió don Hernando Alvarez Azevedo, como procurador de don Pedro Atahualpa cacique principal del pueblo Urco-Urco. . . .

2. ADC. Corrg. Prov. Leg. 61, 1679–1705. 1699. Indios de Ayllo Collatia del Quiquijana contra Cap. Juan Franc. de Ochoa.

3. ANP. L.3, C.23, 1763. Autos que sigue el doctor don Joseph Martines contra los indios del Ayllo de Charachapi de la Provincia de Tinta sobre unas tierras.

4. Bueno, *Jerarquia Eclesiastica Peruana*. No page numbers.

5. *Cuzco 1689*, 236–52.

6. Hopkins, "Colonial History of the Hacienda System," chap. 1, especially pages 24–25.

7. Hopkins, "Colonial History of the Hacienda System," 24–25.

8. Hopkins, "Colonial History of the Hacienda System," 32–33.

9. Burga, *De la encomienda a la hacienda capitalista*, 50–51.

10. Burga, *De la encomienda a la hacienda capitalista*, 117–22.

11. ANP. D. I., L.9, C.194. 1709. Autos que siguió el maestre de campo don Antonio de Luna y Cardenas, como albacea y heredero de doña Josefa Lopez de Paredes.

12. ADC. Corrg. Prov. Leg. 62, 1706–13. Don Pedro de Antesana cacique de Ocongate . . . y otros por averseles dejado Dn. Pablo de Caravajal encomendero que fue. . . .

13. ADC. Corrg. Prov. Leg. 62, 1708–18. 1716. Don Andres Quispicasa cacique principal de Marcaconga.

14. ADC. Intend. Ord. Leg. 24, 1790–91. 1790. Expediente promovido por Doña Maria Obando yndia noble a nombre de su nieto Dn. Justo Savarara (Sawaxaura) para la venta de unos quartos en solar de yndios en el Aillo de Mohina.

15. ANP. Tierras de Comunidades. L.9, C.79. 1785. Sicuani. Expediente promovido por don Andres Mejia vecino del pueblo de Sicuani.

16. ADC. Corrg. Prov. Leg. 65, 1738–50. Tierras de Guascarquiuar.

17. ADC. Intend. Ord. Leg. 69, 1812. Ylario Yañes vecino y residente del pueblo de Quiquijana . . . seis topos de tierra q denuncio para se vendan.

18. ADC. Intend. Ord. Leg. 59, 1806–7. 1806. Acomayo. Dn. Estevan de Olarte vesino de Pueblo de Acomayo . . . un pedaso de tierras baldias.

19. ADC. Corrg. Prov. Leg. 70, 1776–79. Escritura de arrendamiento de la estancia de Pullapulla, propia del comun de yndios del Pueblo de Yanaoca.

20. ADC. Corrg. Prov. Leg. 70, 1776–79. 1778. Pampamarca. Escritura de arrendamiento de la hazienda de Tintamarca a favor de Dn. Joseph de Unda.

21. ADC. Corrg. Prov. Leg. 60, 1601–77. 1668. Cap. D. Agustin Jara de la Cerda contra los caciques de Urcos y Andahuaylillas.

22. For a similarly equitable treatment of indigenous peoples before the law see, for example, Spores, "Spanish Penetration and Cultural Changes," 92.

23. ADC. Corrg. Prov. Leg. 61, 1679–1705. Acos. Don Mateo Parco Gualpa principal y gobernador de Pueblo de San Francisco de Guayqui.

24. ANP, D. I., L.(?), C.312. 1763. Memorial que Sebastian Fuentes Pongo Yupanqui, indio del pueblo de Acomayo . . . elevó al Superior Gobierno, querellándose contra el corregidor.

25. ADC. Intend. Prov. Leg. 91, 1788–90. 1790. Expediente de los yndios de Luracachi y Marangani, sobre el derecho a unas tierras.

26. ADC. Corrg. Prov. Leg. 61, 1679–1705. 1697. Cacique de Oropesa contra Manuel de Dueñas.

27. ADC. Intend. Prov. Ord. Leg. 99, 1807–9. 1807. Acopia. Expedte. promo-

vido por los yndios de Acopia solicitando no se entrometa Dn. Manuel Farfan ni sus yndividuos en tierras de comunidad.

28. ANP. D. I., L.3, C.53. 1608. Testimonio de los autos que siguieron los indios de San Pedro de la Rivera de Quiquijana . . . contra los herederos de
Gonzalo Becerra de Guevara.

29. ADC. Corrg. Prov. Leg. 61, 1679–1705. 1699. Indios de Ayllo Collatia del
Quiquijana contra. Cap. Juan Franc. de Ochoa.

30. ADC. Corrg. Prov. Leg. 61, 1679–1705. 1690. Don Agustin Guallpa, Don
Franco Canqui y Don Blas Canqui y Don Bartme Tapia contra Andres
Campo.

31. ADC. Corrg. Prov. Leg. 62, 1706–18. 1718. Acopia. Don Juan Choque, Dn.
Felipe Choque (y otros) en nombre del comun.

32. ADC. Corrg. Prov. Leg. 60, 1601–77. 1662. Don Bernabe Gualpa, cacique
de Mohina, reducido en Oropesa.

33. Bueno, *Jerarquia eclesiastica.*

34. ADC. Corrg. Prov. Leg. 61, 1679–1705. 1696. Don Diego Quispehumpiri y
Don Francisco Rimache, caciques de Urcos en nombre del pueblo comun.

35. ANP. D. I., C.197, 1712. Títulos de las tierras y punas, que siendo visitador
de tierras el maestro Fr. Domingo de Cabrera Lartaum, se repartieron a los
indios del ayllo Vicho. . . .

36. ADC. Corrg. Prov. Leg. 66, 1752–65. 1754. Don Joseph Cusipaucar Maita,
cacique principal de Oropesa.

37. ADC. Intend. Ord. Leg. 20, 1789. Don Francisco Xavier de Arrillaga casique de ayllo Guasao en voz y nombre de toda la comunidad.

38. ANP. Tierras de Comunidades (T. C.). L.3, C.23, 1763. Charachapi. Autos
que sigue el doctor don Joseph Martines contra los indios del Ayllo de Charachapi, de la Provincia de Tinta sobre el derecho a unas tierras; ANP. Leg. 7,
Cuad. 71, 1777. Documentos presentados por el Dr. Dn. Joseph Martinez en
la causa con los indios de San Pablo de la provincia de Tinta (Cuzco).

39. ANP. Tierras de Comunidades (T. C.). L.3, C.23, 1763. This is one of the
few instances encountered in which a *natural* chose to give testimony in
Spanish. Most often even though a *natural* could speak Spanish well official
testimony was given in Quechua.

40. ANP. Tierras de Comunidades (T. C.). L.3, C.23, 1763.

41. ADC. Intend. Crim. Leg. 120, 1785–88. 1786. Quehuar. El comun de yndios de ayllo Quehuar contra Maria Cheque, Simon y Benta Aymituma y sus hijos sobre usurpazn de tierras hecha por estos a dho. comun.

42. ADC. Intend. Ord. Leg. 23, 1790. Don Juan Antonio de Figueroa Sargto mayor poseedor y dueño de la hacienda de Suipococha . . . en los terminos de Acos.

43. ADC. Intend. Prov. Crim. Leg. 123, 1791–92. Guaro. Don Juan de Dios Xara, vecino de Huaroc.

5. Ethnic Land Conflict and the State

1. ADC. Corrg. Prov. Leg. 62, 1706–14. Causa sivil de despojo que sigue el cacique segunda persona del ayllo Machacamarca en el nombre de su comun contra los yndios y otros particulares del pueblo de Catca.

2. Stavig, "Ethnic Conflict," 766.

3. Glave, "Comunidades campesinas," 67–68.

4. BNP. Ms. B1479. La causa que se sigue por parte de los indios del pueblo de Combapata, provincia de los Canas y Canchis contra los del pueblo de Checacupe, sobre unas tierras y pastos. Tinta. 1647.

5. Glave, "Comunidades campesinas," 67–68

6. Glave, "Comunidades campesinas," 67.

7. BNP. Ms. B1479. These lands were high points that sometimes had religious significance, and the conflicts could have had a religious component that neither community wished to divulge.

8. Orlove, *Alpacas, Sheep and Men*, 84–86. Also see Flores Ochoa, ed., *Pastores de puna*; and Rhoades and Thompson, "Adaptive Strategies."

9. Golte, *Repartos y rebeliones*, Map 25. Poblacion Indigena por Cacique. Maps begin on page 207. Some agricultural regions had settlement patterns similar to Canas y Canchis, while other herding regions, like those around Lake Titicaca with a flatter topography, had settlement patterns in which the Indian-*curaca* ratio was between those of Quispicanchis and Canas y Canchis.

10. Golte, *Repartos y rebeliones*, Map 25.

11. ADC. Corrg. Ord. Leg. 27, 1700–1711. 1703. Thomas Condori, yndio natural

del pueblo de San Francisco Guayqui. For the importance of alcohol in disputes see Stavig, "Violencia cotidiana," 460–61.

12. ADC. Corrg. Prov. Leg. 62, 1706–18. Quiquijana, 1716. Pedro Tiraquimbo indio . . . repartimiento de Cacha contra Matheo Guaman.

13. ADC. Corrg. Prov. Crim. Leg. 79, 1745–73. Yanaoca, 1771. Miguel Niña Choque indio contra Nicolas Quente.

14. ADC. Corrg. Prov. Leg. 64, 1731–37. Quiquijana, 1737. Doña Francisca Chimba, viuda de Pedro Tiraquimbo.

15. ADC. Corrg. Prov. Leg. 62, 1706–18. Urcos, 1715. Joseph Guaman contra Sebastiana Sisa.

16. ADC. Intend. Ord. Leg. 11, 1787. Pomacanche. Solicitud para construir una casa D. Roque Luna en la plaza del ayllo Pomachapi.

17. ADC. Corrg. Prov. Leg. 69, 1772–75. Sicuani, 1775. Antonio Torres y Dionicio Choque, yndios del pueblo de Sicuani contra Mateo Zavala y Petrona Linares sobre el derecho a un solar.

18. ADC. Intend. Prov. Ord. Leg. 99, 1807–9. Marangani, 1809. Adjudicazion de las tierras de Querera a favor de los yndios de Marangani y ayllo Lurucachi, Felix Poco y Tomas Poco.

19. ADC. Corrg. Prov. Leg. 61, 1679–1705. Andaguaylillas, 1704. Doña Ynes Yepes contra Don Marcos Senteno, ayllo Sallac. A *forastero* was a person—or a descendant of a person—not living in his community of origin. People often became *forasteros* to avoid obligations such as *mita* and tribute to which *originarios* were subject.

20. ADC. Intend. Ord. Leg. 13, 1787. Expte relativo a la denuncia que hace Luis de Oroz de unas tierras llamadas Motca en Quispicanchis que parece fueron de los Tupamaros. For genealogy of the rebel leader see Rowe, "Genealogía y rebelión," 74.

21. ADC. Corrg. Prov. Leg. 60, 1601–77. Surimana, 1617. Expediente del indio Felipe Condorcanqui gobernador de Surimana.

22. ANB. SGI, 1781, n. 248. Testimonio en f16 de las cartas de los rebeldes, comisiones, e informe que Diego Xptoval Tupac Amaru hizo al exmo . . . virrey de Lima, en respuesta del indulto gral que libró; Golte, *Repartos y rebeliones*, 95.

23. O'Phelan, *Rebellions and Revolts*, 256–73.

24. Morner, *Perfil de la sociedad rural*, 138, 144, 146; Stavig, "Ethnic Conflict."

25. ADC. Corrg. Prov. Leg. 62, 1706–18. 1714. Causa sivil de despojo que sigue el cacique segunda persona del ayllo Machacamarca en nombre de su comun contra los yndios y otros particulares del pueblo de Catca.

26. ADC. Corrg. Prov. Leg. 60, 1601–77. 1633. Don Diego yndio viejo natural de Pichigua (hurinsaya). Grandson's case is included in this document.

27. AAC. 22.1, LXVII, 2, 26. Miserables-Poblacion Indigena. 1787. Clemente Zapata, alcalde mayor, cacique y gobernador de Layo, por si, y los principales y comun.

28. ADC. Intend. Ord. Leg. 11, 1787. Exped. relativo a la solicitud del cacique de Pueblo Nuevo sobre unas fanegadas de tierra en litijo con los yndios de Acopia.

29. For actions of curacas see Larson, "Caciques, Class Structure"; Spalding, "Social Climbers" and "Kurakas and Commerce"; and Stern, "Struggle for Solidarity."

30. Cahill, "Curas and Social Conflict," 256–57; O'Phelan, "El sur andino."

31. ADC. Corrg. Prov. Crim. Leg. 81, 1776–84. 1778. Criminal contra don Faustino Mexia cacique interino que fue del ayllo Chumo.

32. ADC. Corrg. Prov. Leg. 62, 1706–18. Acomayo, 1711. Don Juan Ysidro de Fuentes en nombre de los indios comunes.

33. For a discussion of this process see Spalding, "Kurakas and Commerce."

6. Labor in the Spanish Realm

1. *Cuzco 1689*, 159.

2. ADC. Corrg. Prov. Leg. 61, 1679–1705. 1687. Mita de Quispicanchis.

3. ADC. Corrg. Prov. Leg. 63, 1719–30. 1725. Tributo de Urcos. Don Pedro Quispihumpiri cacique.

4. ADC. Corrg. Prov. Crim. Leg. 81, 1776–78. 1778. Criminal contra Ventura Tapia y su muger vesinos del Cuzco por yncendio de la Real Carsel de este pueblo.

5. ADC. Corrg. Prov. 1771. Varios papeles que se interceptaron a Dn Euginio Sinanyuca el dia 12 de Oct. de 1780 referentes a varios comisiones.

6. ADC. Intend. Ord. Leg. 99, 1807–9. Obraje de Andahuaylillas de Dn. Jose Herrera, viuda Dna. Jacinta Balleros.

7. ADC. Intend. Ord. Leg. 42, 1797-98. 1797. Expedte iniciado por el coronel de exercito D. Juan Antonio Figueroa sobre que a los indios q. trabajaron en la fabrica de moler metales pagan su trabajo segun ordenanza.

8. ANP. Compania de Jesus. Contenciosos. Leg. 13, 1614. Urcos. Compania de Jesus contra el cacique de Urcos.

9. ADC. Corrg. Prov. Leg. 61, 1684, 1679-1705. Indios de septima. Doña Maria Marquez viuda del Capitan Juan Roldan de Huerta regidor de Cuzco.

10. ADC. Intend. Ord. Leg. 24, 1790-91. Vale de siento cuarenta ps. q. dara el Sr. Dn. Ramon Moscoso al governador del pueblo de Pomacanche Dn. Roque Luna.

11. Hopkins, "Colonial History of the Hacienda System," 219-32; see also ADC. Intend. Crim., Leg. 108, 1794-96. Causa Criminal sobre excesos del Cacique Choquecahua. Why it is listed with a later date is unknown. Hopkins cites the document as Figure 7-35, p. 447.

12. Hopkins, "Colonial History of the Hacienda System," 219-32.

13. Hopkins, "Colonial History of the Hacienda System," 219-32.

14. Wightman, *Indigenous Migration and Social Change*, 83.

15. ADC. Intend. Prov. Crim. Leg. 124, 1792-94. 1792. Sicuani. Criminal contra Jose Mateo alias el Viscayano pr la muerte . . . de Juan criado de Capitan Dn Manuel Antuñano.

16. ADC. Corrg. Prov. Leg. 60, 1601-77. 1676. Quispicanchis. Doña Juana de la Minera . . . cuatro yndios yanaconas que tengo agregados.

17. Wightman, *Indigenous Migration and Social Change*, 85.

18. Wightman, *Indigenous Migration and Social Change*, 85.

19. Wightman, *Indigenous Migration and Social Change*, 85-86, 147-48.

20. ADC. Intend. Ord. Leg. 56, 1804-5. 1804. Oropesa. Expediente seguido pr el indio Lorenzo Quispe sobre no se le cobre doble tributo pr el cobrador de Oropesa Francisco Alvarez pr estar matriculado en este ciudad en el Ayllo Yanacona.

21. Glave, *Vida símbolos y batallas*, 71. Cuadro 5.

22. Glave, *Vida símbolos y batallas*, 75-83. Cuadro 7.

23. For further discussion of this process see chap. 7 on the Potosi *mita*.

24. *Cuzco 1689*, 243.

25. AAC. 8.3-14.-1.2, LXXIV, 2, 34, f.7. Pleitos. 1747. Don Felipe Pardo, Presbitero en los autos sobre que Don Miguel Cano de Herrera dueño de las haciendas de Lauramarca que estan en la Doctrina de Ocongate; see also Wightman, *Indigenous Migration and Social Change*, 115–16.

26. *Cuzco 1689*, 156–58; Morner, *Perfil de la sociedad rural*, 47.

27. ADC. Intend. Crim. Leg. 106, 1791–92. 1792. Acomayo. Autos criminales seguidos a denuncia del Sr. Fiscal de S.M., D. Antonio Zuares Rodrigz contra D. Luis Farfan de Yraola, casique del Pueblo de Acomayo, Partido de Quispicanchis de ocultazn de Yndios tributarios y otros excesos.

28. ADC. Intend. Ord. Leg. 25, 1791. Rafael Quispe . . . casique de los ayllos de Pumamarca and Ayarmarca de la Parroquia de Sn. Sebastian . . . Tengo a mi cargo nueve Indios forasteros.

29. Wightman, *Indigenous Migration and Social Change*, 145.

30. Super, "Nutritional Regimes," 10; Santisteban, *Los obrajes*, 101, 154–55.

31. Santisteban, *Los obrajes*, 101, 154–55; Wightman, *Indigenous Migration and Social Change*, 144–45 and notes 49–50 in chap. 6.

32. ADC. Corrg. Prov. Leg. 65, 1738–50. 1642. Guaro. Don Lorenco Tito, Don Lorenco Paucar y Don Felipe Oyua caciques de Andagualillas en nombre de otros caciques y comun. This document was with material for the eighteenth century.

33. *Cuzco 1689*, 161.

34. *Cuzco 1689*, 156–58; ADC. Corrg. Prov. Leg. 60, 1601–77. 1675. Don Matheo Cusiguallpa y Don Pedro Carlos Inga . . . indios de septima en el obraje de Maestro de Campo Don Diego de Esquivel y Xarava.

35. Esquivel y Navia, *Noticias Cronológicas*, 424.

36. For a discussion of credit and debt see Bauer, "Rural Workers in Spanish America"; ADC. Corrg. Prov. Leg. 61, 1679–1705. 1700. Juan Francisco de Ochoa. Obraje en Guaro. Debts owed: 0–9 pesos—118 (workers), 10–19 p.—90, 20–39 p.—54, 40–59 p.—11, 60–79 p.—1, 80–99 p.—1, 100–49 p.—1, 150+ p.—1.

37. ADC. Corrg. Prov. Leg. 61, 1679–1705. 1705. Obraje de Guaroc. Debts owed: 0–9 pesos—102 (workers), 10–19 p.—50, 20–39 p.—77, 40–59 p.—21, 60–79 p.—3, 80–99 p.—2, 100–50 p.—2.

38. ADC. Corrg. Prov. Leg. 65, 1738–50. 1750. Obraje Marabamba.

39. *Cuzco 1689*, 166.

40. ADC. Corrg. Prov. Leg. 62, 1706–18. 1713. Marques de Moscoso, obraje de Marabamba; *Cuzco 1689*, 161.

41. ADC. Intend. Ord. Leg. 56, 1804–5. 1804. Expedte iniciado pr. Tomas Qpe Tito solicitando la livertad de su hijo Jose Qpe Tito del obraje de Quispicanche.

42. ADC. Intend. Ord. Leg. 64, 1809. Lucre. Expediente seguido por el yndio Matias Tito contra su recaudador de tributos Marcos Chillitupa.

43. ADC. Intend. Prov. Ord. Leg. 95, 1800–1801. 1801. Expediente inisiado por el Protector interino de Naturales a nombre de la yndia Tomasa Guamani, sobre el maltrato que experimentaron Yldefonsa Umpiri y su abuela en el chorillo de Amancay [*sic.*, Abancay] propia de Dn. Antonio Gallegos.

44. BNP 1798, C1070. Expediente sobre que los telares corrientes que tienen los indios tributarios en el partido de Quispicanchis deberán pagar encabezonamiento.

45. ADC. Intend. Ord. Leg. 22, 1790. Autos seguidos por Matheo Turpo Casique de pueblo de Ocongate . . . contra Ylario Perez.

46. ADC. Intend. Ord. Leg. 37, 1796. El capitan de dragones por su magestad Dn. Mariano Santos . . . The hacienda was in Paruro.

47. ADC. Corrg. Prov. Leg. 66, 1752–65. Coporaque. Mathais Molero, cacique de Livitaca, esposo y conjunta persona con Dna. Gregoria Reira.

48. AAC. 9.1, 1-15-1.2, LIV, 1, 4. Contratos. Ramon Paulino de Vera, vecino del pueblo de Sicuani, casique gobernador en el, pide se le den en arrendamiento 500 ovejas pertenicientes a la iglesia del dicho pueblo.

49. Glave, "La producción de los trajines," 30–32; Hanke, *Los virreyes españoles*, 108.

50. AGI. Escribania 858–c. Memorial. 1678. Exelentisimo señor los Caciques de la Provincia de Canas Y Canches disen que en ella . . . en tiempos pasados havia gran numero de españoles Carnereros.

51. ADC. Corrg. Prov. Leg. 67, 1766–69. 1766. Baltacar Calvo contra Pedro de la Llana de Yanaoca. For more on *trajines* see the work of Glave.

52. Intend. Prov. Ord. Leg. 92, 1791–93. 1791. Causa executiva seguida en la Prov de Lampa a Pedimto de Dn. Pedro Jose de Sarabia contra Dn. Mariano Zinayuca vesino del Pueblo de Coporaque pr. cantidad de pesos.

53. ANP. Aduanas del Cuzco. c-16. L. 161. C. 7, 1775. En la ciudad del Cuzco en 12 de Julio de 1775. . . . Remite a la Villa de Potosi: seis pearas de ropa de la tierra de obraje, quatro de azucar con el harriero Josef Tupamaro.

54. ADC. Corrg. Prov. Leg. 63, 1719–30. 1730. General Dn. Andres Joseph de Villela, caballero del orden de Calatrava y Corregidor y Justicia Mayor que fue de Quispicanchis.

55. ANP. Aduanas del Cuzco. c-16. L.161. C.7, 1775.

56. ADC. Intend. Ord. Leg. 6, 1785. Checacupi. Expediente sobre . . . testamento del D. D. Miguel de Yturyaira, cura de Checacupi.

57. ADC. Intend. Ord. Leg. 1, 1784. Expedte . . . sobre la denuncia hecha por Dn. Miguel Payba en razon de . . . unas haziendas y molinos. The will was from 1682.

58. AAC. 7–22.2–29.1, I, 4, 77. Pareceres, Peticiones, Solicitud. Petición de Pedro Guzman y Sebastian Sinca, caciques gobernadores del pueblo de Layo, al Obispo del Cuzco, para que se nombre otro cura.

59. AAC. LXII, 2, 23, fol. 5. Parrocos, Parroquias. Concubinas en Pitumarca . . . Dn. Miguel Carasas.

60. ADC. Intend. Ord. Leg. 48, 1800. El comun de los pueblos de Checacupi y Pitumarca puesto a los pies de V.S. desimos que nro cura el D.D. Loaisa nos tiene en estado de un total desesperacion.

61. ADC. Corrg. Prov. Crim. Leg. 79, 1745–73. 1755. Combapata. Causa Criminal seguida . . . contra Diego de Leon y Rosa Cancha su muger, Indios, por persecusiones del Don Phe Asensio Delgado Cura.

7. Community, Identity, and the Potosi *Mita*

1. From the motto on the coat of arms of the Villa Imperial de Potosi.

2. For an attempt to end the *mita* see Cole, "Abolitionism Born of Frustration."

3. Borja, *Memorias de los Virreyes*, 72.

4. Solórzano y Perei(y)ra, *Politica Indiana*, 262.

5. Acosta, *Natural and Moral History*, 197.

6. Cobb, "Potosi, a Mining Frontier," 51; Cieza de Leon, *Travels*, 387.

7. Arzáns de Orsúa y Vela, *Historia*, 1:286.

8. Acosta, *Natural and Moral History,* 197.

9. Arzáns de Orsúa y Vela, *Historia,* 3:85; Cañete y Dominguez, *Guía Histórica,* 38.

10. Cieza de Leon, *Travels,* 387.

11. Capoche, *Relación General,* 177.

12. Brading and Cross, "Colonial Silver Mining," 569; and L. Fisher, *Silver Mines,* 6, 127. According to Fisher a mark weighed 8 ounces and was valued 8.5 pesos at the mint.

13. Brading and Cross, "Colonial Silver Mining," 571.

14. Brading and Cross, "Colonial Silver Mining," 561.

15. Jimenez de Espada, *Relaciones Geográficas de Indias,* 1:381–82.

16. Wallerstein, *Modern World System,* 183.

17. Brading and Cross, "Colonial Silver Mining," 573.

18. Padden, *Tales of Potosi,* xxv. See also Arząns de Orsúa y Vela, *Historia,* 1:8; Brading and Cross, "Colonial Silver Mining," 573; Shurz, "Mexico, Peru and the Manila Galleon"; and Cobb, "Supply and Transportation," 28.

19. Hakluyt, "Discourse of Western Planting," 313–19.

20. Smith, *General Historie of Virginia,* 219.

21. Arząns de Orsúa y Vela, *Historia,* 1:3.

22. Leon Pinelo, *Paraiso en el Nuevo Mundo,* 323–28, as cited in Hanke, *Bartolomé Arząns de Orsúa y Vela's History,* 9. When Cervantes had Don Quixote tell Sancho Panza how deeply he valued his companionship he had the knight declare, "if I were to reward you as you deserve . . . the mines of Potosi would not suffice."

23. Elliott, *Imperial Spain,* 204.

24. Acosta, *Natural and Moral History,* 204–5.

25. Elliott, *Old World and the New,* 96.

26. Elliott, *Old World and the New,* 96.

27. Hamilton, *American Treasure,* 283.

28. Hamilton, *American Treasure,* vii.

29. Braudel and Spooner, "Price in Europe," 447–48; for a differing view see Hammerstrom, "'Price Revolution' of the Sixteenth Century."

30. Braudel and Spooner, "Price in Europe," 447; ADP. Concepción, 1762–83. Checasupa, 1768.

31. Cieza de Leon, *Travels,* 387.

32. Cobb, "Potosi and Huancavelica," 64, 134–35. Encomenderos were not supposed to employ Indians in their own mines.

33. Capoche, *Relación General,* 26.

34. Cobb, "Potosi and Huancavelica," 65.

35. Cobb, "Potosi and Huancavelica," 92–93; Arzáns de Orsúa y Vela, *Historia,* I, 286.

36. ANB. E. P. Bravo, 1568, f39v. (MC97e) 1566, VIII, 27. Cuzco. Carta de Poder: Don Carlos Inca, vecino, a Pedro de la Torre, vecino de la ciudad de La Plata por diversos efectos incluyendo de minas e indios; Barnadas, *Charcas.*

37. Glave, "Producción de los trajines," 30.

38. Glave, "Producción de los trajines," 35.

39. Matienzo, *Gobierno del Perú,* 15.

40. Hemming, *Conquest of the Incas,* 407; Cañete y Dominguez, *Guía Histórica,* 106–7; Rodas, "El Reclutamiento," 471–75. The provinces included in the *mita* were Porco, Chayanta, Paria, Carangas, Sicasica, Pacajes Omasuyos, Paucarcolla, Chuquito (these last four are on the shores of Lake Titicaca), Cavana and Cavanilla, Quispicanches, Azangaro and Asilla, and Canes y Canches.

41. Glave, *Vida símbolos y batallas,* 64.

42. Glave, *Vida símbolos y batallas,* 66; Morner, *Perfil de la sociedad rural del Cuzco,* 116; ANB. MI47 (Minas 1365) Nueva Numeración General de 1733. Archivo General de la Nación. Buenos Aires (AGN. B.A.) Sala 9, 14-8-10. Mita. Ordenanzas de virreyes. Potosí. 1683–774. 1692 Mita; Factors such as changes in provincial boundaries and lacuna in the data make province-wide *mita* evaluations problematic.

43. Capoche, *Relación General,* 135.

44. *Mercurio Peruano,* 1792. Edicion Fuentes, I, 208, as cited in René-Moreno, "La Mita de Potosí en 1795," 8.

45. ADC. Corrg. Prov. Leg. 60, 1601–77. 1655. Pomacanche mita. Maestro del Campo Joseph de los Rios y.

46. ADC. Corrg. Prov. Leg. 61, 1679–1705. 1687. Mita de Papres.

47. ANB. E. C. 1770, 81. Don Manuel Maruri, regidor de Potosi y receptor del derecho de alcabalas, sobre que se continuan el pago de las que estan obligados a pagar los enteradores de mita y sus segundos de los efectos de comestibles y ropa de la sierra que introducen en la villa para su expendido en las tiendas, plazas y canchas.

48. ADC. Corrg. Prov. Leg. 61, 1679–1705. 1690; Mita. Pomacanche. For a discussion of the transfer of wealth out of the communities see Sánchez-Albornoz, *Indios y tributos en el Alto Perú.*

49. ADC. Corrg. Prov. Leg. 60, 1601–77. 1646. Mita. Quispicanchis. ADC. Corrg. Prov. Leg. 60, 1601–77. 1674. Mita. Marcaconga.

50. ADC. Corrg. Prov. Leg. 61, 1679–1705. 1690. Mita. Pomacanche, Sangarará.

51. ADC. Corrg. Prov. Leg. 61, 1679–1705. 1687. Mita de Papres.

52. ADC. Corrg. Prov. Leg. 60, 1601–77. 1646. Mita de Quispicanchis.

53. *Cuzco 1689,* 127–73, 236–52.

54. ADC. Corrg. Prov. Leg. 60, 1601–77. 1646. Mita de Quispicanchis. ADC. Corrg. Prov. Leg. 61, 1679–1705. 1690. Mita. Pomacanche, Sangarará.

55. ANP. Superior Gobierno (S. Gob.) L.8, C.146, 1729. Expediente promovido ante el Superior Gobierno, sobre la regulacion de los tributos de la Provincia de Canas y Canches, para que se les pague a los indios del servicio de minas, la bonificación de leguaje, cuando concurren a lugares apartados. ANB. MSS2 (Ruck). 1603. Para que el corregidor de Potosí y los demás ... hagan pagar lo que se ocupan en yr y bolver a sus pueblos, fl53–154v.

56. *Cuzco 1689,* 243.

57. *Cuzco 1689,* 241. For a similar policy in the Lake Titicaca region see BNP. B585.1673. Despacho de la mita de Potosi. Puno, Nov. 2, 1673.

58. ANB. MI47 (Minas no. III) Mano de obra minera no. 686. 1692. IV, 27, Lima. Repartimiento general de indios de mita para las minas e ingenios de Potosi hecho al orden del conde de la Monclava, virrey del Peru. And ANB 147 (Minas 1392) 1736. VI, 24–1736 XI.i Potosi. Entrega de indios de mita: El capitán general de ella a los interesados de las provincias de Porco, Canas y Canches, Chuquito.

59. Sánchez-Albornoz, *Indios y tributos,* 142–49.

60. Sánchez-Albornoz, *Indios y tributos,* 103; Rowe, "Incas under Spanish

Colonial Institutions," 176. The amount required varied according to distance from Potosi, and it also changed with the passage of time. In general, the further one went from Potosi the greater the cost of a substitute.

61. ADC. Intend. Ord. Leg. 41, 1797. Expedte seguido por Mateo Gamarra sobre que el Subdo se releve del cargo de nombramento de Capitan enterador a la mineria del trapiche de la Villa de Potosi.

62. ADC. Intend. Ord. Leg. 41, 1797.

63. ADC. Corrg. Prov. Leg. 60, 1601–77. 1633. Don Diego Arqui yndio viejo natural de Pichigua (hurinsaya).

64. AGN. B. A. Sala 9, 6–2–5, 22. Meml de las Provincias y Pueblos qe estan obligados a enuiar yndios para la mita del cerro de Potosi con distincion de quales son buenos medianos y malos, 2 fs.

65. Sánchez-Albornoz, "Mita, migraciones y pueblo," 59; for percentages of all provinces see Stavig, "Indian Peoples," 351.

66. Tandeter, *Coercion and Market,* 19.

67. AHP. C. R. 26. Yanaconas. In the late sixteenth century several people with origins in the upper Vilcanota were registered in Potosi as *yanacona* of the crown. Among those who took such action were: Domingo Ato, aged thirty, from Tinta and married; Francisco Guanco, a twenty-year-old man from Sicuani who had lived in Potosi since he was a small child; and Juan Saucani from Guaro(c), whose father had been a *huayrador,* and who was married and had a four-month-old baby.

68. ANP. Derecho Indigena (D. I.) L.XXIV C.706. 1786. Autos promovidos en virtud del decreto expedido por el Superior Gobierno para que se empadronasen a los indios llamados ausentes con los originarios. Contains 1692 materials. For totals see Stavig, "Indian Peoples," 354.

69. ANP. D. I. LXXIV C.706. 1756, 1692. Autos promovidos en virtud del decreto expendido por el Superior Gobierno para que se empadronasen a los indios llamados ausentes con los originarios; Morner, *Perfil de la Sociedad Rural del Cuzco,* 144.

70. ANP. D. I. LXXIV C.706. 1756. Autos promovidos en virtud del decreto expedido por el Superior Gobierno para que se empadronasen a los indios llamados ausentes con los originarios.

71. *Cuzco 1689,* 241.

72. Sánchez-Albornoz, *Indios y tributos,* 142–49.

73. Cole, "Potosi Mita under Hapsburg Administration," 222–23.

74. ANB. Minas 7. 126. no. 8. 1798. Don Bartolomé Uancoiro y don Sebastian Condori, enteradores de la mita del pueblo de Acopia . . . sobre que los hermanos Baltasar y Agustin Ramos exhiben sus partidas de bautizo, por donde constará la obligacion que tienen de servir la mita de Potosi, como originarios de dicho pueblo.

75. Evans, "Census Enumeration."

76. Acosta, *Natural and Moral History,* 207–8.

77. Cañete y Dominguez, *Guía Historica,* 112.

78. Tandeter, "Propiedad y gestión."

79. Rodas, "La Mita," 17–18; Cole, "Abolitionism Born of Frustration." The Conde de Lemos, one of the viceroys most sympathetic to the plight of the workers, ordered *mitayos* be allowed to leave at the end of the day to sleep in their own residences. But this regulation seems not to have been enforced once the viceroy's term of office was up, if it was ever enforced to any extent.

80. Du Biscay, *Account of a Voyage,* 50.

81. Capoche, *Relación General,* 158–59.

82. Acosta, *Natural and Moral History,* 212.

83. Thierry Saignes provided me with the information based on Repartimiento General del Marques de Montesclaros, 1610, Bibliotheque Nationale de Paris, ms. espagnol n. 175, ff. 257–318, and AGI. Charcas 51(?). 1617 Lista de mitayos presentes y faltos en Potosi; For totals see Stavig, "Indian Peoples," 361–62.

84. ADP. San Pablo 1749–87. 1750, 6v.

85. Capoche, *Relación General,* 173–76.

86. Padden, *Tales of Potosi,* 117–18.

87. Capoche, *Relación General,* 175.

88. Jimenez de Espada, *Relaciones Geográficas,* 373.

89. ANB. M. T. 147. (Minas 1367a, Mano de obra minera 721a.)

90. ADP. San Pablo. 1749–87. Difunciones.

91. BNP. C.1000. 1770. Autos seguidos a pedimiento de los indios enteradores de la real mita sobre no deben pagar obvenciones; and BNP. C.301. 1772. Dis-

posiciones para que los doctrineros de indios no usen de la violencia para de-terrar la idolatría.

92. Jimenez de Espada, *Relaciones Geográficas*, 1:381–82.

93. Levillier, *Audiencia de Charcas*, 1:68–70; Jimenez de Espada, *Relaciones Geográficas*, 1:379.

94. ANB. M125, no. 13. f.220–29. Mitayos.

95. ANB. CPLA. 24, f.480–82 (MC832). 1651. XII, 13, Potosi. Acuerdo del Cabildo . . . para remedio de la falta de lluvias; ANB. CPLA. t.20, f339v (MC701a) 1635. X, 24. Potosi. Capítulo de acuerdo. . . . En vista de la falta de agua para la mol-ienda.

96. Cieza de Leon, *Travels*, 392.

97. Levillier, *Audiencia de Charcas*, III, 27, 86; Cobb, "Potosi and Huancave-lica," 82; ANB. CPLA. (MC92) 1565. IX, 19, Potosi. Acuerdo del cabildo . . . cura-cion de los indios . . . de romadizo; ANB. CPLA. t.5, f. 410. (MC296a) 1589. XII, 20, Potosi. Acuerdo del cabildo . . . la peste de viruelas y sarampion entre los indios; ANB. CPLA. t.5, f.407 (MC294a [ord]) 1589.XI, 23, Potosi. Acuerdo del cabildo. . . . Se habian hecho processions; ANB. CPLA. t.5, f.406 (MC294c) 1589. XI, 16. La Plata. Provision de la audiencia de Charcas . . . teniendo noticia de la pestilencia de viruelas; Dobyns, "Outline of Andean Epidemic History," 510; Arzáns de Orsúa y Vela, *Historia*, 2:427, 447, 467–68, and 3:17–18, 25, 43.

98. Arzáns de Orsúa y Vela, *Historia*, 3:82–96.

99. Arzáns de Orsúa y Vela, *Historia*, 3:92.

100. ADP. Defunciones. San Sebastian, Concepción.

101. ANB. E. Can. no. 68 t.126, no. XIII (M9291). 1719. XII, 15. Carangas. Don Juan Bautista Uri-Siri alcalde mayor y capitan enterador de la mita . . . en nombre de los demas capitanes enteradores . . . sobre que se suspenda la mita hasta que cese la peste en Potosi.

102. ANP. L.10, C.234. 1727. Diligencias que se actuaron en orden a la revisita y numeracion que de los indios tributarios de los repartimientos de Lampa, Azangaro, Canas y Canches; ANB. M147 (Minas 1365) 1733. VI, 15, Lima. Nueva numeracion general de indios sujetos a la mita de Potosi; ANB. (Minas 1392) 1736. VI, 24– 1736. XI, 1. Entrega de indios de mita. . . . En la Retasa del Pueblo de Cullupata huvo ciento sesenta, tributarios los ciento veinte, y siete originarios (should be 142), y los dies y ocho Forasteros de que revajan treinta, y tres los dies, y ocho por Forasteros, y quinse para el servicio de la

Yglesia Republica, y Restan para la deduccion de la mita ciento veinte, y siete Yndios originarios, cuia septima parte son diez, y ocho Yndios, y seis para de continuo trabajo con dos descansos. ANB. M. t.147 (Minas 1367 y Mano de Obra No. 7219). 1733. Extracto de las provincias que vienen a mitar a esta villa de Potosi su, cerro Rico y Rivera; see also Tandeter, "Trabajo forzado," 516.

103. ADC. Corrg. Prov. Leg. 69, 1772–75. Yauri. Diego Merma, yndio del Pueblo de Yauri contra Mateo Lima y Thomas Pallani indios del mismo pueblo por ciento y viente ovejas.

104. ADC. Intend. Prov. Ord. Leg. 94, 1797–99. 1797. Siquani. no. 44. Robo en Pichigua. Lucas Chancayarni.

105. ADC. Corrg. Prov. Leg. 71, 1780–84. 1780. Siquani. Ordinaria contra los bienes de Pasqual Quispe a pedimto a Dn Domingo Anco por 28 ps que este demanda.

106. ADC. Corrg. Prov. Leg. 70, 1776–79. 1777. Sicuani. Antonio Hanco (Ancco), indio del Aillo Lari contra Doña Thomasa Requelme sobre un solar.

107. Intend. Prov. Ord. Leg. 99, 1807–8. 1809. Marangani. Adjudicazn de las tierras de Querera a favor de los yndios de Marangani y Ayllo Lurucachi. Felix Poco y Thomas Poco.

108. ADC. Corrg. Prov. Leg. 61, 1679–1705. 1705. Marcaconga. Don Juan Tanqui.

109. Cook, *People of the Colca Valley*, 65–79.

110. ANB. Minas 127, no. 6 (MC1517) 1750–54. III, 26. Mita. El doctor don Martin de Landaeta, cura propio del beneficio de Ambana, provincia de Larecaja, contra Sebastian Palli y Diego Palli originarios del pueblo de Marangani provincia del Cuzco.

111. Glave, *Vida símbolos y batallas*, 88.

112. Glave, *Vida símbolos y battalas*, 68.

113. Wightman, *Indigenous Migration and Social Change*, 133–34.

114. ADC. Corrg. Prov. Criminales Leg. 80, 1773–75. 1773. Marangani. Criminal sobre la muerte de Diego Sunca.

115. ANP. L.10, C.234. 1727. Diligencias que se actuaron en orden a la revista y numeracion que de los indios tributarion de los repartimientos de Lampa, Azangaro, y Canas y Canchis.

116. All references come from the ANB. ANB. CPLA. t.5 f.436v (MC301). 1590.

VII, 1 Lima. Provision del virrey ... corregidores que con su descuido ocasion la continua desercion de mitayos. ANB. MSS 9. no. 97, fs. 294–311. 1616; ANB. CPLA. 16, fl69–169v (MC600) 1619. XI, 3. Potosi. Acuerdo del Cabildo. Viendose la proposicion, inserta, presentada por los azogueros sobre los nuevos inconvenientes contra el entero de la mita. ANB. Minas 125, no. 1. 1640. Título conferido por don José ... de Elorduy, corregidor de Potosi ... para el entero de la mita. ANB. Minas t.145, no. 4 (MC879) 1660. X, 7. Madrid. Copia de real cédula dirigida a esta Audiencia de la Plata: Enviese relación de los corregidores y demás encargados de ella.

117. Sánchez-Albornoz, *Indios y tributos*, 144.

118. ADC. Corrg. Prov. Crim. Leg. 81, 1776–84. 1780. Coporaque. Criminal contra Jose Chaco o Ylachaco por usurpacion de RS. tributos al Rey, y a los yndios quando fue cobrador de este ramo en el ayllo Ancocagua de este mismo pueblo.

119. Sánchez-Albornoz, *Indios y tributos*, 144.

120. ADC. Corrg. Prov. Leg. 70, 1776–79. 1777. Antonio Hancco, indio del Aillo Lari contra Doña Thomasa Requelme sobre un solar.

121. BNP. C373. 1789. Representacion hecha por los caciques de este partido de Tinta, e informes de sus respectivos curas sobre extinguie la mita que va a la villa de Potosi.

122. BNP. C373. 1789.

123. BNP. C373. 1789.

124. BNP. C373. 1789.

125. ANB. MSS (Ruck) 575, t.9 f. 135–136v. 1791. IX, 10. Lima. Despacho del conde Lemos, virrey del Peru; de conformidad con el auto acordado de la Audiencia de Lima, de 1791. VII, 22. que se expidió en consideración a lo que pidieron los caciques del partido de Tinta para que se extingue la mita.

126. ADC. Inten. Ord. Leg. 43, 1798. Sicuani. Expedte. iniciado pr. Clemte Sulca solicitando no turnar en ir a la mita de Potosi.

127. Stavig, "Ethnic Conflict," 743.

128. ADC. Inten. Ord. Leg. 53, 1802–3. 1803. Layo. Autos seguidos por el yndio Lucas Cano contra el cacique Gabriel Guamán y Alcalde mayor Ventura Sarvia del Pueblo de Layo sobre prision y embargo de sus ganados injustamente.

129. ADC. Intend. Ord. Leg. 52. 1802. Langui. Expediente promovido por el

yndio Matias Aquino sobre no volver a turnar la mita de Potosi y libertad de pagar por los profugos.

130. ADC. Intend. Ord. Leg. 52, 1802. Langui. Expediente promovido pr el yndio Matias Aquino sobre no bolber a turnar la mita de Potosi y libertad de pagar pr los profugos.

131. ADC. Intend. Ord. Leg. 52, 1802.

132. ADC. Corrg. Prov. Crim. Leg. 80, 1773–75. 1775. Coporaque. Quejas de los caciques de Coporaque por el mal tratamiento que sus indios reciben en la mita de Potosi.

133. ADC. Corrg. Prov. Crim. Leg. 80, 1773–75. 1775.

134. Rowe, "Incas under Spanish Colonial Institutions," 176.

8. Rebellion, Cultural Redemption, and Thupa Amaro

1. Campbell, "Ideology and Factionalism," 122; and L. Fisher, *Last Inca Revolt*, 45–48; Vega, "Los sacerdotes," 2–7; for a similar use of formal legal structure in an uprising see Langer "Andean Rituals of Revolt."

2. L. Fisher, *Last Inca Revolt*, 46.

3. O'Phelan, "Las reformas fiscales Borbónicas," 353; O'Phelan, *Rebellions and Revolts*, 256–73.

4. Campbell, "Ideology and Factionalism," 114–15.

5. Szeminski, "Why Kill the Spaniard?" 16.

6. O'Phelan, "Las reformas fiscales Borbónicas," 342, 353.

7. Taylor, *Drinking, Homicide, and Rebellion*.

8. Zavala, *El servicio personal de los indios*, 3:61. See also Larson and Wasserstrom, "Coerced Consumption," 58–59.

9. Spalding, *Huarochirí*, 270; J. Fisher, *Government and Society in Colonial Peru*, 12; O'Phelan, *Rebellions and Revolts*, 260.

10. Golte, *Repartos y rebeliones*, 140–47 (Cuadro 33), 207 (Map 1) and n. 18; O'Phelan, *Rebellions and Revolts*, 284–98 (Appendix I).

11. Golte, *Repartos y rebeliones*, 140 (Cuadro 33).

12. Golte, *Repartos y rebeliones*, 140 (Cuadro 33).

13. ADC. Corrg. Prov. Crim. Leg. 79, 1745–73. 1768. Dn. Joseph Thupa Amaro,

cacique pral y Governador del Pueblo de Pampamarca contra cobrador Dn. Geronimo Cano; Rowe, "Genealogía y rebelión," 74–75.

14. *Cuzco 1689*, 165.

15. O'Phelan, *Rebellions and Revolts*, 99–101.

16. Golte, *Repartos y rebeliones*, Map 17.

17. Golte, *Repartos y rebeliones*, 120.

18. O'Phelan, *Rebellions and Revolts*, 108.

19. O'Phelan, *Rebellions and Revolts*, 108; L. Fisher, *Last Inca Revolt*, 13.

20. BNP. 1766. c3969. Informes de los curas de Oropesa, San Andrés de Checa y Tinta, acerca de la consulta formulada por el cabildo del Cuzco respecto a los repartimientos hechos por los corregidores.

21. BNP. 1766. c3969. Also see Golte, *Repartos y rebeliones*, 114–18; L. Fisher, *Last Inca Revolt*, 13. Fisher cites Juan and Ulloa, *Noticias Secretas de América*, 240–45. There is some indication that in the later *repartos* the *naturales* at least were allowed to choose among items they were to receive.

22. Golte, *Repartos y rebeliones*, 95; L. Fisher, *Last Inca Revolt 1780–1783*, 39; Stavig, "Ethnic Conflict," 744.

23. Golte, *Repartos y rebeliones*, 141–47. "Chaca" should be "Checa" or "Cacha."

24. ADC. Corrg. Prov. Crim. Leg. 80, 1773–75. 1774. Don Lucas Poma Inga, cacique . . . de Cusipata de Quiquijana contra don Carlos Ochoa.

25. ADC. Intend. Prov. 1786. Expediente relativo a que se verifique la fabrica de puentes en Tinta poniendo una cantidad de pesos que dejo . . . el corregidor Reparaz (is a 1785 case with 1786 materials). There are several cases that give this picture of the daily decisions of Reparaz. For a case that gives a different view, see ADC. Corrg. Prov. Crim. Leg. 79, 1745–73. El Comun de Indios del ayllo Lurucachi del Pueblo de Marangani. Interestingly, in this case it was Corregidor Arriaga who found a judicious solution to community complaints.

26. Rowe, "Genealogía y rebelión," 74–76.

27. ADC. Corrg. Prov. Leg. 67, 1766–69. [H]ucha a minas de Condoroma, 1767. What exactly one can make of this is uncertain, for a wide variety of people, including Thupa Amaro, had interests in Condoroma mines. O'Phelan, *Rebellions and Revolts*, 271.

28. Rowe, "Genealogía y rebelión," 74–76.

29. For the impact of alcohol on Indians in colonial Mexico see Taylor, *Drinking, Homicide, and Rebellion.*

30. O'Phelan, *Rebellions and Revolts,* 135.

31. ADC. Corrg. Prov. Prov. Crim. Leg. 79, 1745–73. 1768. Don Cristobal Sinanyuca cacique de Collana de Coporaque . . . se ha ausentado. The outcome of the charges against the three accused is unknown. Sinanyuca, like Arriaga, had problems with church officials, which influenced his role in the rebellion. For a questioning of the role of E. Sinanyuca and the Indians of Coporaque, see Hinojosa, "Población y conflictos campesinos."

32. For information on Indian peasants' proclivity to revolt and the Maras-Urubamba rebellion see O'Phelan, *Rebellions and Revolts,* 118, 174–81; O'Phelan, "Cuzco 1777," 113–28. O'Phelan suggests that "Indian peasants, as an isolated sector, were perhaps less likely [than mestizos, *curacas, criollos*] to promote general rebellion."

33. For instance, Viceroy Chinchón had raised the tax in 1627. See O'Phelan, *Rebellions and Revolts,* 161.

34. O'Phelan, *Rebellions and Revolts,* 167.

35. O'Phelan, *Rebellions and Revolts,* 167.

36. O'Phelan, *Rebellions and Revolts,* 194–203

37. O'Phelan, *Rebellions and Revolts,* 265.

38. O'Phelan, *Rebellions and Revolts,* 198–202.

39. O'Phelan, *Rebellions and Revolts,* 203.

40. O'Phelan, *Rebellions and Revolts,* 264.

41. Campbell, "Social Structure of the Túpac Amaru Army," 685–89. In these pages there is a table containing names, residence, social status, age, marital state, occupation, rank, and sentences of the commanders. O'Phelan, *Rebellions and Revolts,* 219, 264.

42. O'Phelan, *Rebellions and Revolts,* 180.

43. Burga, "La crisis del siglo XVIII." Much of this section draws on Stavig, "Ethnic Conflict."

44. ADC. Corrg. Prov. Leg, 63, 1719–30. 1720. Peste, Quiquijana.

45. Burga, "La Crisis del siglo XVIII," 8. Though recording practices were not necessarily uniform from year to year, the figures give an overall indica-

tion of population growth. The situation was similar in Coporaque. See Hinojosa, "Población y conflictos," 236–37.

46. ADC. Corrg. Prov. Leg. 65, 1738–50. 1745. Tierras de Guascarguiguar; Burga, "La Crisis del siglo XVIII," 8.

47. Mörner, *Perfil de la sociedad rural del Cuzco*, 144–46.

48. ADC. Corrg. Prov. Leg. 63, 1719–30. 1720. Peste, Quiquijana.

49. For such abuse in the late seventeenth century, see Sánchez-Albornoz, *Indios y tributos*, 91–110, 142–49. See also Spalding, "*Kurakas* and Commerce," 592, 594–99.

50. ADC. Corrg. Prov. Leg. 79, 1745–1773. 1772–79. El comun de Indios del Ayllo Lurucache del Pueblo de Marangani contra su cacique dn Santos Mamani sobre varios excesos; see also Hopkins, "Colonial History of the Hacienda System," 197–213, especially 207.

51. Hopkins, "Colonial History of the Hacienda System," 212.

52. Cahill, "Curas and Social Conflict," 256–57. Cahill notes that there was "discernible in the late eighteenth century . . . caciques, many of whom were forasteros installed by corregidores or subdelegados to do their bidding." See also O'Phelan, "El sur andino."

53. Hopkins, "Colonial History of the Hacienda System," 234–35.

54. ADC. Corrg. Prov. Crim. Leg. 79, 1745–73. 1773. Criminal contra Nicolas Sencia, Clemente Huahuamani, Marcos Huahuamani y Cayetano Mamani, Yndios del mismo pueblo sobre la muerte acaecida a Estevan Alfaro, Indio; ADC. Corrg. Prov. Crim. Leg. 79, 1745–73. 1772. Criminal contra Faustino Guaguamamani (name is written different ways in the document); see also Hopkins, "Juego de enemigos," 168.

55. AAC. Quejas, 29.1, XII, 1, 16. 1752. Queja de Miguel Lloclla maestro cantor de la iglesia de Pomacanchi, contra el curaca Juan Esteban Pacheco, por atropellos.

56. ADC. Corrg. Prov. Crim. Leg. 77, 1769–70. Contra Lucas Cahua yndio del ayllo Ancocagua . . . en el Pueblo de Coporaque por queja de su cacique.

57. Flores Galindo, *Europa y el país de los incas*, 50, 67; for a discussion of *Inkarrí*, see Ossio, *Ideología mesiánica del mundo andino*.

58. Rowe, "Colonial Portraits of Inca Nobles," 258–68; Campbell, "Ideology and Factionalism," 125; L. Fisher, *Last Inca Revolt*, 30.

59. Flores Galindo, "In Search of an Inca," 194–95, 202.

60. Rowe, "El movimiento nacional inca del siglo XVIII," 21, 25.

61. Stern, "Age of Andean Insurrection," 53.

62. Szeminski, "Why Kill the Spaniard?" 173.

63. Campbell, "Ideology and Factionalism," 116; Szeminski, "Why Kill the Spaniard?" 177.

64. L. Fisher, *Last Inca Revolt,* 40.

65. ADC. Corrg. Prov. Leg. 81, 1776–84. 1780. Criminal contra Francisco negro livertino doméstico del cura.

66. L. Fisher, *Last Inca Revolt,* 41; Glave, *Vida símbolos y batallas,* 61–63.

67. L. Fisher, *Last Inca Revolt,* 104.

68. O'Phelan, *Rebellions and Revolts,* 224; L. Fisher, *Last Inca Revolt,* 112–14; Vega, *Jose Gabriel Tupac Amaru,* 84.

69. Vega, "Los sacerdotes que lucharon por la Patria," 4.

70. O'Phelan, *Rebellions and Revolts,* 225; Vega, "Los sacerdotes que lucharon por la Patria," 2–7.

71. Szeminski, "Why Kill the Spaniard?" 170.

72. Szeminski, *Utopia Tupamarista,* 19; Szeminski, "Why Kill the Spaniard?" 169.

73. Szeminski, "Why Kill the Spaniard?" 170; see also Hidalgo Lehuede, "Amarus y cataris," 117–38. In Chiapas during the Tzeltal revolt Indians also saw themselves as the true Christians. See works by Wasserstrom and Gosner.

74. Szeminski, "Why Kill the Spaniard?" 176–78. Mass was held daily by Túpac Catari's forces, and in one instance Catarista rebels who did not demonstrate proper respect to Our Lady of Copacabana were executed by their own people.

75. Szeminski, "Why Kill the Spaniard?" 177–78.

76. Campbell, "Ideology and Factionalism," 126.

77. Szeminski, "Why Kill the Spaniard?" 168.

78. L. Fisher, *Last Inca Revolt,* 95–96; Campbell, "Ideology and Factionalism," 126.

79. Szeminski, "Why Kill the Spaniard?" 178.

80. Szeminski, "Why Kill the Spaniard?" 191.

81. L. Fisher, *Last Inca Revolt*, 363, 366.

82. L. Fisher, *Last Inca Revolt*, 192–211; O'Phelan, *Rebellions and Revolts*, 240.

83. L. Fisher, *Last Inca Revolt*, 236–38.

84. Szeminski, "Why Kill the Spaniard?" 237.

85. Szeminski, "Why Kill the Spaniard?" 223.

86. Szeminski, "Why Kill the Spaniard?" 379.

87. O'Phelan, *Rebellions and Revolts*, 217.

88. Campbell, "Ideology and Factionalism," 115, 124; O'Phelan, *Rebellions and Revolts*, 249.

89. Morner and Trelles, "Un intento de calibrar las actitudes hacia la rebelión," 12–13.

90. BNP. 1780, c2812. Expediente sobre la causa seguida por Melchor Choquecondori y Soto indio principal del pueblo de Pampamarca, sobre la sucesion del cacicazgo del pueblo de Ayllo Capac. Lima, Agos. 14, 1780.

91. O'Phelan, *Rebellions and Revolts*, 214–15.

92. L. Fisher, *Last Inca Revolt*, 238.

93. Glave, *Vida símbolos y batallas*, 142; L. Fisher, *Last Inca Revolt*, 107. She places Guamba Tupa on the loyalist side.

94. L. Fisher, *Last Inca Revolt*, 209–11, 232–34; O'Phelan, *Rebellions and Revolts*, 219–20, 237.

95. Morner and Trelles, "Un intento de calibrar," 26–27. Even though rebel percentages do not total 100 percent, I have left them as they appear. Morner and Trelles have developed different models that produce different figures. I have selected the models that I think best represent the situation, but one should consider the numbers more as close approximations rather than exact figures.

96. Morner and Trelles, "Un intento de calibrar," 27–28.

97. Campbell, "Ideology and Factionalism," 122–23.

98. Campbell, "Ideology and Factionalism," 123–24.

99. ADC. Intend. Crim. Leg. 120, 1785–88. 1787. Testimonio de los autos criminales seguidos de oficio contra Narciso Santos Mamani yndio de Lurucache . . . por Francisco Martinez.

Notes to Pages 252–62

100. Glave, *Vida símbolos y batallas*, 137. The information on Sinanyuca comes from Glave's account and from the anthology *Tupac Amaru y la Iglesia—Antología*, which contains a section entitled "El caso Sinanyuca," 165–201.

101. Glave, *Vida símbolos y batallas*, 137–41.

102. Glave, *Vida símbolos y batallas*, 141–46.

103. Glave, *Vida símbolos y batallas*, 147–48.

104. Glave, *Vida símbolos y batallas*, 148. "Beberemos en el cráneo del traidor, usaremos sus dientes como un collar, de sus huesos haremos flautas, de su piel haremos un tambor, después bailaremos."

105. O'Phelan, *Rebellions and Revolts*, 240.

106. ADC. Corrg. Ord. Leg. 57, 1781–82. Criminal contra Estevan Castro quien murió aorcado por emasario del rebelde Js. Tupa Amaro. Case was in 1780.

107. ADC. Intend. Ord. Leg. 25, 1791. Autos que sigue Brigida Guaman yndia natural de la Doctrina de Acomayo contra su cura . . . Fray Baltasar Gastelu.

108. ADC. Intend. Prov. Leg. 120, 1785–86. 1786. Criminal contra Ygnacio Castelo . . . sobre las injurias que ha inferido a Maria Herrera mujer del cacique Simon Callo y otros echos.

109. Valcarcel, *Túpac Amaru*, 243; L. Fisher, *Last Inca Revolt*, 218–19.

9. *Más Allá*

1. Flores Galindo, "In Search of an Inca," 193–95.

2. Flores Galindo, "In Search of an Inca," 194–95.

3. Flores Galindo, "In Search of an Inca," see entire article, 193–210.

4. Walker, "Voces discordantes," 96.

5. Elliott, "Discovery of America," 49.

6. Walker, "Voces discordantes," 90, 95.

7. "El naufragio de Tupac Amaru," 4–5; C. Valcarcel, Tupac Amaru, chap. 34.

BIBLIOGRAPHY

Abbreviations

AHR   American Historical Review

HAHR   Hispanic American Historical Review

HISLA Revista Latinoamericana de Historia Económica y Social

JLAS   Journal of Latin American Studies

LARR   Latin American Research Review

Acosta, Father Joseph de. *Natural and Moral History of the Indies*. Edited by Clements Markham. London: Hakluyt Society, 1880.

Adorno, Rolena, ed. *From Oral to Written Expression: Native Andean Chronicles of the Early Colonial Period*. Syracuse NY: Maxwell School of Citizenship and Public Affairs, 1982.

———. *Guamán Poma: Writing and Resistance in Colonial Peru*. Austin: University of Texas Press, 1986.

———. "The Language of History in Guamán Poma's Nueva Corónica y Buen Gobierno." In *From Oral to Written Expression: Native Andean Chroniclers of the Early Colonial Period*. Edited by Rolena Adorno. Syracuse NY: Maxwell School of Citizenship and Public Affairs, 1982.

Aguirre, Carlos, and Charles Walker, eds. *Bandoleros, abigeos y montoneros. Criminalidad y violencia en el Perú, siglos XVIII–XX*. Lima: Instituto de Apoyo Agrario, 1990.

Allen, Catherine. "To Be Quechua: The Symbolism of Coca Chewing in Highland Peru." *American Ethnologist* 8, no. 1 (1981).

Andrien, Kenneth J. *Crisis and Decline: The Viceroyalty of Peru in the Seventeenth Century*. Albuquerque: University of New Mexico Press, 1985.

————. "The Sale of Fiscal Offices and the Decline of Royal Authority in the Viceroyalty of Perú 1633–1700." *HAHR* 61, no. 2 (1982).

Aparicio, Manuel Jesus. "Historia de la Provincia de Canchis." In *K'anchi, La provincia de Canchis a través de su historia.* Edited by Vicente Guerra Carreño. Lima: Empresa Editora Humboldt, 1982.

Arriaga, Father Pablo José de. *Extirpation of Idolatry in Peru.* Edited and translated by L. Clark Keating. Lexington: University of Kentucky Press, 1968.

Arzáns de Orsúa y Vela, Bartolomé. *Historia de la Villa Imperial de Potosi.* Edited by Lewis Hanke and Gunnar Mendoza. Providence RI: Brown University Press, 1965.

Assadourian, Carlos Sempat. "Dominio colonial y señores étnicos en el espacio andino." *HISLA* 1 (1983).

————. "Los señores étnicos y los corregidores de indios en la conformación del Estado colonial." *Anuario de Estudios Americanos* XLV (1987).

————. *El sistema de la economía colonial mercado interno, regiones y espacio económico.* Lima: Instituto de Estudios Peruanos, 1982.

Ayans, Antonio de (1596). "Breve relación de los agravios que reciven los indios que ay desde cerca del Cuzco hasta Potosí." In *Pareceres jurídicos en asuntos de Indios (1605–1718).* Edited by Rubén Vargas Ugarte. Lima, 1951.

Bakewell, Peter. *Miners of the Red Mountain: Indian Labor in Potosí, 1545–1650.* Albuquerque: University of New Mexico Press, 1984.

Barnadas, Josep M. Charcas: *Orígenes históricos de una sociedad colonial.* La Paz: CIPCA, 1973.

Basadre, Jorge. *El Conde de Lemos y su tiempo.* Lima: Editorial Huascarán, 1948.

————. "El régimen de la mita." *Letras* 8 (1937).

Bauer, Arnold J. "La cultura mediterránea en las condiciones del nuevo mundo: elementos en la transferencia del trigo a las Indias." *Historia* 21 (1986).

————. "Rural Workers in Spanish America: Problems of Peonage and Oppression." *HAHR* 59, no. 1 (1979).

————. *Treaders and Flailers. Mediterranean Culture in New World Conditions: Elements in the Transferral of Wheat to the Indies.* Davis CA: Working Paper Series. Agricultural History Center. University of California, Davis, 1987.

Bibliography

Behar, Ruth. "Sexual Witchcraft, Colonialism, and Women's Powers: Views from the Mexican Inquisition." In *Sexuality and Marriage in Colonial Latin America*. Edited by Asunción Lavrin. Lincoln: University of Nebraska Press, 1989.

Benino, Nicolás de. "Relación muy particular del cerro y minas de Potosí y de su calidad y labores." In *Relaciones geográficas de Indias*. Vol. 1. Edited by Marcos Jimenez de la Espada. Madrid: Ediciones Atlas, 1965.

Bertonio, Ludovico. *Vocabulario de la lengua aymara*. Cochabamba: CERES, 1984.

Betanzos, Juan Diez de. "El Dios Viracocha y Los Canas." In *K'anchi, La provincia de Canchis a través de su historia*. Edited by Vicente Guerra Carreño. Lima: Empresa Editora Humboldt, 1982.

————. *Narrative of the Incas*. Edited and translated by Ronald Hamilton and Dana Buchanan. Austin: University of Texas Press, 1996.

Biscay, Acarete du. *An Account of a Voyage up the River de La Plata and Thence Over Land to Peru*. n.p., 1698.

Bloch, Marc. *French Rural History: An Essay on Its Basic Characteristics*. Berkeley: University of California Press, 1970.

Bolton, Ralph. "The Qolla Marriage Process." In *Andean Kinship and Marriage*. Edited by Ralph Bolton and Enrique Mayer. Washington DC: American Anthropological Association, Special Publication No. 7, 1977.

Bolton, Ralph, and Enrique Mayer, eds. *Andean Kinship and Marriage*. Washington DC: American Anthropological Association, Special Publication No. 7, 1977.

Borah, Woodrow. "The Spanish and Indian Law: New Spain." In *Inca and the Aztec States, 1400–1800: Anthropology and History*. Edited by George A. Collier, Renato I. Rosaldo, and John D. Wirth. New York: Academic Press, 1982.

Borja, Virrey Don Francisco de. *Memorias de los Virreyes*. Lima, 1859.

Boxer, C. R. *Church Militant and Iberian Expansion 1440–1770*. Baltimore: Johns Hopkins University Press, 1978.

Boyer, Richard. *Lives of the Bigamists: Marriage, Family and Community in Colonial Mexico*. Albuquerque, University of New Mexico Press, 1995.

————. "Women, *La Mala Vida*, and the Politics of Marriage." In *Sexuality and Marriage in Colonial Latin America*. Edited by Asunción Lavrin. Lincoln: University of Nebraska Press, 1989.

Bibliography

Brading, David A. "Images and Prophets: Indian Religion and the Spanish Conquest." In *Indian Communities of Colonial Mexico: Fifteen Essays on Land Tenure, Corporate Organization, Ideology and Village Politics*. Amsterdam: CEDLA, 1990.

Brading, David, and Harry E. Cross. "Colonial Silver Mining: Mexico and Peru." *HAHR* 52, no. 4 (1972).

Braudel, Fernand, and Frank Spooner. "Price in Europe from 1450 to 1750." In *Cambridge Economic History of Europe*. Vol. 4. Cambridge: Cambridge University Press, 1967.

Bronner, Fred. "Peruvian Encomenderos in 1630: Elite Circulation and Consolidation." *HAHR* 57, no. 4 (1977).

Brown, Kendall W. *Bourbons and Brandy: Imperial Reform in Eighteenth-Century Arequipa*. Albuquerque: University of New Mexico Press, 1986.

Brundage, Burr Cartwright. *Lords of Cuzco: A History of the Inca People in Their Final Days*. Norman: University of Oklahoma Press, 1967.

Bueno, Cosme. *Jerarquía eclesiástica peruana. Descripción de las provincias pertenecientes al obispado del Cuzco*. Lima, 1767.

Burga, Manuel. "La crisis del siglo XVIII y las rebeliones indígenas." *Inkarrí*, 2 April 1981.

———. *De la encomienda a la hacienda capitalista: El valle del Jequetepeque del siglo XVI al XX*. Lima: Instituto de Estudios Peruanos, 1976.

———. "La utopía andina." *Allpanchis* 20 (1982).

Burkett, Elinor. "Indian Women and White Society: The Case of Sixteenth-Century Peru." In *Latin American Women: Historical Perspectives*. Edited by Asunción Lavrin. Westport: Greenwood Press, 1978.

———. "La mujer durante la conquista y la primera pocal colonial." *Estudios Andinos* 5, no. 1 (1976).

Burkhart, Louise M. *Slippery Earth. Nahua-Christian Moral Dialogue in Sixteenth Century Mexico*. Tucson: University of Arizona Press, 1989.

Cahill, David. "Curas and Social Conflict in the Doctrinas of Cuzco, 1780–1814." *JLAS* 16, no. 2 (1984).

Calancha, Antonio de la. *Crónica moralizada del orden de San Augustin en el Perú*, Barcelona, 1638.

Campbell, Leon G. "The Army of Peru and the Tupac Amaru Revolt." *HAHR* 56, no. 1 (1976).

———. "Ideology and Factionalism during the Great Rebellion, 1780–1782."

Bibliography

In *Resistance, Rebellion, and Consciousness in the Andean Peasant World, Eighteenth to Twentieth Centuries.* Edited by Steve J. Stern. Madison: University of Wisconsin Press, 1987.

—————. "Recent Research on Andean Peasant Revolts, 1750–1820." *LARR* 14, no. 1 (1979).

—————. "Social Structure of the Túpac Amaru Army in Cuzco, 1780–81." *HAHR* 61, no. 4 (1981).

Cañete y Dominguez, Pedro Vicente. *Guía histórica, geográphica, física, política, civil y legal del Gobierno e Intendencia de la Provincia de Potosí.* Potosí: Editorial Potosí, 1952.

Capoche, Luis (1585). "Relación general de la Villa Imperial de Potosí." In *Relaciones históricas literarias de la América Meridional.* Biblioteca de autores españoles. Madrid: Edicones Atlas, 1959.

Carter, W. E. "Trial Marriage in the Andes?" In *Andean Kinship and Marriage.* Edited by Ralph Bolton and Enrique Mayer. Washington DC: American Anthropological Association, Special Publication No. 7, 1977.

Chayanov, A. V. *Theory of Peasant Economy.* 1923. Reprint, Madison: University of Wisconsin Press, 1986.

Choque Canqui, Roberto. "El papel de los capitanes de indios en la provincia de Pacajes en el entero de la mita de Potosí." *Revista Andina* 1 (1983).

Cieza de Leon, Pedro de. *El Señorío de los Incas.* Lima: Instituto de Estudios Peruanos, 1967.

—————. *Travels of Pedro de Cieza de Leon.* Edited and translated by Clements Markham. London: Hakluyt Society, 1864.

Cobb, Gwendolin B. "Potosi, a Mining Frontier." In *Greater America: Essays in Honor of Herbert Eugene Bolton.* Berkeley: University of California Press, 1945.

—————. "Supply and Transportation for the Potosi Mines, 1545–1640." *HAHR* 29, no. 1 (1949).

Cobo, Bernabé. *Historia del Nuevo Mundo.* Vol. 3. Sevilla, 1893.

—————. *History of the Inca Empire.* Edited and translated by Roland Hamilton. Austin: University of Texas Press, 1979.

—————. *Inca Religion and Customs.* Edited and translated by Roland Hamilton. Austin: University of Texas Press, 1990.

Cole, Jeffrey A. "An Abolitionism Born of Frustration: The Conde de Lemos and the Potosi Mita, 1667–73." *HAHR* 63, no. 2 (1983).

Bibliography

————. *Potosi Mita, 1573–1700: Compulsory Indian Labor in the Andes.* Stanford CA: Stanford University Press, 1985.

————. "The Potosi Mita under Hapsburg Administration. The Seventeenth Century." Ph.D. dissertation. Amherst: University of Massachusetts, 1981.

Colección Documental del Bicentenario de la Revolución Emancipadora de Tupac Amaru, Vols. 1–2. Lima: Comision Nacional del Bicentenario de la Rebelion Emancipadora de Túpac Amaru, 1980.

Collier, George A., Renato I. Rosaldo, and John D. Wirth, eds. *Inca and Aztec States, 1400–1800.* New York: Academic Press, 1982.

Cook, N. David. *Demographic Collapse: Indian Peru, 1520–1620.* New York: Cambridge University Press, 1981.

————. *People of the Colca Valley: A Population Study.* Boulder CO: Westview Press, 1982.

Cordech de Sans, Juan. *Estructura psicodinámica de la prostitución.* Barcelona: Universidad de Barcelona, Facultad de Medicina, 1964.

Cornblit, Oscar. "Society and Mass Rebellion in Eighteenth-Century Peru and Bolivia." In *Latin American Affairs.* Edited by Raymond Carr. Oxford: Oxford University Press, 1970.

Crespo Rodas, Alberto. "El reclutamiento y los viajes en la 'mita' del Cerro de Potosí." In *La Minería Hispana e Ibero Americana.* Leon: Catedra di San Isidoro, 1970.

Cushner, Nicholas P. *Lords of the Land: Sugar, Wine, and Jesuit Estates of Coastal Peru, 1600–1767.* Albany: State University of New York Press, 1980.

Cuzco 1689. Economía y sociedad en el sur andino. Informes de los párrocos al obispo Molliendo. Prologue and transcription by Horacio Villanueva Urteaga. Cuzco: Centro Bartolomé de Las Casas, 1982.

Davies, Keith A. *Landowners in Colonial Peru.* Austin: University of Texas Press, 1984.

de Certeau, Michel. *Practice of Everyday Life.* Translated by Steven F. Rendell. Berkeley: University of California Press, 1984.

Desan, Suzanne. "The Uses and Abuses of 'Community' in Natalie Zemon Davis and Edward P. Thompson." Paper presented at the 1987 Chartier Mini-Conference, Berkeley.

"Descripción Corográfica de la Provincia de Tinta. *Mercurio Peruano,* no. 139, 140, 141. May 3, 6, 10, 1792." In *K'anchi, La provincia de Canchis a través de su historia.* Edited by Vicente Guerra Carriño. Lima: Empresa Editora Humboldt, 1982.

Diez de San Miguel, Garci. *Visita hecha a la Provincia de Chucuito por Garci Diez de San Miguel en el año 1567.* Lima: Casa de la Cultura, 1964.

Dobyns, Henry F. "An Outline of Andean Epidemic History to 1720." *Bulletin of the History of Medicine* 37, no. 6 (1963).

Durand Flores, Luis. *Independencia e integración en el Plan Político de Tupac Amaru.* Lima: Comision Nacional del Bicentenario de la Rebelion Emancipadora de Túpac Amaru, 1973.

Elliot, J. H. *Imperial Spain, 1469–1719.* New York: Academic Library, 1966.

———. *Old World and the New, 1462–1650.* London: Cambridge University Press, 1970.

Esquivel y Navia, Diego de. *Noticias cronológicas de la gran ciudad del Cuzco.* Lima: Fondo de Cultura Peruana, 1980.

Evans, Brian M. "Census Enumeration in Late Seventeenth-Century Alto Perú: The Numeración General of 1683–84." In *Studies in Spanish American Population History.* Edited by David J. Robinson. Dellplain Latin American Studies, no. 8. Boulder CO: Westview Press, 1981.

Farris, Nancy. *Maya Society under Colonial Rule. The Collective Enterprise of Survival.* Princeton: Princeton University Press, 1984.

Fisher, John. R. *Government and Society in Colonial Peru: The Intendant System.* London: University of London's Athlone Press, 1970.

———. *Silver Mines and Silver Miners in Colonial Peru, 1776–1824.* Liverpool: University of Liverpool, Centre for Latin American Studies Monograph Series, no. 2, 1977.

Fisher, Lillian Estelle. *Last Inca Revolt, 1780–1783.* Norman: University of Oklahoma Press, 1966.

Flores Galindo, Alberto. *Arequipa y el sur andino: ensayo de historia regional (siglos XVII–XX).* Lima: Editorial Horizonte, 1977.

———. *Aristocracia y plebe: Lima, 1760–1830.* Lima: Mosca Azul, 1984.

———. *Buscando un Inca.* Lima: Instituto de Apoyo Agrario, 1987.

———. *Europa y el país de los incas: La utopía andina.* Lima: Instituto de Apoyo Agrario, 1986.

———. "In Search of an Inca." In *Resistance, Rebellion, and Consciousness in the Andean Peasant World, Eighteenth to Twentieth Centuries.* Edited by Steve J. Stern. Madison: University of Wisconsin Press, 1987.

Bibliography

———. "Los rostros de la plebe." *Revista Andina* 1, no. 2 (1983).

———. "La revolución tupamarista y los pueblos andinos (una crítica y un proyecto)." *Allpanchis* 15 (1981).

Flores Galindo, Alberto, ed. *Comunidades campesinas: Cambios y permanencias.* Chiclayo: CES Solidaridad, 1987.

———. *Túpac Amaru II—1780.* Lima: Retablo de Papel Editores, 1976.

Flores Ochoa, Jorge, ed. *Pastores de puna.* Lima: Instituto de Estudios Peruanos, 1977.

Gade, Daniel W., and Mario Escobar. "Village Settlement and the Colonial Legacy in Southern Peru." *Geographical Review* 72, no. 4 (1982).

Garcilaso de la Vega, "El Inca." *Royal Commentaries of the Incas.* Translated by Harold V. Livermore. Austin: University of Texas Press, 1966.

Geertz, Clifford. *Interpretation of Cultures.* New York: Basic Books, 1973.

Genovese, Eugene. *Roll, Jordan, Roll: The World the Slaves Made.* New York: Vintage Books, 1974.

Gibbs, Donald. "Cuzco 1680–1710: An Andean City Seen through Its Economic Activities." Ph.D. dissertation. University of Texas at Austin, 1979.

Gibson, Charles. *Aztec under Spanish Rule.* Stanford CA: Stanford University Press, 1964.

Glave, Luis Miguel. "Comunidades campesinas en el sur andino, siglo XVII." In *Comunidades campesinas: Cambios y permanencias.* Edited by Alberto Flores Galindo. Chiclayo: CES Solidaridad, 1987.

———. "Comunidades campesinas en los andes. Proceso histórico e identidad cultural." Unpublished manuscript, 1989.

———. "La producción de los trajines: Coca y mercado interno colonial." *HISLA* 6 (1985).

———. *Vida símbolos y batallas. Creación y recreación de la comunidad indígena. Cusco, siglos XVI–XX.* Lima: Fondo de cultura económica, 1992.

Glave, Luis Miguel, and María Isabel Remy. *Estructura agraria y vida rural en una region andina: Ollantaytambo entre los siglos XVI y XIX.* Cuzco: Centro Bartolomé de las Casas, 1983.

Golte, Jurgen. *Repartos y rebeliones.* Lima: Instituto de Estudios Peruanos, 1980.

González Holguín, Diego. *Vocabulario de la lengua general de todo el Perú llamado lengua quichua o del Inca.* Lima: Imprenta Santa Maria, 1952.

Gorbak, Celina, Mirtha Lischetti, and Carmen Paula Muñoz. "Batallas Rit-

Bibliography

uales del Chiaraje y del Tocto de la Provincia de Kanas (Cuzco-Perú)." *Revista del Museo Nacional* 31 (1962).

Gossen, Gary, H. "The Other in Chamula Tzotzil Cosmology and History: Reflections of a Kansan in Chiapas." *Cultural Anthropology* 8, no. 4 (1993).

Griffiths, Nicolas. *The Cross and the Serpent: Religious Repression and Resurgence in Colonial Peru.* Norman: University of Oklahoma Press, 1996.

Gruzinski, Serge. "Individualization and Acculturation: Confession among the Nahuas of Mexico from the Sixteenth to the Eighteenth Centuries." In *Sexuality and Marriage in Colonial Latin America.* Edited by Asunción Lavrin. Lincoln: University of Nebraska Press, 1989.

Guamán Poma de Ayala, Felipe. *El primer nueva corónica y buen gobierno.* 3 vols. Mexico: Siglo Veintiuno, 1980.

Guerra, Francisco. *Pre-Columbian Mind.* New York: Seminar Press, 1971.

Guha, Rananjit. "The Prose of Counter-Insurgency." In *Selected Subaltern Studies.* Edited by Ranajit Guha and Gayatri Chakravorty Spivak. New York, Oxford University Press, 1988.

Gutierrez, Ramon. *When Jesus Came, the Corn Mothers Went Away: Marriage, Sexuality and Power in New Mexico 1500–1844.* Stanford CA: Stanford University Press, 1991.

Hakluyt, Richard. "Discourse of Western Planting." In *Original Writings and Correspondence of the Two Richard Hakluyts.* Edited by E. G. R. Taylor. London: Hakluyt Society, 1935.

Hamilton, Earl J. *American Treasure and the Price Revolution in Spain, 1501–1650.* Cambridge MA: Harvard University Press, 1934.

Hammerstrom, Ingrid. "The 'Price Revolution' of the Sixteenth Century: Some Swedish Evidence." *Scandinavian Economic History Review* 5 (1957).

Hanke, Lewis. *Bartolomé Arzáns de Orsúa y Vela's History of Potosi.* Providence RI: Brown University Press, 1965.

———. *Los virreyes españoles en América durante el gobierno de la Casa de Austria, Perú.* Biblioteca de autores españoles. Madrid: Ediciones Atlas, 1978.

Harris, Olivia. "Complementarity and Conflict: An Andean View of Women and Men." In *Sex and Age as Principles of Social Differentiation.* Edited by J. LaFontaine. London: Academic Press, 1978.

———. "Condor and Bull: The Ambiguities of Masculinity in Northern Potosi." In *Sex and Violence: Issues in Representation and Experience.* Edited by Peter Gow and Penelope Harvey. London: Routledge, 1994.

———. "The Power of Signs: Gender, Culture and the Wild in the Bolivian Andes." In *Nature, Culture and Gender.* Edited by Carol P. MacCormack and Marilyn Strathern. Cambridge: Cambridge University Press, 1980.

Harris, Olivia, Brooke Larson, and Enrique Tandeter, comp. *La participación indígena en los mercados surandinos.* La Paz: CERES, 1987.

Harrison, Regina. "The Theology of Concupiscence: Spanish-Quechua Confessional Manuals in the Andes." In *Coded Encounters: Writing, Gender, and Ethnicity in Colonial Latin America.* Edited by Francisco Javier Cevallos-Candau, Jeffrey A. Cole, Nina M. Scott, and Nicomedes Suárez-Araúz. Amherst: University of Massachusetts Press, 1994.

Harvey, Penelope. "Domestic Violence in the Andes." In *Sex and Violence: Issues in Representation and Experience.* Edited by Peter Gow and Penelope Harvey. London: Routledge, 1994.

Hemming, John. *Conquest of the Incas.* New York: Harcourt Brace Jovanovich, 1970.

Hidalgo Lehuede, Jorge. "Amarus y cataris: aspectos mesiánicos de la rebelión indígena de 1781 en Cusco, Chayanta, La Paz y Arica." *Chungara* 10 (March 1983).

Hinojosa, Iván. "Población y conflictos campesinos en Coporaque (Espinar) 1770–1784." In *Comunidades campesinas: Cambios y permanencias.* Edited by Alberto Flores Galindo. Chiclayo: CES Solidaridad, 1987.

Hobsbawm, Eric. *Bandits.* London: Weidenfeld and Nicolson, 1969.

———. "Peasants and Politics." *Journal of Peasant Studies* 1, no. 1 (1973).

———. *Primitive Rebels: Studies in Archaic Forms of Social Movements in the Nineteenth and Twentieth Centuries.* Manchester: Manchester University Press, 1959.

Hopkins, Diane Elizabeth. "The Colonial History of the Hacienda System in a Southern Peruvian Highland District." Ph.D. dissertation. Cornell University, 1983.

———. "Juego de enemigos." *Allpanchis* 17, no. 20 (1982).

Hunefeldt, Christine. *Lasmanuelos, Vida Cotidiana de una Familia Negra en La Lima Del S. XIX.* Lima: Instituto de Estudios Peruanos, 1992.

Isbell, Billie Jean. "La otra mitad esencial: Un estudio de complementaridad sexual en los Andes." *Estudios Andinos* 5, no. 1 (1976).

Izko Gastón, Javier. "Condores y Mast'akus. Vida y muerte en los valles nor-

Bibliography

tepotosinos." In *Tiempo de Vida y Muerte. Estudio de caso en dos contextos andinos de Bolivia.* Edited by Javier Izko Gastón, Ramiro Molina Rivero, and René Pereira Morató. La Paz: Conampo, 1986.

Jacobsen, Nils. "Livestock Complexes in Late Colonial Peru and New Spain: An Attempt at Comparison." In *The Economies of Mexico and Peru During the Late Colonial Period, 1760–1810.* Edited by Nils Jacobsen and Hans-Jurgen Puhle. Berlin: Colloquium Verlag, 1986.

Jimenez de Espada, Marcos, ed. *Relaciones geográficas de Indias.* Madrid: Editorial Atlas, 1965.

Joseph, Gilbert. "Tracking the 'Social Bandit': A Reexamination of Peasant Resistance in Mexico and Latin America." Paper presented at VII Mexico/Chicano Symposium: "Rebellions in Mexican History." University of California, Irvine, April 1989.

Julien, Catherine J. "Inca Administration in the Titicaca Basin as Reflected at the Provincial Capital of Hatunquolla." Ph.D. dissertation. University of California, Berkeley, 1978.

———. "Inca Decimal Administration in the Lake Titicaca Region." In *Inca and Aztec States, 1400–1800: Anthropology and History.* Edited by George A. Collier, Renato I. Rosaldo, and John D. Wirth. New York: Academic Press, 1982.

Kauffman-Doig, Federico. *Sexual Behavior in Ancient Peru.* Lima: Kompaktos, S.C.R.L., 1977.

Kellogg, Susan. *Law and the Transformation of Aztec Culture, 1500–1700.* Norman: University of Oklahoma Press, 1995.

Keith, Robert G. *Conquest and Agrarian Change: The Emergence of the Hacienda System on the Peruvian Coast.* Cambridge MA: Harvard University Press, 1976.

———. "Encomienda, Hacienda and Corregimiento in Spanish America: A Structural Analysis." *HAHR* 51, no. 3 (1971).

———. "Origen del sistema de hacienda: El valle de Chancay." In *Hacienda, comunidad y campesinado en el Perú.* Edited by José Matos Mar. Lima: Instituto de Estudios Perunos, 1976.

Kicza, John E., ed. *Indian in Latin American History: Resistance, Resilience and Acculturation.* Wilmington DE: Scholarly Resources, Inc., 1993.

Kinsey, Alfred C. *Sexual Behavior in the Human Male.* Philadelphia: W. B. Saunders Co., 1948.

Bibliography

Kinsey, Alfred C., et al. *Sexual Behavior in the Human Female.* Philadelphia: W. B. Saunders Co., 1953.

Klein, Herbert S. "Hacienda and Free Community in Eighteenth-Century Alto Peru: A Demographic Study of the Aymara Population of the Districts of Chulumaní and Pacajes in 1786." *JLAS* 7, no. 2 (1975).

Kubler, George. "The Neo-Inca State, 1537–1572." *HAHR* 27, no. 2 (1947).

———. "The Quechua in the Colonial World." In *Handbook of South American Indians.* Vol. 2. Edited by Julian Steward. Washington DC: U.S. Government Printing Office, 1964.

Langer, Eric. "Andean Banditry and Peasant Community Organization, 1882–1930." In *Bandidos: The Varieties of Latin American Banditry.* Edited by Richard W. Slatta. New York: Greenwood Press, 1987.

———. "Andean Rituals of Revolt: The Chayanta Rebellion of 1927." *Ethnohistory* 37, no. 3 (1990).

Larson, Brooke. "Caciques, Class Structure and the Colonial State in Bolivia." *Nova Americana* 2 (1979).

———. "'Exploitation' and 'Moral Economy' in the Southern Andes: A Critical Reconsideration." Paper presented at the CLASCO conference in Lima, 1986.

———. *Colonialism and Agrarian Transformations in Bolivia: Cochabamba, 1550–1900.* Princeton NJ: Princeton University Press, 1988.

Larson, Brooke, Olivia Harris, and Enrique Tandeter, comp. *La participación indígena en los mercados surandinos.* La Paz: CERES, 1987.

Larson, Brooke and Robert Wasserstrom. "Coerced Consumption in Colonial Bolivia and Guatemala." *Radical History Review* 27 (1983).

Lavallé, Bernard. "Divorcio y nulidad de matrimonio en Lima (1650–1700): La desavenencia conyugal como indicador social." *Revista Andina* 4, no. 2 (1986).

———. "Las doctrinas de indígenas como núcleos de explotación colonial Siglos XVI–XVII." *Allpanchis* 19 (1982).

Lavrin, Asunción, ed. *Sexuality and Marriage in Colonial Latin America.* Lincoln: University of Nebraska Press, 1989.

———. "Introduction." In *Sexuality and Marriage in Colonial Latin America.* Edited by Asunción Lavrin. Lincoln: University of Nebraska Press, 1989.

———. "Sexuality in Colonial Mexico: A Church Dilemma." In *Sexuality*

Bibliography

and Marriage in Colonial Latin America. Edited by Asunción Lavrin. Lincoln: University of Nebraska Press, 1989.

Lehmann, David, ed. *Ecology and Exchange in the Andes.* Cambridge: Cambridge University Press, 1982.

León Pinelo, Antonio de. *Paraíso en el Nuevo Mundo.* Edited by Raul Porras. Lima: Imprenta Torres Aquirre, 1943.

Levillier, Roberto, ed. *Audiencia de Charcas, Correspondencia de presidentes y oidores.* 3 vols. Madrid: Imprenta de Juan Paeyo, 1918–1922.

———. *Don Francisco de Toledo, supremo organizador del Peru, su vida, su obra (1515–1582).* 4 vols. Madrid: Espasa-Calpe S.A., 1935–40.

———. *Gobernantes del Perú, cartas y papeles.* Madrid: Sucesores de Rivadeneyra, 1926.

Lewin, Boleslao. *La rebelión de Túpac Amaru y los orígenes de la emancipación americana.* Buenos Aires: Hachette, 1957.

Lima, Consejo Provincial. *Doctrina Christiana y Catecismo para instrucción de los indios.* Lima, 1584.

———. *Tercero Cathecismo y exposición de la Doctrina Christiana, por sermones.* Lima, 1585.

Lockhart, James. *Men of Cajamarca: A Social and Biographical Study of the First Conquerors of Peru.* Austin: University of Texas Press, 1972.

———. *Spanish Peru, 1532–1560: A Colonial Society.* Madison: University of Wisconsin Press, 1968.

Lockhart, James and Enrique Otte, trans. and eds. *Letters and People of the Spanish Indies.* Cambridge: Cambridge University Press, 1976.

Lohman Villena, Guillermo. *El corregidor de indios en el Perú bajo los Austrias.* Madrid: Ediciones Cultura Hispánica, 1957.

Lorente, Sebastian, ed. *Relaciones de los virreyes y audiencias.* 2 vols. Madrid: Imprenta M. Rivadeneyra, 1871.

Lounsbury, Floyd G. "Some Aspects of the Inka Kinship System." In *Anthropological History of Andean Polities.* Edited by John V. Murra, Nathan Wachtel, and Jacques Revel. Cambridge: Cambridge University Press, 1986.

MacCormack, Sabine. "The Heart Has Its Reasons: Predicaments of Missionary Christianity in Early Colonial Peru." *HAHR* 65, no. 3 (1985).

———. "Pachacuti: Miracles, Punishments, and Last Judgment: Visionary Past and Prophetic Future in Early Colonial Peru." *AHR* 93, no. 4 (1988).

Bibliography

———. *Religion in the Andes*. Princeton: Princeton University Press, 1991.

MacLean y Esteños, Roberto. "Sirvinacuy o tincunacuspa." *Perú Indígena* 2, no. 4 (1952).

Mallon, Florenica, E. "The Promise and Dilemma of Subaltern Studies: Perspectives from Latin American History." *AHR* 99, no. 5 (1994).

Masters, William H., Virginia E. Johnson, and Robert C. Kolodny. *Human Sexuality*. New York: Harper Collins, 1992.

Masuda, Shozo, Izumi Shimada, Craig Morris, et al. *Andean Ecology and Civilization*. Tokyo: University of Tokyo Press, 1985.

Matienzo, Juan de. *Gobierno del Perú (1567)*. Edited by Guillermo Lohman Villena. Lima and Paris: Institut Francais d'Etudes Andines, 1967.

McCaa, Robert. "Marriageways in Mexico and Spain 1500–1900." *Continuity and Change* 9, no. 1 (1994).

Millones, Luis. "Un movimiento nativista del siglo XVI: el Taki Onkoy." In *Ideología mesiánica del mundo andino*. Edited by Juan Ossio. Lima: I. Prado Pastor, 1973.

———. "Religion and Power in the Andes: Idolatrous Curacas of the Central Sierra." *Ethnohistory* 26, no. 3 (1979).

Moore, Barrington, Jr. *Injustice: The Social Bases of Obedience and Revolt*. White Plains NY: M. E. Sharpe, 1978.

Moore, Sally Falk. *Power and Property in Inca Peru*. New York: Columbia University Press, 1958.

Morner, Magnus. *Andean Past: Land, Societies, and Conflicts*. New York: Columbia University Press, 1985.

———. *Perfil de la sociedad rural del Cuzco a fines de la colonia*. Lima: Universidad del Pacifico, 1978.

———. *Race Mixture in the History of Latin America*. Boston: Little, Brown, 1967.

———. "The Spanish Hacienda: A Survey of Recent Research and Debate." *HAHR* 53, no. 2 (1973).

Morner, Magnus, and Efraín Trelles. "Un intento de calibrar las actitudes hacia la rebelión en el Cuzco durante la acción de Túpac Amaru." In *Dos ensayos analíticos sobre la rebelión de Túpac Amaru en el Cuzco*. Stockholm: Estudios Históricos sobre Estructuras Agrarias Andinas, no. 2, 1985.

———. "A Test of Causal Interpretations of the Túpac Amaru Rebellion." In *Resistance, Rebellion, and Consciousness in the Andean Peasant World*,

Eighteenth to Twentieth Centuries. Edited by Steve Stern. Madison: University of Wisconsin Press, 1987.

Murúa, Martín de. *Historia del origen y genealogía real de los Reyes Incas del Perú.* Madrid: Instituto San Toribio de Mogrovejo, Consejo Superior de Investigaciones Científicas, 1946.

Murra, John V. "An Aymaran Kingdom in 1567." *Ethnohistory* 15, no. 2 (1968).

———. "Cloth and Its Functions in the Inca State." *American Anthropologist* 64 (1962).

———. "The Economic Organization of the Inca State." Ph.D. dissertation. University of Chicago, 1956.

———. *Formaciones económicas y políticas del mundo andino.* Lima: Instituto de Estudios Peruanos, 1975.

———. "The Mit'a Obligations of Ethnic Groups to the Inca State." In *Inca and Aztec States, 1400–1800: Anthropology and History.* Edited by George A. Collier, Renato I. Rosaldo, and John D, Wirth. New York: Academic Press, 1982.

———. "Rite and Crop in the Inca State." In *Culture in History: Essays in Honor of Paul Radin.* Edited by Stanley Diamond. New York: Columbia University Press, 1960.

"El Naufragio de Túpac Amaru." *El País* Revista 4–5. Madrid, 20 Jan. 1997.

Nizza da Silva, Maria Beatriz. "Divorce in Colonial Brazil: The Case of São Paulo." In *Sexuality and Marriage in Colonial Latin America.* Edited by Asunción Lavrin. Lincoln: University of Nebraska Press, 1989.

Onis, Harriet de, trans. *Incas of Pedro Cieza de León.* Norman: University of Oklahoma, 1959.

O'Phelan-Godoy, Scarlett. "Cuzco 1777: El movimiento de Maras Urubamba." *Histórica* 1, no. 1 (1977).

———. "Elementos étnicos y de poder en el movimiento tupamarista 1780–1781." *Nova Americana* 5 (1982).

———. "La rebelión de Túpac Amaru: Organización interna, dirigencia y alianzas." *Histórica* 3, no. 2 (1979).

———. *Rebellions and Revolts in Eighteenth-Century Peru and Upper Peru.* Köln: Bohlau Verlag, 1985.

———. "El sur andino a fines del siglo XVIII: Cacique o corregidor." *Allpanchis* 11/12 (1978).

———. "Túpac Amaru y las sublevaciones del siglo XVIII." In *Túpac Amaru*

II—1780. Edited by Alberto Flores Galindo. Lima: Retablo de Papel Editores, 1976.

Orlove, Benjamin. *Alpacas, Sheep and Men. The Wool Export Economy and Regional Society in Southern Peru.* New York: Academic Press, 1977.

―――. "Inequality among Peasants." In *Peasant Livelihood.* Edited by Rhoda Halperin and James Down. New York: James Dow, 1977.

Ossio, Juan M., ed. *Ideología mesiánica del mundo andino.* Lima: I. Prado Pastor, 1973.

Ouweneel, Arij. "Altepeme and Pueblos de Indios: Some Comparative Theoretical Perspectives on the Analysis of the Colonial Indian Communities." In *Indian Communities of Colonial Mexico: Fifteen Essays on Land Tenure, Corporate Organization, Ideology and Village Politics.* Amsterdam: CEDLA, 1990.

Padden, R. C., ed. *Tales of Potosi.* Providence RI: Brown University Press, 1975.

Pease G. Y., Franklin. *Del Tawantinsuyu a la historia del Perú.* Lima: Instituto de Estudios Peruanos, 1978.

―――. "The Formation of Tawantinsuyu: Mechanisms of Colonization and Relationship with Ethnic Groups." In *Inca and Aztec States, 1400–1800: Anthropology and History.* Edited by George A. Collier, Renato I. Rosaldo, and John D. Wirth. New York: Academic Press, 1982.

Pizzaro, Pedro. "Descubrimiento y Conquista del Perú." In *La Colección de Libros y Documentos Referentes a la Historia del Perú.* Vol. 6. Lima, 1917.

―――. *Relation of the Discovery and Conquest of the Kingdoms of Peru,* Phillip Ainsworth Means, trans. New York: Cortes Society, 1921.

Platt, Tristan. "The Andean Experience of Bolivian Liberalism, 1825–1900: Roots of Rebellion in 19th–Century Chayanta Potosí." In *Resistance, Rebellion, and Consciousness in the Andean Peasant World, Eighteenth to Twentieth Centuries.* Edited by Steve Stern. Madison: University of Wisconsin Press, 1987.

―――. *Estado boliviano y ayllu andino.* Lima: Instituto de Estudios Peruanos, 1982.

―――. "Mirrors and Maize: The Concept of *yanantin* among the Macha of Bolivia." In *Anthropological History of Andean Polities.* Edited by John V. Murra, Nathan Wachtel, and Jacques Revel. Cambridge: Cambridge University Press, 1986.

Polanyi, Karl. *Great Transformation.* Boston: Beacon Press, 1944.

Bibliography

Popkin, Samuel. *The Rational Peasant*. Berkeley: University of California Press, 1979.

Powers, Karen. *Andean Journeys*. Albuquerque: University of New Mexico Press, 1995.

————. "The Battle for Bodies and Souls in the Colonial North Andes: Intraecclesiastical Struggles and the Politics of Migration." *HAHR* 75, no. 1 (1995).

Price, Richard. "Trial Marriage in the Andes." *Ethnology* 4 (1965).

Ramirez, Susan. *World Upside Down: Cross-Cultural Contact and Conflict in Sixteenth-Century Peru*. Stanford CA: Stanford University Press, 1996.

Rasnake, Roger Neil. "Kurahkuna of Yura: Indigenous Authorities of Colonial Charcas and Contemporary Bolivia." Ph.D. dissertation. Cornell University, 1982.

Recopilación de leyes de los reynos de las Indias, mandados imprimir y publicar por la Ma. Católica del Rey D. Carlos II. Facsimile ed. Madrid, 1943.

Reddy, William. *Rise of Market Culture*. Cambridge: Cambridge University Press, 1984.

Relaciones de los vireyes y audiencias que han governado el Perú. Lima: Imprenta del Estado por J. Edel Campo, 1867–72. (See also Lorente.)

René-Moreno, Gabriel. "La Mita de Potosi in 1795." *Revista del Instituto de Investigaciones Históricas de la Univ. Tomás Friás, Potosi* 1 (1959–60).

Rhoades, Robert, and Stephen Thompson. "Adaptive Strategies in Alpine Environments: Beyond Ecological Particularism." *American Ethnologist* 2, no. 3 (1975).

Ricard, Robert. *Spiritual Conquest of Mexico*. Translated by Lesley Byrd Simpson. Berkeley: University of California Press, 1966.

Romero, C. A. "Tincunakuspa." *Revista Trimestral de Estudios Antropológicos* 1 (1923).

Rosenblat, Angel. *La poblacion indígena y el mestizaje en América*. Buenos Aires: Editorial Nova, 1954.

Rostorowski de Diez Canseco, María. *Etnía y sociedad: Costa Peruana prehispánica*. Lima: Instituto de Estudios Peruanos, 1977.

Rowe, John H. "Ayllus, mercado y coacción colonial: el reto de las migraciones internas en Charcas Siglo XVII." In *La participación indígena en los mercados surandinos: Estrategias y reproducción social, siglos XVI a XX*.

Edited by Olivia Harris, Brooke Larson, and Enrique Tandeter. La Paz: CERES, 1987.

———. *Caciques, Tribute and Migration in the Southern Andes: Indian Society and the 17th Century Colonial Order (Audiencia of Charcas).* London: University of London, Occasional Papers, 1985.

———. "Colonial Portraits of Inca Nobles." In *Civilizations of Ancient America.* Edited by Sol Tax. Vol. 1. Chicago: University of Chicago Press, 1951.

———. "De la borrachera al retrato; los caciques andinos entre dos legitimidades Charcas." *Revista Andina* 9 (1987).

———. "The Ethnic Groups in the Valleys of Larecaja: From Descent to Residence." In *Anthropological History of Andean Polities.* Edited by John V. Murra, Nathan Wachtel, and Jacques Revel. Cambridge: Cambridge University Press, 1986.

———. "Genealogía y rebelión en el siglo XVIII." *Histórica* 6, no. 1 (1982).

———. "Inca Policies and Institutions Relating to the Cultural Unification of the Empire." In *Inca and Aztec States, 1400–1800: Anthropology and History.* Edited by George A. Collier, Renato I. Rosaldo, and John D, Wirth. New York: Academic Press, 1982.

———. "The Incas under Spanish Colonial Institutions." *HAHR* 37, no. 2 (1957).

———. "The Kingdom of Chimor." *Acta Americana* 6 (1948):1–2.

———. "El movimiento nacional inca del siglo XVIII." In *Túpac Amaru II—1780.* Edited by Alberto Flores Galindo. Lima: Retablo de Papel Editores, 1976.

———. "Thupa Amaro: Nombre y Apellido." *Boletín de Lima* 4, no. 24 (1982).

Saignes, Thierry. "Algún día todo se andará; los movimientos étnicos en Charcas Siglo XVII." *Revista Andina* 6 (1985).

Salomon, Frank. "Ancestor Cults and Resistance to the State in Arequipa, ca. 1748–1754." In *Resistance, Rebellion, and Consciousness in the Andean Peasant World, Eighteenth to Twentieth Centuries.* Edited by Steve J. Stern. Madison: University of Wisconsin Press, 1987.

———. *Native Lords of Quito in the Age of the Incas: The Political Economy of North Andean Chiefdoms.* Cambridge: Cambridge University Press, 1986.

———. "Vertical Politics on the Inka Frontier." In *Anthropological History of*

Bibliography

Andean Polities. Edited by John V. Murra, Nathan Wachtel, and Jacques Revel. Cambridge: Cambridge University Press, 1986.

Sánchez-Albornoz, Nicolás. *Indios y tributos en el Alto Perú.* Lima: Instituto de Estudios Peruanos Ediciones, 1978.

———. "La saca de mulas de Salta al Perú, 1778–1808." *Anuario del Instituto de Investigaciones Históricas* 8 (1965).

———. "Mita, migraciones y pueblos. Variaciones en el espacio y en el tiempo." *Revista Boliviana* 3, no. 1 (1983).

———. *Population of Latin America: A History.* Translated by W. A. R. Richardson. Berkeley: University of California Press, 1974.

Santo Tomás, Fray Domingo de. *Lexicon, o vocabulario de la lengua general del Perú.* Facsimile. Edited by Raul Porras Barrenechea. Lima: Imprenta Santa Maria, 1951[2?].

Scott, James L. *Moral Economy of the Peasants: Rebellion and Subsistence in Southeast Asia.* New Haven CT: Yale University Press, 1976.

———. *Weapons of the Weak: Everyday Forms of Peasant Resistance.* New Haven CT: Yale University Press, 1985.

———. "Resistance without Protest and without Organization: Peasant Opposition to the Islamic Zakat and the Christian Tithe." *Comparative Studies in Society and History* 29, no. 3 (1987).

Serulnikov, Sergio. "Disputed Images of Colonialism: Spanish Rule and Indian Subversion in Northern Potosí, 1777–1780." *HAHR* 76, no. 2 (1996).

Silva Santisteban, Fernando. *Los obrajes en el Virreinato del Perú.* Lima: Publicaciones del Museo Nacional de Historia, 1964.

Silverblatt, Irene. *Moon, Sun, and Witches: Gender Ideologies and Class in Inca and Colonial Peru.* Princeton: Princeton University Press, 1987.

———. "'The Universe has turned inside out. . . . There is no justice for us here': Andean Women Under Spanish Rule." In *Women and Colonization: Anthropological Perspectives.* Edited by Mona Etienne and Eleanor Leacock. New York: Praeger, 1980.

Slatta, Richard W., ed. *Bandidos: The Varieties of Latin American Banditry.* New York: Greenwood Press, 1987.

Smith, C. T. "Depopulation of the Central Andes in the Sixteenth Century." *Current Anthropology* 2, nos. 4–5 (1970).

Smith, John. *General Historie of Virginia, New England and the Summer Isles.* London: Michael Sparkes, 1624.

Bibliography

Socolow, Susan. "Acceptable Partners: Marriage Choice in Colonial Argentina, 1778–1810." In *Sexuality and Marriage in Colonial Latin America*. Edited by Asunción Lavrin. Lincoln: University of Nebraska Press, 1989.

Solorzano y Pereira, Juan de. *Política Indiana*. Vol. 1. Biblioteca de autores españoles. Madrid: Ediciones Atlas, 1972.

Spalding, Karen. "The Colonial Indian: Past and Future Research Perspectives." *LARR* 7, no. 1 (1972).

———. *De indio a campesino*. Lima: Instituto de Estudios Peruanos, 1974.

———. "Exploitation as an Economic System: The State and the Extraction of Surplus in Colonial Peru." In *Inca and Aztec States, 1400–1800: Anthropology and History*. Edited by George A. Collier, Renato I. Rosaldo, and John D. Wirth. New York: Academic Press, 1982.

———. *Huarochirí: An Andean Society under Inca and Spanish Rule*. Stanford CA: Stanford University Press, 1984.

———. "Kurakas and Commerce: A Chapter in the Evolution of Andean Society." *HAHR* 53, no. 4 (1973).

———. "Social Climbers: Changing Patterns of Mobility among the Indians of Colonial Peru." *HAHR* 50, no. 4 (1970).

Spores, Ronald. "Spanish Penetration and Cultural Change in Early Colonial Mexico." In *Indian Communities of Colonial Mexico: Fifteen Essays on Land Tenure, Corporate Organization, Ideology and Village Politics*. Amsterdam: CEDLA, 1990.

Stavig, Ward. "La comunidad indígena y la gran ciudad: Los naturales del Cusco y la ciudad minera de Potosí durante la colonia." In *Comunidades campesinas: Cambios y permanencias*. Edited by Alberto Flores Galindo. Chiclayo: CES Solidaridad, 1987.

———. "Ethnic Conflict, Moral Economy, and Population in Rural Cuzco on the Eve of the Thupa Amaro II Rebellion." *HAHR* 68, no. 4 (1988).

———. "Face-to-Face with Rebellion. Individual Experiences and Indigenous Consciousness in the Thupa Amaro Insurrection." In *Indigenous Revolts in Chiapas and the Andean Highlands*. Edited by Kevin Gosner and Arij Ouweneel. Amsterdam: CEDLA, 1996.

———. "Ladrones, cuatreros y salteadores: indios criminales en el Cusco rural a fines de la colonia." In *Bandoleros, abigeos y montoners. Criminalidad y violencia en el Perú, siglos XVII–XX*. Edited by Carlos Aguirre and Charles Walker. Lima: Instituto de Apoyo Agrario, 1990.

Bibliography

———. "'Living in Offense of Our Lord': Indigenous Sexual Values and Marital Life in the Colonial Crucible." *HAHR* 75, no. 4 (1995).

———. "Violencia cotidiana de los naturales de Quispicanchis y Canas y Canchis en el siglo XVIII." *Revista Andina* 3, no. 2 (1985).

Stern, Steve J. *Peru's Indian Peoples and the Challenge of Spanish Conquest: Huamanga to 1640*. Madison: University of Wisconsin Press, 1982.

———. *Secret History of Gender. Women, Men & Power in Late Colonial Mexico*. Chapel Hill: University of North Carolina Press, 1996.

———. "The Social Significance of Judicial Institutions in an Exploitative Society: Huamanga, Peru, 1570–1640." In *Inca and Aztec States, 1400–1800: Anthropology and History*. Edited by George A. Collier, Renato I. Rosaldo, and John D. Wirth. New York: Academic Press, 1982.

———. "The Struggle for Solidarity: Class, Culture and Community in Highland Indian America." *Radical History Review* 27 (1983).

Stern, Steve J., ed. *Resistance, Rebellion, and Consciousness in the Andean Peasant World, Eighteenth to Twentieth Centuries*. Madison: University of Wisconsin Press, 1987.

Super, John C. "Nutritional Regimes in Colonial Latin America." In *Food, Politics, and Society in Latin America*. Edited by John C. Super and Thomas C. Wright. Lincoln: University of Nebraska Press, 1985.

Szeminski, Jan. *La utopía tupamarista*. Lima: Pontificia Universidad Católica de Peru—Fondo Cultural, 1983.

———. "Why Kill the Spaniard? New Perspectives on Andean Insurrectionary Ideology in the Eighteenth Century." In *Resistance, Rebellion, and Consciousness in the Andean Peasant World, Eighteenth to Twentieth Centuries*. Edited by Steve Stern. Madison: University of Wisconsin Press, 1987.

Tandeter, Enrique. *Coercion and Market: Silver Mining in Colonial Potosí, 1692–1826*. Albuquerque: University of New Mexico Press, 1993.

———. "Forced and Free Labour in Late Colonial Potosí." *Past and Present* 93 (1981).

———. "Propiedad y gestión en la minería potosina de la segunda mitad del siglo XVIII." Paper presented at El Sistema Colonial en Mesoamérica y los Andes. VII Simposio Internacional. CLASCO. Comisión de Historia Económica. Lima, 1986.

———. "Trabajo forzado y trabajo libre en el Potosí colonial tardío." *Desarrollo Económico* 80 (1981).

Bibliography

Taylor, William. *Drinking, Homicide, and Rebellion in Colonial Mexican Villages*. Stanford CA: Stanford University Press, 1979.

Tedlock, Barbara. "From Participant Observation to the Observation of Participation: The Emergence of Narrative Ethnography." *Journal of Anthropological Research* 47, no. 1 (1991).

Thompson, E. P. *Customs in Common*. London: Merlin Press, 1991.

———. "The Moral Economy of the English Crowd in the Eighteenth Century." *Past and Present* 50 (1971).

Tord, Javier. "El corregidor de indios del Perú; comercio y tributos." *Historia y Cultura* 8 (1974).

Trelles, Efraín. *Lucas Martinez Vegazo; funcionamiento de una encomienda peruana inicial*. Lima: Pontificia Universidad Católica, 1980.

Tupac Amaru y la Iglesia-Antología. Lima: Unidad de Comunicaciones del Banco Continental, 1983.

Twinam, Ann. "Honor, Sexuality, and Illegitimacy in Colonial Spanish America." In *Sexuality and Marriage in Colonial Latin America*. Edited by Asunción Lavrin. Lincoln: University of Nebraska Press, 1989.

Valcarcel, Carlos Daniel. *Túpac Amaru. El Revolucionario*. Lima: Moncloa Campodonico, 1970.

———. *La Familia del Cacique Túpac Amaru*. Lima: University Nacional Mayor de San Marcos, 1947.

Valera, Blas. *Relación de las costumbres antiguas de los naturales del Pirú*. Biblioteca de autores españoles. Madrid: Edicones Atlas, 1968.

Van Young, Eric. "The Raw and the Cooked: Elite and Popular Ideology in Mexico, 1800–1821." In *Indian Communities of Colonial Mexico: Fifteen Essays on Land Tenure, Corporate Organization, Ideology and Village Politics*. Amsterdam: CEDLA, 1990.

Vega, Juan José. *Jose Gabriel Tupac Amaru*. Lima: Editorial Universo, 1969.

Wachtel, Nathan. *Vision of the Vanquished: The Spanish Conquest of Peru through Indian Eyes, 1520–1570*. Translated by Ben and Sián Reynolds. Sussex: Harvester Press, 1977.

Walker, Charles, and Carlos Aguirre, eds. *Bandoleros, abigeos y montoneros. Criminalidad y violencia en el Perú, siglos XVIII–XX*. Lima: Instituto de Apoyo Agrario, 1990.

———. "Voces discordantes: Discursos alternativos sobre el indio a fines de la colonia." In *Entre la retórica y la insurgencia: las ideas y los movimientos*

Bibliography

sociales en los Andes, siglo XVIII. Compiled by Charles Walker. Cusco: Centro Bartolomé de Las Casas, 1996.

Wallerstein, Immanuel. *Modern World-System.* Vol. 1, *Capitalist Agriculture and the Origins of the European World-Economy in the Sixteenth Century.* New York: Academic Press, 1974.

Wightman, Ann. *Indigenous Migration and Social Change: The Forasteros of Cuzco, 1570–1720.* Durham NC: Duke University Press, 1990.

Wolf, Eric. "Closed Corporate Peasant Communities in Mesoamerica and Central Java." *Southwestern Journal of Anthropology* 13, no. 1 (1957).

———. *Peasants.* Englewood Cliffs NJ: Prentice Hall, 1966.

———. "The Vicissitudes of the Closed Corporate Community." *American Ethnologist* 13, no. 2 (1986).

Womack, John. *Zapata and the Mexican Revolution.* New York: Alfred A. Knopf, 1968.

Yamamoto, Norio. "Papa, llama y chaquitaclla. Una perspectiva etnobotánica de la cultura andina." In *Recursos Naturales Andinos.* Edited by S. Masuda. Tokyo: University of Tokyo, 1988.

Zavala, Silvio, ed. *El servicio personal de los indios en el Perú. (Extractos del siglo XVIII).* 3 vols. México: El Colegio de México, 1978–80.

Zimmerman, Arthur Franklin. *Francisco de Toledo: Fifth Viceroy of Peru, 1569–1581.* Caldwell ID: Caxton Printers, 1938.

Zuidema, R. T. "The Inca Kinship System: A New Theoretical View." In *Andean Kinship and Marriage.* Edited by Ralph Bolton and Enrique Mayer. Washington DC: American Anthropological Association, Special Publication No. 7, 1977.

Zulawski, Ann. *"Forasteros* and *Yanaconas:* The Work Force of a Seventeenth Century Mining Town." Paper presented at the 1986 Annual Meeting of the American Historical Association, New York City.

INDEX

Index

Index

Index

haciendas: chastised on behalf of slain workers, 64; *naturales* labor on, 133–38; use of *yanaconas/forasteros* labor on, 139–44
Hakluyt, Richard, 167
Hamilton, Earl, 169
Hancho, Ysidro, 152
Hanco, Antonio, 196
Hanco, Domingo, 196
head tax, 261
herding traditions: cameloid, 12–14; ethnic identity maintained by, 90–91; llamas, 155. *See also* livestock industry
Herrera, Maria, 255
Hincho, Doña Maria, 24, 25, 26, 27, 30, 241
Hobsbawm, Eric, 25
homicide, 28, 49–52, 282 n.8
Hualpa, 164
Huayrachapi (*ayllu*), 97
Humachi, Manuel, 191
Humpiri, Juan, 50–51
Hurtado de Laguna, Doña Bernarda, 142

Inca, 238–39. *See also* Thupa Amaro, José Gabriel
Incacuna (*ayllu*), 90
Incan nationalism, 236–39. *See also* Thupa Amaro rebellion (1780)
Incas: disdain for criminals by, 64–66; identification with heritage of, 236–39; incest practiced by, 36; land disputes by, 112; marital life of the, 47–48; rape punishment by, 34; *Yanacona* and *forasteros* of the, 138–39. *See also* indigenous peoples
incest, 36–38
indigenous head tax, 261
indigenous peoples: Catholic practice of confessions for, 28–30; Christian sexual mores and, 28–29; colonial period values of, 25–26; conflicted values of Spanish and, 26–27; debt structure of *obraje* labor by, 147–50; ethnic fragmentation of, 2–5; ethnic land conflict among, 111–28; family relationships among, 30; growing interaction with Spanish by, 258; impact of European values on, 56–57; impact of Thupa Amaro rebellion on, 258–62; Incan nationalism and, 236–39; incest practiced by, 36–38; invasion of lands by, 108–9; involved in crime, 58–83; marital life of, 48–49; rape and, 31–36; *sirvinacuy* (trial marriage) practiced by, 38–47; skin color of, 10; Spanish demands on, 211–12; special legal status of, 85–86; use of legal system by, 105–8. *See also* ethnic identity; labor; *mita* labor
indigenous policy (Spain), 260–61
inflation, 169–70
Inga, Pedro Carlos, 147
Inkarrí beliefs, 236
Inti Raymi festival, 1–2, 16
irrigation agreements, 103–4

Jara (de la Cerda), Agustín, 94
Julio, Juan, 68–69

labor: associated with livestock industry, 153–57; colonial compulsion of *mita*, 20, 125–26, 130–33; *forasteros*, 138–44, 197–98, 210, 234, 271 n.29, 290 n.19; hacienda, 133–38; land disputes and obligations of, 125–26; *obraje* (convict), 70–72, 144–51; pastors, 153–55; provided to Catholic priests, 157–60; sent to

Index

Index

Minera, Juana de la, 140

mita labor: communities burdened with, 173–93; depopulation due to, 186, 197–98; disruption of compliance with, 193–94; *faltriquera* replacement for, 179–81; hardships/abuse of, 186–88, 203–6; impact on community population of, 181–82; land conflict and, 125–26; ordered by Toledo, 165, 172–73, 181; property disputes caused by, 196; as relationship with the state, 20; required tasks of, 130–32; resistance to, 163, 185–86, 198–99, 200–202; tribute payment and, 132–33. *See also* labor

mitayos: coca usage by, 188–89; Cuzco/Chuquito delivery of, 182–83; deaths of, 188; diseases suffered by, 189, 192–93, 201; goods traded by, 175–77; impact on families of, 177–78, 194, 196; *leguaje* paid to, 178, 201, 202; populations of, 195; premature return of, 203–5; sent to Potosi silver mine, 162–64, 170; violence against, 192

Mohina (*ayllu*), 92

Mollebamba (*ayllu*), 102

Mollo, Roque, 204, 206

Monclova, Viceroy, 181

Montalvo, Pedro, 76

Montesclaros, Marques de, 155

Montesinos, Diego, 37

Morales, Andres, 122

Moscoso, Ramón, 250

Moscoso y Peralta, Bishop Juan Manuel, 158–59, 239, 240, 241–42, 244, 250, 252, 253

mules, 216

muleteers, 156–57

Muñoz de Arjona, Pedro, 59, 60, 215

Murra, John, 90

Natural & Moral History of the Indies (Acosta), 168–69

naturales. See indigenous peoples

nature: climate (18th century), 13–17; as part of supernatural world, 22–23. *See also* agriculture

"New Laws" (1540s), 19

New Spain, 13

Ninachi, Joseph, 188

Ninaronto, Pedro, 97, 98

Noguera, Francisco, 226, 246

Noguera, José, 119

Noguera, Patricio, 248

Noticias Cronologicas de la Gran Cuidad Del Cuzco (Esquivel y Navia), 147

Oblitas, Antonio, 207, 246

obraje (convict) service, 70–72, 144–51

Ochoa, Carlos, 218–20

Olarte, Gregorio de, 95

"*Ollantay*" (Quechua play), 238

O'Phelan Godoy, Scarlett, 209, 212

Ordoñes, Bartolomé, 59

Orellana (Spanish official), 184

originarios: conflict with *forasteros*, 233–34; giving up status of, 144, 163; ordered to return to provinces, 183–84; tribute payments/*mita* service by, 184

Oropesa, 97

Pacco, Melchor, 78

Pacha, Juan, 177

palabra de casamiento (Spanish betrothal), 42

Palata, Viceroy de la, 181

Pallani, Thomas, 194

Palli, Diego, 197

Palli, Sebastian, 197

Palomino, Don Carlos, 107

Index

Index

Index

Index

Utcca (Udcó), Domingo, 52

Vaihua, Asencia, 82
Valle Umbroso, Marques de, 13–14, 131, 146–47, 150
values: analysis of colonial period through, 25–26; community structure reinforcement of, 82–83; conflicts between Spanish and indigenous, 26–27; conflicts over bigamy, 55; disdain for criminals as, 64–66; impact of European cultural, 56–57; regarding adultery, 50–51; regarding domestic violence, 52–53; regarding rape, 31–36; regarding virginity, 39–40; syncretism of religious, 26, 56. *See also* ethnic identity; sexual mores
Vayalla, Feliz, 81
Vega. *See* Garcilaso de la Vega
Vera, Louisa de, 149
Viana, Gregorio de, 221
Vicho (*ayllu*), 91
Vilca, Jose, 96
Vilca, Visente, 77
Vilcay, Martin, 190
Vilcay, Roque, 190–91
Villa Imperial, 190, 191, 193
village grid pattern, 20

Viracocha (Andean creator-God), 1, 17
virginity, 39–40

water rights disputes, 101–4
Wightman, Ann, 141
women: criminal behavior by, 79–80; debt of those in *obraje*, 148–49; domestic violence against, 50–54, 280 n.84; influence over men by, 279 n.70; land disputes involving, 116–17, 118–19; rape of, 31–36. *See also* children

Xavier de Arrillaga, Francisco, 104
Xavier, Luis, 156–57

yanaconas labor, 138–44, 299 n.67
Yanaoca, 93–94, 124, 125
Yancay, Andrea, 109
Yañes, Ylario, 93
Yanquera, Mathias, 54
Yauri, 240
Yepes, Gregorio de, 242
Ynquillay, Joana, 54–55
Yucra, Carlos, 121
Yupanqui, Sebastian Fuentes Pongo, 95–96
Yura (Bolivia), 6